3RD EDITION

Teacher's Book

Pearson Education Limited
KAO Two
KAO Park
Hockham Way
Harlow, Essex
CM17 9SR
England
and Associated Companies throughout the world.

pearsonenglish.com/speakout3e

First published 2022
Second impression 2023

ISBN: 978-1-292-40740-1

Set in BBC Reith Sans

Printed in Slovakia by Neografia

Acknowledgements
Written by Kate Fuscoe

Contents

SCOPE AND SEQUENCE

	READING	LISTENING/VIDEO	SPEAKING	WRITING
		Understand people saying 'hello'	Introduce yourself	Write a chat message to introduce yourself; use capital letters, full stops and question marks
	Read an article about people with two jobs		Talk about people and their jobs	
		Understand people asking and answering simple questions	Ask and answer simple questions **FUTURE SKILLS** Self-management	
		BBC Street Interviews about what's in your bag	Talk about what's in your bag	Write a lost and found post
	Read a blog about two people		Talk about groups of people	
		Understand someone talking about their family around the world	Talk about your friends and family	Write a description of a photo; use *and*
		Understand short conversations	Have short conversations	
		BBC Programme *Best Home Cook*	Ask about three people	Write a message about a friend
	Read a blog about people's favourite things		Talk about people's things	Write about favourite things; use *and, but*
		Understand a radio phone-in about people's desks	Talk about your desk **FUTURE SKILLS** Collaboration	
		Understand conversations about shopping for clothes	Have shopping conversations	
		BBC Street Interviews about people's shopping habits	Ask and answer questions	Write a personal profile
ıd of words				
		Understand people from different countries talking about lunch	Talk about food	Write an email to a friend
	Read an article about an influencer's daily routine		Ask and answer about your daily routine	
		Understand conversations in a café	Order in a café	
		BBC Programme *Earth From Space*	Ask about someone's routine	Write a quiz

	READING	LISTENING/VIDEO	SPEAKING	WRITING
	Read a text about a good colleague		Talk about people	Write about a good friend; use pronouns
		Understand everyday conversations	Do a quiz and talk about your abilities	
		Understand people making requests and offers	Make requests and offers	
		BBC Street Interviews about birthdays	Talk about your birthday	Write about your birthday
	Read an article about lost things		Say where things are	
		Understand people talking about their neighbourhood	Talk about your perfect town	Write a post about your area; use commas
		Understand conversations about finding a place	Ask where a place is	
		BBC Programme *The Travel Show*	Talk about six hours in a city	Describe a city tour
		Understand a podcast about things that make people happy and healthy	Ask about everyday activities	Write an online post; punctuation
	Read an article about people's childhood heroes		Ask about famous people **FUTURE SKILLS** Collaboration	
		Understand conversations about not feeling well	Have conversations about health problems	
		BBC Street Interviews about keeping fit	Do a sport and exercise survey	Write a Top Tips post
		Understand someone talking about a weekend break	Talk about past actions	
	Read a group chat about people's weekends		Talk about past activities **FUTURE SKILLS** Communication	Write a group chat; linkers: *and, but, then*
		Understand conversations about buying travel tickets	Ask for travel information	
		BBC Programme *Kodo drummers*	Talk about something you want to try	Complete a questionnaire

SOUNDS AND SPELLING p151 **REVISION GAME** p160 **AUDIOSCRIPTS** p162 **VIDEOSCRIPTS** p172 **VERB TABLE** p175

Welcome to *Speakout 3rd Edition*

Welcome to the new edition of our best-selling, eight-level general English course for adults, designed for in-class, online and hybrid use. Developed in partnership with BBC Studios, ***Speakout 3rd Edition*** is the go-to course for teachers looking for comprehensive four-skills coverage, with a particular emphasis on developing learners' confidence in speaking.

Speakout 3rd Edition is the result of extensive research with users of *Speakout 2nd Edition* from around the world. It builds on the tried-and-tested methodology of the series, but has been brought up to date with 100% new content, a revised syllabus based on the Global Scale of English and a fresh new look and feel. With a clearer layout and lesson flow, and an enhanced digital environment offering even more flexibility, the new edition Presentation Tool and Student's eBook can be used on any device – computer, tablet and mobile phone – and all activities from the eBook and the Online Practice report to the gradebook.

We have kept the features that teachers say they love, including global topics, authentic BBC video and audio, international accents and motivating discussion questions, and we have added some exciting new features, such as Future Skills focus boxes, standalone Mediation lessons, an enhanced pronunciation syllabus, and interactive speaking practice activities which provide students with out-of-class, on-the-go speaking practice.

Speakout 3rd Edition features all-new BBC programme clips, street interviews, and vlogs filmed by people from around the world, all of which bring authenticity to the course and encourage students to be more motivated and confident in learning English. The Global Scale of English is embedded in the course, making it clear for learners and teachers *why* they are doing every task as well as providing a tangible framework for assessment and measurement of progress. 'How to …' lessons and Future Skills boxes bring real-world strategies into the course, meaning that employability and personal growth are embedded within the lesson content. There are also independent Mediation lessons at the back of every Student's Book from A2 to C1–C2 to further develop learners' soft and employability skills. The course is also mapped to the Adult Benchmark Tests, which provide clear, at-a-glance reporting, helping learners become more purposeful about their learning, and to Pearson English International Certificate, which is for learners wishing to take a test that gives them a proficiency certificate (see page 24 for details).

We are also delighted to introduce our interactive 'Speak Anywhere' speaking practice activities. These digital speaking roleplays are an extension of the 'How to …' lessons and are designed to give learners freer practice using the target language of the lesson, and also to give them some general fluency practice on the lesson topic. Students can do these activities on their own, outside the classroom, on a computer, tablet or mobile phone, and receive feedback on their performance within the activity.

Accessibility is of paramount importance for ***Speakout 3rd Edition***, as Pearson English is committed as a company to providing education which is available to all. We offer extensive support for learners with many different accessibility needs, such as:

- All our digital content has an accessibility layer powered by a built-in screenreader. This allows learners to fully engage with the exercises and complete them successfully. We also offer a 'keyboard navigation only' mode.
- All informative images are equipped with Alternative text suitable for the learners' level.
- Media players are equipped with speed changing capability, as well as dynamic transcripts for audios, and subtitles and transcripts for videos.
- Content can be resized up to 400% without any disruption to user experience and a high contrast theme can be applied.
- Accessibility support for print components includes audio support for reading texts for the visually impaired and guidance for teachers on how to help students with Dyslexia.

The Global Scale of English GSE

The Global Scale of English (GSE) is a numerical scale which measures English language proficiency. It is also a framework of learning objectives which describe what a learner can do at each level of proficiency on the scale for each of the four skills: speaking, listening, reading and writing. The Global Scale of English enables teachers and students to answer the following questions accurately:

- How good is my English?
- What progress have I made towards my learning goal?
- What do I need to do next to improve?

The Global Scale of English is fully aligned to the Common European Framework of Reference for Languages (CEFR), but the numerical scale enables proficiency to be measured more accurately, more regularly and within a CEFR level. This keeps learners motivated as they see regular evidence of progress.

The GSE chart on the back of each Student's Book shows the range of objectives that are covered within that level. Knowing this range helps you select course materials with the right level of challenge for your students to help them make progress.

Speakout 3rd Edition has been created using the GSE Learning Objectives for Adult Learners. These ensure that the content and activities are at the correct level and inform the lesson goals given at the start of each unit.

where? 6

VLOGS

Q: Where are you and what can you see?

1 Read the question.

2 Watch the video. How many speakers can see trees? How many speakers can see books?

GSE LEARNING OBJECTIVES

6A READING | Read an article about lost things: rooms and furniture
Say where things are: prepositions of place
Pronunciation: sentence stress

6B LISTENING | Listen to people talking about their neighbourhood: places in town (1)
Talk about your perfect town: *there is, there are*
Pronunciation: linking with *there*
Write a post about your area; use commas

6C HOW TO ... | ask where a place is: places in town (2); signs in buildings
Pronunciation: weak forms with *to, of* and *the*

6D BBC PROGRAMME | Understand a show about Ade Adepitan in Rome
Talk about six hours in a city: *the*
Describe a city tour

57

Measuring proficiency using the GSE

The Global Scale of English underpins everything we create at Pearson English, including coursebooks and assessments.

By using our Benchmark Tests alongside ***Speakout 3rd Edition***, you will be able to see the progress being made by learners during their course of study and receive rich score reports which identify strengths and weaknesses along with recommendations on how to address them using ***Speakout 3rd Edition***. For this level of ***Speakout 3rd Edition***, we recommend Benchmark Test Level A. Find out more about this test at www.pearsonenglish.com/exams-offer.

Your learners may also want to take a test that gives them a proficiency certificate. For this level of ***Speakout 3rd Edition***, we recommend Pearson English International Certificate (PTE General) A1. Find out more about this test at www.pearsonenglish.com/exams-offer.

▲ GSE Learning Objectives on Unit Opener pages are written in a shorter, more accessible way to allow learners to understand what they will be learning in each lesson.

GSE Teacher Resources

You can find a full list of the GSE Learning Objectives covered in this Student's Book in the table at the back of this Teacher's Book (see pages 222–233).

For more information about how the GSE can support your planning, teaching and assessment, go to www.pearsonenglish.com/gse. Visit the GSE Teacher Toolkit – freely available online at www.english.com/gse/teacher-toolkit/user/lo – to set learning goals, find grammar resources and check the level of a text.

Student components

Student's Book with eBook and Online Practice

The student's digital components work together to provide a seamless experience between accessing resources, completing activities and reviewing results.

Student's eBook

- Syllabus built on the Global Scale of English (GSE)
- Interactive activities with instant marking
- Student results report to the Gradebook
- Embedded audio and BBC video clips
- See the walkthrough on pages 12–17 for unit details

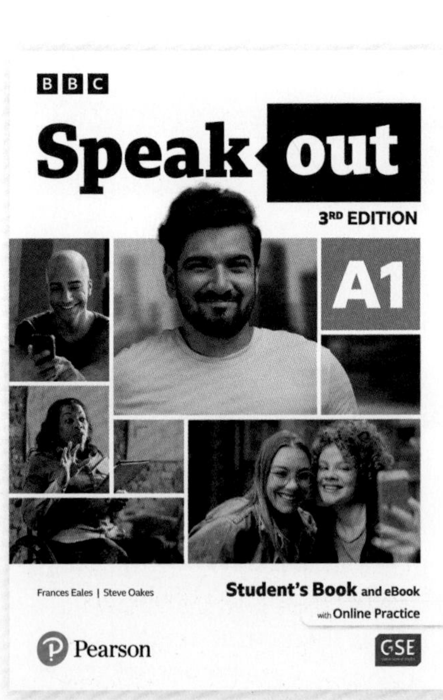

Student's Book

- Print version of the Student's eBook
- Access code for the Student's eBook and Online Practice

Online Practice

- Digital version of the activities in the Workbook with instant marking
- Student results report to the Gradebook

Gradebook

- Student's eBook and Online Practice activities report to the Gradebook so students and teachers can review performance and progress

Workbook

- Print version of the Online Practice activities
- Audio available online
- Includes Adult Benchmark Test task types

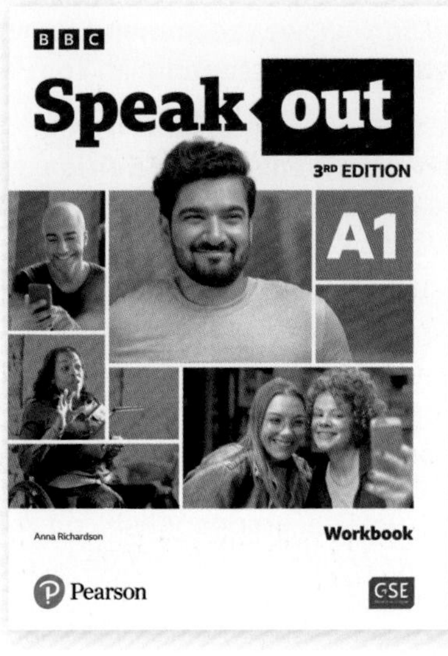

Teacher components

Teacher's Book with Teacher's Portal Access Code

The Teacher's Book includes access to the *Teacher's Portal*, where you can find everything you need to make your teaching more effective in class and online.

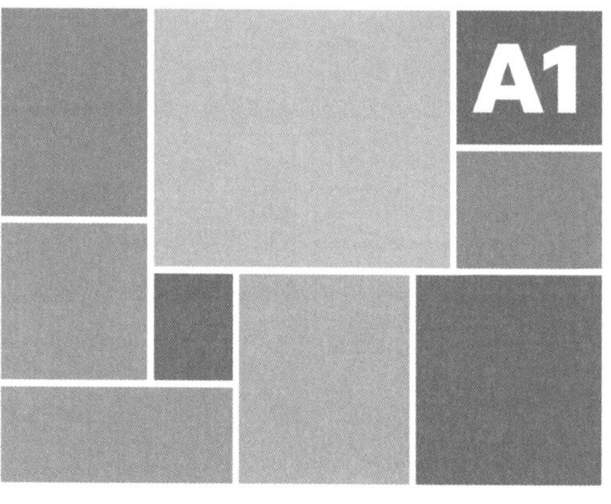

Kate Fuscoe

Teacher's Book
with Teacher's Portal Access Code

Teacher's Book

- Global Scale of English (GSE) Learning Objectives for every lesson
- Full teaching notes and Answer Keys for every activity
- Mediation lesson plans, plus output and evaluation guidance
- Digital activity ideas and cultural background notes
- Extra ideas and support for teaching mixed ability classes, and teaching students with dyslexia
- Audioscripts and videoscripts

Presentation Tool

- Student's eBook and Workbook with interactive activities for display in class and online
- Page-faithful view of the Student's Book for easy navigation between the Student's Book and the Presentation Tool
- Show answers one by one or all at once
- Embedded audio and video for seamless teaching in class
- Teaching notes for each lesson
- Teacher toolkit, including whiteboard

Online Practice

- Assign Online Practice activities in Assignments
- View student performance in the Gradebook

Tests Package

- All tests are offered in two versions: ready-to-print PDFs and editable Word documents. They can also be administered online via the Test Generator
- All tests have A and B versions, and there are specially adapted versions of the tests for students with dyslexia

See page 24 for more details.

Gradebook

- View individual student and class results for all student activities: from the Student's eBook, the Online Practice and the Test Generator

Teacher's Resources

- Photocopiable activities with full teaching notes and Answer Key
- Teaching with ***Speakout 3rd Edition videos***
- GSE Mapping Booklets showing how each level of the course aligns with the GSE and the CEFR
- Exam alignment tables showing detailed correlation between the Adult Benchmark Tests, Pearson English International Certificate, Cambridge Exams and each level of ***Speakout 3rd Edition***
- Downloadable PDF of the Teacher's Book
- Student's Book, Workbook and Tests Package audio and audioscripts
- All in-course BBC video and videoscripts
- Student's Book and Workbook Answer Keys
- Interactive phonetic chart

Virtual classroom

The virtual classroom enables you to teach fully interactive lessons online using the integrated video conferencing tools, with breakout rooms, chat and more. You can assign tasks and have a real-time view of student performance.

All digital components are accessible on computer, tablet and mobile phone so you and your students can enjoy the full functionality of the course anywhere.

All content is compliant with the WCAG 2.1 AA accessibility standard.

How the course works

Unit walkthrough

Course summary

Speakout 3rd Edition has eight levels: A1, A2, A2+, B1, B1+, B2, B2+ and C1–C2.

Each level contains eight units, each with four lessons, plus a Unit Opener and a Review section.

Each unit contains two main input lessons (Lessons A and B), a functional language, or 'How to …', lesson (Lesson C), and the BBC video lesson (Lesson D).

The Grammar Bank and Vocabulary Bank at the back of the book are integral parts of the lessons when they occur. Language presented in these sections is considered to be taught, and is then recycled in subsequent activities. It may also appear in the unit review and the tests content.

Writing activities in the main input lessons have a Writing Bank at the back of the book, which contains the skills development work and the final output task.

The Sounds and Spelling section at the back of the book contains eight standalone lessons. The Review page at the end of every unit includes a cross reference to this section.

The Tests Package contains tests to be used after each unit (including full unit tests and quick unit quizzes), after every two units, mid-course, and at the end of the course.

Unit Opener

Student's Book

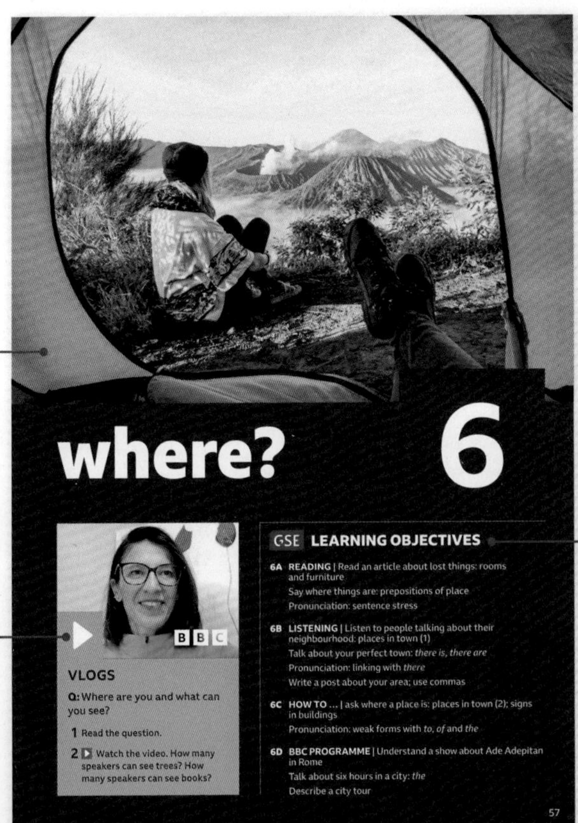

Stunning visuals related to the unit topic help to engage students and stimulate discussion.

The Unit Opener features BBC vlogs filmed by real people from around the world together with a mini-task to engage learners with the broad unit topic. The vlogs provide a good warmer for Lesson A.

The vlogs are embedded in the eBook, and can also be found in the Teacher's and Student's Resources.

The Learning Objectives for each unit are adapted from the (GSE) Learning Objectives that the lesson is built on. GSE Learning Objectives can be found on pages 222–233.

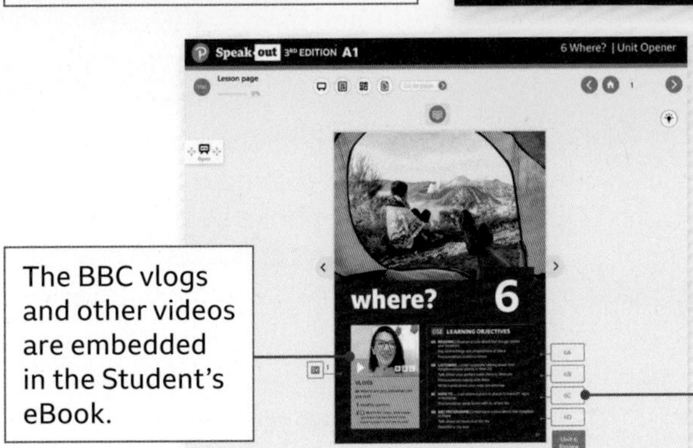

The BBC vlogs and other videos are embedded in the Student's eBook.

The buttons next to the GSE Learning Objectives are clickable and take you directly to each lesson.

All videos have subtitles that can be turned on and off.

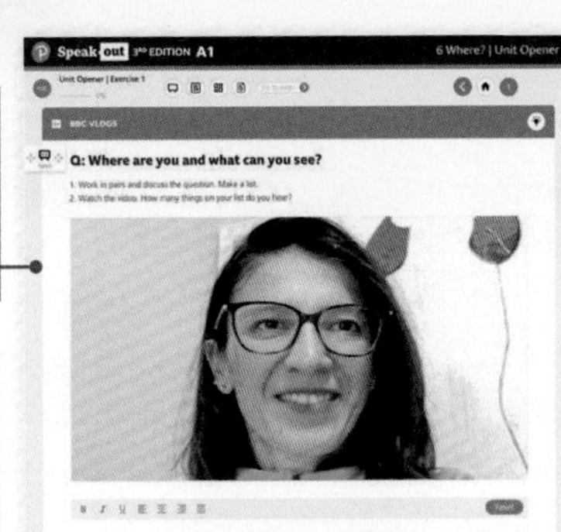

Lesson A – main input lesson 1

All four skills are taught systematically in each unit. Lessons A and B are the two main 'input' lessons. Lessons A and B consist of two pages, and practise vocabulary, grammar, pronunciation and two of the four skills. Each activity is based on a Global Scale of English (GSE) Learning Objective.

The core grammar and vocabulary is contextualised in the Listening and Reading tasks.

Grammar is taught in all four lessons, and there is a page of Reference and Practice for each grammar point in the Grammar Bank. The Grammar Bank is designed primarily for self-study, but can also be used in class.

Each lesson starts with a clear summary of lesson contents.

The Vocabulary Bank is clearly signposted on the lesson page. It is integral to the lesson, and contains either a continuation of the lexical set presented in the lesson, or presents a new set related to the lesson. The language in the Vocabulary Bank is used in subsequent tasks in the lesson.

Each unit features Future Skills. Also known as 'soft', '21st century' or 'transferable' skills, these skills are becoming increasingly important. Modern learners need to develop not just English language skills, grammar and vocabulary, but also skills which will help them become fully rounded citizens of the global community. *Speakout 3rd Edition* is aligned to the Pearson Personal and Social Capabilities (PSC) Framework.

Every lesson contains opportunities for personalised speaking practice.

The final GSE-based output task here is a Speaking task, bringing together the vocabulary and grammar learnt in the lesson. The Workbook also contains speaking practice activities which students can do alone.

In the Student's eBook, content is optimised for digital, so activity types may vary slightly between digital and print editions. The activities are designed to practise the same GSE Learning Objectives and language items.

After learners have completed the Student's Book activities, you can go through the answers with them using the check answers one-by-one or check answers all at once buttons in the Presentation Tool.

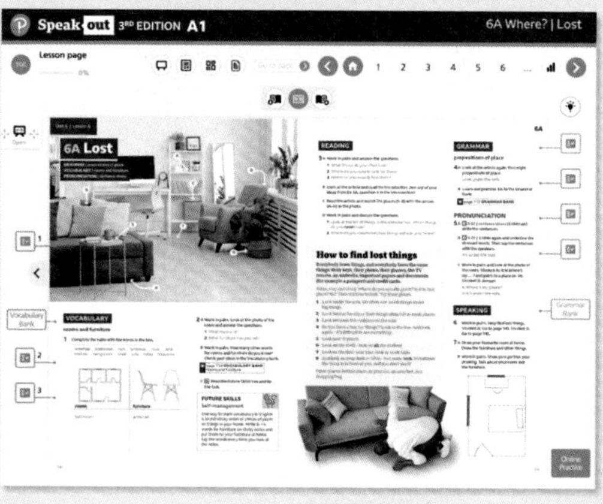

Student's eBook activity

Learners can practise the same lesson Learning Objectives in the Online Practice or using the print Workbook.

If you are using the print Workbook with your class, you also have a page-faithful view of the Workbook to refer to. This links to the Online Practice activities for easy answer checking.

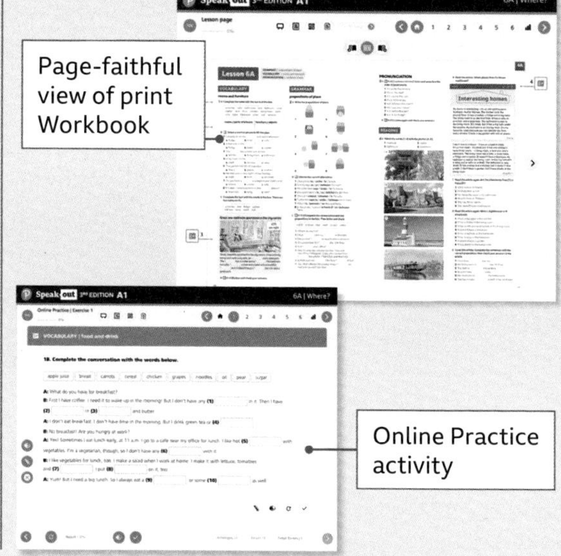

Page-faithful view of print Workbook

Online Practice activity

Lesson B – main input lesson 2

Lesson B is the second of the two main input lessons. It consists of two pages, and practises all four skills, plus vocabulary, grammar and pronunciation.

Speakout 3rd Edition teaches grammar inductively. There is an activity on the lesson page that requires the learner to make a deduction and complete the rule. Learners can refer to a full grammar explanation in the Grammar Bank, and also complete practice activities.

Vocabulary sets are contextualised in the Listening input.

The final GSE-based output task here is a Writing task, bringing together the vocabulary and grammar learnt in the lesson. The scaffolding activities are in the Writing Bank at the back of the book.

The Workbook also contains writing practice activities which students can do alone.

There is a prominent pronunciation syllabus providing practice of individual sounds, stress, intonation and features of connected speech. Learners can record themselves in the Student's eBook activities and Online Practice activities.

Audio for all activities is embedded in the Presentation Tool and Student's eBook, and can also be downloaded from the Resources. The audioscripts are at the back of the Student's Book and Workbook, and there are audioscripts in situ in the Student's eBook and Online Practice activities.

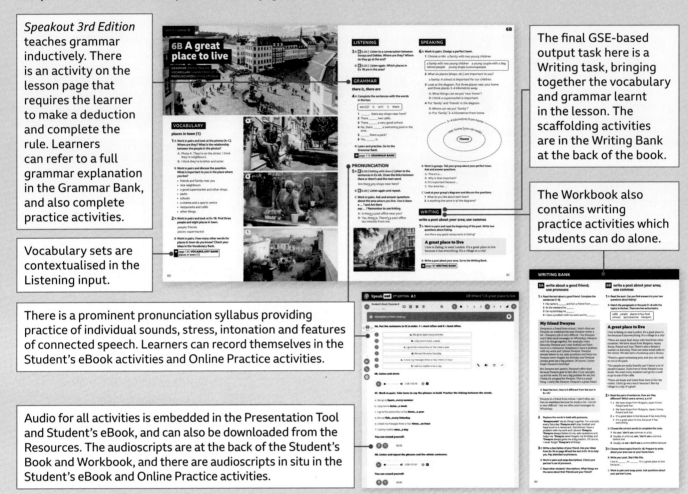

The teacher has access to a variety of resources directly from the Presentation Tool, including Teaching Notes and Answer Keys.

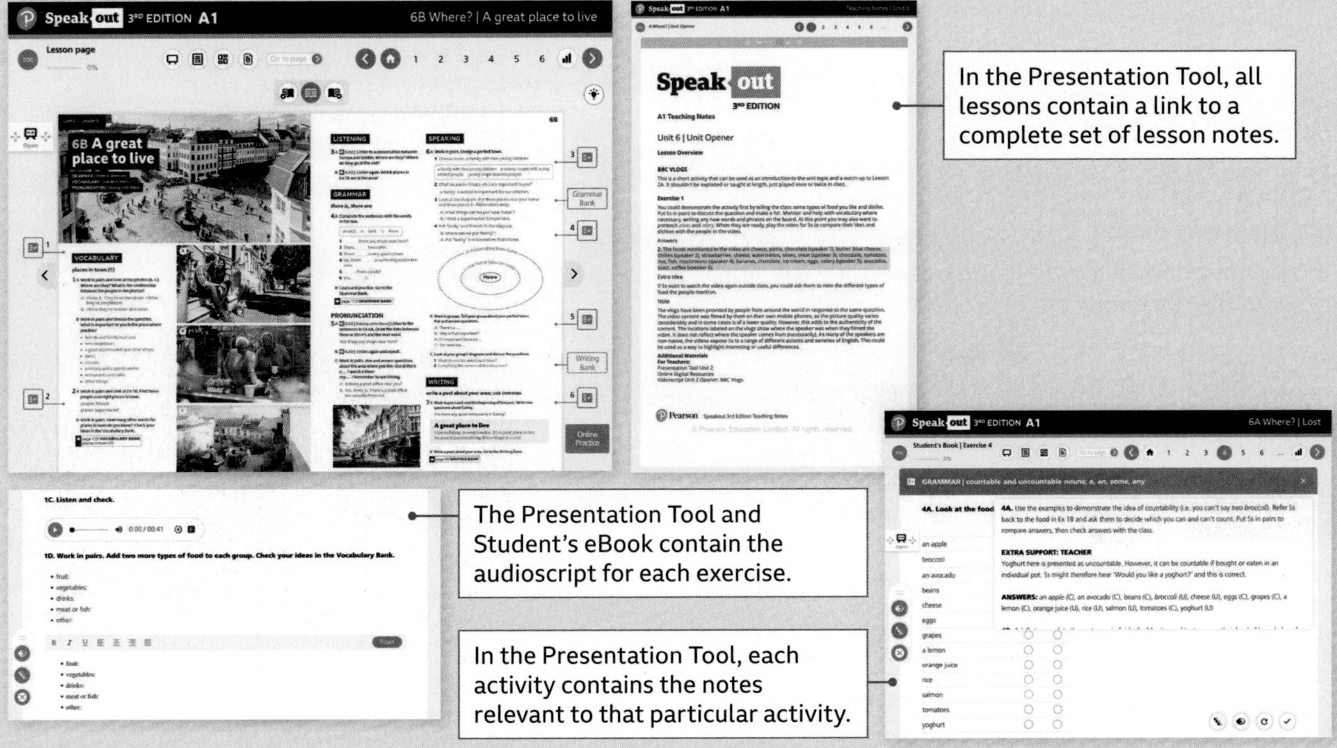

In the Presentation Tool, all lessons contain a link to a complete set of lesson notes.
The Presentation Tool and Student's eBook contain the audioscript for each exercise.
In the Presentation Tool, each activity contains the notes relevant to that particular activity.

Lesson C – functional language, or 'How to ...' lesson

In the 'How to ...' section, students learn and put into practice real-world language that will help them in everyday situations, e.g. asking where a place is, shopping for clothes and ordering in a café.

This lesson teaches practical, real-world skills that also align to the GSE.

Vocabulary is introduced in context to stimulate interest in the topic.

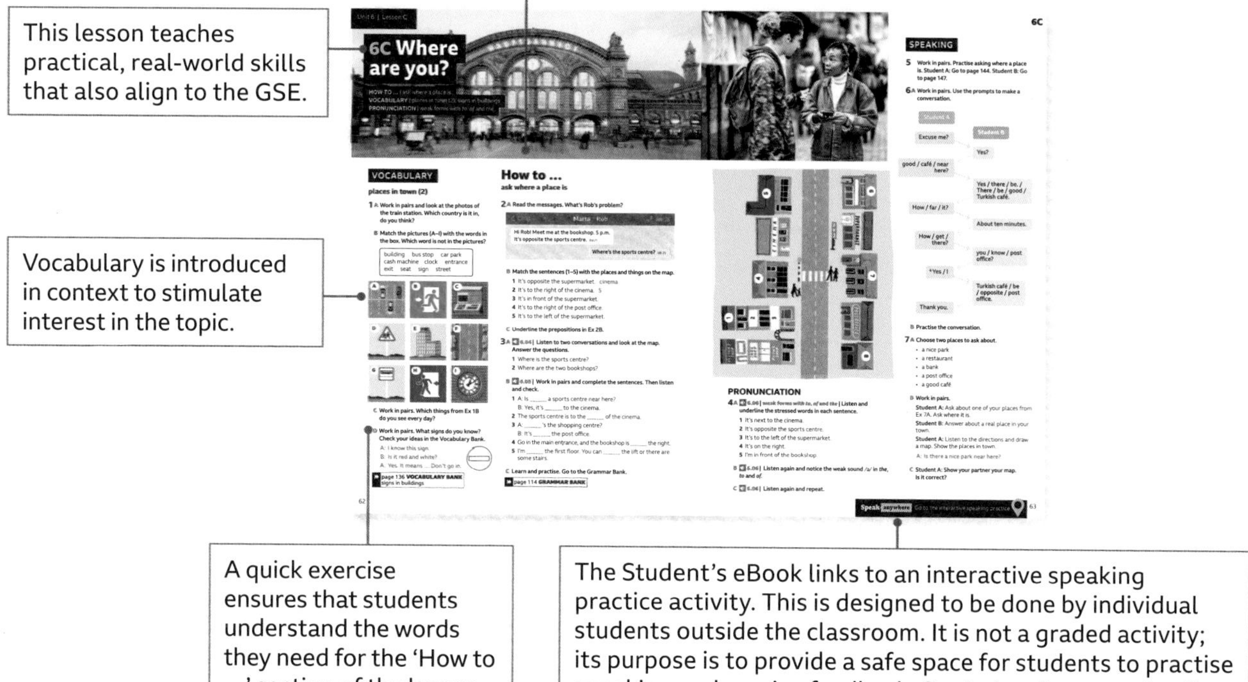

A quick exercise ensures that students understand the words they need for the 'How to ...' section of the lesson.

The Student's eBook links to an interactive speaking practice activity. This is designed to be done by individual students outside the classroom. It is not a graded activity; its purpose is to provide a safe space for students to practise speaking and receive feedback. See below for more details.

'Speak Anywhere' – interactive speaking activities

The Speaking Practice button in the Student's eBook takes learners to 'Speak Anywhere', an interactive speaking activity based on the topic and Learning Objectives of Lesson C. Students speak to a bot, and have a conversation on an everyday topic, such as ordering a meal in a restaurant or asking where a place is.

This activity is designed to be a fun activity for learners to do alone. It gives them a star rating for how well the bot could understand them, and a star rating for use of the target language from the lesson. It is a standalone activity for the learner and does not report to the Gradebook.

As with all the other activities in ***Speakout 3rd Edition***, the 'Speak Anywhere' activities can be done on a computer, tablet or mobile phone.

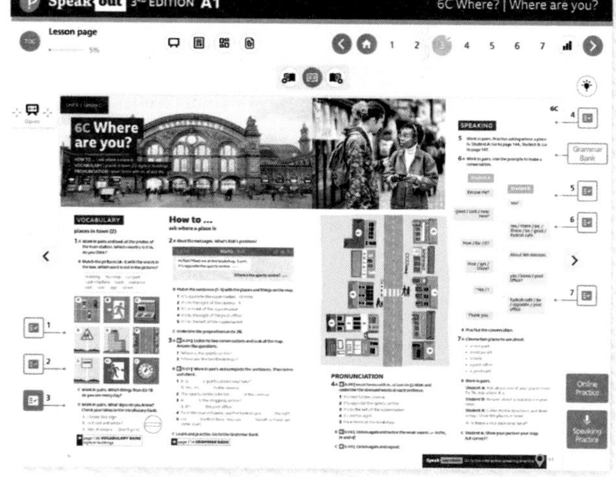

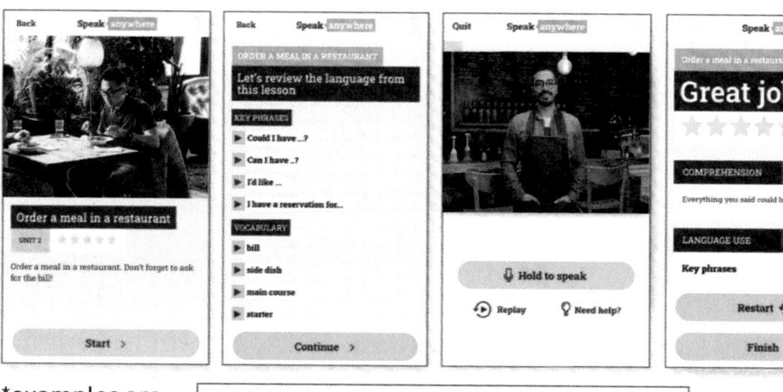

*examples are from level A2

'Speak Anywhere' *on mobile phone

'Speak Anywhere' *on computer

Lesson D – BBC video lessons

Lesson D might be the most enjoyable lesson in the book – the BBC video lesson! Units alternate between a programme clip from the BBC archive (even units), and bespoke BBC street interviews (odd units). Each lesson features a range of tasks to exploit the video fully.

Preview tasks and a summary of the video help to engage learners' interest, activate schemata and set expectations.

In the View section, students watch the video twice. During the first viewing, students complete a gist task; the second viewing is followed by tasks to check learners' more detailed understanding.

Videos are embedded in the Student's eBook and the Presentation Tool, and can also be downloaded from the Resources.

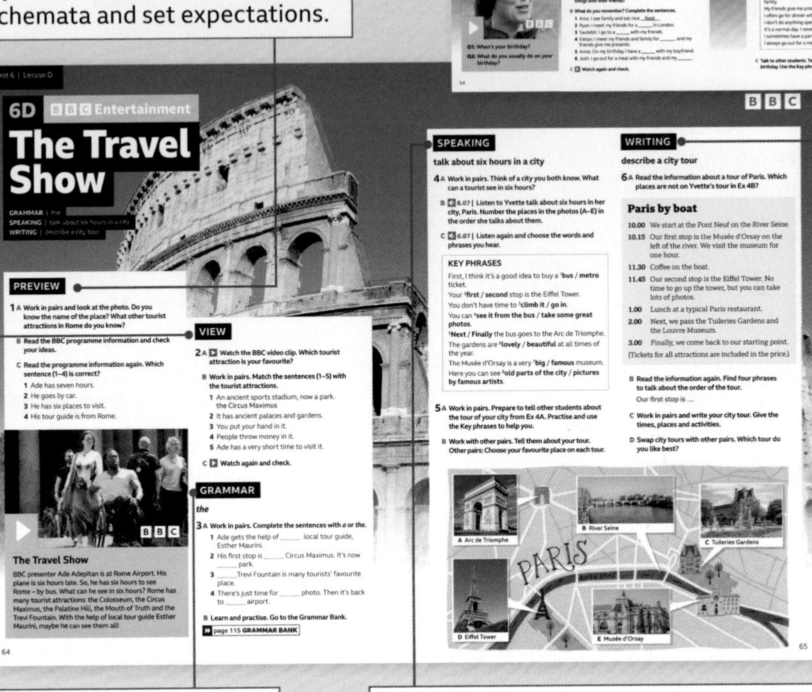

Each BBC video lesson ends with a Writing task.

The BBC video lesson teaches a grammar point that occurs in the video. This grammar point is an integral part of the grammar syllabus and is based on a GSE Learning Objective.

There is a substantial Speaking section, providing opportunities for personalised pairwork and groupwork related to the topic of the video.

The Workbook and Online Practice activities provide further practice of the target language from Lesson D. It isn't necessary for students to watch the videos again to do these activities.

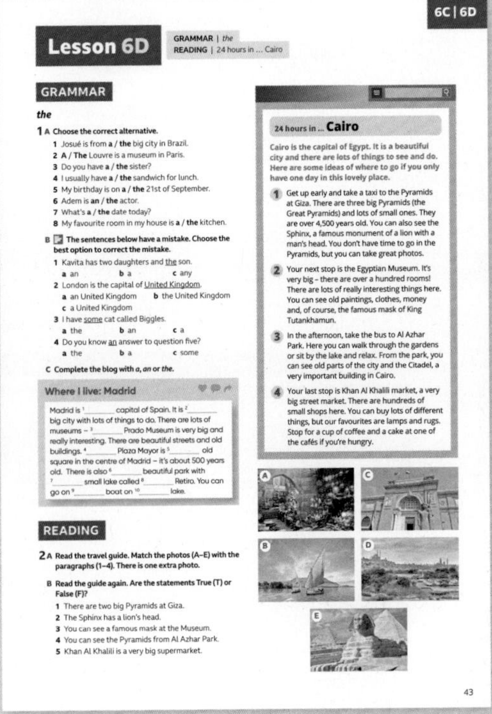

Workbook

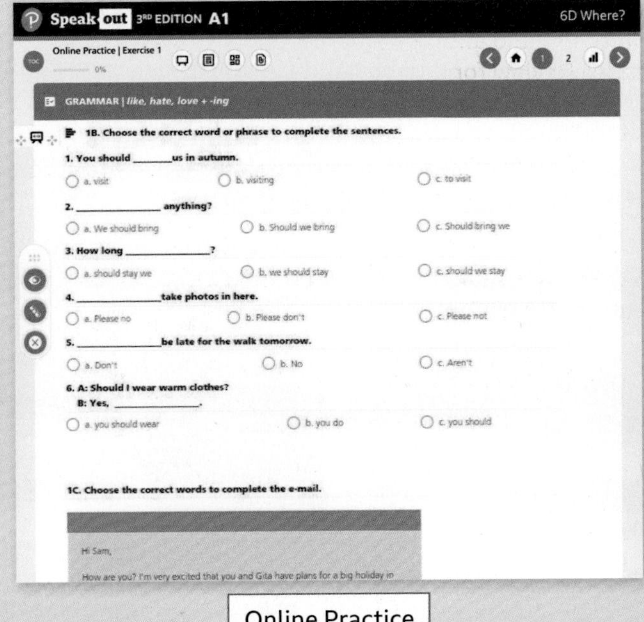

Online Practice

Review

There is a one-page Review at the end of each Student's Book unit. The Review provides practice of the language from the unit. It is designed to consolidate learners' understanding, and includes listening and pairwork speaking activities.

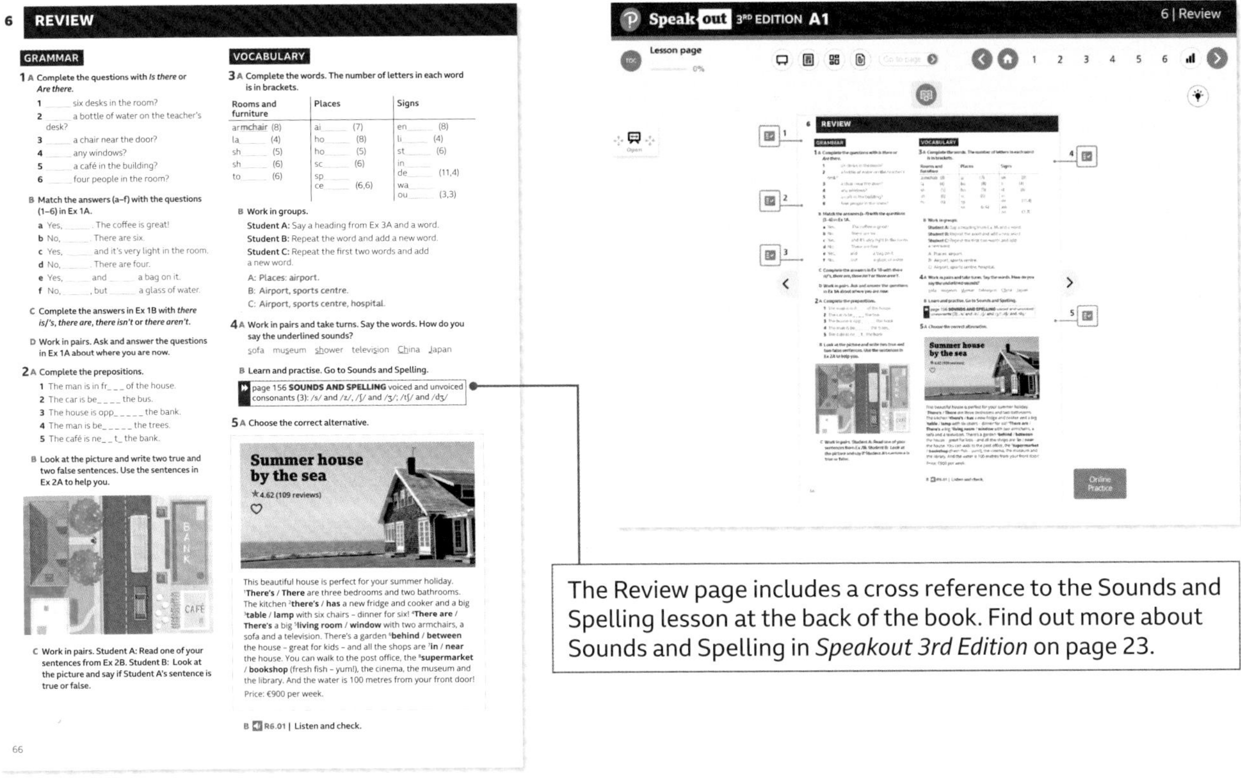

6 REVIEW

GRAMMAR

1 A Complete the questions with *Is there* or *Are there*.

1 ____ six desks in the room?
2 ____ a bottle of water on the teacher's desk?
3 ____ a chair near the door?
4 ____ any windows?
5 ____ a café in the building?
6 ____ four people in the room?

B Match the answers (a–f) with the questions (1–6) in Ex 1A.

a Yes, ____. The coffee is great!
b No, ____. There are six.
c Yes, ____ and it's very light in the room.
d No, ____. There are four.
e Yes, ____ and ____ a bag on it.
f No, ____, but ____ a glass of water.

C Complete the answers in Ex 1B with *there is/'s, there are, there isn't* or *there aren't*.

D Work in pairs. Ask and answer the questions in Ex 1A about where you are now.

2 A Complete the prepositions.

1 The man is in fr_ _ _ of the house.
2 The car is be_ _ _ _ the bus.
3 The house is opp_ _ _ _ _ the bank.
4 The man is be_ _ _ _ _ the trees.
5 The café is ne_ _ t_ the bank.

B Look at the picture and write two true and two false sentences. Use the sentences in Ex 2A to help you.

C Work in pairs. Student A: Read one of your sentences from Ex 2B. Student B: Look at the picture and say if Student A's sentence is true or false.

66

VOCABULARY

3 A Complete the words. The number of letters in each word is in brackets.

Rooms and furniture	Places	Signs
armchair (8)	ai____ (7)	en____ (8)
la____ (4)	ho____ (8)	li____ (4)
sh____ (5)	ho____ (5)	st____ (6)
sh____ (6)	sc____ (6)	in____ de____ (11,4)
to____ (6)	sp____ ce____ (6,6)	wa____ ou____ (3,3)

B Work in groups.
Student A: Say a heading from Ex 3A and a word.
Student B: Repeat the word and add a new word.
Student C: Repeat the first two words and add a new word.

A: Places: airport.
B: Airport, sports centre.
C: Airport, sports centre, hospital.

4 A Work in pairs and take turns. Say the words. How do you say the underlined sounds?
sofa museum shower television China Japan

B Learn and practise. Go to Sounds and Spelling.

page 156 **SOUNDS AND SPELLING** voiced and unvoiced consonants (3): /s/ and /z/, /ʃ/ and /ʒ/; /tʃ/ and /dʒ/

5 A Choose the correct alternative.

Summer house by the sea
4.62 (109 reviews)

This beautiful house is perfect for your summer holiday. [1]**There's / There** are three bedrooms and two bathrooms. The kitchen [2]**there's / has** a new fridge and cooker and a big [3]**table / lamp** with six chairs – dinner for six! [4]**There are / There's** a big [5]**living room / window** with two armchairs, a sofa and a television. There's a garden [6]**behind / between** the house – great for kids – and all the shops are [7]**in / near** the house. You can walk to the post office, the [8]**supermarket / bookshop** (fresh fish – yum!), the cinema, the museum and the library. And the water is 100 metres from your front door!
Price: €900 per week.

B R6.01 | Listen and check.

The Review page includes a cross reference to the Sounds and Spelling lesson at the back of the book. Find out more about Sounds and Spelling in *Speakout 3rd Edition* on page 23.

The Student's eBook provides access to the Online Practice reviews. In the Online Practice and the Workbook, there is a two-page Review after every two units, a Cumulative Review after Units 1–4 and another after Units 5–8, as well as a Cumulative Review for Units 1–8.

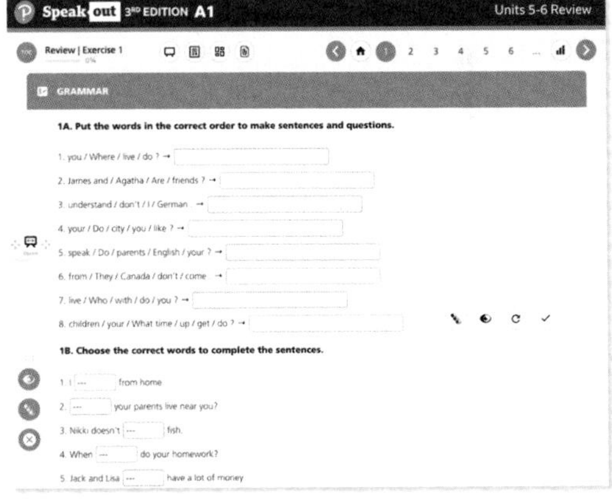

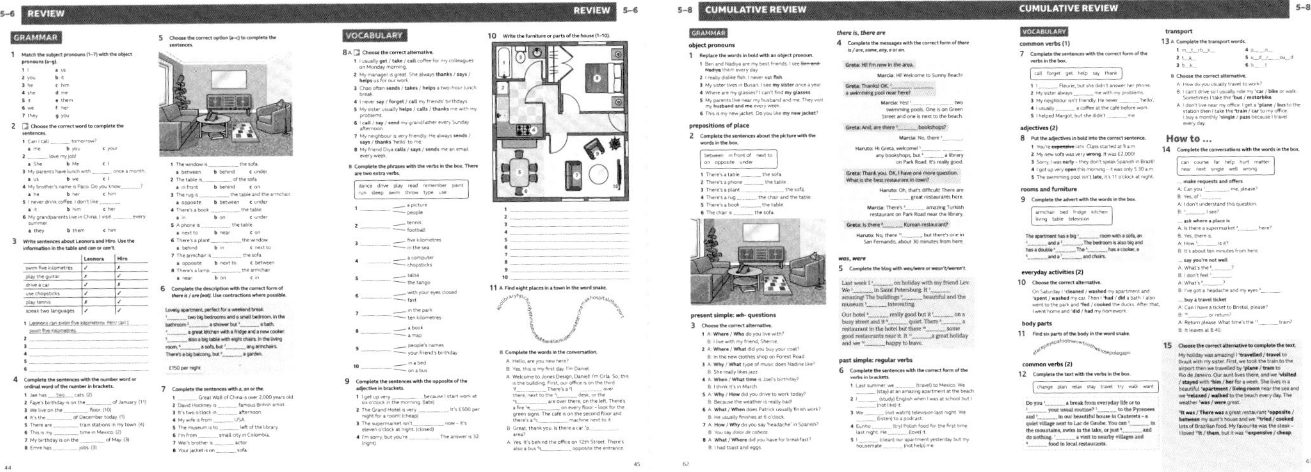

Course methodology

A note from the authors

OVERVIEW

Speakout 3rd Edition is designed to inspire both learners and teachers through engaging topics and authentic BBC material that brings those topics to life. At the same time, it offers a robust and comprehensive focus on grammar, vocabulary, functions and pronunciation. As the name of the course suggests, speaking activities are prominent, but that is not at the expense of the other core skills, which are developed systematically throughout. With this balanced approach to topics, language development and skills work, our aim has been to create a course full of lessons that genuinely engage learners and really 'work' in practice.

Each unit begins with vlogs involving speakers from around the world answering a question related to the unit topic. These clips are informal, authentic and unscripted. They provide short, manageable models of language for students to work from, as well as acting as highly motivating 'tasters' for the unit. The four lessons that follow the vlogs are all related to the unit topic and contain a rich variety of skills and language work – everything you would expect of a modern language course and more.

We recognise that motivation is key to language learning, and in order to help learners stay engaged in the learning process and to track their progress, every section of every lesson has clear, identifiable learning goals. These goals are based on the Learning Objectives from the Global Scale of English (GSE) and focus on grammar, vocabulary, functional language and skills, all carefully pitched at the target level. The language builds incrementally throughout each lesson so that by the end, learners can engage in an extended speaking and/or writing task which offers them opportunities to use all the new language they have learnt in that lesson. There is also a substantial pronunciation syllabus.

Each unit ends with a BBC video lesson which features either a clip from a BBC programme (drama, documentary, news, entertainment or travel) or BBC street interviews where people are filmed on the street answering carefully chosen questions relating to the topic. These videos are a springboard to extended speaking and writing tasks.

Topics and content

In ***Speakout 3rd Edition***, we focus on topics that are relevant to students' lives. Authenticity is important to learners, so we have chosen audio and video material sourced directly from the BBC, as well as drawing on other real-world sources for reading texts and listening activities. At lower levels, we have sometimes adapted materials by adjusting the language to make it more manageable for students whilst keeping the tone as authentic as possible.

Every unit contains a variety of rich, authentic input material, including the vlogs, street interviews, and BBC programmes featuring some of the best the BBC has to offer.

Grammar

Knowing how to recognise and use grammatical structures is central to our ability to communicate with one another. We believe that a guided discovery approach, where students are challenged to notice new forms, works best. At the same time, learning is scaffolded so that students are supported at all times in a systematic way. Clear grammar presentations are followed by written and oral practice. There is also the chance to notice and practise features of pronunciation that are connected to the grammar area being taught.

In ***Speakout 3rd Edition***, you will find:

- **Grammar in context** – The target grammar is almost always taken from the listening or reading texts, so that learners can see the grammar in context, and understand how and when it is used.
- **Noticing** – We involve students in the discovery of language patterns by asking them to identify aspects of meaning and form, and to complete rules or tables.
- **Clear language reference** – The Grammar Bank provides a clear summary of rules and usage. This serves as a reference that students can return to again and again, as well as providing related practice activities.
- **Focus on use** – We ensure that there is plenty of practice, both form- and meaning-based, in the Grammar Bank to give students confidence in manipulating the new language. On the main input page, we often include personalised practice, which is designed to be genuinely communicative and to offer students the opportunity to say something about themselves or the topic. There is also regular recycling of new language in the Review pages, and again the focus here is on moving learners towards communicative use of the language.

Vocabulary

Developing a wide range of vocabulary is key to increasing communicative effectiveness; developing a knowledge of high-frequency collocations and fixed and semi-fixed phrases is key to increasing spoken fluency. An extensive understanding of words and phrases helps learners become more confident when reading and listening, and developing a range of vocabulary is also important for effective writing. Equally vital is learner-training, equipping students with the skills to record, memorise and recall vocabulary for use at the right moment.

In ***Speakout 3rd Edition***, this is reflected in:

- **A prominent focus on vocabulary** – We include vocabulary in almost all lessons whether in a lexical set linked to a particular topic, as preparation for a speaking activity, or to aid comprehension of a video clip or reading text. Where we want students to use the vocabulary actively, we encourage them to talk about their own lives or opinions. The Vocabulary Bank extends the vocabulary taught in the lessons, often using photographs and pictures to support students' understanding, and providing audio support, too.
- **Focus on 'chunks'** – As well as lexical sets, we also regularly focus on how words fit together with other words. We get students to notice how words are used in a text and to focus on high-frequency 'chunks' such as verb-noun collocations or whole phrases.
- **Focus on vocabulary systems** – We give regular attention to word-building skills, a valuable tool in expanding vocabulary. At higher levels, the Vocabulary sections deal with systems such as affixation, multi-word verbs and compound words in greater depth.
- **Recycling** – Practice exercises ensure that vocabulary is encountered on a number of occasions: within the lessons, in the Vocabulary Bank at the back of the book, in subsequent lessons and on the Review page.

Functional Language (How to ...)

One thing that both teachers and learners appreciate is the need to manage communication in a wide variety of encounters, and to know what's appropriate to say in given situations. These can be transactional exchanges, where the main focus is on getting something done (e.g. buying something in a shop or calling to make an enquiry), or interactional exchanges, where the main focus is on socialising with others (e.g. talking about the weekend or responding appropriately to good news). As one learner commented, 'Grammar rules aren't enough – I need to know what to say.' In ***Speakout 3rd Edition***, the focus on functional language comes in the 'C' Lesson in each unit, under the new heading of 'How to ...'.

The third lesson in every unit of ***Speakout 3rd Edition*** looks at one such situation and focuses on the functional language needed. Learners hear or see the language used in context and then practise it in mini-situations, in both written and spoken formats.

Something that students often find frustrating when learning a language is the lack of opportunity to speak English outside class. At the end of the third lesson, students can do the 'Speak Anywhere' interactive speaking practice activity. These digital speaking 'roleplays' use speech recognition technology to give students the opportunity to build their confidence by having a realistic conversation with a bot on the topic of the lesson, and then receive feedback.

Also linked to the third lesson are the Mediation lessons. These standalone lessons appear at the back of the book and are based on GSE Mediation Learning Objectives.

Speaking

The dynamism of many lessons depends on the success of the speaking tasks, whether the task is a short oral practice of new language, a discussion comparing information or opinions, a personal response to a reading text, or a presentation where a student might speak uninterrupted for several minutes. Students develop fluency when they are motivated to speak. For this to happen, engaging topics and tasks are essential, as is the sequencing of stages and task design. For longer tasks, students often need to prepare their ideas and language in a structured way. This all-important rehearsal time leads to more motivation and confidence as well as greater accuracy, fluency and complexity in language use. Also, where appropriate, students should hear a model before they speak, in order to have a realistic goal.

There are several strands to speaking in ***Speakout 3rd Edition***:

- **Communicative practice** – After introducing new language (vocabulary, grammar or functional language), there are many opportunities in ***Speakout 3rd Edition*** for students to use that language in activities which focus on communication as well as accuracy. These include personalised exchanges, conversations and roleplays.
- **Focus on fluency** – In every unit of ***Speakout 3rd Edition***, we include opportunities for students to respond spontaneously. They might be asked to respond to a series of questions, to a short video or to a text, or to take part in conversations, discussions and roleplays. These activities involve a variety of interactional formations, i.e. in pairs or as groups.
- **Speaking strategies and sub-skills** – Throughout ***Speakout 3rd Edition***, students are encouraged to develop speaking strategies and sub-skills highlighted in the GSE. Some examples include using fixed expressions to keep a conversation going, asking for clarification, managing a phone conversation and giving reasons for a viewpoint.

- **Extended speaking tasks** – In the final lesson of each unit, as well as in other speaking tasks throughout the course, students are encouraged to attempt more adventurous and extended use of language in tasks such as problem solving, developing a project or telling a story. These tasks go beyond discussion; they include a model, rehearsal time, useful language and a concrete outcome.

Listening

For most users of English (or any language), listening is the most frequently utilised skill. A learner who can speak well but who has problems understanding language to at least the same level is unlikely to be a competent communicator or user of the language. We feel that listening can be developed effectively through well-structured materials. As with speaking, the choice of interesting topics and texts works hand in hand with carefully considered sequencing and task design. At the same time, listening activities can act as a springboard to stimulate discussion in class.

There are several strands to listening in ***Speakout 3rd Edition***:

- **Focus on authentic recordings** – We believe that it is motivating for all levels of learner to listen to authentic material. As such, each unit starts with vlogs and also includes either a clip from a BBC programme, or a street interview filmed in locations around central London. At the higher levels, there are also authentic, unscripted BBC radio and podcast extracts. All are invaluable in the way they expose learners to real language in use as well as different varieties of English. Where audio recordings, particularly at lower levels, are scripted, they nevertheless aim to reflect the patterns of natural speech.
- **Focus on sub-skills and strategies** – Tasks across the recordings in each unit are designed with a number of sub-skills and strategies in mind. The latter are taken from the GSE and include, for example, listening and predicting what will come next, extracting key details, identifying chronological sequences, and understanding technical instructions.
- **As a context for new language** – We see listening as a key mode of input, and ***Speakout 3rd Edition*** includes many listening texts which contain target grammar, vocabulary or functional language in their natural contexts. Learners are encouraged to notice this new language and how and where it occurs, sometimes by using the audioscripts as a resource.
- **As a model for speaking** – In the third and fourth lessons of each unit, the recordings serve as models for speaking tasks. These models reveal the ways in which speakers use specific language to structure their discourse, for example with regard to turn-taking, hesitating and checking for understanding. These recordings also serve as a goal for the learners' own speaking.

Reading

Reading is a priority for many students, whether it's for study, work or pleasure, and can be practised alone, anywhere and at any time. Learners who read regularly tend to have a richer, more varied vocabulary, and are often better writers, which in turn supports their oral skills. Within the classroom, reading texts can introduce stimulating topics and act as springboards for class discussion.

There are several strands to reading in ***Speakout 3rd Edition***:

- **Focus on authentic texts** – As with ***Speakout 3rd Edition*** listening materials, there is an emphasis on authenticity. Many of the reading texts draw on real-world sources, including newspapers, magazines, media websites and books. We have chosen up-to-date, relevant texts to stimulate interest and motivate learners to read, and the texts represent a variety of genres that correspond to the text types that learners will probably encounter in their everyday lives.
- **Focus on sub-skills and strategies** – In ***Speakout 3rd Edition***, we strive to maintain authenticity in the way readers interact with a text. We always give students a reason to read and provide tasks which bring about or simulate authentic reading, including real-life tasks such as summarising, extracting specific information, reacting to an opinion or following an anecdote. We also focus on strategies for decoding texts, such as guessing the meaning of unknown vocabulary, understanding pronoun referencing and paying attention to discourse markers. As with the listening and speaking sub-skills, the reading sub-skills syllabus is based on the GSE.
- **Noticing new language** – Noticing language in use is a key step towards the development of a rich vocabulary and greater all-round proficiency, and this can be most easily achieved through reading. In ***Speakout 3rd Edition***, reading texts often serve as contexts for introducing grammar and vocabulary as well as discourse features.
- **As a model for writing** – In the writing sections, the texts serve as models for students in terms of overall organisation as well as style and language content.

Writing

Many students need to develop their formal writing for professional and exam-taking purposes, while others prefer to focus on less formal genres. For this reason, ***Speakout 3rd Edition*** covers both formal text types such as essays, formal emails and reports, and informal genres such as discussion forums, personal emails and social media posts.

There are several strands to writing in ***Speakout 3rd Edition***:

- **Focus on genres** – In every unit, there is a section that focuses on a genre of writing, for example emails. We provide a model to show the conventions of the genre and, where appropriate, we highlight fixed phrases associated with it. We then ask students to produce their own piece of writing. While there is always a written product, we also focus on the writing process, including stages such as brainstorming, planning and checking.
- **Focus on sub-skills and strategies** – While dealing with the genres, we include a section which focuses on a sub-skill or strategy that is generally applicable to all writing. Sub-skills include paragraphing, organising content and using linking words and pronouns. Strategies include activities like writing a first draft quickly, keeping your reader in mind and self-editing. We present the sub-skill by asking students to notice the feature. We then provide an opportunity for students to practise it.
- **Lesson D writing task** – At the end of the final lesson in each unit, following the final speaking task, we include a writing task. The idea is for students to develop fluency in their writing. While we always provide a model, the emphasis here is on using writing to generate ideas and personal responses.
- **Writing as a classroom activity** – We believe that writing can be very usefully employed as an aid to speaking and as a reflective technique for responding to texts – akin to the practice of writing notes in the margins of books. It also provides a change of pace and focus in lessons. Activities such as short dictations, note-taking, brainstorming on paper and group story writing are all included in ***Speakout 3rd Edition***.

Pronunciation

For many learners the ability to pronounce English in a comprehensible way is very important. It is also vital in helping them to understand spoken English. In ***Speakout 3rd Edition***, we have taken a practical, integrated approach to developing students' pronunciation, highlighting features that often cause problems in conjunction with a given area of grammar, particular vocabulary items, or functional language. Where relevant to the level, a grammar, vocabulary or functional language focus is followed by a focus on a feature of pronunciation, for example, word stress, sentence stress, intonation or the weak forms of auxiliary verbs. Students are given the opportunity to listen to models of the pronunciation, notice the key feature and then practise it. In the Vocabulary Bank, we give the pronunciation of each item. At A1 level, there is a comprehensive focus on common sounds and their spelling, as well as on potentially confusing sound–spelling relationships.

Future Skills

We recognise that in addition to language skills, students need to be equipped with a range of other skills to improve their levels of employability and help them to thrive in the future. For this reason, we include a Future Skills feature in roughly half the lessons. The key skills taught are: collaboration, communication, creative and critical thinking, leadership, self-management, and social responsibility. These sections comprise short notes highlighting the relevant skills as they occur naturally in the flow of the lesson, followed by mini-tasks that encourage students to develop those skills.

Teaching A1 Learners

Teaching any particular level of language learner presents the teacher with a unique set of challenges and rewards. Some are particular to that level only, while others are applicable to a number of levels. Here we will try to offer a few thoughts and guidelines for teaching A1 learners.

A1 can be the most rewarding level to teach; every lesson brings learners tangible advances in knowledge and skills, as they leave the lesson able to do or say something that an hour or two before was completely unknown to them. The particular challenges a teacher faces with A1 learners require less in terms of knowledge of the language and more in terms of technique, in particular the ability to convey the meaning of new language and instructions to people who may have heard little or no English in their lives.

It's sometimes said that there are no true A1 learners in English among adult learners, because of the omnipresence of the language, but of course there are many who are beginning their study of English with no more than a handful of words and phrases and perhaps very little experience of learning a language in a classroom. This point is perhaps one of the most important to keep in mind – that your A1 students may find the context and routines of your classroom completely alien. Their expectations will be informed by their previous learning experiences, and may include a view of the teacher's role as authoritarian and directive. Routines and formats we take for granted, like checking an exercise in pairs, completing communicative activities with more attention to meaning than form, and working out grammar rules and meanings of words from context, may be new and strange to the A1 learner. For this reason, considerable attention needs to be given to orienting A1 learners to what's expected of them, to how to complete basic procedures, and most of all to taking the initiative in indicating when they don't understand something. The nodding, smiling face of an A1 learner may be hiding an utterly confused individual too afraid to show their disorientation, and it's vital that the teacher establishes a clear communication with students from the start, so that minutes and lessons don't pass where one or more students don't know what's going on.

Here are our Top Tips to help at this level:

- When planning your lessons, think through in detail how you will set up activities. It can be useful for A1 learners to hear instructions in English and become familiar with some basic expressions, and that should be part of your routine. It's also important to invest time in demonstrating to students how an activity is supposed to be done. This is essentially learner training; training students how to function in a modern language classroom.
- Be realistic in your expectations of what A1 learners can produce; while some learners at this level can comfortably carry out speaking tasks in the Student's Book, some will be very reticent about saying anything at all. Aside from providing encouragement and support, often there is little you can do to hurry the pace of their learning.
- Review of vocabulary is important at any level, but at A1 it is crucial. In part because the sound system of English is new, A1 learners find retention of vocabulary extremely difficult. Try to work vocabulary review games and activities into your warmers, fillers and coolers.
- Whenever learners do written tasks, whether they're copying from the whiteboard or completing a task in their books or tablets/laptops, closely monitor what they write. It's common for A1 learners to have serious difficulties with English spelling, and important that the record that they go home with is accurate.
- If you have a monolingual group and speak the learners' first language, consider doing so very selectively. It's useful for learners to hear English as much as possible, and careful planning of instructions can make these valuable listening practice. And the more you rely on learners' L1 to communicate, the more they will – and the greater difficulty they'll have becoming functional in English.
- If you have a multilingual group, consider providing extra support and/or homework for learners who are not able to rely on having similar words or grammar in their language or who have particular skills needs, for example coping with a different script.
- Grade your language so that it is easy to understand. As obvious as this may seem, it's important to remind yourself before and during a lesson. Grading language is a teaching skill that comes naturally for some teachers and which other teachers need to work on. Developing your own ability in this area will benefit your students enormously.
- Use gestures, visuals, real objects and concept questions when introducing language.
- If you're the kind of teacher who likes to adapt the Student's Book, consider limiting the extent to which you do this at A1. A first English course can be daunting for beginners, and the Student's Book can serve as a kind of anchor for them; and if they found a lesson completely overwhelming, it's much easier for them to go home and review the lesson if it came directly from the Student's Book.
- Be consistent about giving and checking homework, such as exercises online. A large proportion of learning – particularly retention – happens during self-study rather than during formal lessons.
- Finally, keep in mind that a language lesson may be an emotionally very stressful experience for A1 learners, more than at any other level. For this reason things that make each individual feel recognised and 'human' – encouragement, praise, the use of students' names, even a well-placed smile or eye contact (where culturally appropriate) – can go a long way towards learners leaving a lesson feeling positive and motivated, and looking forward to the next one.

Antonia Clare, Frances Eales, Steve Oakes and JJ Wilson

Sounds and Spellings

The importance of sounds for A1 students

At A1 level, it's important for students to become aware of some basic elements of English pronunciation which will help lay a good foundation for the rest of their learning. In the main lessons, they learn about sentence stress and intonation as well as some useful patterns such as the pronunciation of the third person *-s* in the present simple and *-ed* endings in the past simple. The lessons also include an initial introduction to how to link words in connected speech. However, for many students the sounds of a new language will present a number of specific challenges and this often depends on their first language and which sounds are very different for them or do not exist in their language. A focus on sounds at this level can help learners with all four language skills:

- **Listening:** When we know about the sounds of a language, we can become better at 'bottom-up listening', that is we can build up words and phrases from hearing their sounds. Of course, at the same time we use a lot of 'top-down listening', that is guessing what is being said from context and background knowledge.
- **Speaking:** When we learn to speak a new language, we often need a good amount of practice in making sounds and words. We may have to learn to use our mouth and voice in a way that is new to us. It's very confidence-building when we can pronounce words and phrases in a way that's understood by other people.
- **Reading:** When we're reading, most of us sub-vocalise the sound of words as part of our process of understanding what we're reading. Students need to be able to recognise the typical pronunciation of certain combinations of sounds to increase their ability to read fluently.
- **Writing:** Although these days many of us have spell-checking software and often write informally in messages and on social media where accurate spelling may not be so vital, many of us want or need to learn to write accurately in another language. Therefore it's important to focus on spelling and its relationship with sounds right from the beginning of our language learning.

The content of the Sounds and Spelling section

In the Sounds and Spelling section students have the opportunity to learn about some key recurrent elements of English pronunciation and writing:

- syllable stress in words and the schwa /ə/ sound often used in unstressed parts of words
- voiced and unvoiced consonant sounds
- short and long vowel sounds
- typical spellings for the three elements above
- common words which have 'special' spellings
- the final silent *e* and how this affects pronunciation

Using phonetic* symbols

Phonetic symbols can be a very useful tool for A1 students. They are particularly helpful:

- when students want a record of how a word is pronounced (and don't have access to an online recording!)
- when the spelling and sounds of a word are different, e.g. ***women*** /ˈwɪmɪn/, ***listen*** /ˈlɪsən/
- when two or three letters are only one sound, e.g. ***repeat*** /rɪˈpiːt/, ***colour*** /ˈkʌlə/

You may feel that it's a bit too challenging at this level for your students to learn the symbols, especially if they are coping with a new alphabet. However, we suggest that you think of the phonetic alphabet as a tool kit, and introduce the individual 'tools' to your students as needed, rather than approaching the phonetic alphabet as a system that students have to learn in its entirety as soon as possible.

**phonetic* = the sounds of all languages; *phonemic* = the sounds of one language – we use phonetic in the teacher's notes because it is a more internationally recognised word.

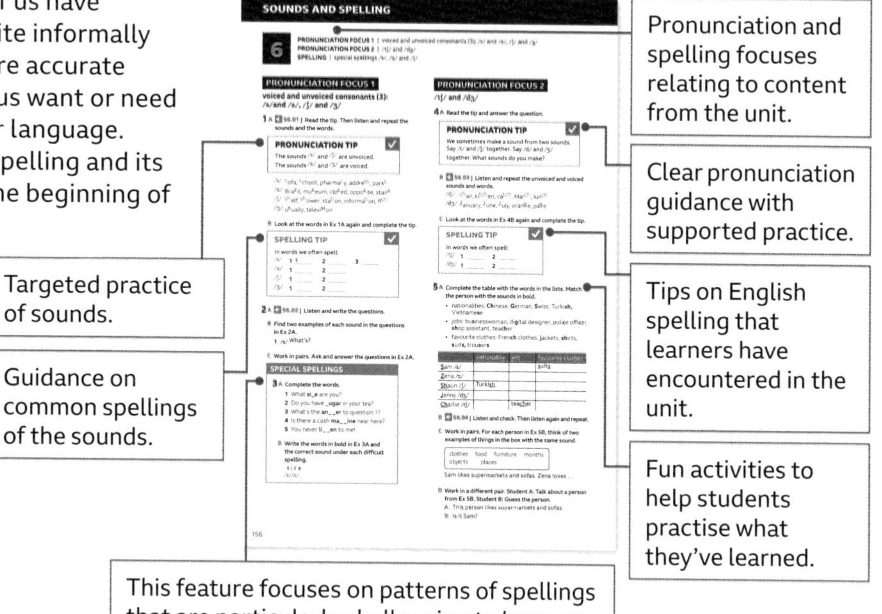
SOUNDS AND SPELLING
Pronunciation and spelling focuses relating to content from the unit.
Clear pronunciation guidance with supported practice.
Tips on English spelling that learners have encountered in the unit.
Fun activities to help students practise what they've learned.
Targeted practice of sounds.
Guidance on common spellings of the sounds.
This feature focuses on patterns of spellings that are particularly challenging to learners.

Testing and assessment while using *Speakout 3rd Edition*

In-course testing

Speakout 3rd Edition offers a comprehensive package of tests. All tests are supplied in A and B formats (different tests which can be used for retakes) and there is also a version suitable for use with students with dyslexia. Tests are available as both ready-to-print PDFs and editable Word documents in the Teacher's Resources area on Pearson English Connect at www.pearsonenglish.com/speakout3e, or as tests assignable online via the Test Generator. The Tests Package audio, audioscripts, Answer Keys and marking guidelines for Writing and Speaking are also available in the Teacher's Resources area.

Types of test

Quick Day 1 Entry Test – a quick multiple-choice diagnostic test to allow teachers to identify any gaps in students' grammar knowledge from the previous level before beginning the current level

Full Unit Tests – a three-part test for every unit, testing Grammar, Vocabulary and Functional Language (Part A); Listening, Reading and Writing (Part B); and Speaking (Part C)

Quick Unit Quizzes – twenty-five multiple-choice questions testing Grammar, Vocabulary and Functional Language from the unit

Progress Tests – four tests for each level, for use after Units 2, 4, 6 and 8, with cumulative testing of the preceding two units; consists of Grammar, Vocabulary and Functional Language (Part A); Listening and Reading (Part B); and Speaking and Writing (Part C)

Mid-course Test – a multiple-choice cumulative test for use after Unit 4 of each level, testing Grammar, Vocabulary and Functional Language from the preceding four units

Full End of Course Test – a three-part cumulative test for use after Unit 8 of each level, testing Grammar, Vocabulary and Functional Language (Part A); Listening, Reading and Writing (Part B); and Speaking (Part C)

Quick End of Course Test – Part A of the Full End of Course Test is multiple-choice, and may be used as a standalone test

Adult Benchmark and Pearson English International Certificate

Speakout 3rd Edition is mapped to Adult Benchmark and Pearson English International Certificate.

Adult Benchmark

Benchmark takes the time, complexity and subjectivity out of the assessment process. This straightforward yet powerful tool makes it easy to measure real progress, fast. And with just a few basic requirements, the test can even be taken from home. Use the Benchmark Tests alongside any English course to smooth and accelerate the journey to fluency.

Pearson English International Certificate

Pearson English International Certificate (PTE General) gives learners official certification of their English language skills at any level. Awarded by Edexcel, International Certificate is recognised by universities and employers in many countries around the world. The exam tests authentic communication skills in real-world contexts and is available in both paper-based and computer-based formats.

Lead-in

LESSON OVERVIEW

The activities on the Lead-in page are designed to present various sets of basic vocabulary, some or all of which may be familiar to your Ss, and some basic functional language for the classroom. Use the Lead-in page to assess your Ss' existing knowledge (as an informal diagnostic test, as you listen to and assess their current language skills, if any) and/or to revise or teach the target language in each activity.

Online Teaching

If you're using these exercises online, you might find the following tips useful:

- **Ex 1A:** Display the page on your device and use a pointer to name the items, inviting Ss to repeat. Then go on to the matching task.
- **Vocabulary Bank, international words / classroom language, Exs 1B:** For each listen and repeat exercise, remind Ss to put their microphones on mute. Display the photos/ pictures and play the recording for Ss to repeat. Then point and ask Ss to repeat.

Additional Materials

For Teachers:

Presentation Tool Lead-in

Online Digital Resources

Vocabulary Bank Lead-in

For Students:

Online Practice Lead-in

Workbook Lead-in

VOCABULARY

international English

EXTRA SUPPORT: TEACHER The work on international words at the beginning of the Lead-in should give Ss some confidence that they already know a lot of English! They will probably have other ideas about international words and you could add a few more that you know will be familiar. Note that there is a focus on *a/an* in the Vocabulary Bank for Lesson 1B, but this isn't covered in the Lead-in, where all the items presented use *a*.

1 A Refer Ss to the photos and say the words. Then ask Ss to match the photos with the words. Go through the answers, pointing to the photos and eliciting the words.

EXTRA SUPPORT: TEACHER At this stage Ss won't know the pronunciation of the alphabet to give their answers to a matching activity like this, or like Exs 1A in the Vocabulary Bank. You could go ahead to Lesson 1C and work on just the alphabet, or you could teach letters as you go along in the Lead-in, or simply project the photos so Ss can tell you the words as you point to each photo. Alternatively, you may decide simply not to worry about the pronunciation of the letters at this stage.

ANSWERS:

A a restaurant	**B** a photo	**C** a pizza
D a park	**E** a coffee	**F** a bus

B L.01 | Play the recording. Ask Ss to listen and repeat chorally. When you have done this, call on a few individual Ss to repeat and praise their efforts.

C Put Ss in pairs to write five more English words. To prompt this, you could show some pictures of words that you think they'll know.

EXTRA SUPPORT: TEACHER Other international words which Ss might know are: *airport, café, internet, menu, sandwich, hospital, tea, television.* There may also be ideas from a particular group of Ss who share a language about 'borrowed' words from English. Many computer-/internet-/technology-related words may be the same.

D Refer Ss to the Vocabulary Bank on page 124 to check if any of their ideas are there.

VB **page 124 VOCABULARY BANK** international words

The Vocabulary Bank pages are an integral part of the lessons and Ss will be referred to them frequently. You might want to explain this to your Ss at this point and show them where the Vocabulary Bank appears in the book. The activities should only be omitted from the lessons if you are confident that your Ss already know the vocabulary. If you don't use the practice exercises in class, it would be a good idea to set them as homework.

international words

1 A Ask Ss to match the international words (1–10) with the photos (A–J). They should work alone at first, then compare in pairs before going through the answers. Drill thoroughly chorally and individually.

EXTRA SUPPORT: DYSLEXIA Dyslexic learners may find that covering the words they are not currently matching with a photo helps them to focus.

EXTRA SUPPORT: TEACHER In case any false beginners ask, the reason *university* doesn't use 'an' is because it doesn't start with a vowel sound. Information on this comes in the Vocabulary Bank for Lesson 1B.

ANSWERS:

1 I **2** B **3** G **4** D **5** F
6 C **7** A **8** J **9** E **10** H

B VB.L.01 | Ask Ss to look at the photos and not the words. Explain that this is to help them remember and associate the meaning and the word. Then play the recording for them to listen and repeat.

C Put Ss in A/B pairs. Student A points to a photo, Student B says the word. Move around and listen. After a few turns, ask them to change roles. At the end, drill any words that were causing problems.

numbers 0–10

2 A Start to count, using your fingers and saying the numbers. Encourage Ss to join in with you. Refer Ss to the box and ask them to write the words in the box next to the numbers. Don't check the answers yet.

EXTRA SUPPORT: DYSLEXIA Ss with dyslexia can find lists of words or phrases presented in boxes difficult to process. To help them with this activity, provide the number words in the box as a vertical list, which is easier to read, for Ss to match with the figures in the exercise. The figures and number words could also be presented as two vertical lists side-by-side for Ss to draw lines between them.

B L.02 | Ask Ss to listen and check their answers. Then play the recording again for them to listen and repeat.

EXTRA SUPPORT: TEACHER You might want or need to tell Ss that, in addition to 'zero', '0' can be said as 'nought' (BrE) and also as 'oh' (e.g. in phone numbers).

ANSWERS:

1 one	**2** two	**3** three	**4** four
5 five	**6** six	**7** seven	**8** eight
9 nine	**10** ten		

C L.03 | Tell Ss they should listen and write the numbers as words not numerals. Pause and repeat items as necessary. Ask Ss to compare in pairs then go through the answers.

EXTRA SUPPORT Beginner level Ss can have problems with reading and spelling, especially those with beginner literacy or dyslexia. Help Ss with the (confusing) pronunciation/spelling of *one*, *two* and *eight*. You could also point out the silent letters at the end of words (e.g. *five*, *nine*) and explain how this silent *e* makes the vowel sound long. Ss could highlight silent letters in colour and rewrite the words several times.

EXTRA SUPPORT: DYSLEXIA Dyslexic learners can find simultaneous listening and writing a challenge. You could give them two options for each number and they then circle the number they hear.

ANSWERS AND AUDIOSCRIPT:

five, nine, one, seven, ten, zero, six, three, eight, two, four

D Demonstrate this activity with a stronger student, then put Ss in A/B pairs. Student A says a number. Student B says the next number, then chooses another number to say. With stronger classes, you can do this around the class with Ss calling on each other to continue. This could also provide an ice-breaker activity for the class, with each student saying their name and then the number.

days of the week

3 A Point to the calendar on your computer, device or watch and say the day (e.g. 'Today is Tuesday.'). See if Ss can name the other days. Refer them to the task and ask them to number the days, starting with Monday as '1' (as in the example). Don't go through the answers yet.

EXTRA SUPPORT: TEACHER Monday is day one in some cultures but be aware that in others the weekend occurs on different days. In Arabic for example, the name for Sunday translates as 'Day one' or 'First day'. The weekend is Saturday and Sunday in western cultures, but in eastern cultures it may be Thursday and Friday.

B L.04 | Play the recording for Ss to listen and check. Confirm the answers with the class, then play the recording again for Ss to listen and repeat. Pay close attention to *Tuesday* and *Thursday* as Ss often confuse these. Remind Ss that days need a capital letter in English.

ANSWERS AND AUDIOSCRIPT:

Monday, Tuesday, Wednesday, Thursday, Friday, Saturday, Sunday

C Put Ss in pairs. Tell them to cover the words in Ex 3A and name the weekdays and the weekend days. Listen and correct as needed.

EXTRA SUPPORT Introduce a *Look Say Cover Write Check* system with the days of the week. Ss work alone, look at each word in turn, say it aloud, then cover and write it again alongside. They then reveal it and check. Ss need to be extra attentive to spelling and capitalisation. Suggest that they repeat this procedure every two days and at the end of the week they should know the words.

classroom language

EXTRA SUPPORT: TEACHER Depending on your class, Ss may not be expecting the lesson to be conducted in English. Explain at the start that this is your intention and point out the benefits of spending some time in an English-medium bubble, even just for a few hours a week. The introduction of classroom language is to support this.

4 A Explain to Ss that they will learn some phrases for use during the lesson. Look at the conversations and ask Ss to complete them with the words provided. Look at the example and with weaker classes, complete the next sentence together, then move around the class and see how Ss are doing. Ask Ss to check in pairs. Don't check the answers yet.

EXTRA SUPPORT: DYSLEXIA Ss with dyslexia have difficulty with looking at text in two different places as text is already unstable for them. Provide the words in the box as a vertical list that Ss can place alongside the exercise and move up and down as they make their choice of word to fill each gap.

B L.05 | Ask Ss to listen to the conversations and check their answers. Play each conversation separately, pausing after each item and allowing Ss to compare answers in pairs, before checking the answers as a class, writing them on the board. Then play the recording again and invite Ss to say the sentences with the speakers.

ANSWERS:

2 know	**3** English	**4** Thank
5 page	**6** don't	**7** repeat
8 understand		

EXTRA IDEA Put Ss in pairs to practise the conversations. When they have finished, ask them to change roles. If you have time, get Ss to practise the conversations in open pairs across the classroom, nominating two Ss each time. The other Ss listen. This encourages Ss because they are saying something correctly, as they are reading from a script, as well as developing the confidence to hear their own voice speak English aloud in the group.

C Refer Ss to the Vocabulary Bank on page 124.

page 124 **VOCABULARY BANK** classroom language **VB**

classroom language

1 A Read the verbs and phrases (1–12) with the class. Ask Ss to match them with the pictures (A–L) working alone, then compare in pairs. Go through the answers.

EXTRA SUPPORT: DYSLEXIA To help Ss with dyslexia, you could divide the pictures and their corresponding verbs and phrases into two sets of six or even three sets of four for Ss to work on one set at a time. Covering the words they are not working on will also help reduce distraction.

ANSWERS:

1 D	**2** C	**3** L	**4** K	**5** A	**6** B
7 H	**8** G	**9** J	**10** F	**11** E	**12** I

B VB.L.02 | Tell Ss to look at the pictures, not the words, listen and repeat chorally.

C Put Ss in groups of three or four and ask a stronger student to give a classroom instruction. The other Ss do the action. Ss continue in their groups, taking turns to be Student A.

EXTRA IDEA Work with Ss to create classroom posters with key instructions on them. When Ss start to use their own language, you or their peers can point to one of these posters to remind them of the English phrase.

1 welcome!

GSE LEARNING OBJECTIVES

1A Hello

- LISTENING | Understand people saying 'hello': hello and goodbye
- Introduce yourself: present simple *be*: *I*, *you*; countries and nationalities
- Pronunciation: intonation in greetings
- Write a chat message to introduce yourself; use capital letters, full stops and question marks

GSE INFORMATION

LISTENING
22 Can understand the main information when people introduce themselves (e.g. name, age, where they are from).

GRAMMAR
24 Can use subject pronouns with the correct form of the verb 'be' in the simple present.

VOCABULARY
10–29 Can use language related to greeting and saying hello.

10–29 Can use language related to introductions.

SPEAKING
13 Can ask someone what their nationality is.

10–29 Can use language related to nation, nationality and language.

WRITING
24 Can write a few basic sentences introducing themselves (e.g. name, age, where they are from), given prompts or a model.

1B Two jobs

- READING | Read about people with two jobs: jobs
- Pronunciation: word stress in jobs
- Talk about people and their jobs: present simple: *be*: *he*, *she*, *it*

GSE INFORMATION

VOCABULARY
10–29 Can use language related to jobs.

READING
28 Can extract personal details in a limited way.

GRAMMAR
24 Can use subject personal pronouns.

SPEAKING
27 Can say what someone's job is, using familiar common job names.

1C Checking in

- HOW TO ... | ask and answer simple questions: the alphabet
- Pronunciation: the alphabet

GSE INFORMATION

VOCABULARY
11 Can say the letters of the alphabet.

10 Can write the letters of the alphabet in upper and lower case.

HOW TO ...
22 Can understand the main information when people introduce themselves (e.g. name, age, where they are from).

SPEAKING
25 Can ask and answer simple questions in areas of immediate need or on very familiar topics.

1D What's your name?

- BBC STREET INTERVIEWS | Understand street interviews about what's in your bag: common objects
- Talk about what's in your bag: singular and plural nouns; *a*, *an*; *have*, *has*
- Write a lost and found post

GSE INFORMATION

PREVIEW
10–29 Can use language related to household objects and possessions.

VIEW
30 Can identify simple information in a short video, provided that the visual supports this information and the delivery is slow and clear.

22 Can understand the main information when people introduce themselves (e.g. name, age, where they are from).

GRAMMAR
25 Can use common forms of 'have' in the present tense.

WRITING
25 Can write simple sentences about things that they and other people have.

SPEAKING
28 Can exchange personal details (e.g. where they live, things they have).

For full coverage of GSE Learning Objectives go to page 222.

BBC VLOGS

This is a short activity that can be used as an introduction to the unit topic and a warm-up to Lesson 1A. It shouldn't be exploited or taught at length, just played once or twice in class.

Introduce yourself to the class, saying *My name's ... . I'm from ...* . As you do this, gesture to yourself and write the statements on the board. Then to their left write the two questions, i.e. *What's your name?* and *Where are you from?* Explain that Ss will watch a video of people answering these questions. They should listen and count how many speakers are from England. Play the video for Ss to answer the question. Put them in pairs to check their ideas, then play the video once more if necessary. Check the answer with the class.

ANSWER:

Two speakers are from England.

EXTRA IDEA If Ss want to watch the video again outside class, you could ask them to listen for the other countries. (Note that Ss will need to write the names of five countries in Lesson 1A, Ex 6, so this may be good preparation for that.)

If your class is weaker, provide greater support to exploit the video material by giving them these countries as a list, and asking Ss to tick the countries as they hear them: *Australia, China, England, Japan, Poland, Portugal, Serbia, Spain, the United States.*

NOTE The vlogs have been provided by people from around the world in response to the same question. The video content was filmed by them on their own mobile phones, so the picture quality varies considerably and in some cases is of a lower quality. However, this adds to the authenticity of the content.

The locations labelled on the vlogs show where the speaker was when they filmed the video. It does not reflect where the speaker comes from (necessarily).

As many of the speakers are non-native, the videos expose Ss to a range of different accents and varieties of English. This could be used as a way to highlight interesting or useful differences.

Additional Materials

For Teachers:

Presentation Tool Unit 1

Online Digital Resources

Videoscript Unit 1 Opener: BBC Vlogs

1A Hello

GRAMMAR | present simple *be*: *I, you*

VOCABULARY | hello and goodbye; countries and nationalities

PRONUNCIATION | intonation in greetings

LESSON OVERVIEW

In this lesson, Ss learn greetings for different times of the day, and countries and nationalities. They practise asking and saying where they are from, using different countries. Ss are introduced to intonation and how we can use it to show friendliness. The lesson ends with a writing activity where Ss write a chat message to introduce themselves and practise using basic punctuation.

Online Teaching

If you're teaching this lesson online, you might find the following tips useful:

- **Exs 1B and 1C:** Display the task and share your screen. After Ss listen to the conversations, annotate the task to show the correct answers.
- **Ex 3A:** Display the conversation on your device and share your screen. In feedback, elicit the answers and write them in. Ask individual Ss to read sentences aloud.
- **Ex 3C:** Ask Ss to type their answers in the chat box so that they can learn about each other.
- **Writing Bank 1A, Ex 2B:** Ask Ss to share their messages via a collaborative document to read each other's writing.

Additional Materials

For Teachers:

Presentation Tool Lesson 1A

Photocopiable Activities 1A

Grammar Bank 1A

Vocabulary Bank 1A

Writing Bank 1A

For Students:

Online Practice 1A

Workbook 1A

TO START

Say 'hello' in a bright way and wave your hand to show that you are greeting. If appropriate, you could shake hands with one or two learners and encourage them to say hello to you and even each other.

EXTRA SUPPORT: TEACHER Starting the lesson in English and giving instructions in English may be new for many learners. Ss benefit from picking up language in this way, so persist with it and explain, in Ss' first language if necessary, why you are doing it.

EXTRA SUPPORT: DYSLEXIA Dyslexic learners in particular benefit from understanding exactly what they are learning in a lesson so that they understand what they are working towards. In this and every lesson, explain clearly what the learning objectives of the lesson are near the start.

LISTENING

1 A 1.01 | Focus attention on photos A and B. Tell Ss they will hear two conversations and they should match each conversation with a photo (A or B). Play the first conversation and put Ss in pairs to discuss their answer, then play the second conversation. Allow them to confirm or change their answer in their pairs, then elicit Ss' answers. If necessary, play the conversations again.

EXTRA SUPPORT: TEACHER Ss may be anxious about listening to English and their anxiety can mean they find even simple tasks challenging. Support them by explaining before they listen that you don't expect them to understand every word, and that you will play the recording twice. They should just focus on the task and they will find listening easier each time.

ANSWERS:
1 B **2** A

AUDIOSCRIPT 1.01

Conversation 1

J = James S = Sonia

J: Erm, hi.
S: Hello.
J: Are you a student?
S: Yes, I am. Are you?
J: Yes, I am. What's your name?
S: I'm Sonia.
J: I'm James. Nice to meet you.
S: Nice to meet you, too. Where are you from, James?
J: I'm from Canada.
S: Oh, where in Canada?
J: From Vancouver. And you, Sonia?
S: I'm from the UK, from Manchester.

Conversation 2

A = Anna J = Jack

A: Good morning, everyone. Today, Jack Brown is with us. Jack?
J: Hi, everyone. I'm Jack, Jack Brown.
A: Good morning, Jack.
J: I'm in China. So for me it's 'good afternoon'.
A: Are you in Beijing?
J: No, today I'm in Shanghai.
A: So, let's go round the table and …

B Focus attention on the information in the table. Point out the example and as you do so say *James is from Canada. He's from Vancouver.* Ask Ss to match the other names with a country and a city, by drawing a line. Point out that there are three extra cities they don't need. Ss can compare answers in pairs, but don't check the answers as a class yet.

EXTRA SUPPORT: DYSLEXIA Ss with dyslexia can find listening and reading or writing at the same time, challenging. In this exercise, you could play the recording in segments, pausing after each speaker to allow time for them to read the names and answer. When they have finished, play the recording without stopping so Ss can listen and check.

C 1.01 | Play the recording again. Check answers as a class.

ANSWERS:
Sonia – the UK – Manchester
Jack – China – Shanghai

GRAMMAR

present simple *be*: *I, you*

2 A Focus attention on the exercise and gaps. Point out that this is an extract from the first conversation in the recording and that *'m* is the short form of *am*. Read the first line aloud then elicit the first answer as an example, then ask Ss to complete the rest of the sentences. When they have finished, check answers with the class and write them on the board.

EXTRA SUPPORT With weaker classes, point to yourself and say 'I', then gesture to one or more Ss and say 'you'. Then say 'I am', emphasising the verb, and 'you …' to see if Ss can produce the verb. Repeat both forms a few times chorally, with Ss gesturing to themselves for 'I am' and to another student for 'you are'. Write these on the board. Point out that *I'm* and *you're* are the contracted forms.

ANSWERS:
1 Are **2** am **3** 'm

EXTRA IDEA Ask Ss to practise reading the conversation aloud in pairs. When they have finished, they can change roles. You could also point out that this is the present simple form of the verb *be* and that when we make questions the verb and subject change place. Show this on the board with arrows.

B The Grammar Bank on page 92 can be used in the lesson or for homework. Decide how and when the exercises will benefit your class.

GB page 92 **GRAMMAR BANK**

Go through the notes with Ss or let them read them alone. Check understanding where necessary, focusing especially on how we replace a missing letter with an apostrophe. Point out that contracted forms, where the subject and its verb or the verb and *not* join with an apostrophe, are completely usual and Ss should aim to use these rather than full forms. There are some occasions when we don't contract because it's hard to say. For example: the first person (*am*) and the negative (*not*) are not contracted (~~*amn't*~~).

1 This exercise practises the form of *be*. Read the instruction with the class and point out that A and B are two people, then ask Ss to work alone and write the words in the gaps in the conversation. Ss check in pairs, then check answers with the whole class.

EXTRA SUPPORT: DYSLEXIA Provide two alternatives for each gap, one correct and one distractor, for Ss to choose from. This is more closely focused and reduces the writing load.

ANSWERS:
2 I **3** Are **4** not **5** are **6** you **7** am **8** I

EXTRA SUPPORT: TEACHER You could point out that *are* in gap 3 needs a capital letter because it is at the beginning of a sentence, but don't worry about this too much at this point as Ss will learn more about using capital letters later in this lesson and will be taught the full alphabet in Lesson 1C.

EXTRA IDEA Ss will benefit from practising reading the conversation aloud in pairs, changing roles when they have finished. Fast finishers can practise again with a new partner.

2 This exercise practises contracted forms. Look at the example with the class, then ask Ss to change five verbs to contracted forms, then check in pairs. Tell them to refer to the Grammar Bank notes to check what can/can't be contracted if they need to. Check answers with the class. Make sure that Ss have not contracted forms where they should not have (e.g. ~~*Where're*~~ and for short answers). As a follow-up, you could put Ss in pairs to practise the conversations.

EXTRA SUPPORT: DYSLEXIA To help Ss focus on the main point of the exercise, first highlight the verbs that need changing, then ask Ss to make the changes.

ANSWERS:
1 A: (2) ~~I am~~ **I'm** in South Africa.
B: Really! (3) ~~You are~~ **You're** in South Africa! Where in South Africa?
A: (4) ~~I am~~ **I'm** in Cape Town today and in Johannesburg tomorrow. Are you well?
B: Yes, I am. And you?
A: (5) ~~I am~~ **I'm** very well, thank you.
2 A: Hello. Are you a teacher?
B: No, (1) ~~I am~~ **I'm** not.
A: OK, (2) ~~you are~~ **you're** a student.
B: Yes, I am. (3) ~~I am~~ **I'm** Elif Buruk.
A: Where are you from, Elif?
B: (4) ~~I am~~ **I'm** from Turkey.
A: OK. (5) ~~You are~~ **You're** in class A1.

3 A Focus attention on the gapped conversation. This exercise is a bit harder as Ss need to choose and write the correct verb or pronoun and use capital letters when necessary.

EXTRA SUPPORT With weaker classes, and for Ss with dyslexia who can find it difficult to read and process sentences with gaps, write the options on the board for them to choose from, i.e. *'m, am, Are, are, I* (x2), *not, you*. If your class is mixed ability, encourage stronger Ss to work without this support.

B 1.02 | Play the recording for Ss to check their answers. Check answers with the class, write them on the board, then ask Ss to listen again. Drill the conversation with the class chorally and individually, focusing on the questions.

ANSWERS:
2 I **3** are **4** I **5** Are **6** am **7** you **8** not **9** 'm

EXTRA IDEA Ss at this level need to build speaking confidence. For extra practice, ask them to read the conversation aloud in closed pairs. Then ask two confident Ss to read the conversation across the class, in an open pair. If Ss are keen, ask more pairs to read. Encourage all efforts and resist directly correcting too much. At the end, drill a few troublesome words or phrases chorally.

C Complete the sentence about yourself on the board. Point out where capital letters are needed, i.e. for first name, city and country. Then ask Ss to complete the sentence with their own information. Move around the class and support as needed.

D Use your own information and the example in Ex 3A as a model for a conversation with a stronger student. Put Ss in pairs to talk about their name, city and country. When they have finished, ask one or two pairs to repeat their conversation for the class.

VOCABULARY

hello and goodbye

4 Look at the clock or your watch very obviously and say the appropriate greeting for the time shown. Refer Ss to the box and ask them to write in the greetings for each picture, then check in pairs. Check answers with the class. Point out that afternoon is usually 12.00–6.00 p.m. and evening usually refers to after 6.00 p.m. Drill the greetings chorally.

EXTRA SUPPORT: DYSLEXIA Write the list of greetings on the board vertically, in case Ss have difficulty with the horizontal arrangement in the box.

EXTRA SUPPORT: TEACHER Ss may be confused about the difference between *Good evening* and *Good night*. Explain that *Good evening* is a greeting when we arrive somewhere, and *Good night* is used when we are leaving (or going to bed). Point out that *Goodbye* is one word, whereas the other expressions with *Good* are two words. You could also tell Ss which expressions are less formal (i.e. *Hi*, *Hey*, *Bye*, *See you*).

ANSWERS:
2–3 Hi, Hey
4 Good morning
5 Good afternoon
6 Good evening
7–9 Bye, Goodbye, See you
10 Good night

PRONUNCIATION

intonation in greetings

EXTRA SUPPORT: TEACHER The intonation focus here is important for many learners as in many languages the pitch range is much narrower than in English, and learners using their 'native' pitch range risk sounding unfriendly. The practice of 'bad' intonation in Ex 5B helps reinforce the difference in sound and the importance of a wider range. However, if you feel this section is not relevant for your Ss, there is additional pronunciation material in the Vocabulary Bank for this lesson, focusing on word stress in the names of countries and nationalities.

5 A **1.03 |** Focus attention on the pictures of the faces, A and B. Explain that Ss will hear two conversations and that they need to match each one with a face. Play the first conversation and elicit ideas, but don't confirm the answer yet. Play the second conversation, then elicit ideas and confirm the answers. Ask Ss to say why they chose the faces to go with each recording and elicit/emphasise the importance of intonation in communicating feelings.

ANSWERS:
1 B **2** A

AUDIOSCRIPT 1.03
A: Hello, I'm Sonia.
B: Hi, Sonia. I'm James. Nice to meet you.

B Read the instruction with the class. Model the activity yourself by choosing a greeting from Ex 4 and saying it in a very flat or a lively way, so that Ss can call out A or B. Put Ss in pairs to say a greeting to their partner who should listen and say A or B.

C Put Ss in new pairs to introduce themselves. Move around the class and listen for accuracy and friendly intonation. When they have finished, ask if any Ss want to repeat their conversation in front of the class.

EXTRA IDEA You could give Ss a rolecard with a name, city and country to use when introducing themselves. This may add some variety to the conversations, especially if your Ss are all from the same place or area.

EXTRA CHALLENGE You could have a clock or call out different times or use pictures (sun/moon) and change these during the activity so that Ss have to keep changing their hellos and goodbyes according to the time of day. With a stronger class you might also have a picture of two people in a formal setting and two in an informal setting so that Ss have to adjust their choice of greeting.

SPEAKING

6 Put Ss in pairs and ask them to write five countries. Remind them that countries need a capital letter. Fast finishers can write more than five. When they have finished, refer Ss to the Vocabulary Bank on page 125 to check if any of their ideas are there.

VB page 125 **VOCABULARY BANK** countries and nationalities

Note that the Vocabulary Bank activities are an important part of the lesson. They should only be omitted if you are confident that your Ss already know this vocabulary. If you don't use the exercises in class, it would be a good idea to set them as homework.

EXTRA SUPPORT: TEACHER If necessary, teach any countries that are not in the Vocabulary Bank but are relevant to your class. With weaker classes or if you are short of time, you could simply concentrate on the countries most relevant to your Ss.

1 A Look at the countries in the table with the class, pointing out that while both *the US* and *the USA* are correct, the most common way for speakers to refer to the country is *the US* and Ss will meet this in their reading and listening. The full term 'the USA' can sound like British people saying 'I'm from Great Britain', i.e. rather old-fashioned.

Show how the nationalities follow one of three suffix patterns or are irregular. Complete a further example as a class, then ask Ss to continue alone, then check in pairs. Go through the answers as a class, making sure Ss have correct spelling (e.g. *Spanish* not ~~*Spainish*~~). It may be helpful to complete the table on the board, and it can then also be used in Ex 1B to show the stress.

EXTRA SUPPORT With weaker classes, elicit Ss' ideas and write them on the board. Then go through the irregular nationalities as a group and add them to the board.

EXTRA SUPPORT: TEACHER Depending on your class, Ss may not be aware that the US / the USA = *American* and the UK = *British*. You may therefore need to provide these nationalities.

ANSWERS:

1 Australian	**8** South African
2 Brazilian	**9** South Korean
3 Colombian	**10** Spanish
4 Indian	**11** Turkish
5 Italian	**12** British
6 Mexican	**13** Vietnamese
7 American	**14** Japanese

B VB1.01 | Refer Ss to the completed table. Ask them to listen and underline the stressed syllable in each country and nationality. Point out that there is only one main stress, even in longer words, and that the stress is always on a syllable with a vowel sound. There is no syllable stress on one-syllable words. Play the recording, pausing as needed. Check the answers.

ANSWERS:

Argentina, Argentinian
Australia, Australian
Brazil, Brazilian
Colombia, Colombian
India, Indian
Italy, Italian
Mexico, Mexican
the US, the USA, American
South Africa, South African
South Korea, South Korean
Poland, Polish
Spain, Spanish
Turkey, Turkish
the UK, British
China, Chinese
Vietnam, Vietnamese
Japan, Japanese
France, French
Germany, German
Switzerland, Swiss

C VB1.01 | Play the recording again for Ss to listen and repeat chorally. Follow with further individual drills if you feel Ss need it.

D Ask Ss to look at the table and practise saying a country and the nationality in pairs, like a kind of tennis game. Student A says a country and Student B answers with the nationality, then B says a new country and A answers, and so on, trying to keep a constant rhythm. Fast finishers and stronger learners can close their books and continue.

7 A Put Ss in groups of three or four. Ask Ss to note a city and its country, not their own. Monitor to make sure everyone in the group has a different one, but tell Ss not to tell each other at this point. They don't need to write a sentence.

EXTRA IDEA: DIGITAL If Ss are unsure of cities in their chosen country, they could look them up using their devices. For Ex 7B it will be best if they don't choose anywhere too obscure, though.

B Look at the example with the class and demonstrate with a stronger student first, with the student taking the role of A and guessing. Ask Ss to ask and answer in their groups. When they have finished, ask Ss if they guessed correctly.

WRITING

write a chat message to introduce yourself; use capital letters, full stops and question marks

8 A Focus attention on the text and say it's a chat on a website. Ask Ss to read and answer the question, then check in pairs. Check the answer with the class. If necessary, point out that Berna and Carmen introduce themselves, so they aren't friends.

ANSWER:
Berna and Carmen are not friends.

B Refer Ss to the Writing Bank on page 88.

WB ▶ page 88 **WRITING BANK**

1 A Focus attention on the chat and elicit where you would see it (online / in a chat room). Point out that this is a continuation of the chat Ss saw on page 9. Draw attention to the words in bold and ask Ss how they are similar (they all start with a capital letter). Ss read the chat and match the rules with the words in bold, then check in pairs. Check answers with the whole class and elicit a summary of when we need to use capital letters.

EXTRA SUPPORT: DYSLEXIA It may help dyslexic learners if you read the list of reasons for using capital letters to the class to help them identify what they are looking for. Alternatively, pair Ss with a partner who can read the reasons to them.

ANSWERS:

1 Where	**4** London
2 I (in 'I'm Carmen.')	**5** Spain
3 Berna	**6** Turkish

B Ss can look for examples in the chat messages to help them complete the rules, and then compare answers in pairs. Check answers with the whole class. You could ask Ss if they have the same or different rules for capital letters in their language(s).

EXTRA SUPPORT: DYSLEXIA It may help dyslexic learners if you read the versions of the rules with both alternatives in place aloud to the class before they choose.

ANSWERS:
1 at the end **2** question

C Ss correct the chat using capital letters, full stops and question marks where necessary, then check in pairs. Allow plenty of time for this. Check answers with the class.

EXTRA SUPPORT: DYSLEXIA Simplify this activity for Ss with dyslexia by reducing the number of missing capitals to just one per line. Suggest a focus on the punctuation first, and then the capitalisation rather than tackling both aspects together.

ANSWERS:
Hi, **I**'m **M**artín.
Where are you from?
I'm from **M**exico.
Are you **A**merican?
Yes, but **I**'m in **A**ustralia now.

2 A Ss should write a chat message to their partner, and, as this is the first unit, reassure them and allow plenty of time for this. As a guide, you can expect Ss to write two or three sentences. Monitor and offer help where necessary, reminding Ss about correct capitalisation and punctutation in particular.

B When they have finished, ask Ss to pass their message to a partner and reply in writing. If Ss are keen, they can do this several times, answering messages from different Ss. In feedback, ask a few Ss to share any new information they found out with the class.

EXTRA: ALTERNATIVE IDEA If your Ss come from the same place and you want to create variety, you could assign Ss names, cities/countries and other personal information, or give a list of countries for them to choose from (e.g. the Vocabulary Bank).

EXTRA IDEA: DIGITAL Ask Ss to send their chat introductions on their phones, or if teaching online, use the chat function.

TO FINISH

Write the following questions on the board:
Where do you write a chat message like this?
Do you go online?

Ss discuss the questions in pairs. When they have finished, elicit their ideas and have a brief class discussion about how they could use online settings to practise their English.

1B Two jobs

GRAMMAR | present simple *be*: *he, she, it*
VOCABULARY | jobs
PRONUNCIATION | word stress in jobs

LESSON OVERVIEW

In this lesson, Ss learn vocabulary for jobs. The context is a reading about two people and their weekends. This leads into the grammar where Ss are introduced to the third person singular form of the verb *be*. The lesson ends with a communicative speaking activity where Ss talk about someone they know.

Online Teaching

If you're teaching this lesson online, you might find the following tips useful:

- **Ex 2A:** Drill the word stress individually in the main room, by pointing at a photo and nominating Ss in turn.
- **Ex 3:** Use breakout rooms for Ss to mime in pairs.
- **Ex 5A:** Ask Ss to write their answers in the chat so you can assess individuals and they can learn from each other.

Additional Materials

For Teachers:
Presentation Tool Lesson 1B
Photocopiable Activities 1B
Grammar Bank 1B
Vocabulary Bank 1B

For Students:
Online Practice 1B
Workbook 1B

TO START

Start the lesson by saying and writing on the board: *I'm a teacher. It's my job.* See if any Ss volunteer to share their jobs (or family members' jobs) with the class and help them with the correct pronunciation. Tell Ss that jobs is today's lesson topic.

EXTRA SUPPORT: DYSLEXIA Dyslexic learners in particular benefit from understanding exactly what they are learning in a lesson so that they understand what they are working towards. In this and every lesson, explain clearly what the learning objectives of the lesson are near the start.

VOCABULARY

jobs

1 A This warm-up exercise assumes some knowledge of jobs vocabulary. Put Ss in pairs to help each other name the jobs they can see. Don't check the answers yet.

EXTRA SUPPORT With weaker classes, you may want to skip Ex 1A and start with the matching in Ex 1B, which provides the vocabulary for the jobs.

B Demonstrate the activity by asking Ss to identify which photo (A–D) is a doctor. Put Ss in pairs to match the remaining photos with the jobs. Go through the answers.

ANSWERS:
1 A **2** – **3** D **4** C **5** B
'teacher' is not in the photos.

PRONUNCIATION

word stress in jobs

2 A 1.04 | Look at the example with the class and elicit that the underlined syllable is longer and louder. Play the recording for Ss to underline the stressed syllable in the rest of the jobs. Put Ss in pairs to compare, then go through the answers and drill with correct stress. Point out that while English does not have a written accent system, stress is an important part of being able to use a word, so they should systematically record the stress on new vocabulary. It's a good idea to mark the stress in a different colour, to emphasise that it's not part of the word.

EXTRA SUPPORT If Ss struggle to hear the stress, they could try finding the stressed syllable in their names, applying the stress in the wrong place and then in the right place.

EXTRA SUPPORT: DYSLEXIA Underlining can be a problem for dyslexic learners, because text is already visually unstable and it can make the words appear to run together. You could ask Ss to put a box on the stressed syllable, ideally in a different colour to show that it's not part of the word.

ANSWERS:
1 a doctor **2** a teacher **3** a waiter
4 a taxi driver **5** a singer

B Refer Ss to the Vocabulary Bank on page 125.

VB page 125 **VOCABULARY BANK** jobs

Note that the Vocabulary Bank activities are an important part of the lesson. They should only be omitted if you are confident that your Ss already know this vocabulary. If you don't use the exercises in class, it would be a good idea to set them as homework.

1 A Refer Ss to the photos and ask them to write the letter of the photo next to the word. Ss should work alone, then check in pairs. Check answers with the class.

EXTRA SUPPORT: DYSLEXIA In this exercise, Ss with dyslexia might find it helpful to cover the words they are not focusing on at any one time. This might also help reduce distractions when they do Exs 2B and 2C as well.

ANSWERS:
1 B **2** G **3** F **4** H **5** E
6 I **7** C **8** J **9** A **10** D

B VB1.02 | Refer Ss to the photos and ask them to look at the photos and repeat as they hear the words on the recording. They don't need to write anything. Play the recording.

2 A Put Ss in pairs and refer them to the two example sentences. Ask them to use these to choose the correct word to complete rules 1–3. The general rule about *a/an* with singular nouns will be covered in Lesson 1D.

ANSWERS:
1 a(n) **2** a **3** an

B Look at the examples, drawing attention to the initial letter of each job, then ask Ss to work alone to write *a* or *an* in front of the jobs in Ex 1A. Ask Ss to compare answers in their pairs, then go through the answers as a class.

EXTRA SUPPORT If your class is not confident about the vowels, you could write all five (*a, e, i, o, u*) on the board for reference.

ANSWERS:
3 a **4** a **5** a **6** an
7 a **8** a **9** a **10** an

C VB1.03 | Look at the example and say *a bus driver* with the correct stress and drawing attention to the underlined syllables. Then ask Ss to listen and underline the stress in the jobs in Ex 1A. Ask Ss to compare answers, then go through the answers as a class. Drill as needed. Several examples have two words. You could point out that when the job has two words, as in the example, the first word (but not the article *a/an*) usually takes the main stress (though not in the case of a *digital designer*).

ANSWERS:
2 an actor
3 a nurse
4 a police officer
5 a shop assistant
6 an office worker
7 a businessman, a businesswoman
8 a digital designer
9 a football player
10 an artist

3 A Do an example with the class, where you mime a job for Ss to identify, then put Ss in pairs to take turns to mime and guess the jobs. They don't need to write. Move around and listen. When they have finished, drill any jobs that were mispronounced.

B Ask Ss to work alone and write their job. If they are not working, they can say *student*, or can choose the job they'd like or write the job of a parent or family member. Be on hand to help with vocabulary and spelling.

EXTRA IDEA If Ss' own job (or future job) is not featured in the Vocabulary Bank, encourage them to check it in a dictionary and help them locate the stress to pronounce it correctly. It may be necessary to teach *unemployed* and *retired*. These are adjectives, covered at A2, so point out that the different structure, e.g. *I'm ~~a~~ retired.*, does not need *a*.

3 Draw a job on the board, e.g. a doctor listening with a stethoscope, and ask 'What job is this?' Then, when Ss call out, refer them to the question in the model conversation, i.e. *Are you a … ?* and the short answer forms *Yes, I am.* and *No, I'm not*. Either do another example or invite a confident student to do one, then put Ss in pairs to continue. Ss can either draw jobs, or if they prefer, they can continue to mime jobs, as they did in the Vocabulary Bank.

READING

EXTRA SUPPORT: DYSLEXIA There is a recording of the reading text available to help dyslexic learners.

4 A Refer Ss to the text and ask them to match the person in each paragraph with two of the photos in Ex 1A. Give Ss a few minutes, then put them in pairs to discuss. They don't need to read the text aloud. When they have finished, elicit the answers.

EXTRA SUPPORT: TEACHER As a first reading, Ss are looking for the main ideas. This should be a quick task, as they are practising gist reading. For the second reading, in Ex 4B, which requires more detailed understanding, Ss will need more time. Ss don't need to know the technical terms or be told to read more quickly/slowly, but it can be helpful to give a time frame to encourage them to read in the right way.

EXTRA SUPPORT: DYSLEXIA For dyslexic learners, play the recording of the text or read it aloud yourself, with Ss tracking the text as you do so. Designated Ss can listen to the recording on individual devices. They can listen to it again to help them complete Ex 4B.

ANSWERS:
Carol Harris: A, B
Silvio Rossi: C, D

B Draw Ss' attention to the table and point out that they need to find the answers in the text, which they should read silently. Do the first one together and write it on the board to show that they don't need to write sentences. Ask Ss to continue alone, then check in pairs before going through the answers as a class. Complete the table on the board so that Ss can see if their answers are right.

EXTRA SUPPORT: DYSLEXIA This is the first reading of the course. Allow plenty of time, even if it appears simple. Ss may struggle to read and process the text, then fit their answers in the table. You could provide alternatives for each answer, so that Ss just have to choose from the two provided and circle the correct one.

ANSWERS:

name	job in the week	job at the weekend	happy or not?
Carol Harris	doctor	singer	yes
Silvio Rossi	taxi driver	waiter	yes

EXTRA IDEA Ss add an extra row to the table and complete it with their own information, or that of a family member or friend.

GRAMMAR

present simple *be*: *he, she, it*

5 A Point out that the first answer is done as an example and invite Ss to tell you the second answer. Highlight this on the projected task or write it on the board. Ss continue alone, then check in pairs. Check answers with the class and write the verbs on the board. With stronger classes, ask if the verb is positive or negative and how we know that sentence 5 is a question.

ANSWERS:
2 's **3** isn't, 's **4** is **5** Is

B Ss refer to the sentences in Ex 5A to complete the rules. The first one is done for them. Ask them to continue alone or, with weaker groups, do it as a class. Go through the answers and allow time for questions.

ANSWERS:
2 isn't **3** Is

C The Grammar Bank on page 93 can be used in the lesson or for homework. Decide how and when the exercises will benefit your class.

page 93 **GRAMMAR BANK** **GB**

This practises the form and use of the verb *be* with *he*, *she* and *it*. Read the notes with the class or give them a few minutes to read alone then answer any questions they have. Draw Ss' attention especially to the way that the verb and subject change position when we make questions. Point out also the apostrophe for a missing letter, and the two options for the negative – *she isn't* and *she's not*. If Ss want a preferred option, *isn't* is probably more commonly used.

EXTRA SUPPORT: TEACHER As a policy, *Speakout* strives for gender neutrality and inclusion in its language. Throughout the levels there are examples of this type of language, e.g. *Talk to a partner and ask them* … , rather than *Talk to a partner and ask him/her* … . Effectively this is a third person plural substituting for a third person singular in order to be gender neutral. While it is not necessary, or wise at A1 level, to draw Ss' attention to this, if Ss notice it at any point be prepared to explain that this is common in English when we do not wish to make assumptions about people's gender. The third person singular *it* can not be used in such contexts.

GB 1 **Focus attention on the first sentence and discuss as a class why the example answer is correct (*businesswoman* → *she*) and point out that only one alternative is correct in each case. Elicit the second answer and discuss in the same way (*city* → *it*). Ask Ss to continue alone to choose the correct alternative and then compare answers in pairs. Check answers with the class and drill the correct sentences in feedback.**

ANSWERS:

2 It's	**3** He's	**4** isn't
5 Is Imani	**6** What's	**7** it is
8 she's not	**9** isn't	**10** Where's

2 **Look at the example and ask Ss what is missing from the prompts (the verb and a preposition). Point out that in the exercise they need to write the sentences including a verb and sometimes another word, too. Ss write the sentences alone, then check in pairs. Check answers with the class and write the full sentences on the board in the correct form for Ss to check spelling. Drill chorally if it feels appropriate. Pairs could also practise saying the correct questions and answers.**

EXTRA SUPPORT: DYSLEXIA The main focus in this exercise is the verb *be*. Make the exercise more accessible for dyslexic learners by filling in the prepositions and only gapping the verb *be*.

ANSWERS:

2 It's in Vietnam.
3 She's from the USA.
4 He's from South Korea.
5 Yes, she is.
6 No, she isn't.
7 No, she isn't. She's Australian.
8 No, it isn't. It's in Colombia.
9 No, he isn't. He's from the UK.

3 **Read the example with the class, then ask Ss to complete the rest of the questions. Move around and check Ss are using capital letters where needed. In feedback, check answers with the class and write the questions on the board.**

EXTRA SUPPORT: DYSLEXIA This type of exercise, which mixes questions starting with auxiliary verbs and different question words might be difficult for Ss with dyslexia. In this case, you could go through as a class and establish which ones need question words before Ss start. You could also reduce the number of missing words to just one in each sentence, primarily focusing on the verb *be*.

ANSWERS:

2 Is, in	**3** Is, a	**4** Where's
5 Is	**6** What's	**7** Where's, from
8 What's	**9** Is	

6A **Look at the exercise and explain that in each conversation A is showing a photo of a friend to B, and that some sentences are out of place. Fill the first gap as a class, then ask Ss to continue alone and write the correct sentences. Ss can compare in pairs before you check answers as a class.**

EXTRA SUPPORT: DYSLEXIA Ss with dyslexia may struggle with ordering activities. You could work through the exercise as a class, reading out both the gapped conversations and the sentences. Alternatively, you could provide the missing sentences for each conversation on a separate piece of paper for Ss to move up and down next to the conversations to identify the correct one to fill each gap.

ANSWERS:

1 c **2** b **3** a **4** b **5** c **6** a

B **Put Ss in pairs to practise the conversations. When they have finished, ask them to change roles.**

EXTRA IDEA: DIGITAL Ask Ss to record the conversations on their phones, then listen back and check their pronunciation.

SPEAKING

7 **Put Ss in A/B pairs and refer them to the relevant pages.**

1 **Ask Ss to look at the photos and information. Point out or elicit that they only have information about three of the photos and that they should write three *yes/no* questions about each of the other three photos to find out about the people and city in them.**

2 **When Ss have written their questions, model the activity with a strong student, asking one or two questions and writing the short answers (*Yes, he/she/it is.* and *No, he/she/it isn't.*) on the board, based on the information given. Then ask Ss to work in their pairs for Student Bs to ask and Student As to answer about photos A–C. Faster Ss can ask more questions. Move around the class and monitor.**

3 Once Student Bs have asked all their questions, Ss change roles and Student As ask questions about photos D–F for Student Bs to answer, based on the information given. Continue to move around and monitor. When they have finished, drill any problematic words. Ss can show each other their books to find out the correct information about the photos once they've finished the activity.

8 Ask Ss to take out their phones and find pictures of friends they can show. If possible, demonstrate with a photo of your own, saying *This is ….* and inviting questions. Put Ss in pairs to show their photos and ask questions. Stronger learners can extend the conversation.

TO FINISH

Ask Ss if they speak English outside the class and how they could find opportunities to do so. For example, they could create a class group in a messaging app where they can exchange messages in English.

1C Checking in

HOW TO … | ask and answer simple questions
VOCABULARY | the alphabet
PRONUNCIATION | the alphabet

LESSON OVERVIEW

In this lesson, Ss learn to say the letters of the alphabet. The context is a set of conversations at reception desks. This leads into the functional language, where Ss also listen to and practise polite phrases. The lesson ends with a speaking activity where Ss exchange personal information and practise spelling their personal details.

Online Teaching

If you're teaching this lesson online, you might find the following tips useful:

- **Ex 2A:** Display the table on your device and share your screen. Complete it with Ss' help. When you have finished, use the pointer to elicit and drill individual sounds.
- **Ex 3B:** Dictate the spelling. Ss write their answers in the chat so they can compare.
- **Ex 7D:** Put Ss in groups of three in breakout rooms. While two have their conversation, the third listens to their pronunciation of the alphabet, then they change.

Additional Materials

For Teachers:
Presentation Tool Lesson 1C
Photocopiable Activity 1C
Grammar Bank 1C

For Students:
Online Practice 1C
Workbook 1C

TO START

Say your name and then write on the board: *My name is* _ _ _. with a line for each letter and invite Ss to try and spell out your name. Help and correct them. Explain that using the alphabet is today's topic.

EXTRA SUPPORT: DYSLEXIA Dyslexic learners in particular benefit from understanding exactly what they are learning in a lesson so that they understand what they are working towards. In this and every lesson, explain clearly what the learning objectives of the lesson are near the start.

VOCABULARY

the alphabet

1 A Focus attention on 1–6 and put Ss in pairs to try saying them. When they have finished, check answers with the class. Drill the abbreviations chorally and individually.

EXTRA SUPPORT: TEACHER In case Ss ask you about the abbreviations:

1 BBC – British Broadcasting Corporation
2 EU – European Union
3 OK – Oll Korrect (i.e. a slang misspelling of 'all correct')
4 UK – United Kingdom
5 USA – United States of America
6 www – World Wide Web

Note that the above are all initialisms, which are abbreviations formed from initial letters.

B 1.05 | Refer Ss to the chart and point out how each letter has upper-case (capital, in dark green) and lower-case (small, in light green) forms. Play the recording for Ss to listen and repeat. Pay special attention to tricky letters such as the vowels and *Q* and *R*.

PRONUNCIATION

the alphabet

2 A Refer Ss to the table. Say *name* and show how the vowel sound appears in bold in the word. Work down the column and say the words, each time pointing out the vowel sound (or write the words on the board with the vowel sounds marked). Then begin going through the alphabet, starting with *A* and match each letter with its word. Point out the small numbers in front of the first letter in each group. When you get to *C*, ask Ss which number the letter goes with and gesture to the board. Continue with this for as long as Ss need, then ask them to continue in pairs. Don't check the answers yet.

B 1.06 | Play the recording for Ss to check their answers, then check answers with the class. Play the recording again for Ss to listen and repeat.

EXTRA SUPPORT: TEACHER Some Ss may struggle with pronouncing the names for certain letters, so drilling is important here to help give them practice and confidence.

Ss may initially be confused by the fact that the table refers to both sounds and letters. The lack of sound–spelling correspondence in English is a challenge. In spelling, the vowels are *a, e, i, o, u* and the consonants are *b, c, d, f, g, h, j, k, l, m, n, p, q, r, s, t, v, w, x, y, z*. However, as an example, standard British English has twelve vowel sounds and eight diphthongs.

When these vowels and diphthongs appear at the beginning of a noun, we use the article 'an' and not 'a'. There is some possible confusion though: for example, with *u*, which is sometimes pronounced with a consonant sound /j/ before it, e.g. *university*, and so takes the article 'a'; sometimes an initial *h* is silent, e.g. *an hour*. Ss don't need to be told all this at this stage, but you may need to make them aware if they make mistakes.

EXTRA: ALTERNATIVE IDEA To check the answers to Ex 2A, you could drill the sounds chorally, saying the word and the letters that follow it, and eliciting the missing ones as you go. Use a pointer to drill individual letters randomly, especially the vowels. Ss can continue pointing and pronouncing in pairs.

ANSWERS:

n**a**me /eɪ/	**1** A *H* **J** K
thr**ee** /iː/	**2** B **C** D **E** G P **T** V
t**e**n /e/	**3** F L **M** N **S** X **Z**
n**i**ne /aɪ/	**4** I **Y**
n**o** /əʊ/	**5** O
y**ou** /uː/	**6** Q U **W**
c**ar** /ɑː/	**7** R

EXTRA CHALLENGE Choose a few everyday words seen in previous lessons, for example *she, doctor, Italian, name*. Say the letters and ask Ss to write them. Ask Ss to pronounce the words after they have written them.

3 A Refer Ss to 1–6 and ask them to say them. Point out that we say each letter, so *V-I-P*, rather than *vip*. Be aware that some abbreviations though are now commonly said by younger people as words or acronyms, e.g. *ASAP* and *LOL*. Point this out if you think it's relevant to your Ss.

EXTRA IDEA: DIGITAL If Ss are interested in finding out about the abbreviations, they can go online and find their meanings as an out-of-class activity, rather than taking up classroom time for you to explain them. Discuss which Ss recognise and which are informal / used in instant messaging and see if Ss can suggest any more that they know.

B Put Ss in A/B pairs and refer Student As to pages 124–125. Ask them to choose five words and spell each word in turn to their partner who should write the letters. It's important that Student Bs don't look at Student A's pages but write what they hear. When they have finished, A checks B's spelling and they change roles. Move around and monitor. Drill any problematic letters at the end.

EXTRA IDEA You can extend this practice by having Ss spell the names of famous people, places, etc. to each other.

How to …
ask and answer simple questions

4 A **Focus attention on the pictures and ask Ss what they are or where they would see them. Accept any reasonable answers (*ID cards*, *hotel*, etc.). Look at picture A together and discuss which is the first name (Amelia) and which is the surname (Clarke). Point out that the family name (surname) comes second in English. Ss read the words in the box and find examples, then check in pairs. Check answers with the class. Don't worry if Ss can't pronounce the names.**

EXTRA SUPPORT With weaker classes, review how to say numbers 1–9 before starting this exercise. You could count them around the class. Point out that in phone numbers we usually say 'O' (oh) and not zero.

ANSWERS:

first name: Amelia, Imagen (incorrect version of Imogen but don't point this out as Ss have to find the mistake in Ex 4C), Eduardo

surname: Clarke, Menzie, Lopez

address: 7 River Road

phone number: 913 845 662

EXTRA IDEA If Ss are wearing ID cards, or have easy access to them, ask them to show each other, identifying any of the features in the box they include.

B **1.07 | Tell Ss that they are going to listen to three conversations and that they should relate each one to a picture (A–C). Play the recording, then ask Ss to check in pairs. Check answers as a class.**

ANSWERS:

1 B **2** C **3** A

AUDIOSCRIPT 1.07

Conversation 1

A: Can I help you?
B: Yes. I'm here for the conference.
A: What's your name?
B: Imogen Menzie.
A: How do you spell your surname?
B: M-E-N-Z-I-E.
A: OK, here it is. First name Imogen?
B: That's right. I-M-O-G-E-N.
A: Here's your name card. The conference is in room 238.
B: Thank you. Oh wait, there's a mistake …

Conversation 2

C: Hello.
D: Hello. I'm a new student.
C: OK. What's your name?
D: Eduardo Lopez.
C: How do you spell your surname?
D: L-O-P-E-Z.
C: Just a moment. L-O-P-A-Z?
D: No, L-O-P-E-Z.
C: Sorry, L-O-P-E-Z?
D: Perfect.
C: And your first name … E-D-U-A-R-D-O … ?
D: That's right.
C: Great. And what's your phone number?
D: It's 9-1-3-8-4-5-6-6-0.
C: Sorry, can you repeat that, please?
D: 9-1-3-8-4-5-6-6-0.
C: OK, Eduardo. Here's your student card.
D: Thank you!
C: No problem.

Conversation 3

E: What's your surname?
F: It's Clarke.
E: Clarke … Hmm … How do you spell that?
F: C-L-A-R-K-E.
E: Your name isn't here.
F: Really?
E: What's your first name?
F: Amelia.
E: Amelia Clarke. Just a moment … Ah, here it is.
F: Oh good.
E: Erm, what's your phone number?
F: It's 3-2-8-6-3-2-8.
E: Sorry, 3-2-8-6-3-8-2?
F: 2-8.
E: OK, 3-2-8-6-3-2-8.
F: Yes.
E: OK, great, thank you. Here's your key card. You're in room 729.
F: Thank you. Oh wait, there's a mistake …

EXTRA SUPPORT: TEACHER When talking about phone numbers, room numbers and numbers on things like credit cards, it's common for people to say the numerals individually, e.g. seven two nine.

C **1.07 | Tell Ss there are some mistakes on the cards in Ex 4A, either with the name or a number. They should listen again and identify and correct the mistakes on the cards. Play the recording, then ask Ss to check in pairs. Play the recording again if necessary, then check answers as a class.**

ANSWERS:
Conversation 1: ~~Imagen~~ → Im**o**gen
Conversation 2: ~~913 845 662~~ → 913 845 66**0**
Conversation 3: ~~829~~ → **7**29

5 A Read the words in the box with the class and make sure Ss know what they mean. The conversations are extracts from the longer ones they've just heard. Ss should write the words in the gaps, using each word once only, then check in pairs. Don't check answers with the class yet.

EXTRA SUPPORT: DYSLEXIA Dyslexic learners may find the activity easier to process if you supply the words in the box as a vertical list for them to work with.

B 1.08 | Play the recording for Ss to listen and check their answers. Ask them to check in pairs, then check answers with the class.

EXTRA: ALTERNATIVE IDEA Play the recording through once, without stopping. Then play it again, pausing after each conversation and checking the answers as you go. Drill the questions chorally. Ss can practise the conversations in pairs, first using the information provided then again substituting their own information where possible.

ANSWERS:

2 spell	**4** surname
3 phone, repeat	**5** first name

C The Grammar Bank on page 94 can be used in the lesson or for homework. Decide how and when the exercises will benefit your class.

GB page 94 **GRAMMAR BANK**

This focuses on the form and use of functional language for basic questions. Read the notes with the class or give them a few minutes to read alone then answer any questions they have. Check pronunciation of the phrases, as well as of the different titles that are used. Point out that Ss may hear some English speakers use *Mrs* to address a married woman and *Miss* to address an unmarried woman. However, suggest they use *Ms* + surname to address all women, regardless of their marital status in the same way that they use *Mr* + surname to address all men.

1 Look at the example. Point out that Ss don't need to add any words. Ss put the words in order alone, then check in pairs. Check answers with the class. You could also put Ss in pairs to practise the conversation.

EXTRA SUPPORT: DYSLEXIA Reordering words can pose a challenge for learners with dyslexia. Change the exercise to a gap-fill, with a key word missing in each sentence. You could also provide the missing words as a vertical list for Ss to select from as this will be easier to read and process.

ANSWERS:
2 What's your name?
3 How do you spell your surname?
4 No, that's not right. (It's S-T-R-A-T …)
5 What's your address?
6 Can you repeat that, please?
7 Just a minute. (Here's your card.)
8 No problem. Goodbye.

2 Look at the example with the class to explain that they need to identify mistakes and then correct them. Point out that the mistakes could be with the grammar, or a wrong word or spelling. Ask Ss first to underline or highlight where they think there's a mistake, then to discuss and correct them in pairs. Check answers with the class.

EXTRA SUPPORT Support dyslexic and beginner literacy learners by working as a class to identify the words that need to be corrected, then asking Ss to work in pairs to correct them. Alternatively, you could give them the conversation with the mistakes already highlighted for them to focus on making the corrections.

ANSWERS:
A: What's ~~you're~~ **your** first name?
A: … What's your phone ~~numbers~~ **number**?
A: Sorry, is ~~he~~ **it** 322 6237?
A: What**'s** your address?
A: How do you ~~sing~~ **spell** the street name?
A: OK, great, ~~thanks~~ **thank** you.

3 Look at the example with the class. Point out that when Ss see *be* they must choose the correct form of the verb, and explain that various other words will also need to be inserted to complete the conversation. Complete another example, then ask Ss to continue alone, before discussing in pairs. Check answers with the class. Ss can read the conversation in pairs once it has been completed.

EXTRA SUPPORT: DYSLEXIA Help dyslexic learners by presenting the completed sentences with the verb gapped and just have Ss write the correct form of *be*.

ANSWERS:

B: Hello. My name's Kumar. Nadia Kumar.
A: How do you spell Nadia?
B: N-A-D-I-A.
A: Can you repeat your surname, please?
B: Kumar.
A: Is it/that K-U-M-E-R?
B: No, that's not right. It's K-U-M-A-R.
A: Just a minute. Here's your card, Ms Kumar.
B: Perfect. Thank you.

6 **Put Ss in A/B pairs and refer them to the relevant pages. They should not show their partner their page. Explain that they need to ask and answer questions to complete the missing information in their table. Refer Ss to the example conversation and choose two stronger Ss to read the example and model the activity for the class. If necessary, ask them to demonstrate another question and answer, then set pairs to start. Move around the class and support, making sure that Ss don't show each other their answers. When they have finished, ask Ss to compare their tables and see if they wrote the information correctly.**

SPEAKING

7 A Make sure Ss understand the words and phrases in the speech bubbles. Ss complete the conversation alone, then check in pairs. Don't check answers yet.

EXTRA SUPPORT: DYSLEXIA Provide two possible alternatives for Ss to choose from for each gap, one correct and one distractor. Advise Ss to mask the rest of the exercise while they are focusing on each gap, to avoid distraction.

B Refer Ss to Audioscript 1.07 to check their answers. Pairs can practise the conversations after the answers are confirmed.

EXTRA: ALTERNATIVE IDEA If you prefer, you can play Conversation 2 from Audio 1.07 again for Ss to check their answers, making sure they understand that the version in Ex 7A is two extracts from the recording, not the complete conversation.

ANSWERS:

2 Sorry
3 Perfect (*That's right* is also possible)
4 That's right (*Perfect* is also possible)
5 Thank you

FUTURE SKILLS | Self-management 

C Read the Future Skills box as a class. Ask Ss if they can recall any other short phrases. If Ss don't have a notebook, encourage them to get one before the next class.

D Refer Ss to the forms. With weaker classes, you could elicit the questions needed and write them on the board. Put Ss in pairs to practise asking the questions and completing forms for each other. When Ss have finished, put them in new pairs. Monitor and check they are using the phrases from the lesson correctly, as well as using friendly intonation. Model this with a stronger student to show what you expect.

EXTRA CHALLENGE Tell Ss that when a word has two letters that are the same together, as in 'Anna', we often say 'double' (e.g. 'A, double-N, A') and encourage them to do the same if any name they need to spell in the activity has double letters. The same applies to telephone numbers, where they can also practise using 'O' (oh) instead of 'zero', e.g. '8-4-5, double-6, O (oh)'.

EXTRA: HOW TO ... Designate a few Ss as hotel receptionists. Ask other Ss to roleplay checking in at a hotel as themselves with the 'receptionists', without using any notes or referring to their books if possible.

TO FINISH

Ask the class to share the short phrases they used in Ex 7D (following on from the Future Skills activity). You can direct them to Lesson 1A and/or Grammar Bank 1C when they run out of ideas. Encourage Ss to make a note of any short phrases they haven't noted down already.

EXTRA IDEA: SPEAK ANYWHERE Encourage Ss to practise using the Speak Anywhere interactive roleplay.

1D BBC Street Interviews
What's your name?

GRAMMAR | singular and plural nouns; *a, an*; *have, has*
SPEAKING | talk about what's in your bag
WRITING | write a lost and found post

LESSON OVERVIEW

In this lesson, Ss learn about singular and plural nouns, and the form and use of *a* and *an*. They also learn vocabulary for common objects and the verb *have/has*. The context is a video of interviews with people in the street introducing themselves and saying what's in their bag. Ss then do a speaking activity where they practise talking about what's in their bag. The lesson ends with a writing activity where Ss write a lost and found post.

Online Teaching

If you're teaching this lesson online, you might find the following tips useful:

- **Exs 2A and 3A:** Sometimes videos can be a little slow or jumpy when streamed in an online class environment. If you know this is an issue for you, give Ss time to watch the video on their own device before moving on.
- **Ex 3A:** Share your screen and enable the annotation tool for Ss to add words identifying what's in the bags in Ex 1A.
- **Vocabulary Bank 1D, Exs 1A and 1C:** Project the photos one at a time, or share your screen and use a pointer, to elicit and drill individual words.
- **Ex 7B:** Ss can write their posts in the chat or a collaborative document.

Additional Materials

For Teachers:
Presentation Tool Lesson 1D
Online Digital Resources
Grammar Bank 1D
Vocabulary Bank 1D
Videoscript 1D: BBC Street Interviews

For Students:
Online Practice 1D
Workbook 1D

TO START

Write the following questions on the board: *What's your name? How do you spell it?* Ask a confident student to ask you this question and answer, spelling out your name. Put Ss in pairs to ask each other the questions. When they have finished, elicit their answers and write all the names on the board. Remind them about 'double' letters, e.g. 'A, double-N, A' to spell 'Anna'.

EXTRA SUPPORT: DYSLEXIA Dyslexic learners in particular benefit from understanding exactly what they are learning in a lesson so that they understand what they are working towards. In this and every lesson, explain clearly what the learning objectives of the lesson are near the start.

EXTRA SUPPORT Spelling and recognising correct spelling is a key activity in this lesson. It might be worth eliciting the alphabet into its seven rows for pronunciation (see Lesson 1C, Ex 2A) and having this as a reference on the board during the lesson.

PREVIEW

1 A Start by showing the class your bag and hold up some things that you have in it to elicit the names (e.g. phone, water). Refer Ss to the pictures. Put them in pairs to discuss what they can see. When they have finished, don't go through the answers as Ss will see these words in the Vocabulary Bank.

EXTRA SUPPORT If your class is weaker and you think they won't know any of the vocabulary, go straight to the Vocabulary Bank.

EXTRA SUPPORT: TEACHER *Purse* and *wallet* are gendered items of vocabulary. A purse is an item generally used by females, a wallet is more often used by males. Both can refer to the same type of item, which is for carrying money/cash and cards. In American English, a purse refers to a small bag. In British English this is more usually called a handbag.

B Refer Ss to the Vocabulary Bank on page 126 to check their ideas.

ANSWERS:
A an umbrella, a mobile phone, a purse
B a laptop, two books

VB page 126 **VOCABULARY BANK** common objects

Note that the Vocabulary Bank activities are an important part of the lesson. They should only be omitted if you are confident that your Ss already know this vocabulary. If you don't use the exercises in class, it would be a good idea to set them as homework.

1 A Focus attention on the photos and ask Ss to match them with the words. Elicit the first answer as an example. Ss work individually, then check in pairs. Don't check the answers as a class.

EXTRA SUPPORT: DYSLEXIA It might help dyslexic learners to focus if they cover the rest of the words as they focus on each item.

B VB1.04 | Play the recording so Ss can listen and check. Then refer Ss to the photos and ask them to look at them as they listen and repeat with the recording.

ANSWERS:
1 B **2** H **3** M **4** C **5** E **6** F **7** L
8 I **9** G **10** D **11** A **12** J **13** K

C Put Ss in pairs to take turns to point and identify. Move around the class and listen. When they have finished, give brief feedback on any problem words and drill.

EXTRA IDEA You may also want to teach more items that you expect to come up when Ss look in their own bags in Ex 5A.

VIEW

2 A Read the two questions in the BBC programme information box with the class and explain that they're going to watch different people answering these questions. Refer Ss to the photos of speakers A–I and explain that Ss should watch the first part of the video and number the speakers in the order they hear them. Tell Ss to write the numbers 1–9 in their notebooks before watching, and then the letter of each speaker as they appear. Ss then watch and check in pairs. Then check answers with the whole class.

EXTRA SUPPORT Turn on the subtitles if you feel it would benefit learners.

ANSWERS:
1 *H* **2** *A* **3** B **4** E **5** I
6 D **7** G **8** C **9** F

B Refer Ss to the list of names and point out that these are in the order the people appear in the video. Explain that four have a spelling mistake. Ss need to listen to the spelling of each name and correct where necessary. Play the video, pausing as needed, then ask pairs to compare before going through the answers.

EXTRA SUPPORT: DYSLEXIA You could tell dyslexic learners which four names have spelling mistakes so they can focus their attention on listening for the correct spelling.

ANSWERS:
2 Rach**a**el **4** Shar**r**on **7** B**i**ba **8** La**y**an

3 A Refer Ss to the bags in Ex 1A and remind them of or elicit their contents. Ss watch the second part of the video, in which people talk about their bags, and match the bags with the correct speakers. Check answers with the class.

ANSWERS:
Bag A: Speaker D (Simnit)
Bag B: Speaker F (Tom)

B Put Ss in pairs to try and remember who said what. When they have finished, elicit Ss' ideas but don't confirm any answers yet.

C Ss watch the video again and check their ideas, then compare in pairs. Play the video again, if necessary, then check answers as a class.

ANSWERS:
1 G (Biba) **2** A (Rachael) **3** F (Tom)
4 D (Simnit) **5** E (Sharron) **6** H (William)

GRAMMAR

singular and plural nouns; *a, an*; *have, has*

4 A Elicit the five vowels. Remind Ss that we use *an* before nouns that start with vowel sounds and *a* before nouns that start with consonant sounds. Elicit that we use *have* for all subjects apart from third person singular subjects, where we use *has*. Ask Ss to read the sentences and complete them with the correct words alone, then check in pairs. If you're short of time, you could do this exercise as a class. Check answers with the class.

EXTRA SUPPORT: DYSLEXIA For Ss with dyslexia, provide two alternatives for each gap, the correct answer and a distractor.

ANSWERS:
1 an **2** have, a, a **3** have, a
4 have **5** has

B The Grammar Bank on page 95 can be used in the lesson or for homework. Decide how and when the exercises will benefit your class.

GB ▶ page 95 **GRAMMAR BANK**

Check understanding of the notes with the class, and especially ensure Ss understand the rules for spelling plurals for the different endings. Draw their attention to the part of the 'Notice' section that shows that adjectives don't agree in plurals, especially if this is a feature of Ss' first language.

1 This exercise focuses on articles with singular nouns. Elicit the first answer as an example with the class and elicit why it's *a* (the noun starts with a consonant). Then ask Ss to complete the rest of the exercise individually, then check in pairs. Check answers with the class and write them on the board. Point out the capital letters used for the nationalities *Indian* and *American*.

ANSWERS:

1 a **2** a **3** an **4** a **5** a
6 an **7** a **8** an **9** a **10** a

2 This exercise involves spelling different plural forms. Ss write the words individually, then compare in pairs. Check answers with the class. Refer them back to the spelling rules as needed and remind them that adjectives do not take a plural form. Point out that in compound nouns (e.g. *shop assistant*) the plural is on the second word.

ANSWERS:

2 restaurants
3 Indian names
4 nationalities
5 phone numbers
6 addresses
7 shop assistants
8 American cities
9 taxi drivers
10 sandwiches

EXTRA IDEA Ss practise in pairs with one saying their choice of singular noun, and their partner answering with the plural form.

3 Look at the example as a class. Point out that Ss need to use a number and plural noun or *a/an* and a singular noun. If Ss use *one* instead of *a/an* it's correct, but doesn't practise the *a/an* distinction that is the focus. Ss write the answers individually, then compare in pairs. Check answers with the class.

ANSWERS:

2 three notebooks
3 an umbrella
4 four bottles of water
5 two cafés
6 a supermarket
7 an airport
8 a hotel

SPEAKING

talk about what's in your bag

5A Demonstrate the activity first by looking in your bag, showing Ss some items and eliciting the words for these to the board. If possible, revise *keys* and preteach *key ring*, as these come up later in the Writing section. Ss do the same and should write five or more words. If they don't have a bag, they can refer to what's in their purses, wallets or pockets or on their desk. If it's inappropriate for them to disclose this personal information, they can invent a list of objects for the sake of the activity or draw a bag with objects in it. Move around the class and help with vocabulary as needed.

B Read through the Key phrases as a class and deal with any queries. Demonstrate again by using the Key phrases to talk about your bag, then ask Ss to decide which of the Key phrases are true for them. Monitor and help with variations where necessary.

EXTRA SUPPORT In the examples, Ss see *a/an* before singular nouns. Before plural nouns they see *my* or a number. *Some* is not introduced at this stage. Some Ss may consider *glasses* as a single item, but point out that the word ends in *s* and we don't use *a*.

6A Put Ss in pairs to ask each other about what they have and use the Key phrases in their answers. Go round and help with vocabulary/pronunciation where necessary, writing any new words/phrases on the board. When they have finished, write *We both ….* on the board and ask a few pairs of Ss to say what was the same for them.

B Read the example with the class, pointing out that Ss now need to use the third person singular verb because they are talking about another person. Arrange Ss in new pairs to tell each other about their first partner's bag, purse or wallet. When they have finished, ask a few Ss to share anything interesting they found out from their partner with the class.

C Read the example with the class, pointing out that we use *both* for two people and *all* for three or more people. Ask Ss to write and then say their sentence to the class.

WRITING

write a lost and found post

7 A Demonstrate the meaning of *lost* and *found* by miming that you have lost your pen, and then find it. Focus attention on the posts, then ask Ss to read and match each post (1–2) with its message (a–b). Tell Ss *PM* in the posts means 'private message'. Give Ss a few minutes to read alone, then put them in pairs to compare. Go through the answers.

EXTRA SUPPORT: DYSLEXIA You could record the posts and messages before the class so Ss can listen as they read. Alternatively, you could read them with the class.

ANSWERS:
1 b **2** a

B Read the instruction to the class. Tell them to choose one thing from the list they made in Ex 5A and write a lost post based on the one they read. Move around and help.

EXTRA: ALTERNATIVE IDEA You might bring in pictures of things for Ss to write their lost posts about rather than having them use personal objects. You could give each student a picture and tell them to write a lost post about it. You then collect and redistribute the pictures, and Ss write a private message saying they have found the object (as in Ex 7C). Ss could also write found posts for the same pictures.

EXTRA SUPPORT For weaker classes, you could provide a writing frame with most of the text completed. At the simplest level, Ss just insert the name of the lost object and their name.

C Put Ss in pairs. Each should write a private message telling their partner that they have the lost object. Refer Ss to the models (a and b) in Ex 7A to help them. Move around the class and help as needed.

D Collect Ss' posts and private messages. Put Ss in groups, for example of four, and give them a set of four posts and four private messages to read and match. When they have matched them, change them with another group so each group reads and matches various sets of posts and private messages.

EXTRA: ALTERNATIVE IDEA You could develop this to a whole class activity for stronger classes who can move around the room. This is best managed if you (a) collect Ss' work, (b) number the posts and letter the private messages, (c) put all of the written texts around the room so that (d) Ss can walk around, read the texts, and write down the letter of the private message that matches each post.

EXTRA IDEA: DIGITAL Ask Ss to share their posts online, in a collaborative document or on a webpage.

TO FINISH

Put Ss in new pairs to discuss what they have in their bag (or desk / pencil case) for their English class and what is important or less important for their learning.

1 REVIEW

LESSON OVERVIEW

This lesson is a review of the language – both grammar and vocabulary – presented in this unit. It also includes a link to the Sounds and Spelling section for this unit, which focuses on syllables, stress and /ə/; and /s/, /z/ and /ɪz/ in plurals. The notes below assume that the tasks are completed in class. However, the self-study type exercises (i.e. Exs 1A, 1B, 2A, 4A, 5A, 5B and 7A) could be done out of class and then checked in the following lesson when the communicative tasks are then completed.

Online Teaching

If you're teaching this lesson online, you might find the following tips useful:

- **Ex 1A:** Ask Ss to use a collaborative document in pairs to write their answers and then check.
- **Ex 1C:** Put Ss in breakout rooms for this activity.

Additional Materials

For Teachers:

Sounds and Spelling 1

Unit Test in test package

TO START

Ask Ss to work in pairs and try to remember what language they studied in Unit 1 (Grammar: present simple *be*: *I*, *you*, *he*, *she*, *it*, singular and plural nouns, *a*/*an*, *have*, *has*; Vocabulary: hello and goodbye, countries and nationalities, jobs, the alphabet, common objects; How to ... ask and answer simple questions). Ask them to look at the unit lesson objectives to check their ideas.

GRAMMAR

1 A Look at the example as a class. Put Ss in pairs to discuss and choose the correct alternative. Go through the answers as a class, nominating individuals to read the whole sentence and drilling as needed.

ANSWERS:

2 Mexico **3** Argentinian **4** the UK
5 American **6** Italy

B Read the instruction with the class and give an example yourself, e.g. *George Clooney, Rihanna, Paris*. The famous people need to be living because in Ex 1C Ss will use the present tense. Then ask Ss to write their three names.

C Look at the example, then demonstrate the activity with a stronger learner, e.g. A: 'George Clooney.' B: 'George Clooney is American. He's from the USA.' You may need to introduce *I think ...* and *I don't know!* Put Ss in pairs to have their conversations.

2 A Look at the conversation with the class and elicit the first answer. Point out that contractions are not always possible. Then ask Ss to complete the rest of the conversation alone, then check in pairs. Check answers with the class and write them on the board, pointing out where capital letters are required.

EXTRA SUPPORT: DYSLEXIA You could provide two possible alternatives for each line of the conversation for Ss with dyslexia.

ANSWERS:

1 Are **2** am **3** Are **4** 'm

B Look at the example, then do another example with the class. Explain that you will choose a letter and Ss must ask you questions until they can identify the letter. They then repeat the activity in pairs.

EXTRA: ALTERNATIVE IDEA You could make this a team game, with the team or team member asking the fewest number of questions to reach a correct answer (selected by you or another team member) winning.

3 A Put Ss in pairs and ask them to choose four of the words in the box and then write two examples for each, as in the example. Fast finishers and stronger learners can choose more words and write more examples.

B Look at the example as a class and give a further example yourself, e.g. 'Sam, Nick – names!' Put Ss in different pairs. Ask Ss to take turns to say their examples so that their partner can identify the word from the box in Ex 3A.

EXTRA: ALTERNATIVE IDEA If Ss are competitive, this could be made into a team game in groups, with either the person or team identifying the word from the box in Ex 3A fastest winning a point.

VOCABULARY

4 A Look at the example. Elicit what has been added or changed (*a*/*an*, nationality, word order), then ask Ss to work individually to write phrases, then check in pairs. When they have finished, check answers with the class, asking individual Ss to read phrases aloud and writing them on the board.

ANSWERS:

2 an Australian bus driver
3 a British waiter
4 a Polish singer

B **Read the example with the class, elicit what has been added or changed (again *a/an*, nationality, word order), then put Ss in pairs to take turns giving jobs and countries and making phrases.**

EXTRA SUPPORT Weaker classes might need preparation time to write a list of a few jobs and countries before they start. You could also refer them to Vocabulary Banks 1A and 1B to help.

5 A **Look at the example and establish what letters are missing (the vowels). Elicit what these are and write them on the board (*a, e, i, o, u*). Ss work alone completing the words with the missing vowels, then check in pairs. You could say the words aloud before going through the answers as a class.**

EXTRA SUPPORT Ss with dyslexia or beginner literacy might find this activity a challenge because of the partial presentation of the words. To support them, you could write the words on the board with underscores to show where vowels are missing.

ANSWERS:

2 Hello
3 Good evening
4 Bye
5 Good morning
6 See you
7 Good night
8 Goodbye

B **Ask Ss to highlight 1, 3, 5 and 7 in Ex 5A and then ask them which is first in the day (*Good morning*) then ask them to put the rest in order. Ask Ss to check their answers in pairs, then check the answer with the class and drill the phrases.**

EXTRA SUPPORT: DYSLEXIA To reduce distraction, supply just 1, 3, 5 and 7 from Ex 5A in a list for Ss to number in the correct order.

ANSWER:

The correct order is 5 (Good morning), 1 (Good afternoon), 3 (Good evening), 7 (Good night).

6 A **Refer Ss to the underlined letters and ask them to say the words in pairs. In feedback, go through the answers and drill the sounds and the words.**

ANSWERS:

In *Japan, doctor* and *number* the underlined sound is pronounced /ə/.

In *buses*, the underlined sound is /ɪz/. In *bags*, it's /z/. In *tickets*, it's /s/.

EXTRA SUPPORT: TEACHER Ss may struggle with the fact that the same sound can be produced by different letters (e.g. *or/er*) and that different sounds can be produced by the same letters (e.g. *tickets* /s/ or *bags* /z/). Assure them that this is mainly for their understanding, and you don't expect them to produce perfect pronunciation at this stage!

B **Refer Ss to Sounds and Spelling on page 151.**

page 151 **SOUNDS AND SPELLING**
syllables, stress and /ə/; /s/, /z/, /ɪz/ in plurals

The Sounds and Spelling section can be used to help with particular problems. You might want to select the sections or even particular sounds that are most useful for your Ss. The vocabulary used in each section comes from the current unit or previous units.

SOUNDS AND SPELLING TEACHER'S NOTES page 204

7 A **Explain that *number 1 = top*, i.e. *most common or popular*, and give a few examples in other contexts, such as popular foods or music. Tell Ss they will learn some interesting facts about language. Ask them which letter of the alphabet they think is used most in English, then read the first sentence to check. Point out that Ss need to choose the correct alternative and that knowing the information is not important. Ask Ss to work alone to choose the correct words, then check in pairs. Don't check the answers yet.**

EXTRA SUPPORT: DYSLEXIA Tell Ss to cover the parts of the text they are not working on in order to help focus their attention.

B **R1.01 | Play the recording for Ss to check. Ask them to tick if their answers are correct. You may want to play the recording twice, then go through the answers.**

ANSWERS:

1 is
2 words
3 has
4 Polish
5 has
6 from
7 numbers
8 isn't

TO FINISH

Ss write a few facts about their language, e.g. how many vowels or consonants there are, and share them with the class. In multilingual classes this will be interesting, and additionally Ss may start to reflect on how their language is similar or different to English.

2 people

GSE LEARNING OBJECTIVES

2A Where are they?

- READING | Read a blog about two people: numbers 11–100; common adjectives (1)
- Pronunciation: word stress in numbers
- Talk about groups of people: present simple *be*: *we, you, they*

GSE INFORMATION

VOCABULARY
10–29 Can use language related to numbers.
22 Can recognise cardinal numbers from 11–100.

READING
27 Can understand simple descriptions of places.

GRAMMAR
24 Can use the correct form of 'be' with singular and plural nouns.

SPEAKING
22 Can say where they and other people are in a limited way.

2B Family and friends

- LISTENING | Understand someone talking about their family around the world: family; people
- Pronunciation: syllables
- Talk about your friends and family: possessive adjectives
- Write a description of a photo; use *and*

GSE INFORMATION

VOCABULARY
10–29 Can use language related to family members and relationships.

LISTENING
23 Can extract the names of people or places from short, simple dialogues if delivered slowly and clearly.

GRAMMAR
25 Can use possessive adjectives such as 'my', 'your', etc.

SPEAKING
22 Can ask and answer basic questions about family and friends in a limited way.
28 Can ask and answer simple questions about people they know in a limited way.

WRITING
27 Can write simple sentences about their family and where they live.
25 Can use 'and' to link nouns and noun phrases.

2C Small talk

- HOW TO … | have short conversations: feelings
- Pronunciation: stress in phrases

GSE INFORMATION

VOCABULARY
10–29 Can use language related to asking about feelings.
25 Can use the verb 'be' in the simple present with adjectives.

HOW TO …
23 Can understand questions addressed carefully and slowly.
26 Can recognise words and simple phrases related to familiar topics, if spoken slowly and clearly and supported by pictures.

SPEAKING
24 Can greet people, ask how they are and react to news.
28 Can express how they are feeling using very basic fixed expressions.

2D Best Home Cook

- BBC PROGRAMME | Understand a show about a baking competition
- Ask about three people: *wh-* questions + *be*
- Write a message about a friend

GSE INFORMATION

VIEW
30 Can identify simple information in a short video, provided that the visual supports this information and the delivery is slow and clear.

GRAMMAR
25 Can form questions with 'what' and 'who' and answer them.
25 Can ask where other people are using 'Where is/are … ?'
25 Can ask someone's age using 'How old … ?'

SPEAKING
27 Can ask simple questions about other people (e.g. their name, age, where they live, things they have).

WRITING
27 Can write simple sentences about their family and where they live.
25 Can use 'and' to link nouns and noun phrases.

For full coverage of GSE Learning Objectives go to page 222.

BBC VLOGS

This is a short activity that can be used as an introduction to the unit topic and a warm-up to Lesson 2A. It shouldn't be exploited or taught at length, just played once or twice in class.

Explain that Ss will watch a video with different people saying where they are now. They should listen and note how many speakers say they are in Italy. When they are ready, play the video then ask Ss to compare their answers. Check the answer with the class.

ANSWER:
Three speakers are in Italy now.

EXTRA CHALLENGE To exploit the vlogs further, you could give Ss a list of the places where the speakers are now and have them put them in the correct order. They could also find them on a map or globe. With stronger classes, you could first put Ss in pairs to make a list of countries, then watch and tick the countries that they hear. With weaker classes, you could provide a list of the places mentioned in order for Ss to tick as they hear them. (Where the speakers are now, in order: *Bogotá, Colombia*; *New York*; *Italy*; *London*; *Rome, Italy*; *Ireland*; *Columbus, Ohio*; *Florence, Italy*; *Madrid, Spain*)

NOTE The vlogs have been provided by people from around the world in response to the same question. The video content was filmed by them on their own mobile phones, so the picture quality varies considerably and in some cases is of a lower quality. However, this adds to the authenticity of the content.

The locations labelled on the vlogs show where the speaker was when they filmed the video. It does not reflect where the speaker comes from (necessarily).

As many of the speakers are non-native, the videos expose Ss to a range of different accents and varieties of English. This could be used as a way to highlight interesting or useful differences.

Additional Materials

For Teachers:

Presentation Tool Unit 2

Online Digital Resources

Videoscript Unit 2 Opener: BBC Vlogs

2A Where are they?

GRAMMAR | present simple *be*: *we, you, they*
VOCABULARY | numbers 11–100; common adjectives (1)
PRONUNCIATION | word stress in numbers

LESSON OVERVIEW

In this lesson, Ss learn numbers 11–100. They also learn some common adjectives. The context is a reading (a blog) where people talk about their bike rides around the UK. This is then used to highlight the grammar of the remaining forms of *be*: *we, you* and *they*. Ss also practise word stress in numbers and exchanging personal information. The lesson ends with a further communicative speaking activity where they practise giving information about different people.

Online Teaching

If you're teaching this lesson online, you might find the following tips useful:

- **Ex 2A:** Use a collaborative document with the words in it and ask Ss to mark the stressed syllables. Use a pointer to drill randomly.
- **Ex 5A:** Display the photos on your device and share your screen. Ask Ss to call out or type their answers in the chat box.
- **Ex 5C:** Display the statements on your device and share your screen. Make sure the annotate function is on. Ask different Ss to write T or F next to each one. Highlight where the answers are found in the text.
- **Ex 6A:** Ask Ss to type their answers in the chat box or in a collaborative document in feedback.

Additional Materials

For Teachers:

Presentation Tool Lesson 2A

Photocopiable Activities 2A

Grammar Bank 2A

Vocabulary Bank 2A

For Students:

Online Practice 2A

Workbook 2A

TO START

Write a few important numbers for you on the board. Tell Ss why they are important numbers (e.g. *my age, the age of my children, my lucky number*). Put Ss in pairs to tell each other their own special numbers.

EXTRA SUPPORT: DYSLEXIA Dyslexic learners in particular benefit from understanding exactly what they are learning in a lesson so that they understand what they are working towards. In this and every lesson, explain clearly what the learning objectives of the lesson are near the start.

VOCABULARY

numbers 11–100

1 A Focus attention on the numbers written as words, with Ss repeating after you. Point out that *eleven* and *twelve* are irregular, but then for 13–19 we add *-teen* to the base number. Ask Ss to write the numbers next to the words, as in the example. They can compare in pairs and help each other. Check answers as a class.

EXTRA SUPPORT It's assumed that Ss already know the numbers 0–10, which were also reviewed in the Lead-in. With weaker classes, revise these first. It may also be useful to provide immediate practice of numbers up to 20, which you can do using the classroom and simple concepts/words that Ss can easily understand, e.g. say 'The number of chairs?' and continue with 'students', 'tables', etc. This could also give the opportunity to revise numbers 0–10 at the same time.

B 2.01 | Play the recording for Ss to listen and repeat after the recording chorally. You may want to further drill the words individually at this point, too.

ANSWERS:

eleven	*11*	sixteen	16
twelve	12	seventeen	17
thirteen	13	eighteen	18
fourteen	14	nineteen	19
fifteen	15	twenty	20

C Ss write the numbers alone, then check in pairs. Don't give any answers yet.

D 2.02 | Play the recording for Ss to listen and check, then play it again for them to repeat chorally. Highlight that we say *a hundred* (or *one hundred*). Add further individual drilling if you think Ss need it.

ANSWERS:

60	sixty	80	eighty
70	seventy	90	ninety

EXTRA SUPPORT For weaker classes, draw three columns on the board for *1–10, 11–19*, and *20–100*. Write the numbers *two, three, four* and *five* in the first column and say them with the class, then write *twelve* and *twenty* in the second and third columns respectively, demonstrating the change in pronunciation as you do so, then do the same with the other numbers. Focus Ss' attention on the spelling changes, from *two* to *twelve/twenty, three* to *thirteen/thirty, four* to *fourteen/forty* and *five* to *fifteen/fifty*. Then write in the remaining numbers (*one – eleven*, and *six – sixteen – sixty*, etc.).

PRONUNCIATION

word stress in numbers

2 A 2.03 | Write the number *thirteen* on the board and ask Ss for the stressed syllable. Underline or highlight it. Refer Ss to the numbers and the underlined example on the page, then play the recording for Ss to underline or highlight the stress in the other numbers. Ask them to compare in pairs, then go through the answers as a class. Ss should notice that in the teen numbers the stress is on *-teen* whereas in the numbers in the second column it is on the first syllable. This stress difference is important because the pairs of words sound so similar.

EXTRA SUPPORT: DYSLEXIA Ss with dyslexia can have difficulty with underlining as it makes reading the letters unclear. You could suggest alternative methods such as highlighting the stressed syllable with a highlighter pen in a different colour or adding a box above the stressed syllable, ideally in a different colour.

ANSWERS:

thirteen (stress: teen)	thirty (stress: thir)
fourteen (stress: teen)	forty (stress: for)
fifteen (stress: teen)	fifty (stress: fif)
sixteen (stress: teen)	sixty (stress: six)
seventeen (stress: teen)	seventy (stress: sev)
eighteen (stress: teen)	eighty (stress: eigh)
nineteen (stress: teen)	ninety (stress: nine)

B 2.03 | Play the recording again for Ss to listen and repeat the numbers. You may want to play it a third time for Ss to practise the difference in stress some more.

C Demonstrate the activity by saying a random number from Ex 2A. Ask a volunteer to point to the correct number. Put Ss in pairs to say and point. This is a listening discrimination exercise, and Ss don't need to write anything. Move around the class and listen. When they have finished, drill any words that were causing problems.

EXTRA IDEA For extra work on pronunciation, you could tell Ss that the numbers in the first column (the *-teen* numbers) are in their left hand and the numbers in the second column (the *-ty* numbers) in their right. Say random numbers and Ss should raise the relevant hand. This is a fun kinetic activity and also a useful assessment tool to see which Ss are struggling to hear the difference.

3 A Look at the example and highlight the hyphen. Ask Ss to work alone to write the numbers. Check the answers and write them on the board. Make sure that Ss have correct spelling. Point out that in double digits, the second number is more stressed, e.g. *twenty-seven*.

ANSWERS:
2 forty-nine **3** seventy-three **4** fifty-six

B Ask Ss to say the numbers in pairs. Weaker classes may need to do this as a class. Move around and listen. When they have finished, check as a class.

ANSWERS:
sixty-seven, thirty-four, ninety-eight, fifty-two, twenty-five, eighty-eight

EXTRA IDEA For extra work on numbers, you could play *Bingo!* Provide Ss with a grid of nine boxes or ask them to draw one in their notebooks, then fill it with numbers of their choice. It is best to limit this (e.g. to numbers between 1 and 20). When they are ready, say numbers in random order and have them circle the ones they have. When they have completed their grid, they call out 'Bingo!'. You could play several times using different grids and different number ranges.

C/D Put Ss in A/B pairs and refer them to the relevant pages. Write an email address on the board, different from the ones in the activity (e.g. *patblu99@coldmail.co.uk*). Ask Ss what it is (an email address) and how to say it and elicit/teach how we say @ (at), *.co.uk* (dot co dot UK) and *.com* (dot com). Explain that Ss have different personal information and they must ask each other questions and answer using this information so they can complete the membership cards. With weaker classes, elicit the questions needed and write them on the board. Ask a stronger pair to demonstrate the activity and emphasise that they should listen to each other and not look at each other's books. Student Bs ask Student As first, and they change roles only once Student B's card is complete. Move around the class and listen. When Ss have completed both cards, ask them to check their answers with their partner, particularly to see if they have the spelling correct. Recap on and drill any persistent problems with pronunciation of letters, such as *e*, *i*, *a* and *r*, that Ss often confuse.

EXTRA IDEA If Ss don't mind swapping personal information, they could follow the activity by practising saying their own age, address and email. Alternatively, they can practise saying these at home on their own.

4 A Ask Ss to write the names and ages of three friends in their notebooks. Model this activity on the board (you could use the examples in the book). Tell Ss not to write sentences.

B Say 'My friend is Philip.' and write spaces for the letters of the name on the board, i.e. _ _ _ _ _ _, to elicit the question *How do you spell that/'Philip'?* Write the question on the board. Then say 'He's twenty-four years old.' and elicit the question *How old is he/Philip?* to the board. Point out that we often omit the words 'years old' when talking about age. Drill both questions thoroughly as Ss need to be able to understand and say them. Refer Ss to the example in their book and ask a strong student to demonstrate with you. Make a show of writing the name as you listen to how it is spelt. Then put Ss in pairs to continue. Move around the class and discourage them from showing each other the names, as this takes away the listening element of the activity. When they have finished, Ss can show each other their notebooks and check the spelling. There's no need for whole class feedback, but you can note any problem letters and recap these at the end.

READING

EXTRA SUPPORT: DYSLEXIA There is a recording of the reading text available to help dyslexic learners.

5 A Before Ss read, display the photos without the captions via the Presentation Tool and ask them to talk in pairs about the photos and where they think they are. Use the photos to teach the words *canal* and *sea*, and also teach *mountains*, as Ss will meet these in the blog. If Ss can't come up with any countries, give them a few possibilities to choose from (e.g. *Australia*, *Germany*, *England*, etc.). After a few minutes, check Ss' ideas but don't confirm yet.

EXTRA IDEA A map, either digital or physical, could be a useful aid. Show and find the UK countries with your Ss: England, Scotland, Wales and Northern Ireland. You could identify and locate the capital cities as well, as London appears in the text. It may also be an opportunity to teach the adjectives: English, Scottish and Welsh. Note that most Northern Irish people either identify as Northern Irish, Irish or British, and this can be a delicate topic. (The Republic of) Ireland is a separate country, and Irish is the nationality.

B Focus attention on the blog, then ask Ss to read it and identify the countries in the photos. Give a time limit of two minutes here, to encourage Ss to read quickly and for a purpose.

ANSWERS:
A England **B** England **C** Wales

C **Focus attention on the question and clarify that *True* = correct and *False* = not correct, according to the text. Then ask Ss to read the blog again and mark each statement T or F. Give them three or four minutes, then ask them to compare in pairs. Then go through the answers as a class, nominating individual Ss to give answers. Highlight *2OnABikeUK* and elicit how to say it ('two on a bike UK') and how this relates photo A.**

EXTRA SUPPORT: TEACHER Ss may feel apprehensive about finding unknown words in a text. It's advisable to set a time frame and focus attention on reading to answer the questions. In going through the answers, ask Ss to locate where they are found in the text. This helps them develop their reading skills. When they have finished, you can discuss any words Ss had problems with.

ANSWERS:
2 F **3** F **4** T **5** T **6** F

D **Refer Ss to the gapped sentences and explain that they need to choose a word in bold from the blog to complete each one. Tell Ss that the words in bold are adjectives – words used for describing. Look at the first sentence as a class and elicit the answer, then ask Ss to continue alone before checking in pairs. When they have finished, ask individual Ss to read out their answers. Confirm, drill and further clarify as needed.**

EXTRA SUPPORT: DYSLEXIA For Ss with dyslexia, write the words in bold in the text in a vertical list on the board or on a handout. Dyslexic learners can usually process words presented in lists more easily.

ANSWERS:
1 old **2** cold **3** tired
4 friendly **5** small

E **Refer Ss to the Vocabulary Bank on page 127.**

VB page 127 **VOCABULARY BANK** common adjectives (1)

Note that the Vocabulary Bank activities are an important part of the lesson. They should only be omitted if you are confident that your Ss already know this vocabulary. If you don't use the exercises in class, it would be a good idea to set them as homework.

1 A **Draw attention to the pictures (A–K) and elicit/ teach the adjectives. Point out / Elicit the pairs of opposites and write them in pairs on the board. Ask Ss to match the adjectives with the pictures individually, then check in pairs. Check answers as a class.**

EXTRA SUPPORT: DYSLEXIA Covering the adjectives they are not focusing on will help Ss with dyslexia reduce distractions as they match the adjectives with the pictures.

ANSWERS:
1 E **2** J **3** K **4** G **5** C **6** F
7 I **8** B **9** D **10** H **11** A

B **VB2.01 | Explain that Ss should look at the pictures (A–K) and then play the recording for them to repeat chorally. Further drill individually as needed.**

EXTRA SUPPORT The lack of sound–spelling correspondence in English is a difficulty for all Ss, particularly those with beginner literacy or who are dyslexic, so you may want to introduce a system called *Look Say Cover Write Check*. Ss first look at a new word and say it aloud. They then cover it with their hand and write it alongside. When they have done this, they reveal the original and check they have it correct. They can repeat this process over several days, using a designated notebook.

C **Read the instruction as a class. Point out that question 1 is to practise the adjectives and question 2 specifically practises the pairs of opposites. Demonstrate the activity with a stronger student then ask Ss to continue in pairs. Move around the class and listen, to see how they are doing, and when they have finished have a final drill or recap as needed.**

D **Read the instruction to the class or ask a stronger student to read it. Look at the example together and elicit further options to demonstrate that several options are possible (e.g. a cold coffee, a good coffee). Remind Ss that the adjective goes before the noun and does not have a plural form. Put Ss in pairs to complete the activity.**

EXTRA SUPPORT Weaker classes may need time to make a list of suitable nouns and adjectives that go with them. They can do this in A/A and B/B pairs while you go around and help ensure they are correct. Then re-pair Ss in A/B pairs to work with a new partner and their list.

EXTRA CHALLENGE Show stronger Ss picture cards or flash up pictures of everyday items to elicit the noun and a suitable adjective. This could be a competitive team activity where teams come up with as many accurate pairings as they can.

GRAMMAR

present simple *be*: *we*, *you*, *they*

6 A **Point to yourself and say *I*, then to a student to elicit *you*, then gesture to the class and yourself to elicit *we*. Turn to the board and, with Ss' help, write up a column of the subject pronouns from *I* to *they*. Tell Ss you will be focusing on *we*, *you* and *they* with the verb *be* and refer them to the exercise. Remind them that *I*, *you*, *he*, *she* and *it* were introduced in Unit 1. Point out that *you* is the same for singular and plural in English. Ask Ss to complete the sentences using the blog to help them. Put Ss in pairs to compare answers, then check answers with the class. Ask Ss to read the sentences to each other to practise the forms.**

EXTRA SUPPORT With weaker classes, build up the subjects and verbs on the board, with positive and negative forms, including contracted forms, as a table for Ss to refer to and drill them thoroughly before asking Ss to copy it into their notebooks.

ANSWERS:
1 're **2** we, 're **3** Are **4** aren't

B **The Grammar Bank on page 96 can be used in the lesson or for homework. Decide how and when the exercises will benefit your class.**

GB page 96 **GRAMMAR BANK**

Read through and check understanding of the notes with the class, especially focusing on the use of contractions and features of pronunciation. Point out the silent *r* in *aren't* (/ɑːnt/). If Ss are confident, you could ask individuals to read sections aloud to the class. Point out that *we* includes the speaker and *they* does not.

1 **This practises the meaning and use of the subject pronouns as well as accuracy of the verb. Read the example and check Ss understand that this is a conversation. Ss choose the correct alternatives individually, then check in pairs. Check answers with the class. Put Ss in pairs to practise the conversation, taking turns at both roles.**

ANSWERS:

2 we're	**3** they	**4** they are
5 Are they	**6** they aren't	**7** are they
8 They're		

2 **This practises the correct use of pronouns. Look at the example with the class, then ask Ss to write the rest of the sentences. Remind them that when *I* is included they need to use *we*. When they have finished, ask different Ss to read their answers aloud or you could ask individuals to come to the board to write an answer to check as a class.**

EXTRA SUPPORT To reduce the writing load of the exercise for Ss with beginner literacy or dyslexia, ask them to just write the pronouns and verbs, not the complete sentences.

ANSWERS:
2 We're / We are shop assistants.
3 Are they from Scotland?
4 They're / They are Mr Vega and Ms Fox.
5 Where are you?
6 They aren't / They're not / They are not here.
7 We're / We are at university.
8 Are they here?

3 **Ss complete the conversation individually then check in pairs. Remind them that words that go at the beginning of sentences need a capital letter. Check answers with the class, calling on individuals to read out sentences. If you have time, Ss could practise the conversation in threes (A, B and C) and then rotate roles.**

EXTRA SUPPORT To support beginner literacy and dyslexic learners, provide two alternatives for each gap, one correct and one distractor.

ANSWERS:

2 What	**3** I	**4** 'm	**5** Where
6 We're	**7** you	**8** 're	**9** Are
10 n't	**11** We	**12** it's	**13** are

SPEAKING

7 **Tell Ss that they are now going to talk about other people. Put Ss in A/B pairs and refer them to the relevant pages.**

1 **Ss each look at their photo and the information about the three people. Tell them they need to remember as much of this information as possible.**

2 **When Ss have read their information, ask them to take turns to tell their partner about the people in their photo without looking at the information, as far as possible. Stronger Ss can ask each other questions. While they are speaking, move around and make notes on Ss' use of language for later class feedback. When they have finished, go over any common errors and/or ask a stronger pair to repeat the exercise for the class.**

3 **Tell Ss they are going to talk about 'themselves'. Ask Ss to look at their second photo and choose one person to be 'them'. They also need to name the other two people in their photo. They then complete the information. They can invent information or use information about real friends.**

4 **Ask Ss to tell their partner about the friends in their photo. Stronger Ss can ask each other questions.**

EXTRA: ALTERNATIVE IDEA If Ss are willing to share real personal information, ask them to use photos of their own family and friends on their devices for this activity. Put Ss in groups of three to talk and share. Move around and feed in vocabulary as they need it.

EXTRA IDEA: DIGITAL Ask Ss to use their device to record themselves and listen back to it. This can be useful for pronunciation practice and developing fluency. They can just listen to it themselves or later compare their recordings with others.

TO FINISH

Discuss with Ss where their family and friends are. They can show photos on their phones and ask questions.

2B Family and friends

GRAMMAR | possessive adjectives
VOCABULARY | family; people
PRONUNCIATION | syllables

LESSON OVERVIEW

In this lesson, Ss learn vocabulary to describe family relationships and people in general. The context is a listening where the speaker gives personal information about their family, enabling revision of numbers to say age, and jobs. This leads into the grammar of possessive adjectives, which Ss then practise by talking about their family relationships. The lesson ends with a writing activity where Ss write a description of a photo.

Online Teaching

If you're teaching this lesson online, you might find the following tips useful:

- **Ex 4C:** Display the table on your device and make sure the annotate function is on. In feedback, ask Ss to take turns to complete the table.
- **Ex 4D:** Put Ss in breakout rooms to discuss or ask Ss to type their answers in the chat box in the main room.
- **Ex 6A:** Ask Ss to make a list in a collaborative document. They can then compare this list with the Vocabulary Bank.

Additional Materials

For Teachers:
Presentation Tool Lesson 2B
Photocopiable Activities 2B
Grammar Bank 2B
Vocabulary Bank 2B
Writing Bank 2B

For Students:
Online Practice 2B
Workbook 2B

TO START

Show pictures of some famous families and groups of friends and ask Ss if they can name them (e.g. *the Simpsons*, *Friends*). Ask Ss what the relationships are. Explain that this is the focus of today's lesson.

EXTRA SUPPORT: DYSLEXIA Dyslexic learners in particular benefit from understanding exactly what they are learning in a lesson so that they understand what they are working towards. In this and every lesson, explain clearly what the learning objectives of the lesson are near the start.

VOCABULARY

family

1 **Look at the instruction with the class, pointing out that there are five relationships and four photos so it's not a simple matching task. Talk as a class about photo A. You could encourage the use of vocabulary studied in the last lesson, i.e. adjectives (*She's young.*) and numbers, as well as *about* for expressing ages they're not sure about (*She's about nine.*). You may like to teach *They (don't) look similar.* Ask Ss to discuss their ideas in pairs, then check answers as a class. Point out that *parents* refers only to mother and father, and that *children* is an irregular plural.**

ANSWERS:

1 Justin and Emma in B; Matías and Antonella in D
2 Thomas and Jessica in C; David and Mariana in D
3 David and Mariana (parents) and Matías and Antonella (children) in C
4 Mark (father) and Mia (daughter) in A; David (father) and Antonella (daughter) in D
5 Mariana (mother) and Matías (son) in D

PRONUNCIATION

syllables

2A **Read the example with the class and elicit further examples of syllables to check Ss are confident. Use your fingers to show the syllables as you say the words. Ss then complete the rest of the exercise.**

EXTRA SUPPORT Show Ss that each syllable begins with a consonant. This will help them understand where the division is, i.e. not *broth-er*, but *bro-ther*, which makes pronunciation easier. (Of course, this doesn't work where a word begins with a vowel.) In a monolingual class, you could compare how this works in Ss' first language.

B **2.04 | Play the recording and ask Ss to listen to confirm the number of syllables. Play the recording again for Ss to repeat. Show the stress movement with your hand as they do so.**

ANSWERS:

One syllable: wife, son

Two syllables: *brother, sister,* husband, parents, children, father, daughter, mother

C **Read the rule with the class and elicit the answer. Stronger classes could suggest further examples of two-syllable nouns (e.g. *number, seven, happy*).**

ANSWER:

one

EXTRA SUPPORT: TEACHER Two-syllable nouns tend to be stressed on the first syllable, e.g. *brother*, and two-syllable verbs on the second, e.g. *decide*. There are of course many exceptions. Acknowledge these if Ss bring them up, but don't introduce them.

3 **Focus attention on the example and read it with the class. While the verb *have* hasn't been formally introduced in this context, Ss should nevertheless understand it. Give a further example with your own family if you like, then put Ss in pairs to talk. Weaker classes might need to write first. Stronger classes can be invited to include a bit more information, but don't correct language that they haven't studied yet, such as third person verb forms. When they have finished, you could ask Ss if their partner's family is very similar or different to theirs and why.**

LISTENING

4A **Focus attention on the photo of Mark and Mia and read the instruction with the class. Ask Ss to look at the other photos and discuss in pairs, first writing on the board: *I think [name] is his sister/brother.* When Ss have finished, have a brief whole class discussion, but don't confirm the answers yet.**

B **2.05 | Play the recording for Ss to check. Elicit the answers.**

ANSWERS:

1 Jessica 2 David

AUDIOSCRIPT 2.05

My name's Mark. I'm American, and I'm from New York City, and my family … Well, it's a very international family. I have a sister in France, a brother in Colombia, and our parents are in New York. I'm in Italy, and I have a beautiful daughter, Mia. She's eight and she's a student at school here.

My sister Jessica and her husband Thomas are in France. They have a restaurant in Paris. Jessica's forty-five. She's a good mother, and she's a great sister to me. Their children are in the UK, in London. Their son, Justin, is twenty-one now. He's a writer for a magazine. I don't remember its name. Their daughter Emma is eighteen and she's a student at university.

My brother David and his family are in Colombia. David's thirty-eight. His wife, Mariana, is Colombian. They have two young children, Antonella and Matías. David's a doctor. He often says 'Come and visit! It's perfect for your holiday!' But they're in Colombia and I'm in Italy! We're very happy in Italy, but we really are an international family!

C 2.05 | **Refer Ss to the table and explain that they should listen and complete the missing information. Allow a couple of minutes for them to read the information in the table. Play the recording, then put Ss in pairs to complete and compare their answers. Play the recording again. Elicit the answers and write them on the board.**

EXTRA SUPPORT Ss with dyslexia and beginner literacy can struggle to complete tasks where they are asked to do several things at the same time – in this case, listen, read and write. You could have the information on the board for Ss to choose from or provide two alternatives for each box for Ss to circle the correct one. Playing the recording several times will be helpful as well as allowing time to read the existing information before listening.

ANSWERS:

name	age	country now	job or studies
Mia	8	Italy	*a student at school*
Jessica	45	*France*	*has a restaurant*
Justin	21	the UK	*a writer for a magazine*
Emma	18	*the UK*	a student at university
David	*38*	Colombia	a doctor

D **Put Ss in pairs. Ask them to cover the table and just look at the photos to see what they can remember and tell their partner. Weaker classes may need to read the information again, or one of the pair may need to have their book open and confirm or correct. Reassure Ss it's not a memory test and that this is just an opportunity for speaking practice.**

GRAMMAR

possessive adjectives

5A **Write on the board: *Jessica is his sister. David is his brother.* Refer Ss back to the photos and remind them of the context of Mark and his family. Underline the possessive *his*. Some Ss may find it puzzling that the same possessive adjective is used with both male and female, as in many languages the possessive is determined by the object. Explain that the possessive adjective matches the subject (in this case, Mark – who is a man). Ask Ss to complete the sentences with the possessive adjectives, then check in pairs. Check as a class. In number 4, Ss may be tempted to say *Justin/he* is the subject, but the subject is *magazine*. In number 5, the possessive adjective refers back to David, because of the word *wife*. Number 6 is a bit different, and we must assume the possessive refers to the listener, i.e. *you*. Drill the sentences chorally and individually.**

EXTRA SUPPORT With weaker classes, first go through the possessive adjectives and relate them to the subject they refer to (as in the table in Ex 5B). Before Ss attempt the exercise, ask them to identify the subject in the sentences. This will generally help them choose the correct adjective.

EXTRA SUPPORT: DYSLEXIA Provide Ss with a vertical list of the possessive adjectives for them to refer to and hold next to the sentences to help choose the correct one for each gap. They can refer to this in Ex 5B as well.

ANSWERS:

2 My, her **3** Their **4** its
5 His **6** your

B **Ask Ss to use the sentences in Ex 5A to help them complete the table. Check answers with the class. Drill the pairs of words chorally, (*I–my, it – its, you–your*, etc.).**

ANSWERS:

subject pronoun	possessive adjective
I	**my**
it	its
you	your
he	**his**
she	her
we	*our*
they	their

C **The Grammar Bank on page 97 can be used in the lesson or for homework. Decide how and when the exercises will benefit your class.**

page 97 **GRAMMAR BANK**

GB

This focuses on the form and use of possessive adjectives. Check understanding of the notes, especially of the potential confusion of *they're/their* and *you're/your*. Point out that *it's* is a contraction of the verb *be* (*it is*) and that the possessive *its* has no apostrophe.

1 **Complete the first line of the conversation with the class, then ask Ss to continue choosing the correct alternatives. Move around the class and refer Ss to the notes to help them. When they have finished, nominate different Ss to read out the answers. Ss can practise the conversation in pairs, taking turns at both roles. Confidence can be built by having open pairs read across the class.**

ANSWERS:

1 your	**2** my	**3** Our	**4** her
5 Our	**6** His	**7** he	**8** He's
9 their	**10** It's		

2 Refer Ss to the example and ask them to correct the conversations alone, then check in pairs. Check answers with the class. Ask Ss to practise the conversations in pairs.

EXTRA SUPPORT: DYSLEXIA Ss with dyslexia can find missing word exercises like this difficult. In this case, stage the exercise. First go through as a class and mark where the words are missing. Then ask Ss to decide which words go where. Finally, check as a class. Alternatively, you can highlight where the words are missing for Ss to just select the correct options, which can be provided in groups relevant to specific conversations (e.g. *my, our, their, your* for conversations 1 and 2).

ANSWERS:

1 A: What are **your** names?
2 A: This is a photo of **our** children.
B: What are **their** names?
3 B: Yes, **her** husband's a businessman with a big company.
A: What's **its** name?
4 A: Hi Liz, I'm at the airport, but **your** brother isn't here.
B: Oh, no. Just a moment. I have **his** phone number.

SPEAKING

6A Look at the examples given with the class. Put Ss in pairs to make a list and give a time frame of two minutes to focus them. When they have finished, ask how many words they have and ask the pair with the longest list to read it out while others listen and check. Ask the class for any other words not already mentioned.

B Refer Ss to the Vocabulary Bank on page 127.

VB page 127 **VOCABULARY BANK** people

Note that the Vocabulary Bank activities are an important part of the lesson. They should only be omitted if you are confident that your Ss already know this vocabulary. If you don't use the exercises in class, it would be a good idea to set them as homework.

1A Draw attention to the photos (A–H) and elicit/teach the nouns for the people. Then ask Ss to match the people (1–8) with the photos (A–H). Go through the answers and drill chorally. Elicit which words are male/female and those that could be either (i.e. child, baby, friend, person).

ANSWERS:
1 C **2** H **3** F **4** E **5** A **6** G **7** B **8** D

B **VB2.02 |** Focus attention on the photos. Play the recording and pause for Ss to repeat chorally.

2A Ask Ss how we usually make plurals (by adding *s*). Refer them to this list of irregular plurals and ask them to write the singular form individually, using Ex 1A to support them, then compare answers. Go through the answers as a class.

ANSWERS:
2 man **3** woman **4** child

B **VB2.03 |** Play the recording and pause for Ss to repeat. Further drill a few individuals if you feel they need it.

3 Put Ss in pairs. Ask them to take turns to point at and say the word. Encourage them to listen to and correct each other. Move around the class and listen, then give brief feedback on any problematic pronunciation.

EXTRA CHALLENGE As an extension to the pointing and naming, stronger classes could work in pairs with one pointing and their partner providing the plural noun.

7A Name half the class Student As and the rest Student Bs and direct them to the relevant pages. Explain that they have different information and should use the words in brackets and the question words to make questions to ask for information they don't have. If necessary, review what each question asks about, i.e. *How old … ?* for age, *Where … ?* for place and *What … ?* for thing. Most Ss will need to write these questions, so put them in A/A and B/B pairs to do this. Provide support and discretely check their questions as you move around the class.

EXTRA SUPPORT: DYSLEXIA Exs 7A and 7B could be difficult for Ss with dyslexia, who may find it a challenge to focus on the key information needed for each stage. In this case, you could break the task down into stages, write these on the board and tick them as they are achieved.

Aim: Complete the text with the missing information

1 ☐ *Read the text with a partner and highlight the key information.*
2 ☐ *Write the questions with your partner.*
3 ☐ *Work with a new partner.*
4 ☐ *Ask the questions.*
5 ☐ *Write the answers.*
6 ☐ *Answer your partner's questions.*

Note that this is the order of the stages for Student A. For Student B, stage 6 will come before stages 4 and 5.

Advise Ss to cover the parts of the information they are not referring to when they answer their partner's questions in Ex 7B as this will also help them to focus.

ANSWERS:

Student A

2 What nationality is Filipa? / Where is Filipa from?
3 Where do they live? / Where is their home?
4 How old is Zoe?
5 What is her job?
6 Where is Andreas?
7 Where does he work?

Student B

2 Where is Keith from?
3 Where are their children?
4 Where is Zoe?
5 Where does she work?
6 How old is Andreas?
7 What is his job?

B Put Ss in A/B pairs to ask and answer questions to complete their respective texts. Student A asks their questions first for Student B to answer, then they swap roles. Remind them that they should not look at their partner's information but should listen carefully and ask for spelling if necessary. When Ss have finished, they should show each other their information. This acts as a peer check and there is no need for a whole class check.

EXTRA IDEA Ss can exchange information and repeat the speaking activity with their partner's questions for extra practice. They don't need to write.

8A Model the activity first by writing the names of a few people in your life on the board (e.g. Gary, Jemima, Doug) and inviting questions ('Who's Gary?', 'How old is he?', etc.). Answer Ss' questions ('Gary is my brother.', 'He's thirty-six.'). Then ask Ss to write three to five names of people they know. They should write only names, not sentences.

B Put Ss in pairs to talk about the people. Move around the class and listen. This is a fluency stage, so don't worry too much if Ss make mistakes and only step in if they have a communication problem. They need to develop confidence. If you have time, put them in new pairs and repeat the activity.

WRITING

write a description of a photo; use *and*

9A Put Ss in pairs to look at the photo at the bottom of the page and discuss the question. Elicit their ideas but don't confirm if they are correct or not.

B Refer Ss to the beginning of the description to check. Elicit the answer. Highlight the word *and* ('Mei *and* Ken') and point out that it joins two words, or longer phrases.

ANSWER:

They're from Kobe in Japan.

C Explain that Ss will now write their own descriptions. Refer them to the Writing Bank on page 88.

page 88 **WRITING BANK**

1A Refer Ss to the photo and the full description and give them one minute to find the names of the people. Elicit their answers.

ANSWERS:

The woman is Mei, the man is Ken, the girl is Sora and the boy is Aya.

B Refer Ss to the example and ask them to put *and* in sentences 2 and 3. Ask Ss to compare in pairs, then elicit the sentences.

ANSWERS:

2 She's a teacher **and** her husband Ken is a businessman.
3 They have two children, a daughter **and** a son …

C Refer Ss to the description of the photo again and ask them to find four more examples of *and*. Ask Ss to compare in pairs, then elicit the sentences. Use the examples to show that *and* can join single words ('aged one *and* three') as well as longer phrases that contain a subject and verb (clauses).

ANSWERS:

Mei **and** Ken in the park

… aged one **and** three. Their names are Sora **and** Aya. They're a lovely family **and** we often have video calls with them.

2A Ask Ss to complete the notes, based on their own ideas. Move around to help with vocabulary (e.g. where they are, job titles) as needed. If Ss are having problems thinking of information, you could suggest some nationalities and jobs for them to choose from, or refer them to the relevant parts of the Vocabulary Bank.

B Ask Ss to use their notes to write a description. They can use the text in Ex 1A to help them. Allow plenty of time for this. Move around and be available to help, prompting Ss for capital letters and reminding them to use *and*.

C Ask Ss to compare in pairs or small groups.

EXTRA IDEA: DIGITAL Ss record their descriptions on a dedicated video platform, where other Ss can watch and comment or ask questions.

3 **Ss should write descriptions of three photos and bring them (and the photos) to class.**

EXTRA SUPPORT: DIGITAL Give some weblinks to photos and info about famous people for Ss to write descriptions.

EXTRA IDEA: OUT OF CLASS There are a number of ways you can exploit Ss' writing here in a follow-up activity. For example, in a later class put the photos around the classroom without the descriptions, and give Ss (in pairs) all the descriptions; they then try to match them with the photos. Ss could read and peer correct each other's descriptions. The photos and descriptions could be collated for an online magazine. Ss could also share their photos and descriptions in an online group.

TO FINISH

Ask Ss to think of someone important to them, then share information about them in pairs, e.g. 'Maria is my wife. She's from Portugal. She's also a teacher.'; 'Anish is my friend. He lives in Agra in India. He has two children.'

2C Small talk

HOW TO ... | have short conversations
VOCABULARY | feelings
PRONUNCIATION | stress in phrases

LESSON OVERVIEW

In this lesson, Ss learn language for expressing feelings in everyday conversations. The context is a listening where they hear conversations in different places. This leads into short conversational phrases, which Ss listen to and practise saying using sentence stress. The lesson ends with a speaking activity where Ss practise talking about their feelings on various topics.

Online Teaching

If you're teaching this lesson online, you might find the following tips useful:

- **Ex 1A:** Ask Ss to express how they are feeling in the chat using emojis.
- **Ex 3A:** Use an online whiteboard to show the patterns. Say different phrases and ask Ss to match and then to repeat them.
- **Exs 5B and 6:** Put pairs/groups in breakout rooms to have their conversations. Go round each room monitoring carefully while they practise.

Additional Materials

For Teachers:
Presentation Tool Lesson 2C
Photocopiable Activity 2C
Grammar Bank 2C

For Students:
Online Practice 2C
Workbook 2C

TO START

Ask Ss 'How are you today?' If Ss can't answer, use a thumbs up to elicit *fine/good* and thumbs down to elicit *not very good*. Write the question on the board, tell Ss how you are, then put Ss in pairs to discuss the question. Tell them one of the lesson topics is talking about feelings.

EXTRA SUPPORT: DYSLEXIA Dyslexic learners in particular benefit from understanding exactly what they are learning in a lesson so that they understand what they are working towards. In this and every lesson, explain clearly what the learning objectives of the lesson are near the start.

VOCABULARY

feelings

1 A Focus attention on the table and tell Ss that the words in each row match the meaning of the emoji. Ss discuss and write the remaining words in the correct places in pairs. When they have finished, elicit their answers and drill.

ANSWERS:

1 not very good	**4** really good
2 not bad	**5** great
3 *good*	

EXTRA SUPPORT: TEACHER *Fine* or *Not bad* is the traditional positive response to the question *How are you?* Increasingly, people answer *Good* to this question. *Well* often refers more closely to health. The response *I'm not (very) well.* suggests a (mental/physical) health problem.

B Put Ss in different pairs. Refer them to the example conversation and model this with a stronger student. Remind Ss that there is more than one alternative for most of the emojis. Ask Ss to cover the words in the table and ask each other the question, then look at the words again before repeating the activity.

EXTRA IDEA If Ss are able to move around the classroom, you could open this activity out so that they walk around and greet other Ss, asking how they are and answering. Encourage them to use different responses each time someone asks.

How to ...
have short conversations

2 A 2.06 | Refer Ss to the photos and talk about where they are. Explain that they should listen and match each conversation (1–3) with a photo (A–C). Play the recording, ask Ss to compare their answers in pairs, then check the answers.

ANSWERS:
1 B **2** A **3** C

AUDIOSCRIPT 2.06

Conversation 1

D = Dave J = Jen

D: Hey, Jen, how are you?
J: Hi, Dave. Not bad, thanks. Coffee?
D: Yes, please. Black with sugar.
J: Here.
D: Thanks.
J: How are you?
D: Good, thanks. How's work?
J: It's OK. How are your children?
D: They're great, thanks. Lena's three now and Stella's six. I have a photo.
J: Aw ... They're beautiful!
D: Yes ... Oh, look at the time! Thanks for the coffee.
J: No problem.

Conversation 2

K = Katie N = Nick

K: Hi, Nick.
N: Hey, Katie. Are you OK?
K: Yes, great. You?
N: Good, thanks. It's a beautiful day.
K: Yes, it is. How's your new car?
N: It's really good. We're very happy with it.
K: Great!
N: I'm really hot ... and tired.
K: Me too. Ah here's my street. See you.
N: See you later! Say 'hello' to Greg!

Conversation 3

A = Andy S = Susanna

A: Hey, Susanna! Where's our class?
S: Hi! Er ... Anthony?
A: Andy.
S: Sorry, Andy. Our class? Just a moment. It's 617. Yeah, room 617.
A: How are you?
S: Very well, thanks. You?
A: I'm fine.
S: Hey, Andy, you have art classes, right?
A: That's right.
S: How's your new teacher? Ms Brown?
A: She's really good and she's very friendly.
S: Oh that's good. Ah, here we are, room 617.

B 2.06 | Focus Ss' attention on the words in the box. Point out that one has been done for them (*work* is in Conversation 1). Play the recording again, pausing after each conversation to allow Ss to write. Ask Ss to check in pairs, then check answers with the class.

ANSWERS:
car 2 children 1 teacher 3 work *1*

C **Refer Ss to the conversations. Explain that they are extracts from the longer conversations they just heard. Tell them that each gap represents one word. Ask them to complete the conversations alone, then check in pairs. Don't go through the answers yet.**

EXTRA SUPPORT This exercise may challenge weaker Ss as it relies on them recalling a lot of precise information from the conversations in the recording. If Ss are struggling, you could proceed straight to the listening in Ex 2D for them to listen for and identify the missing words and/or provide them, jumbled, on the board, for Ss to choose from.

EXTRA SUPPORT: DYSLEXIA As well as providing the missing words, preferably in a vertical list which they will find easier to read, dyslexic learners will benefit from having the activity broken down into more manageable chunks (e.g. listing the answers to 1–8 and 9–14 for them separately).

D **2.07 | Play the recording, pausing after each conversation, for Ss to check/correct their answers. Ask pairs to compare, then go through the answers as a class and write them on the board. Present them as part of the complete phrases, and drill the phrases.**

EXTRA SUPPORT: TEACHER It's important that Ss can both see and hear how the missing words in the activity work as part of whole phrases. When learners are learning 'chunks' or phrases as a whole, it's as important for them to learn the stress pattern as it is when learning individual words. Getting the right pattern will help Ss sound natural when speaking as well as helping them to hear and identify common phrases. Circles can show this visually, as could using Cuisenaire® rods or any other method you use to indicate stress.

ANSWERS:

2 please	**3** with	**4** 's
5 are	**6** at	**7** Thanks
8 No	**9** day	**10** happy
11 you	**12** See	**13** new
14 friendly		

PRONUNCIATION

stress in phrases

3 **A** **Tell Ss the phrases in the activity come from the conversations they have just heard. Look at the first phrase with Ss and say it slowly, counting the syllables with your fingers. Show them how stress pattern d matches it, pointing out that each circle represents a syllable and the larger circles are for the stressed syllables. As Ss have seen word stress before, this transition to sentence stress should not cause too many difficulties. Ss should continue alone then check in pairs. Don't confirm the answers yet.**

EXTRA SUPPORT Before Ss complete Ex 3A, write two circle patterns from the exercise (OOo, OoOO) on the board and hum the sounds, stressing the larger circles. Ask Ss to copy you. Then hum one of the patterns and ask Ss to identify which it is. Ask Ss what the circles represent (syllables) and what the larger ones mean (stressed syllables).

B **2.08 | Play the recording for Ss to check their answers. Go through the answers as a class. Drill the phrases.**

ANSWERS:

2 a **3** b **4** c

FUTURE SKILLS | Self-management 

C **Refer Ss to the Future Skills box and read it with them. Ask Ss to identify the stress pattern of the phrases by saying them to their partner. Go through the answers and drill.**

ANSWERS:

Thanks for the coffee. OooOo

How are the children? OooOo

EXTRA: FUTURE SKILLS Elicit useful phrases for work or college. (e.g. saying hello and goodbye, small talk, etc.). Write these on the board and ask pairs to identify the stress patterns, then add them to their notes. Classes not in the workplace could write variations on the expressions seen (e.g. Thanks for the tea., How are the cats?) and draw their stress pattern.

D **The Grammar Bank on page 98 can be used in the lesson or for homework. Decide how and when the exercises will benefit your class.**

page 98 **GRAMMAR BANK**

GB

This focuses on short phrases for starting and ending a conversation. Check understanding of the way the tables are organised, especially the singular and plural changes.

1 **Ss match the questions (1–8) with the answers (a–h) alone, then check in pairs. Check answers with the class. Point out that *How are things?* is a general expression.**

EXTRA SUPPORT: DYSLEXIA To make the exercise easier for Ss with dyslexia to process, you could divide the list of questions into two halves (1–4 and 5–8) each with the relevant answers. They can draw lines to match them.

ANSWERS:

2 g **3** b **4** a **5** h **6** d **7** e **8** c

GB 2 **Focus attention on the example and explain that Ss need to choose two possible answers in each case. Ss complete the exercise alone, then check in pairs. Check answers with the class, then put Ss in pairs to practise the conversations. They should swap roles and practise again, using the other possible response.**

ANSWERS:
2 Bye.; See you.
3 She's OK.; She's fine.
4 White, no sugar.; Black, please.
5 Yes, it is.; Yes.
6 I'm very happy with it.; It's not bad.

3 **Look at the example as a class and discuss how the capital letters and full stops can help Ss put the words in order. Ss should work alone and write the conversation. Move around the class and help Ss as needed. Ask pairs to compare, then go through the answers as a class.**

EXTRA SUPPORT: DYSLEXIA As word ordering can be challenging for dyslexic learners, adapt the exercise to a gap-fill with a key word (or words) gapped in each sentence. For further support, provide the missing words as a vertical list or two alternatives for each gap.

EXTRA: ALTERNATIVE IDEA If you are short of time, ask half the Ss to order Maria's sentences and the other half to order Kemi's and then pair Ss to show each other their answers and practise the conversation in pairs.

ANSWERS:
2 Hi, Maria. How are things?
3 Good, thanks. Coffee?
4 Yes, please. Black, no sugar.
5 How are your children?
6 They're very well.
7 Thanks for the coffee.
8 No problem.

4 **Look at the example as a class and point out that a variety of different types of words are missing. Refer Ss to the Grammar Bank notes to help identify them. Ss complete the conversation, then check in pairs. When they have finished, go through the answers and drill the exchanges before asking pairs to practise the conversation.**

EXTRA SUPPORT: DYSLEXIA For Ss with dyslexia, provide the missing words jumbled in a vertical list on the board or on paper. You could also divide the conversation into two halves to help make the processing of the information easier.

ANSWERS:

2 are	**3** 'm/am	**4** too
5 's/is	**6** She	**7** your
8 It	**9** very/really	**10** time
11 for	**12** See	

4A **Put Ss in pairs and refer them to the prompts. Use the example to point out that Ss need to insert the correct form of *be* where necessary and that various other words will also need to be inserted to complete the conversation. Ss work together and write the conversation. Move around the class and help them as needed. Go through the answers.**

EXTRA: ALTERNATIVE IDEA If you are short of time, divide the class in two and ask one half to complete only Student A, and the other half to complete only Student B. Then put them in A/B pairs to show each other their answers and practise the conversation.

EXTRA SUPPORT: TEACHER These flow charts are a feature of most of the *How to …* sections. As this is the first time Ss will use one, it is set up in a controlled way with them writing the sentences before practising the conversation orally. In later units, they should be encouraged to just use the prompts to prepare themselves to speak, without any written preparation.

EXTRA SUPPORT Inserting missing words can be a challenge for beginner literacy and dyslexic learners as they tend to miss out or jump over words, parts of words or even lines of text. You could provide the conversation in lines, not in flow-chart format, with one word missing in each sentence and a clear gap to show where it goes.

ANSWERS:
B: I'm OK, thanks. How are you?
A: I'm fine. It's a beautiful day.
B: Yes, it is. How's work?
A: Good. How's your work?
B: It's not bad. How are your children?
A: They're good.
B: Great. See you later!
A: See you later!

B **Put Ss in pairs to practise the conversation. When they have finished, they can change roles.**

EXTRA IDEA Ask Ss to read the conversation across the class, with different Ss taking the role of A and B. This can help Ss develop confidence in speaking in front of the group. To encourage Ss to listen to each other, switch speakers in the middle of the conversation.

C **Ask Ss to change five things and then repeat the conversation. Stronger Ss can simply underline the words to change, while weaker ones will need to write. Ask them to change roles when they have finished. Stronger pairs can close their books and repeat.**

EXTRA: HOW TO … Ask Ss to work in pairs and write their own short conversation, including some of the language from the lesson. When they have finished, select a few confident/willing pairs to perform for the class.

SPEAKING

5 A **Refer Ss to the table and explain that they will now talk about feelings. Ask them to complete the first column (*You (A)*) with a word or emoji. They don't need to write a sentence. Some Ss might worry that they don't have a new job, car, etc. – explain that they should use their imagination. While they're working, go round and make sure they are completing the task correctly. Ideally, they should use a range of feelings, not necessarily their own true ones.**

B **Read the example with the class, draw attention to the phrase *How's your … ?* and drill. Then ask Ss to work in groups of three and take turns to roleplay the conversation and complete the second column (*Student B*) with either words or emojis to show how their partner feels. Monitor and encourage them to use the phrases from the lesson. When they have finished, ask Ss to ask the other student in their group and practise the conversations again, completing the third column (*Student C*).**

EXTRA IDEA: DIGITAL Ask Ss to record their first conversation, then listen back together and think about how to improve. Ss can then practise the conversation again with their second partner.

6 **Invite Ss to ask you about one of the things in the box and answer them. Remind them to use *How's your … ?* and point out that *children* and *parents* are plural, so we need to change the question. Elicit this to the board (*How are your … ?*). Put Ss in pairs to have a conversation about three of the things in the box. This time they should express how they really feel. Move around and listen, then at the end ask one or two pairs to repeat a conversation for the class.**

TO FINISH

Ask Ss to discuss in small groups how they feel about their English class. You could list the different elements (reading, pronunciation, etc.) and Ss use emojis or words to state what they like or don't like so much.

EXTRA IDEA: SPEAK ANYWHERE Encourage Ss to practise using the Speak Anywhere interactive roleplay.

2D BBC Food

Best Home Cook

GRAMMAR | *wh-* questions + *be*
SPEAKING | ask about three people
WRITING | write a message about a friend

LESSON OVERVIEW

In this lesson, Ss learn the form and use of *wh-* questions with the verb *be*. They also learn some vocabulary specific to the video content. The context is a video clip of a popular TV show about making cakes and baking. Ss practise asking and answering *wh-* questions about people they know, then read a message introducing someone who will visit their city. The lesson ends with a writing activity where Ss practise introducing a friend or family member talked about previously, in a similar message.

Online Teaching

If you're teaching this lesson online, you might find the following tips useful:

- **Ex 1A:** Share your screen and have a whole class discussion of the pictures. Ss can contribute verbally or if in a very large group, use the chat.
- **Ex 2B:** Sometimes videos can be a little slow or jumpy when streamed in an online class environment. If you know this is an issue for you, give Ss time to watch the video on their own device before moving on.
- **Ex 6A:** Display the exercise and message on a shared screen and invite Ss to add their answers in the chat after a fixed time limit.
- **Ex 6B:** Ss write independently then use a collaborative noticeboard to display their messages and read each other's.

Additional Materials

For Teachers:
Presentation Tool Lesson 2D
Online Digital Resources
Grammar Bank 2D
Videoscript 2D: BBC Food

For Students:
Online Practice 2D
Workbook 2D

TO START

Show some pictures of cakes and bread and ask Ss to identify them. Elicit or teach the words *cake* and *bake* (to cook in an oven; showing a picture of an oven could help explain this). *Best Home Cook* is an internationally recognisable format, so if there is a similar programme in the Ss' country, you could show a clip and elicit the name.

EXTRA SUPPORT: DYSLEXIA Dyslexic learners in particular benefit from understanding exactly what they are learning in a lesson so that they understand what they are working towards. In this and every lesson, explain clearly what the learning objectives of the lesson are near the start.

PREVIEW

1 A Ask Ss to work in pairs to match the words (1–7) with the pictures. When they have finished, go through the answers and further clarify as needed. Point out that all the words are nouns and that *a judge* has a general meaning, not just somebody in a court of law, as 'someone who decides'.

EXTRA SUPPORT Some weaker classes may not be able to identify all the pictures. You can complete the task as a class if necessary.

EXTRA IDEA With stronger classes, you could point out that the suffix *-er*, when added to a verb, often forms the noun for the person who does the action of the verb. There are various examples in this exercise: *baker*, *presenter*, *manager* and *winner*.

ANSWERS:
2 E **3** B **4** F **5** A **6** G **7** C

B Refer Ss to the programme information and check that they understand *task* (a job to do). Ask them to look at the photo, read the information and decide if the sentences (1–3) are true or false. Then put them in pairs to check. When they have finished, go through the answers.

EXTRA SUPPORT: DYSLEXIA Read the text aloud or have another student read it out to support dyslexic learners as they read.

ANSWERS:
1 T **2** F **3** F

VIEW

2 A Refer Ss to page 150 and read the example conversation with the class. Put Ss in pairs to look at the seven cakes and choose the best three. Point out that if they can't agree on the three winners it doesn't matter. Discuss Ss' ideas as a class and see if there is any general agreement on the best cakes.

B ▶ Ask Ss to watch the video clip and note who are the three winners. You could write the names from Ex 2A on the board to help with this. Ss don't need to write their answers. After viewing they can compare with their partner from Ex 2A and then discuss as a class their reaction to the winners.

EXTRA SUPPORT Turn on the subtitles if you feel it would benefit learners.

ANSWERS:
Suzie (cake B), Robin (cake E) and Katie (cake G) are the winners.

C ▶ Put Ss in pairs and ask them to match each name from the video clip (1–6) with a piece of personal information (a–f), then check their answers with another pair. Play the video again for Ss to check their answers. Confirm the answers with the class. Write the letter and number pairings on the board.

ANSWERS:
2 d **3** a **4** e **5** f **6** b

D ▶ Ask Ss to read the sentences and check they understand the alternatives. Play the video clip again for Ss to select the correct alternatives, then ask pairs to compare before going through the answers as a class.

EXTRA SUPPORT: DYSLEXIA Ss with dyslexia can find it difficult to watch/listen and read at the same time. To support them in this activity, make sure they understand the sentences and alternatives so they know what to listen for. You could then pause the video clip as necessary to give them time to select their answers.

ANSWERS:
1 Best
2 Claudia
3 36
4 34
5 Italy
6 Manchester

GRAMMAR

wh- questions + *be*

3 A Clarify that the questions Ss will form in this exercise refer back to the sentences in Ex 2D. Ask Ss to complete the questions with a question word, then check in pairs. If your class is weaker, recap the meaning of the question words and what they refer to (*who* = a person, *what* = a thing, etc.). If you're short of time, you could do this exercise together as a class. Check answers with the class. In some cases, an alternative question can be formed, (e.g. 2 Where is the presenter?), though these will of course not relate to the information given in the statements in Ex 2D.

ANSWERS:

1 What **2** Who **3** How
4 How **5** Where **6** Where

B The Grammar Bank on page 99 can be used in the lesson or for homework. Decide how and when the exercises will benefit your class.

GB page 99 **GRAMMAR BANK**

Check understanding of the notes with the class, and focus on the pronunciation of the *wh-* question words and how they have silent letters (e.g. *when* /wen/).

1 This exercise checks the meaning of the question words and revises singular and plural forms of the verb *be*. Look at the example with the class and discuss why *What's* is used (an email address is a thing, and it's singular). Ask Ss to complete the rest of the questions individually, using the words in the box, then check in pairs. Check answers with the class. Drill the complete questions.

EXTRA SUPPORT: DYSLEXIA Provide the words from the box in a vertical list for Ss to hold alongside the exercise.

ANSWERS:

2 Where's
3 Who are
4 How's
5 What are
6 When's
7 Who's
8 Where are
9 How are
10 When

2 Explain that the exercise has four separate conversations. In every conversation, Ss should find one mistake in each question. They can work alone, then check in pairs. Check answers with the class. Ask pairs to read out the questions and answers across the class.

EXTRA SUPPORT With weaker classes, provide two alternatives for each question word, one correct and one distractor. This will also help beginner literacy and dyslexic learners.

ANSWERS:

1 ~~When~~ **How old** are they?
2 ~~How's~~ **What's** / **What is** 'fútbol' in English?
~~What's~~ **Who's** / **Who is** your favourite football player?
3 How ~~old has~~ old**'s** / old **is** Tom?
~~Who's~~ **Where's** / **Where is** he now?
4 ~~When~~ **Where** are the children?
~~What~~ **Who** are they with?

EXTRA IDEA Ss practise the corrected conversations in pairs, taking turns at both roles.

EXTRA IDEA: DIGITAL Ss record one of the conversations in pairs. They listen back to their recording and comment on their pronunciation. If time, they can record a second conversation and upload to a sharing site.

SPEAKING

ask about three people

4A Give an example by writing the names of three people on the board and saying who they are, e.g. *George* ('my brother'), *Mary* ('my best friend') and *Francisca* ('works with me'). Ss then do the same. Move around the class to make sure they are just writing names.

B Refer Ss to the example and then give similar information about your three names on the board, e.g. 'George is my brother. He's a teacher. He's married.' Give Ss a few minutes to think, then ask them to tell their partner about their people. Move around the class and listen, and help with vocabulary if needed. If they enjoy this, Ss can change pairs and repeat.

EXTRA IDEA: DIGITAL Ss make a short video or audio recording about their three people, then play it to a partner who asks questions.

C 2.09 | Refer Ss to the three names (1–3) and give them a minute or two to read through the information about them (a–c). Explain that they should listen and match the names with the information. Play the recording and ask Ss to compare answers, then play it again if needed. Go through the answers.

EXTRA SUPPORT: DYSLEXIA You could provide the names on slips of paper. Ss should select them and place them beside the information as they listen.

ANSWERS:

1 c (sister) **2** b **3** a

AUDIOSCRIPT 2.09

A: Who's Judi?
B: Judi's my sister. I have a photo.
A: Nice photo! How old is she?
B: She's thirty.
A: And who's Dennis?
B: He's a good friend.
A: Where's he from?
B: He's from Singapore.
A: Is he married?
B: Yes, he is. He has a wife and a daughter.
A: Who's Kenji?
B: Kenji is someone from work.
A: Where's Kenji from?
B: He's Japanese. He's from Tokyo.
A: What's his job?
B: He's a sales assistant in our shop. He's really nice.

D 2.09 | Refer Ss to the Key phrases and read them aloud slowly and clearly. Allow time for Ss to ask any questions they have. Explain that they should listen and identify the phrases they hear. Play the recording and ask Ss to compare answers, then play it again if needed. Go through the answers. Drill some of the phrases chorally and individually if Ss struggle with them.

ANSWERS:

All the phrases are used, except: 'Where's she from?', 'She has a good job in a shop.' and 'How old is he?'.

There is a slight change of wording in 'He has a wife and two sons.' which is in the recording as 'He has a wife and a daughter.'

5 Put Ss in different pairs from Ex 4B. Ask them to practise talking about their three people, asking and answering and including the Key phrases. Move around the class and help Ss.

WRITING

write a message about a friend

6A Look at the message as a class and elicit who it's from (Sonia) and who it's to (Jen). Ask Ss if they are friends or if it is a business communication (friends). Explain that xxx means 'kisses' and is very friendly. Ss should read the message and choose the correct alternatives. Give them two or three minutes, then check answers.

EXTRA SUPPORT With weaker classes, you could read the text aloud and then get Ss to read it aloud to each other in pairs. This approach would also help support Ss with beginner literacy or dyslexia.

ANSWERS:

1 her friend **2** Argentinian **3** Martina

B Ask Ss to write their own message, following the structure of the message they read in Ex 6A and using the name and information of one of the three people they talked about in Exs 4 and 5. Point out how the message starts and ends. Tell Ss they should aim to write 40–50 words. Move around the class and help.

EXTRA IDEA: DIGITAL Ss write their messages and send them to each other by email or in a messaging app. Alternatively they could upload them to an online platform where they can read each other's messages and even respond.

TO FINISH

Put Ss in pairs to discuss if they watch reality TV programmes like *Best Home Cook* and if they can name any more examples. It could be fun to translate the names from their first language into English.

2 REVIEW

LESSON OVERVIEW

This lesson is a review of the language – both grammar and vocabulary – presented in this unit. It also includes a link to the Sounds and Spelling section for this unit, which focuses on short and long sounds: /ɪ/, /iː/, /ʊ/, /uː/; and /w/ and /h/ in question words. The notes below assume that the tasks are completed in class. However, the self-study type exercises (i.e. Exs 1, 2A, 2B, 3A, 4A, 4B and 6A) could be done out of class and then checked in the following lesson when the communicative tasks are then completed.

Online Teaching

If you're teaching this lesson online, you might find the following tips useful:

- **Exs 2B and 2C:** Ss can put their calculations in the chat box for other Ss to answer.
- **Ex 6A:** Display the text on your device and share your screen. Make sure the annotate function is on. Ask different Ss to choose the correct alternatives.

Additional Materials

For Teachers:

Sounds and Spelling 2

Unit Test in test package

TO START

Ask Ss to work in pairs and try to remember what language they studied in Unit 2 (Grammar: present simple *be*: *we*, *you*, *they*, possessive adjectives, *wh*-questions + *be*; Vocabulary: numbers 11–100, common adjectives, family, people, feelings; How to ... have short conversations). Ask them to look at the unit lesson objectives to check their ideas. You could ask them what they found hard/interesting/useful in Unit 2.

GRAMMAR

1 **Ss complete the conversation with the words in the box alone. Remind them they need to use capital letters for the beginning of sentences/questions. They then check in pairs. Check answers with the class.**

EXTRA SUPPORT: DYSLEXIA Gap-fill writing, transferring words from one place to another, can be challenging for Ss with dyslexia. In this case, give Ss two alternatives to choose from for the sentences/questions with gaps.

ANSWERS:

1 Who **2** my **3** What **4** their
5 Her **6** his **7** Are **8** aren't
9 Where **10** 're **11** Are **12** aren't

VOCABULARY

2 A **Introduce the idea of calculations by writing some simple ones on the board, e.g. *2 + 2 = 4, 4 - 2 = 2*, and then use these to introduce the words *plus*, *minus* and *equals*. Refer Ss to the exercise and ask them to write the answers in words. When they have finished, Ss can compare answers saying the whole calculations. Go through the answers as a class.**

ANSWERS:

2 sixty **3** thirty-eight **4** forty

B **Ask Ss to work alone and complete the questions. They should also write the answers.**

C **Put Ss in pairs to ask and answer their questions from Ex 2B. Monitor and check they're pronouncing the numbers correctly.**

3 A **Elicit the vowels and write them on the board. Ask Ss to work alone to complete the adjectives, then check in pairs. Go through the answers paying attention to correct pronunciation of the vowels.**

EXTRA SUPPORT English spelling can be challenging for all Ss, especially those with beginner literacy or dyslexia, because of the lack of sound–spelling correspondence. To help with this, say the words in turn for Ss to listen and complete, and discuss silent letters, such as the *r* in *tired*, the *e* in *favourite* and the *i* in *friendly*. Suggest that Ss use a *Look Say Cover Write Check* system, as mentioned in the Extra Support box for Lesson 2A, Vocabulary Bank 2A, Ex 1B. This can help them memorise these spellings.

ANSWERS:

1 big **2** hot **3** new
4 young **5** good **6** beautiful
7 favourite **8** friendly **9** tired
10 bad **11** small **12** cold
13 old **14** great

B **Read the example with the class and do a further example yourself. Then ask Ss to work in groups of three with only Student A able to look at the list. Monitor and check Ss' pronunciation of the letters, and prompt them to rotate the role of looking at the list. When they have finished, recap on any letters or words that Ss are mispronouncing.**

C Look at the example and ask Ss to complete this activity in the same groups of three, taking turns to make sentences. Move around the class and listen. In feedback, ask a few groups to share their answers with the class.

EXTRA: ALTERNATIVE IDEA For Ss who can manage a more complex task, merge Exs 3B and 3C together as follows. Ss identify the adjective in Ex 3B, then all take turns to make a sentence with that adjective (Ex 3C). They then revert to Ex 3B, with a different student selecting a word, then all make a sentence, then the third student chooses a word, etc.

4 A Look at the picture and read the example with the class. Point out there could be more than one possible answer. Ss complete the task alone then check in pairs. Go through the answers as a class.

EXTRA SUPPORT Family tree diagrams will not necessarily be familiar to your Ss. If this is the case, explain that a family tree is a visual of how a family is organised. Go over the connections, showing how generations are expressed from top to bottom, couples are linked horizontally and children descend vertically from that connection. If Ss struggle, work together to build a family tree of a famous family that they know.

ANSWERS:
2 Andy or Bella **3** Bella **4** Chris or Di

B Read the instruction with the class, elicit an example, then Ss write their sentences. Stronger Ss can write more than three. They should also write the answers.

C Put Ss in A/B pairs. Ask Student As to say their sentences and Student Bs to identify the person, then change roles.

EXTRA CHALLENGE Ss draw their own family tree and describe the relationships to a partner. You may need to move around and be available to help with vocabulary to express more complex relationships, such as stepson, second wife, etc.

5 A Focus attention on the words and ask Ss to take turns to say them in pairs. They should focus on the underlined sounds in particular. Go through the answers and drill the words/sounds (the phonetic symbols are given below, though Ss do not need to know them at this stage).

ANSWERS:

six /ɪ/	where /w/
sixteen /iː/	what /w/
good afternoon /uː/	who /h/

EXTRA SUPPORT: DYSLEXIA The underlining and the focus on sections of words that have different sounds expressed by the same spelling pattern mean this activity might be challenging for dyslexic learners. You could go through the activity as a class and use phonetic symbols in a different colour above the letters to show how the sounds differ.

B Refer Ss to Sounds and Spelling on page 152.

page 152 **SOUNDS AND SPELLING** short and long sounds (1): /ɪ/, /iː/, /ʊ/, /uː/; /w/ and /h/ in question words

The Sounds and Spelling section can be used to help with particular problems. You might want to select the sections or even particular sounds that are most useful for your Ss. The vocabulary used in each section comes from the current unit or previous units.

SOUNDS AND SPELLING TEACHER'S NOTES page 205

6 A Ask Ss to read the text and choose the correct alternatives, then put them in pairs to compare answers. Don't go through the answers yet.

EXTRA SUPPORT: DYSLEXIA If possible, record the text before the class, indicating where the alternatives occur, for Ss to listen to as they read, or, if preferred, ask pairs to take turns reading to each other.

B R2.01 | Play the recording for Ss to check their answers. Go through the answers as a class.

ANSWERS:

1 My	**2** are	**3** they're
4 is	**5** Why	**6** we're
7 what	**8** Our	

EXTRA IDEA: DIGITAL Ask Ss to read the text aloud in pairs. When they have practised it, ask them to record it and listen back and help each other improve. They should then record it again and make improvements.

TO FINISH

Ask Ss to work alone and write three new words or phrases they have learnt and want to remember. When they have finished, ask Ss to compare answers. Discuss how Ss can use their notebooks for revising and retrieving after lessons.

3 things

GSE LEARNING OBJECTIVES

3A Favourites

- READING | Read a blog about people's favourite things: things; colours
- Talk about people's things: possessive *'s*
- Pronunciation: possessive *'s*
- Write about favourite things; use *and, but*

GSE INFORMATION

VOCABULARY
10–29 Can use language related to household objects and possessions.

READING
29 Can understand basic factual statements relating to pictures or simple texts.

GRAMMAR
28 Can use ''s' to express possession with singular nouns.

SPEAKING
18 Can use a few simple words to describe objects (e.g. colour, number), if supported by pictures.

WRITING
26 Can write basic sentences describing everyday objects (e.g. colour, size), given a model.

28 Can use 'but' to link clauses and sentences.

3B What's on your desk?

- LISTENING | Understand a radio phone-in about people's desks: desk objects
- Pronunciation: sentence stress
- Talk about your desk: present simple *have* + *yes/no* questions (*I*, *you*, *we*, *they*)

GSE INFORMATION

VOCABULARY
10–29 Can use language related to home office and stationery.

LISTENING
29 Can identify objects, places or people from short spoken descriptions.

GRAMMAR
26 Can ask *yes/no* questions using the present simple.

SPEAKING
26 Can ask basic questions about objects (e.g. colour, size).

3C How much is it?

- HOW TO ... | shop for clothes: clothes
- Pronunciation: intonation

GSE INFORMATION

VOCABULARY
10–29 Can use language related to shops and buying clothes.

10–29 Can use language related to describing clothes.

HOW TO ...
26 Can identify how much something costs in short, simple dialogues about the price, if delivered slowly and clearly.

27 Can ask about the price of something using 'How much is/are ... ?'

SPEAKING
23 Can give basic information about the price of something.

28 Can ask people for things and give people things.

3D Shopping

- BBC STREET INTERVIEWS | Understand street interviews about people's shopping habits: shops
- Ask and answer questions about buying online and in shops: likes, dislikes and opinions
- Write a personal profile

GSE INFORMATION

PREVIEW
10–29 Can use language related to shops and shopping experience.

VIEW
25 Can understand basic information about someone's likes and dislikes.

GRAMMAR
27 Can use the present simple to refer to likes, dislikes and opinions.

SPEAKING
28 Can describe a person's likes and dislikes using simple language.

WRITING
30 Can write a few simple sentences to introduce themselves and provide basic personal information, given prompts or a model.

For full coverage of GSE Learning Objectives go to page 222.

BBC VLOGS

This is a short activity that can be used as an introduction to the unit topic and a warm-up to Lesson 3A. It shouldn't be exploited or taught at length, just played once or twice in class.

Introduce the activity by telling (and showing, if possible) the class your favourite thing and writing on the board: *My favourite thing is my (phone).* Ask Ss: 'What's your favourite thing?' Put Ss in pairs to discuss the question. When they have finished, ask a few Ss for their answers and have a brief class discussion before they watch the video. Write useful vocabulary on the board. At this point you may also want to preteach *bike/bicycle* and explain these mean the same. When they are ready, play the video for Ss to count how many speakers say their bike is their favourite thing.

ANSWER:
Two speakers say their bike (or bicycle).

EXTRA IDEA If Ss want to watch the video again outside class, you could ask them to note the other favourite things that are mentioned.

NOTE The vlogs have been provided by people from around the world in response to the same question. The video content was filmed by them on their own mobile phones, so the picture quality varies considerably and in some cases is of a lower quality. However, this adds to the authenticity of the content.

The locations labelled on the vlogs show where the speaker was when they filmed the video. It does not reflect where the speaker comes from (necessarily).

As many of the speakers are non-native, the videos expose Ss to a range of different accents and varieties of English. This could be used as a way to highlight interesting or useful differences.

Additional Materials

For Teachers:

Presentation Tool Unit 3

Online Digital Resources

Videoscript Unit 3 Opener: BBC Vlogs

3A Favourites

GRAMMAR | possessive *'s*
VOCABULARY | things; colours
PRONUNCIATION | possessive *'s*

LESSON OVERVIEW

In this lesson, Ss learn vocabulary for everyday objects. They also learn how to describe things using colours. The context is a reading where different people describe their favourite things and why they like them. This leads into the grammar of the possessive *'s*. Ss also practise the different pronunciations of possessive *'s*: /s/, /z/ and /ɪz/. Ss then do a speaking activity where they practise describing objects in pairs. The lesson ends with a writing activity where Ss write a description of their favourite things using the linking words *and* and *but*.

Online Teaching

If you're teaching this lesson online, you might find the following tips useful:

- **Ex 1A:** Display the exercise on your device and share your screen. Make sure the annotate function is on. In feedback, ask different Ss to draw lines to connect the words and photos.
- **Exs 1B and 1C:** Put Ss in pairs in breakout rooms for this activity. Monitor their discussion.
- **Writing Bank 3A, Ex 1C:** Ss write their sentences in the chat and compare.

Additional Materials

For Teachers:

Presentation Tool Lesson 3A

Photocopiable Activities 3A

Grammar Bank 3A

Vocabulary Bank 3A

Writing Bank 3A

For Students:

Online Practice 3A

Workbook 3A

TO START

Put Ss in small groups. Introduce the question *What's that?* and the answer *It's a … . / I don't know.* Ask them to point around the room, or display some pictures of everyday items such as from the introductory vlogs, and name what they can. Explain that today's lesson is about learning the names of different things.

EXTRA SUPPORT: DYSLEXIA Dyslexic learners in particular benefit from understanding exactly what they are learning in a lesson so that they understand what they are working towards. In this and every lesson, explain clearly what the learning objectives of the lesson are near the start.

VOCABULARY

things

1 A Focus attention on the photos and ask Ss to write the letters (A–H) vertically in their notebooks, then write the words from the box beside them. Put Ss in pairs to help each other. When they have finished, elicit Ss' answers and drill chorally and individually. Include *a* before each noun in drilling.

EXTRA SUPPORT: TEACHER Ss whose languages do not have an article system (*a*, *an*, *the*) tend to leave out articles before nouns. They also can't always hear them, as they are usually weak forms. It's helpful to drill these as part of the noun, to try and embed their use.

ANSWERS:
A car **B** camera **C** guitar
D bed **E** ring **F** coffee machine
G bike **H** watch

B Keep Ss in the same pairs to say how many things they have without specifying which they are.

C Look at the example, then model the activity yourself and invite Ss to guess (e.g. 'I have two of the things.', 'I think you have …'). Keep Ss in the same pairs as for Ex 1B for their partner to guess what things they have. When they have finished, ask who has the most things and find out which thing is the most popular.

2 Put Ss in pairs to look at the photos and name the colours they can. When they have finished, refer Ss to the Vocabulary Bank on page 128 to check.

ANSWERS:
A blue **E** purple
B black (and white) **F** red
C brown **G** green
D yellow **H** black

EXTRA SUPPORT Weaker classes may not know colours. If this is the case, you could introduce them, or go straight to the Vocabulary Bank.

page 128 **VOCABULARY BANK** colours **VB**

Note that the Vocabulary Bank activities are an important part of the lesson. They should only be omitted if you are confident that your Ss already know this vocabulary. If you don't use the exercises in class, it would be a good idea to set them as homework.

1 A Focus Ss' attention on pictures A–J. Ss match the colour words (1–10) with the pictures individually, then check in pairs. Check answers with the class.

ANSWERS:
1 F **2** C **3** G **4** D **5** H
6 J **7** I **8** A **9** E **10** B

B VB3.01 | Ask Ss to look at the pictures, not the words. Play the recording for Ss to repeat chorally. Include further individual drilling if you feel it's needed.

EXTRA IDEA Ss work in pairs to point and name the colours they can see in the room.

C Ss match the colours 1–2 with pictures A–B. Point out other colours that can be *light* and *dark* (e.g. blue, grey, etc.) and those that can't have shades (i.e. black, white). Check the answers. Drill pronunciation.

ANSWERS:
1 A **2** B

EXTRA IDEA Ask Ss to name other colours that could be light and dark (e.g: blue, grey, brown, pink, etc.). Ss look around the room and identify objects and clothes in the different (light/dark) colours.

D VB3.02 | Ss listen and match the photos (A–D) with the phrases they hear, writing the numbers and letters in their notebooks. Ask Ss to check in pairs. Check answers with the class.

ANSWERS:
A 2 **B** 1 **C** 4 **D** 3

AUDIOSCRIPT VB3.02

1 It's a dark blue bus.
2 It's a light blue bus.
3 They're light brown.
4 It's dark red.

VB **EXTRA IDEA** After the listening you could write the sentences and point out that we can say *It's a* + colour + noun (e.g. *It's a red car.*). We can also say *It's* + colour (e.g. *It's red.*). (Point out that ~~*It's red colour / It's colour red*~~ are not correct.) Ss create and share more sentences to practise this.

2 A Put Ss in A/B pairs. Ask them to take turns to point at the colours in Ex 1A and say them.

B Ask Ss to stay in their A/B pairs and look around the classroom. Student As choose an object and say the colour and Student Bs guess the object. After a while they change roles.

READING

EXTRA SUPPORT: DYSLEXIA There is a recording of the reading text available to help dyslexic learners.

3 A Ask Ss to read and write the things beside the information given, as in the example. You may want to preteach *grandmother* and *perfect*. Put Ss in pairs to discuss their answers. When they have finished, elicit the answers and confirm them on the board.

EXTRA SUPPORT: DYSLEXIA Play the recording of the text for Ss to listen and read at the same time. Alternatively, dyslexic learners can be paired with a student who can support them in the reading. This should help prepare them for Ex 3B where they need to read out sentences.

ANSWERS:
1 **colour:** *car*, bike
2 **country or nationality:** camera, guitar, coffee machine, watch
3 **age:** ring (It says the camera and guitar are 'old', but doesn't give the age.)
4 **family:** camera, ring, watch

B Look at the example. Put Ss in A/B pairs. Ask Student As to close their books and then ask a stronger Student B to demonstrate the activity for the rest of the class to identify the thing. Ask Ss to work in pairs and take turns with their books open to read and closed to name the thing. Move around the class and listen. When they have finished, drill any words that were causing problems.

GRAMMAR

possessive *'s*

4 A Ss correct the sentences by adding *'s* using the text to help them. Ask Ss to compare in pairs then go through the answers. Point out that the *'s* indicates possession and is not a plural, i.e. *my father's camera = the camera of my father.*

ANSWERS:
1 father**'s** 2 grandmother**'s** 3 mother**'s**

EXTRA IDEA As the previous unit deals with possessive adjectives, connecting the two here might be helpful for Ss, e.g. *his camera = my father's camera; her ring = my grandmother's ring; her name = my mother's name.*

B Ask Ss to complete the rule in pairs, using the examples in Ex 4A to help them. Check answers with the class and underline the person in the examples in Ex 4A.

ANSWER:
'*s*

B The Grammar Bank on page 100 can be used in the lesson or for homework. Decide how and when the exercises will benefit your class.

page 100 **GRAMMAR BANK** GB

This focuses on the possessive *'s* and the contexts we use it in. To reinforce understanding, it also contrasts the possessive *'s* with *'s* as a contraction of *is*. Go through the notes with Ss or let them read them alone. Check understanding where necessary. Note that the possessive *'s* for plurals (*s'*) is covered at A2 level.

1 Look at the example with the class. Ss add the possessive *'s* to the sentences alone, then check in pairs. Check answers with the class. The possessive *'s* after the letter *s* in numbers 6 and 8 looks a bit odd but assure Ss it's correct, and model that it is pronounced /ɪz/. You could point out that this group of sounds is the same as that for plurals, which they studied in Sounds and Spelling 1.

ANSWERS:
2 Anna**'s** favourite thing is her phone.
3 Saanvi is Kiara**'s** mother.
4 Our teacher**'s** name is Mr Kaminski.
5 Katie**'s** taxi is here.
6 Where are Luis**'s** glasses?
7 Will Brown**'s** book is very good.
8 Is this Jess**'s** magazine?
9 Are you Ms McKee**'s** students?
10 What is Michele**'s** address?

2 **Read the instruction with the class, then ask Ss to find the other places where the apostrophe is missing in the first conversation. Point out that these are both contractions of the verb form *is* and examples of the possessive *'s*. Then check the answers to the first conversation, but don't identify which answers are contractions and which are possessives yet. Ss move on to the other conversations alone, identifying the missing apostrophes in each, then compare in pairs. Check answers with the class (again, not identifying the forms of the *'s* yet). Ask pairs to practise the conversations.**

ANSWERS:

1 B: [2]It**'s** Alfonso.
A: [3]Is Alfonso**'s** wife**'s** name Gianna?
B: [4]No, her name**'s** Bella. Gianna**'s** their new baby.
2 A: [5]Your bag**'s** very big. What**'s** in it?
B: [6]I have my husband**'s** laptop and my son**'s** schoolbooks. His name is Rob. And I have a football!
A: [7]Is it Rob**'s** football?
B: [8]No, it**'s** my daughter**'s** football!
3 A: [9]Where**'s** Kirstie**'s** boyfriend from?
B: [10]Mike**'s** from Dublin.
A: [11]How old**'s** Mike?
B: [12]I don't know. Twenty-eight? Jen, when**'s** Mike**'s** birthday?

3 **Focus attention on the example. Read the instruction with the class, then ask them to identify each *'s* in Ex 2 as P (possessive *'s*) or C (contraction of *be*). If you are short of time, Ss can simply write P or C above the instances of *'s* in the conversations, rather than write them out. Go through the answers as a class, referring back to the sentences as necessary.**

EXTRA SUPPORT If Ss struggle with this, advise them to try saying the verb without contracting (e.g. *What is your name* = contraction; *friend ~~is~~ name* = not a contraction), to check.

ANSWERS:

2 It's C
3 Alfonso's P, wife's P
4 name's C, Gianna's C
5 bag's C, What's C
6 husband's P, son's P
7 Rob's P
8 it's C, daughter's P
9 Where's C, Kirstie's P
10 Mike's C
11 How old's C
12 when's C, Mike's P

PRONUNCIATION

possessive *'s*

EXTRA SUPPORT: TEACHER The sounds for the possessive *'s* work in exactly the same way as /s/, /z/ and /ɪz/ at the end of words. If you worked on this with the class in Sounds and Spelling 1, you could remind them of this.

5 A **3.01 | Introduce the sounds /s/, /z/ and /ɪz/, demonstrating them in isolation and drilling. You could use a snake image to relate to /s/ (hissing) and a bee image for /z/ (buzzing). Play the recording for Ss to listen to and read the sentences. Draw attention to the words in bold. Ask Ss to listen and identify the correct sound for the words in bold. Go through the answers, drilling both the words and sounds separately.**

ANSWERS:

/s/ Pat's
/z/ *grandmother's*, father's
/ɪz/ Alice's

B **Put Ss in pairs to read the sentences and write the sound they think is made by the *'s* in bold. Don't give any answers yet.**

C **3.02 | Play the recording for Ss to check their answers. Check the answers with the class, then ask Ss to practise saying the sentences in their pairs.**

ANSWERS:

1 Susan's /z/
2 Philip's /s/
3 Felix's /ɪz/
4 Irmak's /s/
5 Darsh's /ɪz/
6 Carol's /z/

D **Read the example, then ask a stronger pair to give another example from the photos. Put Ss in pairs to continue. When they have finished, say a few things yourself and have Ss chorus the answers.**

EXTRA IDEA For further practice, Ss can work in groups. Ask them to put personal items in the middle and take turns to point and name them, e.g. 'Izzy's pen', 'Jack's glasses'.

EXTRA IDEA: DIGITAL Ss make a short video of some objects they have at home. They show the film to their classmates and do the voiceover, e.g. 'This is my mum's coat and this is my dad's umbrella.'

SPEAKING

6 **Put Ss in A/B pairs and refer them to the relevant pages. Explain that they are each going to look at a picture of people and things and there are five differences between them that they need to find. They should not show their picture but take turns to ask questions to find the differences between what they can see and what their partner can see. Point out the example, which shows that the difference is in colour. Ask Ss to start.**

Monitor and check Ss are using the grammar and vocabulary from the lesson correctly. Note down any common errors or examples of good language use for later class feedback.

When they have finished, give feedback on Ss' language use as a class.

ANSWERS:

The five differences are:

Philip has a red/green bike.

Jack has a brown/yellow guitar.

Felix has a black/brown camera.

Susan has a yellow/pink bag.

Carol has an orange / a red book.

WRITING

write about favourite things; use *and*, *but*

7 A **Ss saw in Writing Bank 2B how *and* is used to add information. Ask them to identify which sentence needs *and*, and then discuss/identify the purpose of *but* in the other sentence. Ask Ss if they know what things in the text are referred to, then ask them to check in the text in Ex 3A.**

EXTRA: ALTERNATIVE IDEA With weaker classes, go over how we use *and* and *but* with an example. Write two sentences on the board about yourself, e.g. *I'm a teacher. I'm (a man/woman).* Ask Ss if they can join these to make one sentence (i.e. *I'm a teacher* ***and*** *I'm (a man/woman).*). Give an example of a sentence with *but*, e.g. *I'm (Spanish) but I live in (England).*, and ask Ss to find two sentences in this one (i.e. *I'm (Spanish). I live in (England).*). Point out that when we use *and* we add information and when we use *but* there's a contrast.

ANSWERS:

1 but **2** and

B **Refer Ss to the Writing Bank on page 89.**

page 89 **WRITING BANK**

WB

1 A **Focus attention on the rule and discuss it. Introduce the words *positive* (+) and *negative* (-), and *add* and *contrast*. Elicit an example to ensure Ss understand then ask Ss to match the sentence halves using a linker, *and* or *but*. Ask Ss to discuss in pairs then elicit answers from the class.**

EXTRA SUPPORT Point out that Ss are now making one sentence, so there is no full stop before the linking word and no capital letter in the middle. Ss may query capital *I*, but remind them it's always capital when used on its own in place of a person's name. You could also mention that we commonly use a pronoun (*it*, *she*, etc.) to refer to the subject in the second clause, rather than repeat the noun.

ANSWERS:

1 b (She has a new watch now, but I love her old watch.)

2 c (My bike is green and it's very important to me.)

3 a (It's old and my room is cold, but my bed is my favourite place.)

B **Ss read the first part of each sentence, then choose the correct ending for it, a or b. Ask them to check in pairs then go through the answers with the class. Discuss each time if it is a continuation of the same idea (adding to it) or a contrast.**

EXTRA SUPPORT: DYSLEXIA Ss should cover the sentences and options they are not working on to reduce distraction. It may also be a good idea for them to cover the a/b at the beginning of each sentence as these could also distract / interrupt their reading.

ANSWERS:

1 a **2** b **3** a **4** a **5** a

C **Read the example and give another example to show what to do (e.g. 'My coat is very old, but I like it.'). Then ask Ss to work alone to complete the sentences. Move around and help as needed.**

D **Demonstrate the activity. Repeat your sentence from Ex 1C (e.g, 'My coat is very old, …') and invite Ss to ask questions (e.g. 'What colour is it?'). Put Ss in groups of three or four to read out their sentences and ask/answer questions. When they have finished, ask a few Ss to repeat this for the class.**

2 A **Tell Ss to read the description quickly and find the answers to the questions in Ex 1D. Ask Ss to compare in pairs, then check answers as a class.**

EXTRA SUPPORT: DYSLEXIA Read the description aloud for Ss to follow as they listen.

ANSWERS:
How old is it? about 100 years old
What colour is it? orange, blue and red
Where is it from? Morocco

B **Give Ss a minute or two to choose what they're going to write about. Move around the class and support as needed. Ss write their descriptions. About four sentences – a total of 30–40 words – should be appropriate for this task.**

EXTRA IDEA: DIGITAL Ask Ss to post their descriptions on a class forum, with a photo if possible.

EXTRA IDEA Once Ss have completed their descriptions, ask them to read/show them to a partner and check each other's use of *and* and *but*.

8 A **Ask Ss to work alone and make a list of favourite things. Tell them to make notes about them, as in the example. They shouldn't write sentences.**

B **Put Ss in small groups to tell each other about their favourite things. In case of time constraints, they should take turns to each describe just one thing.**

9 **Ask Ss to bring a photo of a favourite thing to the next lesson. Tell them to check the name in English and prepare to tell other Ss about the thing.**

EXTRA: OUT OF CLASS If Ss enjoy describing their things, a few Ss can talk to the whole group about their photo of a favourite thing at the start of each class.

TO FINISH

Put Ss in pairs to discuss which three favourite things they'd take to a new home or on holiday.

3B What's on your desk?

GRAMMAR | present simple *have* + *yes/no* questions (*I, you, we, they*)
VOCABULARY | desk objects
PRONUNCIATION | sentence stress

LESSON OVERVIEW

In this lesson, Ss learn more vocabulary for everyday objects. The context is a listening where people talk about their desks. This leads into the grammar, *have*, to describe possession, where Ss also learn *yes/no* question forms and short answers. Ss then practise weak and strong forms of *do* in *yes/no* questions. The lesson ends with a speaking activity in which Ss talk about objects and ask for clarification in pairs.

Online Teaching

If you're teaching this lesson online, you might find the following tips useful:

- **Ex 1A:** Ask Ss to show the objects they have on their desk/workspace at home.
- **Ex 5A:** Put Ss in breakout rooms to underline the main stressed words and practise saying the questions. Come back to the main room to check.

Additional Materials

For Teachers:
Presentation Tool Lesson 3B
Photocopiable Activities 3B
Grammar Bank 3B

For Students:
Online Practice 3B
Workbook 3B

TO START

Talk to Ss about what you have on your desk and hold up the objects as you name them, e.g. 'I have a pen, a pencil, a book', etc. Ask Ss to do the same in pairs. Tell Ss today's lesson is about learning the words for different things we have on our desks (or in our work areas).

EXTRA SUPPORT: DYSLEXIA Dyslexic learners in particular benefit from understanding exactly what they are learning in a lesson so that they understand what they are working towards. In this and every lesson, explain clearly what the learning objectives of the lesson are near the start.

VOCABULARY

desk objects

1 A Ss look at the photo and discuss the question in pairs. When they have finished, elicit their answers. Don't worry about accuracy in the verb form if Ss try to use *have* (*I don't have*) as they haven't studied this yet.

B Ask Ss to work in pairs to name the objects in the photo, using the words in the box. Point out that not all the objects in the box can be seen in the picture. When Ss have finished, point at the items and elicit their answers. Drill chorally and individually. There is a mixture of singular and plural nouns in the box. If you think your Ss can manage, draw attention to the final *s* in *glasses, headphones, scissors* and *sticky notes* and point out that we don't need *a/an* with these plural nouns. Drill the others with *a*.

EXTRA SUPPORT: DYSLEXIA It might be helpful to list the words in the box vertically either on the board or on a piece of paper that Ss can place alongside the photo to tick off what they can see.

EXTRA IDEA Work as a class and check understanding of the things that are not in the picture (i.e. bottle of water, book, tablet). You could use photos or actual objects. The vocabulary will come in useful later in the unit.

ANSWERS:
computer, cup of coffee, glasses, headphones, keyboard, mouse, notebook, pen, pencil, phone, plant, scissors, sticky notes

C Look at the example, and then complete another one yourself asking the class to guess (e.g. 'C', 'Computer?', 'Yes.'). Put Ss in pairs to choose three objects and then take turns to say the first letter for their partner to guess. Move around and listen. When they have finished, drill any words that were causing problems.

D Put Ss in pairs. Ask them to close their books and write.

EXTRA IDEA Show Ss a tray with a number (e.g. ten) of everyday items from Ex 1B. Cover the tray with a cloth. Ask Ss to discuss in pairs or small groups and write down as many things as they can remember. Alternatively, show them the tray and then take one item away and see if they can identify which thing you have removed. This can be repeated several times. If a tray is not convenient, you could show a picture on the board and use a shape to place over an item.

LISTENING

2 A 3.03 | Tell Ss they will listen to two people talking about their desk. They should listen to both and decide which person's desk is shown, speaker one (Sandy) or speaker two (Joe). Play the recording, ask Ss to compare and then elicit the answer.

ANSWER:
Joe talks about the desk in the photo.

AUDIOSCRIPT 3.03

TW = Toni White S = Sandy J = Joe

TW: Hello, this is Toni White. Welcome to … *We're all Different*! Today is about people and their desks. What do people have on their desks? How are the desks different? First of all, Sandy. Are you there?

S: Hi, yes, I'm here.

TW: Sandy, do you have a job?

S: No, I don't. I'm a student at college. I'm an art student.

TW: OK, so Sandy, what's on your desk?

S: Well, my desk is small and I have a lot of things on it. I have a computer and a keyboard … a mouse … and … a notebook and a pen. I have a cup of coffee. I also have some sticky notes … scissors … my glasses …

TW: Do you have any pencils? For your artwork?

S: No, I don't have any pencils on my desk.

TW: So, what's different about your desk?

S: Different?

TW: Yes, different. I mean, everybody has a computer, a mouse, scissors …

S: Oh, I see. OK. Well, I have three plants. And oh, my pens are in a cup, a blue cup from Paris.

TW: Very nice. Thank you, Sandy!

S: You're welcome.

TW: And next is Joe. Joe, do you have a job?

J: Yes, I do. I'm a digital designer.

TW: And what do you have on your desk, Joe?

J: Well, of course I have a computer and a keyboard. What else? I have a notebook. For my ideas. And … my glasses … and some headphones from my son. He's sixteen years old.

TW: Do you have a photo? A photo of your son?

J: No, I don't. My family photos are in the living room. What else is on my desk? A plant, and … a cup of coffee. An apple …

TW: So what's different about your desk?

J: Well, I have two notebooks. A big notebook and a small notebook. Different notebooks for different things.

TW: OK, thank you Joe. And next is …

B 3.03 | Tell Ss they will listen again and refer them to the table to read through before they listen. They should listen and tick the things each speaker has on their desk. Play the recording, twice if needed. Ask pairs to compare then go through the answers.

EXTRA SUPPORT: DYSLEXIA Auditory (listening) processing can be a problem for dyslexic learners and this task, which requires them to listen and read at the same time, could be challenging. Read through the list in the table with the class before playing the recording to help Ss focus on what they are listening for. Pause between the speakers, giving time for Ss to compare answers and help each other. When you have corrected the task, Ss can listen again and confirm the correct answers.

EXTRA CHALLENGE Get stronger classes to cover the photo before they listen for the second time, so they are focusing on the words only and not getting visual support.

ANSWERS:

	Sandy	Joe
computer	✓	✓
keyboard	✓	✓
mouse	✓	
notebook	✓	✓
pen	✓	
pencil		
sticky notes	✓	
glasses	✓	✓
headphones		✓
plant	✓	✓

EXTRA CHALLENGE Ask Ss to extend the table with the other items in the box in Ex 1B. They then add two extra columns to the table and in the first tick the items they have on their desk/workspace at home. Then put Ss in pairs to listen to each other talk about what they have and tick the second new column about their partner.

GRAMMAR

present simple *have* + *yes/no* questions (*I, you, we, they*)

3 A Remind Ss of the listening and how the speakers use the verb *have* to talk about what's on their desk. Ss choose the correct alternative alone, then compare in pairs. Move around the room to see how they are doing, but don't correct. Don't check the answers yet.

EXTRA SUPPORT This task is intended to enable Ss with some knowledge to try it. As the language hasn't been introduced, weaker classes may struggle if asked to choose an alternative. In this case, you could just proceed to the listening in Ex 3B and then ask Ss to choose. Play the recording again once you have checked answers.

B 3.04 | Play the recording for Ss to check their answers. Check answers with the class and write them on the board.

ANSWERS:

1 have	**2** I have	**3** don't have
4 have	**5** do	**6** Do you have
7 don't	**8** have	

C The Grammar Bank on page 101 can be used in the lesson or for homework. Decide how and when the exercises will benefit your class.

page 101 **GRAMMAR BANK**

GB

This focuses on the present simple form and use of *have* with *I, you, we* and *they,* and on the auxiliary *do* in questions and negatives. Go through the notes with Ss or let them read them alone. Check understanding where necessary, especially of the form of questions and short answers.

The Grammar Bank also covers *a/an* with singular nouns and *some/any* with plural nouns. Uncountable nouns + *some* is not covered here and is met at A2 level.

EXTRA SUPPORT: TEACHER Ss may ask about *have got*. While *have* and *have got* mean the same, the form is different in negatives and questions. In US English, *have* is more common; in UK English, *have got* is more common – though both are used in either context. Because the two forms differ in the formation of negatives and questions it's best at this level to choose one, in this case *have*, and stick with it.

1 Read the example with the class, and ask Ss when we need *a* and *an*. Hold up a bunch of pens, with the number not being clear, and say *some pens* then ask Ss to complete the rest of the sentences, then check in pairs. Check answers with the class by asking individuals to read out sentences and drilling as needed.

ANSWERS:

1 *a*, an	**2** a	**3** some	**4** any
5 an	**6** any	**7** some	**8** any

GB 2 **Read the example with the class and check Ss understand they don't need to add any words, only to write the words in order to make questions with *have*. Ss write the questions individually, then compare answers in pairs. Check answers with the class.**

EXTRA SUPPORT As word ordering exercises can be challenging for dyslexic learners and involve a lot of writing for beginner literacy learners, you could adapt this exercise and present it as a gap-fill with key words missing. A vertical list of the missing words or phrases could be provided for extra support.

ANSWERS:

2 Do Pat and Viv have any children?
3 Nasir, do you have a desk at home?
4 Carolina, do we have any cups?
5 Do you have any sisters, Craig?
6 Mrs Davies, do the students have any books?

3 **In this exercise, Ss write the short answers to the questions in Ex 2. Read the example with the class and complete item 2 together, pointing out how the subject of the sentence indicates the form of the short answers (e.g. *you* becomes *I* in the example; the nouns are replaced by pronouns, e.g. 'Pat and Viv' becomes *they* in item 2) then ask Ss to work alone. Check answers with the class.**

EXTRA SUPPORT: DYSLEXIA To help Ss make the link between the sentences in Exs 2 and 3, you could provide the completed sentences from Ex 2 before the beginning of the short answers.

ANSWERS:

2 Yes, they do.
3 Yes, I do.
4 No, we don't.
5 Yes, I do.
6 No, they don't.

4 **Give Ss a few minutes to read the conversations and underline or highlight the mistakes (remind them there is one in each line), then put them in pairs to compare their ideas. Confirm where the mistakes are then ask pairs to correct them. The mistakes could be a wrong word, an extra word or a missing word. Check answers with the class. For extra practice, pairs read the corrected conversations together.**

EXTRA SUPPORT: DYSLEXIA Ask Ss to cover the parts of the conversation they are not working on to reduce distraction. You could supply the conversations with the mistakes already highlighted so Ss just need to focus on the correction.

ANSWERS:

1 B: No, I ~~do~~ **don't**, but I have a tablet.
A: And do you **have** a phone?
B: Yes, I ~~don't~~ **do**, but it's not here.
2 A: Do you have ~~some~~ **any** children?
B: Yes, we do ~~have~~. We have two boys.
A: Do ~~they~~ **you** have any photos?
B: Yes, here on my phone. They ~~have~~ **are** six and eight.

PRONUNCIATION

sentence stress

4A **3.05 | Look at the example as a class and read it aloud so Ss can hear the stress on the words. Remind or tell them that stress means louder, longer and higher. (They will be familiar with this if you worked on Sounds and Spelling 1 with them.) Play the recording, pausing after each sentence for Ss to underline or highlight the stressed words. When they have finished, put Ss in pairs to compare their sentences. Check answers with the class and underline or highlight the sentences on the board (or invite Ss to come up and do so).**

EXTRA SUPPORT Underlining can be difficult for Ss with dyslexia or beginner literacy to read. Write the example sentence on the board as you read it out loud and indicate the stress, e.g. by using a different colour for or drawing a box above the stressed words. You could suggest they use a colour highlighter to mark the words in the exercise.

ANSWERS:

1 B: Yes, I do.
2 A: Do you have a photo of your son?
B: No, I don't.

B **3.05 | Say the two possible pronunciations of *do*: weak /də/ and strong /duː/. Play the recording for Ss to listen to the pronunciation of *do* in the questions.**

EXTRA SUPPORT: TEACHER Ss might find it helpful to understand that we stress words that carry meaning. The small words that help the sentence work grammatically (auxiliary verbs, articles, etc.) are not usually stressed. The auxiliary verb is stressed in the short answers as the last word in the sentence.

ANSWER:

'Do' is pronounced /də/ in both questions.

C **3.05 | Before you play the recording again, make sure Ss understand that you want them to try and say each sentence in the same way as the speaker. This is to encourage them to produce the weak forms and stressed words naturally.**

EXTRA SUPPORT: TEACHER Ss at A1 level will rarely speak quickly enough to sound really natural when using very weak forms. The important thing here is for them to stress the main content words and just reduce the *do* slightly to /də/. Ss will see the very weakened form of *do you* (/djə/) in B1.

EXTRA IDEA You could point out the linking between *have* and *a*, i.e. /hævə/.

5 A Look at the example with the class and ask Ss to work in pairs to underline or highlight the main stressed words in the other questions. Monitor and check Ss are identifying stress correctly. Ask Ss to practise saying the questions in pairs and remind them to use the correct pronunciation of *do*. They don't need to answer the questions at this point. Circulate to check Ss are focusing their emphasis on the stressed words naturally. When they have finished, drill the sentences chorally.

ANSWERS:

2 Do you <u>have</u> any <u>headphones</u> with you?
3 Do you <u>have</u> any <u>plants</u> in your <u>room</u>?
4 Do you <u>have</u> a <u>favourite</u> <u>coffee</u> cup?
5 Do you <u>have</u> a <u>favourite</u> <u>pen</u>?

B Read the example with the class, then model another example with a few stronger Ss to demonstrate that various answers are possible and after a short answer, i.e. *Yes, I do. / No, I don't.*, they could add further information, as in the example. Put Ss in new pairs to ask and answer.

EXTRA IDEA Point out that short answers (*Yes, I do. / No, I don't.*) are everyday responses. The simple answer of 'Yes' or 'No' might be acceptable in another language, but in English it is considered quite impolite. A long answer is also not usual, and it can sound a bit rude, impatient or odd (*Yes, I have a camera.*).

EXTRA CHALLENGE Ss could conduct a survey, asking several other Ss and ticking or crossing the questions according to their answers. This has the benefit of allowing more practice of the question forms and short answers. Individuals could be asked to report their results back to the class.

SPEAKING

FUTURE SKILLS | Collaboration

6 A Read the Future Skills box as a class, drill the phrases, then refer Ss to Ex 6B.

EXTRA: FUTURE SKILLS With stronger classes, you could elicit/teach other useful phrases, e.g. *I don't know that word., Can you say that again? What's this in English? How do you say this word? Please can you explain?*

B Put Ss in A/B pairs and refer them to the relevant pages. They should ask each other about what they have in their photo using the question *Do you have … ?* in order to find five things that are the same. Ask a few Ss to feed back. If necessary, teach or remind them of the phrase *We both* … (meaning 'we two' / 'the two of us').

ANSWERS:

Any five of the following:

- a cup of coffee
- glasses
- a notebook
- paper
- a pen
- a plant / plants
- sticky notes

7 Read the instruction to the class or ask a student to read it. Point out the word *both* (two people/things) in the example and drill it. Put Ss in pairs to tell each other what is on their desks/workspaces and identify what is different. When they have finished ask a few pairs to report back, including the word *both* in their sentences if they talk about things that are the same (e.g. 'We both have a computer.').

EXTRA CHALLENGE In their pairs, Ss compare what they have in their bags and make sentences about what is the same (starting *We both* …) and what is different. This may involve new vocabulary so move around and be available to help with this.

TO FINISH

Ss discuss what things they bring to their English class and what's important for them to study well at school or home. You could encourage Ss to bring useful items such as highlighter pens, that they can use to mark stress or highlight notes; to file papers in date order and to get a dedicated vocabulary notebook.

3C How much is it?

HOW TO ... | shop for clothes
VOCABULARY | clothes
PRONUNCIATION | intonation

LESSON OVERVIEW

In this lesson, Ss learn functional language for asking about prices and vocabulary for clothes and sizes. The context is a listening about shopping and buying clothes. This leads into shopping requests where Ss also learn about voice range in phrases. The lesson ends with a speaking activity where Ss roleplay conversations in shops.

Online Teaching

If you're teaching this lesson online, you might find the following tips useful:

- **Vocabulary Bank 3C, Ex 1C:** In the main room, make sure Ss' cameras are on, before asking them to name the clothes they are wearing and write them in the chat box.
- **Ex 5A:** Use a collaborative document to check answers. Nominate a different student to type each answer in.

Additional Materials

For Teachers:

Presentation Tool Lesson 3C
Photocopiable Activity 3C
Grammar Bank 3C
Vocabulary Bank 3C

For Students:

Online Practice 3C
Workbook 3C

TO START

Write on the board: *What's your favourite colour for clothes? Where do you buy clothes?* Answer the questions yourself, to give a model (e.g. 'My favourite colours for clothes are blue and green.', 'I go to the shopping centre.'). Ss discuss the questions in pairs. When they have finished, elicit answers from a few Ss and have a brief class discussion. Tell Ss that clothes and shopping are today's topics.

EXTRA SUPPORT: DYSLEXIA Dyslexic learners in particular benefit from understanding exactly what they are learning in a lesson so that they understand what they are working towards. In this and every lesson, explain clearly what the learning objectives of the lesson are near the start.

VOCABULARY

clothes

1 A Focus attention on the photos and elicit what Ss can see. Ss discuss the questions in pairs. When they have finished, ask a few Ss to share their answers with the class.

ANSWERS:
1 A online **B** in a market **C** in shops
2–4 Students' own answers

B Look at the list of clothes with the class. Clarify the meaning of *light/dark* (remind Ss that they saw this in the Vocabulary Bank for Lesson 3A) by using clothes and things in the room, then put Ss in pairs to find the clothes in the photos. Go through the answers. Drill the words.

EXTRA SUPPORT: TEACHER Ss may want to name the red hoodie that the man in photo A is wearing – in fact some may use 'jacket' since that's an item in the list. If it comes up, you can teach them 'hoodie'.

ANSWERS:
A a white T-shirt
B a blue jacket; a light brown jacket
C a light green shirt, white jeans
'a dark blue coat' is not in the photos.

C Refer Ss to the Vocabulary Bank on page 129.

page 129 **VOCABULARY BANK** clothes **VB**

Note that the Vocabulary Bank activities are an important part of the lesson. They should only be omitted if you are confident that your Ss already know this vocabulary. If you don't use the exercises in class, it would be a good idea to set them as homework.

1 A Ask Ss to match the clothes (1–12) with the photos (A–L). Ss can first work alone, then help each other in pairs. Go through the answers as a class. Point out the silent letters in *coat*, *jeans*, *suit* and *shoes*.

ANSWERS:
1 G **2** J **3** F **4** L **5** I **6** K
7 C **8** D **9** A **10** B **11** H **12** E

B VB3.03 | Play the recording and ask Ss to look at the photos, listen and repeat.

C Put Ss in pairs to write the clothes they can see without looking at their books. If you are teaching online, make sure all Ss' cameras are on before continuing. Weaker classes can refer to their books to check spelling. When they have finished, put two pairs together to compare their ideas.

EXTRA IDEA Ss could play back-to-back guessing. They have ten seconds to look at their partner, then turn round and try to remember their clothes, e.g. 'I think you have black shoes, jeans, a blue T-shirt …'.

EXTRA CHALLENGE With fast finishers, you could ask pairs/groups to list the clothes of a classmate without naming the person. (e.g. 'black shoes, white shirt, …') The others look around and identify which person it is.

D Refer Ss to the photos. Ask them to match the sizes (1–3) with the correct photos (A–C). Go through the answers. Drill pronunciation.

ANSWERS:
1 C **2** A **3** B

How to …
shop for clothes

2 A 3.06 | Focus Ss' attention on the main photos (A–C) once more. Tell them they will hear two conversations and need to match them with the correct photos. Play the recording. Ask Ss to compare their answers in pairs, then check them with the class, asking what Ss heard that gave them the answers.

ANSWERS:
Conversation 1: Photo B
Conversation 2: Photo A

AUDIOSCRIPT 3.06

Conversation 1
B = Becca I = Ian M = man

B: Hey Ian, look at this jacket.
I: Nice! Brown's a good colour for you. How much is it?
B: I don't know. Excuse me?
M: Can I help you?
B: Yes, how much is this jacket?
M: It's thirty pounds.
B: Can I try it on?
M: Yes, of course.
B: Thanks. It's … big. Do you have a small?
M: No, I don't.
I: It's great, Becca. It's good on you. Really.
B: OK. How about twenty-five pounds?
M: No, it's thirty.
B: OK, thirty pounds.

Conversation 2
R = Ryan N = Nia

R: Are you online?
N: Yeah, I'm on sportsclub101.com.
R: Do they have jumpers?
N: No, it's all sports clothes. Oh wait, yes, they have jumpers.
R: Great.
N: Um, yeah. What size are you? Medium?
R: No, large.
N: Large, OK. What colour? They have green, blue and black.
R: Blue … Is it dark blue?
N: Yes, it is.
R: Then blue. How much is it?
N: Forty-nine pounds.
R: OK. Fine.
N: Anything else? I have your jumper and a top for me.
R: That's fine.
N: OK. Where's your credit card?
R: My credit card?
N: Yeah. My credit card is in the bedroom.
R: Oh, OK. My credit card is on the table.
N: Got it, thanks.

EXTRA SUPPORT: TEACHER Some Ss might be surprised to notice bargaining in the conversation in the market. It is considered acceptable to bargain in some contexts in the UK, e.g. markets, but not in regular shops.

B Ss should look at the clothes items in pairs and name them together, including the colours. Then, play the recording for them to listen and tick what they hear. Tell weaker classes they are listening for two of the items, one jacket in conversation 1 and one jumper in conversation 2. Ask Ss to compare answers in pairs. Check answers with the class.

ANSWERS:
brown jacket, dark blue jumper

C 3.06 | Ss listen again for the prices. Ask them to check in pairs. Check answers with the class.

ANSWERS:
The brown jacket is thirty pounds.
The dark blue jumper is forty-nine pounds.

3 A Explain that Ss should complete the conversations in pairs, using the words provided, from what they can remember of the conversations they heard. Don't give any answers yet.

EXTRA SUPPORT: DYSLEXIA Write the options in a vertical list, which is easier to read and process, on the board or on a piece of paper for Ss with dyslexia to choose from.

B 3.07 | Play the recording for Ss to listen and check their answers. Check answers with the class, calling on individuals to say each sentence and writing the correct answers on the board. Drill phrases then ask Ss to practise the conversations in pairs, taking turns at each role.

ANSWERS:
1 *How*, Excuse, much, try
2 size, is

C The Grammar Bank on page 102 can be used in the lesson or for homework. Decide how and when the exercises will benefit your class.

GB page 102 **GRAMMAR BANK**

This focuses on the form and use of phrases for asking about prices and buying clothes. Read the notes with the class or give them a few minutes to read alone then answer any questions they have.

1 Complete the first sentence with the class as an example. Ss continue alone, then check in pairs. Check answers with the class. You could then ask Ss to practise the conversation in pairs.

ANSWERS:

1 me	**2** Can I	**3** is
4 It's	**5** size	**6** you are
7 try	**8** of course	**9** are
10 They're	**11** you	**12** I'm

EXTRA IDEA Highlight, or tell Ss to highlight, the changeable information: coat, €37, medium; shoes, €43, 40. Ask Ss to replace the words/information with their own ideas before repeating the conversation.

2 Ss complete the conversation with one word in each gap alone, then check in pairs. Check answers with the class.

EXTRA SUPPORT: DYSLEXIA Gap-filling exercises can be difficult for Ss with dyslexia. Give Ss the missing words, jumbled in a vertical list on the board to choose from. Ss complete the conversation with the missing words provided.

ANSWERS:

2 Excuse	**3** help	**4** How
5 's/is	**6** on	**7** course
8 have	**9** here	**10** changing

3 Look at the example and remind Ss that the slashes often (but not always) represent missing words and that they also need to change the form of the verb *be*. Ss work alone to write the conversation, then compare answers. Go through the answers, drilling parts of the conversation. Ss can then practise the conversation in their pairs, taking turns at each role. Monitor and check they're using the phrases correctly. In feedback, you could ask a few Ss to practise the conversation in open pairs across the classroom.

EXTRA SUPPORT: DYSLEXIA Creating sentences from prompts can present a challenge for Ss with dyslexia. To simplify the process for them, you could provide the completed sentences with some of the functional language gapped (an option would be to do this just for the customer's part and provide the assistant's lines in full). Depending on what is gapped, their answers may differ slightly.

ANSWERS:
Customer: Yes, how much are the trousers?
Assistant: They're $55.
Customer: Do you have an extra large size?
Assistant: I'm sorry, we don't.
Customer: How much is this T-shirt?
Assistant: It's $5.
Customer: Can I try it on?
Assistant: Yes. What size are you?
Customer: I'm (a) size fourteen.

PRONUNCIATION

intonation

4A 3.08 | Look at pictures 1 and 2 and explain that they relate to voice range. Demonstrate the idea of range and the difference between the pictures with a word or short phrase (e.g. 'Hello'). Ask Ss to read through the pairs of sentences (1–3). Play the recording for Ss to label the sentences with 1 or 2. Ask Ss to compare, play the recording again as needed, then check answers with the class. Ask which range, 1 (large) or 2 (small), sounds friendly.

ANSWERS:
1 a 1; b 2
2 a 2; b 1
3 a 1; b 2
1 sounds friendly.

B 3.08 | Play the recording again, pausing for Ss to repeat.

EXTRA SUPPORT: TEACHER The intention here is to encourage Ss to use a wider voice range and therefore sound more friendly/polite. While it may seem odd to have them repeat both the good and bad model, it has been found that learners become more aware of the problem with narrow range / flat intonation when they consciously produce it in contrast with a positive model, so this is an effective way to raise their awareness. Depending on your class, you could have some fun by encouraging them to exaggerate the intonation, which would also help reinforce the difference in range.

SPEAKING

5 A Refer Ss to the conversation, pointing out the two roles and reminding them that the slashes often (but not always) represent missing words. Then ask Ss to try saying the questions in pairs. Monitor and offer help where necessary. Weaker classes will need to write first. When they have finished, ask a pair to read the conversation across the class and write the correct answers on the board. Drill the whole conversation chorally and individually.

EXTRA SUPPORT With weaker classes, or Ss with beginner literacy needs, provide Ss with the complete conversation, cut up, and ask them to put it in order. Once they have become sufficiently familiar with the conversation, they can turn over parts of it and say the sentences and questions without the prompts.

EXTRA SUPPORT: DYSLEXIA To help dyslexic learners visualise the prompts as a conversation, you could provide them as a single column of dialogue. You could also replace the slashes with gaps where necessary, indicating the number of words needed.

ANSWERS:

1 Can I help you?
2 How much is this shirt?
3 Can I try it on?
4 What size are you?
5 Where are the changing rooms?

B Put Ss in pairs and ask them to practise the questions only, with friendly intonation. Listen and offer feedback and encouragement.

C Ask pairs to practise the conversation, reading from the prompts in their books (you may need to erase the questions on the board to encourage them to do this). Move around, listen and give feedback on their pronunciation

D Tell Ss to swap roles and roleplay the conversation again, making changes to the words in bold (i.e. shirt, ten, large).

EXTRA CHALLENGE Stronger classes should be able to conduct the roleplay without looking after a couple of turns of practice. To provide a bit of support, first write key words from each stage of the conversation on the board in order and under the headings of *Customer* or *Shop assistant* (e.g. *Excuse …* ; *help …* ; *shirt …* ; *ten dollars …* ; etc.) and elicit each phrase. Don't write the questions up. Leave the words on the board. Ss can refer to these key words to help them recall the conversation.

EXTRA IDEA: DIGITAL Ss make an audio recording or video of their conversation, using props or sound effects to add authenticity and fun if they wish.

6 Tell Ss they will now practise shopping conversations. Put them in A/B pairs and refer them to the relevant pages.

1 Ss look at the task and the pictures which give them the information they need for the first part of the roleplay. Ask Ss who is the customer (Student A), who has the shop (Student B) and who speaks first (Student A). Then ask them to start. Move around the class and listen. Stronger Ss can improvise; weaker classes may need the support of some key words and phrases on the board. When they have finished, give some whole class feedback to help them when they repeat the roleplay.

2 Pairs look at their new information and change roles. Move around to monitor and support as necessary.

EXTRA: HOW TO … Designate Ss as customers and shopkeepers. Customers write what clothes they want to buy, and shopkeepers make a list of what clothes they have to sell and their prices. Set up 'shops' in the classroom and ask Ss to move around visiting different shops to find what they want.

TO FINISH

Put Ss in pairs to discuss what clothes they like wearing for different occasions (at home, to work/school, etc.) and at different times (weekdays, weekends, evenings, etc.). You could ask them to refer to the Vocabulary Bank to help when they do this.

EXTRA IDEA: SPEAK ANYWHERE Encourage Ss to practise using the Speak Anywhere interactive roleplay.

3D BBC Street Interviews Shopping

GRAMMAR | likes, dislikes and opinions
SPEAKING | ask and answer questions
WRITING | write a personal profile

LESSON OVERVIEW

In this lesson, Ss learn to express likes, dislikes and opinions. They also learn the names of different shops. The context is a video of interviews with people in the street talking about their shopping habits. Ss then do a speaking activity where they practise talking about their own attitudes to shopping. The lesson ends with a writing activity where Ss write a personal profile.

Online Teaching

If you're teaching this lesson online, you might find the following tips useful:

- **Ex 2B:** Share your screen and enable the annotation tool for individual Ss to complete the sentences.
- **Ex 2A and 3A:** Sometimes videos can be a little slow or jumpy when streamed in an online class environment. If you know this is an issue for you, give Ss time to watch the video on their own device before moving on.
- **Ex 5A:** Ss write their answers in the chat.
- **Ex 5C:** Ss discuss in breakout rooms.

Additional Materials

For Teachers:
Presentation Tool Lesson 3D
Online Digital Resources
Grammar Bank 3D
Vocabulary Bank 3D
Videoscript 3D: BBC Street Interviews

For Students:
Online Practice 3D
Workbook 3D

TO START

Write the word *shopping* on the board or display some pictures of local shops and ask Ss for their reactions. Tell Ss that today's lesson is about shopping.

EXTRA SUPPORT: DYSLEXIA Dyslexic learners in particular benefit from understanding exactly what they are learning in a lesson so that they understand what they are working towards. In this and every lesson, explain clearly what the learning objectives of the lesson are near the start.

PREVIEW

1A Refer Ss to the questions. Give an example yourself to start them off (e.g. 'I shop in the city centre. I buy food and clothes …'). Put Ss in pairs to ask and answer the questions. When they have finished, take general feedback to see what kinds of shops and shopping are popular.

B Put Ss in pairs to make a list of shops. Set a three-minute time limit.

EXTRA SUPPORT If your class is weaker and may not know any vocabulary, they can list shop names (e.g. Primark®) or go straight to the Vocabulary Bank.

C When they have finished, refer Ss to the Vocabulary Bank on page 130 to check their ideas.

page 130 **VOCABULARY BANK** shops VB

Note that the Vocabulary Bank activities are an important part of the lesson. They should only be omitted if you are confident that your Ss already know this vocabulary. If you don't use the exercises in class, it would be a good idea to set them as homework.

1 A Focus attention on the photos and ask Ss to match the words with them. Elicit the first answer as an example. Ss work individually, then check in pairs.

ANSWERS:
1 F **2** B **3** G **4** D **5** J
6 H **7** A **8** C **9** E **10** I

B VB3.04 | Play the recording for Ss to listen and check.

EXTRA IDEA If Ss are interested, you may also want to teach more shops that are locally relevant. If Ss used shop names in Ex 1B, you could go back to them and identify their type.

C Put Ss in pairs to take turns to point and identify. Move around the class and listen. When they have finished, give brief feedback on any problem words and drill.

VIEW

2 A ▶ **Read the two questions in the BBC programme information box with the class and explain that they're going to watch different people answering these questions. Then refer Ss to the instruction and ask them to count how many speakers buy food online as they watch the first part of the video. Tell Ss to count with their fingers, there's no need to write. Ss then watch and check in pairs, then check answers with the whole class.**

EXTRA SUPPORT Turn on the subtitles if you feel it would benefit learners.

ANSWER:
Two speakers buy food online. (Rachael: food; Nic: cat food)

B Put Ss in pairs to try and remember who said what, using the initial letters provided to help them. When they have finished, elicit their answers but don't confirm any answers yet.

EXTRA SUPPORT Provide a vertical list of the missing words for Ss to insert in the gaps. Ask them to match them with the first letters of the words first. This will help support all Ss, including weaker, beginner literacy and dyslexic learners. It's also useful if you are short of time.

C ▶ **Ss watch the video again and check their ideas, then compare in pairs. Play the video once more if necessary, then check answers as a class.**

ANSWERS:

1 house	**2** video	**3** clothes
4 cat	**5** shoes	**6** trainers

3 A ▶ **Refer Ss to the two statements. Suggest they write 1 and 2 on separate lines in their notebooks and tick the number each time they hear the shops in statements 1 and 2 referred to. Ss watch the video, then compare in pairs. Play the video again if Ss want you to.**

ANSWERS:
1 T (Six speakers talk about clothes shops: Rachael, Gloria, Joe, Holly, Nic and Kirsty.)
2 F (Only one speaker talks about video game shops: Vincent.)

B ▶ **Refer Ss to the different shops. Suggest they write the shop names in their notebooks and tick them when they hear them. Ss watch the video, then compare in pairs. Play the video again if Ss want you to.**

EXTRA SUPPORT: DYSLEXIA Provide Ss with a vertical list of shop names with space beside for them to tick as they watch. Tell Ss there is only one that they won't hear.

ANSWER:
They talk about all the shops except for the baker's.

GRAMMAR

likes, dislikes and opinions

4 A Draw a smiley face and a sad face on the board and ask Ss to identify which is *positive* and which is *negative*, to check they understand these words. Ask Ss to look at the sentences and identify which verbs in bold are positive and which are negative. If you're short of time, you could do this exercise as a class. Check answers with the class. Write the verbs under the smiley/sad faces on the board and ask Ss to copy.

ANSWERS:
Positive: love, like
Negative: hate, dislike, don't like

B Ask Ss to choose the correct alternative alone, then check in pairs. Go through the answers as a class with individual Ss reading the sentences aloud.

ANSWERS:
1 think **2** think

C The Grammar Bank on page 103 can be used in the lesson or for homework. Decide how and when the exercises will benefit your class.

▶▶ page 103 **GRAMMAR BANK**

GB

Check understanding of the notes with the class (especially ensure Ss understand that some nouns don't have a plural form). You could draw their attention to the use of the intensifiers *really* and *a lot* and where they are positioned in relation to the verb.

1 Complete the first sentence as an example with the class and elicit why it's *love* (the key word *favourite*). Then ask Ss to continue individually, choosing the correct alternatives, then check in pairs. Check answers with the class and write them on the board. Deal with any questions as they come up and refer Ss back to the notes.

ANSWERS:

1 love	**2** like	**3** don't	**4** hate
5 think	**6** really	**7** love	**8** lot
9 think	**10** don't		

GB **2** **Look at the example with the class. Point out that capital letters can help them identify the first word, though there are other capitals in the conversations, too. Ss write the conversations individually, then compare in pairs. Check answers with the class.**

EXTRA SUPPORT: DYSLEXIA Ss with dyslexia could be given a conversation with a few key words gapped to complete. Their answers may vary slightly, depending on which words are gapped.

ANSWERS:

1 B: I really like Fridays.
A: Me too.
B: And I really hate Mondays.

2 A: Sonia, do you like my new coat?
B: Yes, I do. I think it's beautiful.
A: How's your new apartment?
B: We're really happy with it. We like it a lot.

EXTRA CHALLENGE Elicit the types of words in the conversations that have capital letters in addition to the ones that start the sentences (names of people and days, i.e. proper nouns).

EXTRA IDEA: DIGITAL Ss practise reading their choice of the conversations in pairs, then record themselves and listen back to themselves and others.

3 **Ss find the mistakes individually, then compare in pairs. Check answers with the class.**

EXTRA SUPPORT: DYSLEXIA Identifying and then correcting mistakes can be challenging for Ss with dyslexia. You could provide the incorrect sentences with the mistakes highlighted so they can focus just on the correction part of the exercise.

ANSWERS:

2 We ~~like really~~ **really like** bookshops.
3 Young people ~~no~~ **don't** like black and white films.
4 We hate big ~~city~~ **cities**.
5 correct
6 ~~Think you~~ **Do you think** the new supermarket is good?
7 I ~~not~~ **don't** think Julia's ring is old.
8 A: Do you like babies? B: Yes, I ~~like~~ **do**.
9 correct
10 I like your coat **a** lot.
11 ~~Like Tom and Kate~~ **Do Tom and Kate like** Italian restaurants?
12 We like ~~a lot~~ our new apartment **a lot**.

SPEAKING

ask and answer questions

5A **Refer Ss to the question prompts and answers and give them a few minutes to read through and deal with any vocabulary issues. Suggest they tick the answers which are the same for them. (It doesn't matter if they don't know who the famous people are.) When they have finished, have a show of hands to see how many Ss have the same answers.**

B **Look at the example as a class. Further demonstrate the activity by matching the next question phrase (b) with a question prompt (1–12) with the class, then ask Ss to continue individually. They should write the number and letter in their notebooks, as the example, e.g. 1 a. When they have finished, ask pairs to compare, then go through the answers as a class. Write a full example of each question type (a–d) on the board.**

EXTRA SUPPORT Remind Ss we use *who* for people and *what* for things. In the question phrases, Ss see both a plural and singular verb form for *what*. Weaker classes may benefit from writing some of the questions in full. This will be time consuming, so give a limited number.

EXTRA SUPPORT: DYSLEXIA Provide Ss with the question phrases in a vertical list on a separate piece of paper that they can hold next to the questions to help with matching.

ANSWERS:

1 a **2** a **3** c **4** c **5** b **6** b
7 a **8** d **9** d **10** d **11** d **12** d

C **Explain that the Key phrases are different ways to give full answers to the questions. Read over them as a class. Put Ss in pairs to ask each other the questions in Ex 5A and use the Key phrases in their answers. Go round and help with vocabulary/pronunciation where necessary, writing any new words/phrases on the board.**

D **When they have finished, ask a few pairs of Ss to say what they both like. You could encourage them to use *We both …* as in the example.**

WRITING

a personal profile

6A Explain that Ss will read a personal profile where a student talks about what they like and don't like. Tell Ss the profile answers three of the questions in Ex 5A and that one of these is given in the example. Give Ss a few minutes to read alone, then put them in pairs to match the information with two other question prompts (1–12). Go through the answers.

EXTRA SUPPORT For Ss with dyslexia or beginner literacy, you could record the text before the class for them to listen on their personal devices while they read. Additionally, provide slips of paper with the three completed questions on for them to place near the relevant sections of text.

ANSWERS:
my favourite actress is Zendaya = 3
I like sports, but I don't like football. Tennis is my favourite sport. = 8

B Read the instruction to the class. Tell Ss to choose three questions from the list in Ex 5A and write their own profile, of 20–40 words, based on the one they read in Ex 6A. Move around and help/correct. Stronger Ss can be encouraged to write more words about more than three questions.

EXTRA SUPPORT For weaker classes, you could provide a writing frame with most of the text already completed and some key gaps.

EXTRA IDEA: DIGITAL Ss can post their personal profiles on a class webpage.

C Put Ss in groups and ask them to read each other's profiles. When they have finished, ask groups for feedback on if anyone likes the same things.

EXTRA CHALLENGE You could develop this to a whole class activity, suitable for stronger classes who can move around the room. Collect the texts in and write Ss' names on them. Display the written texts around the room so that Ss can walk around, read the texts, and find the person if they read about someone they share interests with.

TO FINISH

Put Ss in small groups to discuss what computer games / TV programmes / apps they like / don't like using.

3 REVIEW

LESSON OVERVIEW

This lesson is a review of the language – both grammar and vocabulary – presented in this unit. It also includes a link to the Sounds and Spelling section for this unit, which focuses on voiced and unvoiced consonants: /p/ and /b/, /k/ and /g/, /t/ and /d/; and sounds at the end of words. The notes below assume that the tasks are completed in class. However, the self-study type exercises (i.e. Exs 1A, 2A, 2B, 3A, 3B, 4A, 4B and 6A) could be done out of class and then checked in the following lesson when the communicative tasks are then completed.

Online Teaching

If you're teaching this lesson online, you might find the following tips useful:

- **Ex 1B:** Put Ss in breakout rooms in pairs for this exercise.
- **Ex 2A:** Ask Ss to write their answers in the chat, then go over them as a class in the main room.
- **Exs 6A and 6B:** Use a collaborative document to give and check answers.

Additional Materials

For Teachers:
Sounds and Spelling 3
Unit Test in test package

TO START

Ask Ss to work in pairs and try to remember what language they studied in Unit 3 (Grammar: possessive *'s*, present simple *have* + *yes/no* questions (*I, you, we, they*), likes, dislikes and opinions; Vocabulary: things, colours, desk objects, clothes, shops; How to … shop for clothes). Ask them to look at the unit lesson objectives to check their ideas.

GRAMMAR

1 A Read the example with the class, then ask Ss to complete the rest of the sentences using names and the possessive *'s*. Remind them of how family trees work if necessary. Check answers with the class with Ss reading sentences aloud. Check the pronunciation of *David's* /z/, *Ruby's* /z/, Janette*'s* /s/ and *Max's* /ɪz/.

ANSWERS:

2 Max's	**3** Ruby's	**4** Janette's
5 Janette's	**6** Max's	

B **Demonstrate the activity by writing names on the board and giving a brief description of who the person is, e.g. *Sadie* 'my friend's daughter'; *Ahmed* 'my father's friend'). Tell Ss not to include the names of their very close family or their own friends, (i.e. not *my mother, father, brother, sister, friend*, etc.) as the purpose of the activity is to describe who the people are, using the possessive *'s*. Ss work individually to write names. Monitor and check they are not writing sentences. Encourage Ss to think about the pronunciation, particularly the extra syllable /ɪz/. When they have finished, put Ss in pairs to take turns to say a name from their list and ask and answer each other as in the example. When they have finished, ask a few pairs to remember something they learnt from their partner and tell the class.**

2A **Focus attention on the example and remind Ss that slashes usually represent missing words. Elicit the kinds of words that are missing (*do, a/an*, etc.). Ss work alone to write questions, then check in pairs. Check answers with the class, writing the complete questions on the board.**

EXTRA SUPPORT: DYSLEXIA Adapt the task to a gap-fill for dyslexic learners. For more support, provide two alternatives for each gap or a vertical list of the missing words to choose from.

ANSWERS:

2 Do you have an email address?
3 Do they have (any) British friends?
4 Do we have an Italian speaker in the office?
5 Do Ramin and Vineeta have an apartment?
6 Do you have a cat?

B **Look at the example with the class. Ask Ss to complete the rest of the answers then match them with the remaining questions. When they have finished, ask pairs to read out the questions and answers. Write the short answers on the board. Ss could practise the questions and answers in pairs.**

EXTRA SUPPORT: DYSLEXIA Present the questions and answers in two columns for Ss to match. If possible, the answers could be cut up, so Ss can move them to the questions and try them.

ANSWERS:

b don't 5 **c** do 4 **d** don't 3
e don't 1 **f** do 2

3A **Ask Ss to rewrite the sentences, as in the example. When they have finished, ask individuals to read out the correct answers.**

EXTRA SUPPORT To reduce the writing load for learners with dyslexia and beginner literacy, Ss can just identify where the adverb fits. They don't need to rewrite the sentences.

EXTRA SUPPORT: TEACHER Ss are taught at this point that *really* modifies the verb (e.g. *I really think …*). It can equally, of course, modify the adjective (e.g. … *the internet is really great.*). If Ss place it there, no problem.

ANSWERS:

2 I **really** hate supermarkets.
3 I like big cities **a lot**.
4 I **really** think the internet is great. (*I think the internet is really great.* is also possible)
5 I **really** think phones are bad. (*I think phones are really bad.* is also possible)
6 I like red cars **a lot**.

B **Ask Ss to change the sentences to make them true for themselves. Rewrite one or two of the sentences for yourself on the board, to show how it could be changed, e.g. *I really don't like big cities. I like small cities a lot.* Move around and help as needed.**

C **When they have finished, put Ss in pairs to ask each other questions. Ask pairs how similar/different they are and what they have in common.**

VOCABULARY

4A **Explain that Ss should find words vertically or horizontally. Elicit one or two as a class, then ask Ss to work alone and find the rest of the words. If possible, Ss could highlight the words in each category with a different colour. In feedback, check answers with the class and ask Ss to come and highlight the words on the board if you have an interactive whiteboard.**

EXTRA SUPPORT: DYSLEXIA Word search activities can be confusing for dyslexic learners. You could give them the words to look for in each group and ask Ss to look only for one group at a time. They can also use two pieces of L-shaped card or paper with which to make a window to view the letters in specific rows and columns in the grid. They choose a letter, place the inside edge of one piece of card directly to the left or above it and place the other piece so they make a small window around the letter. They then move the second piece along the row or down the column to reveal more letters to see if they make a word. (This is also a good technique for reading generally as it reduces distraction from other lines of text.)

ANSWERS:

P	U	R	P	L	E	W	A	T	C	H
B	X	J	O	M	J	P	I	N	K	E
L	B	E	R	E	S	W	T	Z	E	A
A	L	A	A	S	B	H	R	I	Y	D
C	A	N	N	K	I	I	O	M	B	P
K	H	S	G	I	R	T	U	O	O	H
W	C	R	E	R	T	E	S	B	A	O
V	O	H	O	T	E	D	E	N	R	N
T	A	B	L	E	T	V	R	R	D	E
F	T	S	S	C	I	S	S	O	R	S
S	U	I	T	G	L	A	S	S	E	S
B	R	O	W	N	A	D	R	E	S	S

Colours: black, brown, orange, pink, purple, white

Objects: glasses, headphones, keyboard, scissors, tablet, watch

Clothes: coat, dress, jeans, skirt, suit, trousers

B **Ask Ss to make a list of objects and clothes with their colours alone, including two false items. Move around and help as needed.**

C **Put Ss in pairs to take turns to say their sentences and guess which are true or false, as in the example.**

5 A **Put Ss in pairs to say the words and identify the sounds, then check answers with the class.**

EXTRA SUPPORT: TEACHER The intention is for Ss to begin to notice the contrast between voiced and unvoiced sounds, but don't expect Ss to be perfect at this point or to write the phonetic symbols, as the 'full answer' comes via the Sounds and Spelling section.

ANSWERS:

pencil /p/	car /k/	tablet /t/
bed /b/	guitar /g/	dark /d/

B **Refer Ss to Sounds and Spelling on page 153.**

page 153 **SOUNDS AND SPELLING**
voiced and unvoiced consonants (1): /p/ and /b/, /k/ and /g/, /t/ and /d/; sounds at the end of words

The Sounds and Spelling section can be used to help with particular problems. You might want to select the sections or even particular sounds that are most useful for your Ss. The vocabulary used in each section comes from the current unit or previous units.

SOUNDS AND SPELLING TEACHER'S NOTES page 208

6 A **Write the five vowels (*a, e, i, o, u*) on the board. Ask Ss to read the text and write the missing vowels to complete the words, then put Ss in pairs to compare.**

EXTRA SUPPORT: DYSLEXIA Presenting words with letters missing can cause difficulties for Ss with dyslexia. Adapt the exercise to a word-level gap-fill. Provide Ss with two possible alternatives for each gap. Advise them to cover the lines they are not working on as they read to reduce distractions.

B **R3.01 | Play the recording for Ss to listen and check the answers. Elicit the answers to the board to ensure correct spelling and drill where needed.**

ANSWERS:

1 shirts	**2** jumper	**3** jacket
4 laptop	**5** notebook	**6** sticky notes
7 yellow	**8** blue	**9** green
10 camera		

TO FINISH

Make a list on the board, with Ss' help, of different aspects of a lesson (e.g. grammar, vocabulary, reading, etc.). Ask Ss to number them in order of how much they like them. Put Ss in groups of three or four to discuss what they like and don't like and why. Have a group discussion when they have finished, to help inform future classes.

4 every day

GSE LEARNING OBJECTIVES

4A Time for lunch!

- LISTENING | Understand people from different countries talking about lunch: food and drink
- Talk about food: adverbs of frequency
- Pronunciation: word stress
- Write an email to a friend

GSE INFORMATION

VOCABULARY
10–29 Can use language related to food and drink.

LISTENING
26 Can recognise words and simple phrases related to familiar topics, if spoken slowly and clearly and supported by pictures.

GRAMMAR
33 Can use a range of common adverbs of frequency.

SPEAKING
28 Can express preferences about food and drink using basic fixed expressions.

WRITING
28 Can write short, simple notes, emails and postings to friends.

4B A day in the life

- READING | Read about an influencer's daily routine: everyday activities (1); telling the time
- Ask and answer about your daily routine: present simple: regular verbs (*he*, *she*, *it*)
- Pronunciation: third person *-s*

GSE INFORMATION

VOCABULARY
10–29 Can use language related to everyday activities.

READING
25 Can understand short, simple descriptions of objects, people and animals, given visual support.

GRAMMAR
26 Can use the present simple to refer to daily routines.

SPEAKING
28 Can answer simple questions about their daily activities or routines, given a model.

4C Can I have … ?

- HOW TO … | order in a café: café words
- Pronunciation: intonation in *or* phrases

GSE INFORMATION

VOCABULARY
10–29 Can use language related to food and drink.

10–29 Can use language related to utensils, appliances and tableware.

HOW TO …
29 Can follow simple, everyday transactions (e.g. shopping and eating out) if carried out slowly and clearly.

SPEAKING
24 Can ask for a drink or food in a limited way.

4D Earth From Space

- BBC PROGRAMME | Understand a documentary about three people around the world
- Ask about someone's routine: present simple: *yes/no* questions (*he*, *she*, *it*)
- Write a quiz

GSE INFORMATION

VIEW
30 Can identify simple information in a short video, provided that the visual supports this information and the delivery is slow and clear.

GRAMMAR
26 Can ask *yes/no* questions using the present simple.

SPEAKING
27 Can ask simple questions about other people (e.g. their name, age, where they live, things they have).

WRITING
34 Can write short descriptive texts (4–6 sentences) on familiar personal topics (e.g. family, possessions), given a model.

For full coverage of GSE Learning Objectives go to page 222.

BBC VLOGS

This is a short activity that can be used as an introduction to the unit topic and a warm-up to Lesson 4A. It shouldn't be exploited or taught at length, just played once or twice in class.

Check understanding of *breakfast*, *lunch* and *dinner* by showing typical photos with a suitable time alongside (e.g. 8.00 a.m., 1.00 p.m., 8.00 p.m.). If Ss ask, explain that *a.m.* is before 12.00 midday and *p.m.* is after. Tell Ss which meal is your favourite (e.g. 'My favourite meal is breakfast.') and then put Ss in pairs to tell each other. When they have finished, take a vote to see which meal is the most popular. When they are ready, play the video for Ss to watch for how many speakers say 'breakfast'.

ANSWER:
Four speakers say 'breakfast'.

EXTRA IDEA If Ss want to watch the video again outside class, they can note the foods (and drinks) mentioned (tuna salad, fish, coffee, fruit, pasta with cheese, omelette, tea, cereal with milk, orange juice, eggs). Alternatively, you might have Ss count the number of speakers who say the other meals. (Two say lunch and two say dinner.)

NOTE The vlogs have been provided by people from around the world in response to the same question. The video content was filmed by them on their own mobile phones, so the picture quality varies considerably and in some cases is of a lower quality. However, this adds to the authenticity of the content.

The locations labelled on the vlogs show where the speaker was when they filmed the video. It does not reflect where the speaker comes from (necessarily).

As many of the speakers are non-native, the videos expose Ss to a range of different accents and varieties of English. This could be used as a way to highlight interesting or useful differences.

Additional Materials

For Teachers:

Presentation Tool Unit 4
Online Digital Resources
Videoscript Unit 4 Opener: BBC Vlogs

4A Time for lunch!

GRAMMAR | adverbs of frequency
VOCABULARY | food and drink
PRONUNCIATION | word stress

LESSON OVERVIEW

In this lesson, Ss learn food and drink vocabulary. They also learn adverbs of frequency. The context is a listening where Ss listen to people talking about what they have for lunch. Ss then do a speaking activity where they talk about what they eat and drink at different mealtimes. The lesson ends with a writing activity where Ss write an email to a friend.

Online Teaching

If you're teaching this lesson online, you might find the following tips useful:

- **Ex 3A:** Ask Ss to type their answers in the chat box. This will allow them to compare their ideas with other Ss before they listen.
- **Ex 5A:** Type the jumbled sentences into a collaborative document or display them on your device and share your screen. Make sure your settings allow for annotations and invite Ss to write them in the correct order.
- **Ex 6B:** Put Ss in breakout rooms to discuss. Aim to visit each breakout room briefly to check Ss are on task. Then listen closely to a few pairs to assess them more fully. Listen closely to the other pairs in future lessons.

Additional Materials

For Teachers:

Presentation Tool Lesson 4A
Photocopiable Activities 4A
Grammar Bank 4A
Vocabulary Bank 4A
Writing Bank 4A

For Students:

Online Practice 4A
Workbook 4A

TO START

Choose a few international foods (pizza, sandwich, omelette, etc.). Show some pictures or write the words on the board. Ask Ss to discuss in pairs which ones they like. When they have finished, elicit answers from each group and have a brief class discussion to see which foods are popular.

EXTRA SUPPORT: DYSLEXIA Dyslexic learners in particular benefit from understanding exactly what they are learning in a lesson so that they understand what they are working towards. In this and every lesson, explain clearly what the learning objectives of the lesson are near the start.

VOCABULARY

food and drink

1 **Focus attention on the words in the box. With weaker classes, go through these as a class and drill. Put Ss in pairs to name the foods in the photos (A–C). When they have finished, check answers with the class and drill pronunciation.**

EXTRA SUPPORT: TEACHER There is a mixture of countable and uncountable nouns in the word choice box, and Ss may make mistakes here. As it is not a focus in this lesson, don't correct them as long as communication of the vocabulary is successful.

ANSWERS:
chicken, egg, pasta, rice, sandwich, tomato

PRONUNCIATION

word stress

2 A **4.01 | Ss have seen syllable stress before, so write *apple* on the board and draw two circles, one large and one small, to remind Ss of syllables and stress. Look at the example with the class, then ask Ss to match the words in the box with the correct syllable patterns. Fast finishers can add more words. Check answers with the recording and confirm by writing them on the board.**

ANSWERS:
1 *egg*, fish, rice, steak
2 *apple*, chicken, mushroom, pasta, sandwich
3 banana, tomato

EXTRA IDEA You could remind Ss that many nouns in English have two syllables and the stress in these is often on the first syllable. The unstressed syllable is frequently a weak form (schwa), so even where the vowel is the same in both syllables, it has a different sound (e.g. *pasta* = /ˈpæstə/).

B **4.01 | Play the recording again, pausing for Ss to repeat. Use your arm or hand to gesture where the stress falls.**

EXTRA IDEA You could ask Ss to add more words to each syllable pattern, choosing a recently studied category such as clothes or colours. If your class is competitive, this can be a team game to see how many words teams can add to each pattern.

C **Refer Ss to the Vocabulary Bank on page 131.**

page 131 **VOCABULARY BANK** food and drink

VB

Note that the Vocabulary Bank activities are an important part of the lesson. They should only be omitted if you are confident that your Ss already know this vocabulary. If you don't use the exercises in class, it would be a good idea to set them as homework.

1 A **Look at the photos with the class and name the items, drilling chorally. Ask Ss to match the words (1–20) with the photos (A–T).**

EXTRA SUPPORT: DYSLEXIA Given the number of vocabulary items, dyslexic learners may find it helpful to cover the sections or even words they are not working with to help them focus.

ANSWERS:
1 L **2** P **3** O **4** G **5** D **6** Q **7** E **8** A
9 N **10** F **11** S **12** C **13** I **14** M **15** T **16** H
17 R **18** K **19** J **20** B

EXTRA CHALLENGE Point out the categories (fruit, vegetables, etc.). Fast finishers or stronger classes can add more words to each category, using their devices or dictionaries as needed to find words that are important to them / their diet.

B **VB4.01 | Play the recording for Ss to listen and repeat.**

C **Remind Ss how we make regular plurals and make the first word plural as an example (*apples*). Bring Ss attention to the NOTICE box and tell them some nouns for food don't have a plural form. They are not part of this exercise, but, if Ss ask, you can give a brief explanation (see Extra Support: Teacher, below). Ss continue alone then check in pairs. Go through the answers. Point out that for words ending *o* we use *es* in the plural.**

EXTRA SUPPORT: TEACHER Ss may have questions about the note regarding plurals. With stronger classes, you could preview countable/uncountable nouns and point out that a useful guide is we don't have plurals for things we buy in grams and kilograms (e.g. *meat, cheese*) or liquids. We can say *two chickens* if referring to *whole chickens*.

ANSWERS:

1 apples	**6** potatoes
2 bananas	**7** tomatoes
3 oranges	**8** steaks
4 carrots	**19** eggs
5 mushrooms	**20** sandwiches

D **Look at the example and explain that Ss must find the item in each line that does not fit the group and say why. Ask Ss to work alone first, then discuss their ideas in pairs, giving their reasons. Go through the answers as a class. If Ss have different ideas that can be justified, accept them.**

ANSWERS:

2 banana (It isn't a vegetable.)
3 sandwich (It isn't a drink.)
4 fruit juice (It's the only drink.)
5 orange (It isn't a type of meat.)
6 milk (It's the only drink. It also has one syllable and the other words have three syllables.)

2 A **Point out that Ss need to think about the correct verbs but cross out the alternative in each sentence that is wrong. Elicit the first answer, then ask Ss to answer for the second sentence. Go through the answers as a class and write them on the board.**

ANSWERS:

1 ~~eat~~ **2** ~~drink~~

B **Put Ss in pairs to talk about their breakfast. They can use the statements from Ex 2A as well as their own ideas. Be prepared to help with additional vocabulary. Take brief class feedback.**

LISTENING

3 A **Put Ss in pairs to discuss the questions. Refer them to the Vocabulary Bank to help them with question 2. When they have finished, take brief feedback and ask for a show of hands to see how many people have a small or big lunch.**

B **4.02 | Explain that Ss will hear three people talking about the dishes shown in the photos (A–C). They should listen and number the photos in the order that they hear them. Play the recording, ask pairs to compare, then go through the answers.**

ANSWERS:

1 C **2** B **3** A

AUDIOSCRIPT 4.02

I = Isabel M = Miki A = Aiden

I: My husband is Italian. In Italy, we usually have lunch together in our apartment: my two children, my husband and my husband's mother. We eat together. We always have pasta for lunch. Pasta and tomatoes or pasta and mushrooms and cheese. After the pasta we have meat or fish. Fish is our favourite. Then we often eat fruit, an apple or a banana. We drink water with lunch and after lunch, we drink coffee. I love coffee.

M: For lunch I have a 'bento' box, or Japanese lunch box. I make different food every day. I usually have rice, fish or chicken and vegetables. What do I have in my box today? My box has rice, an egg, tomatoes and other vegetables. After lunch I always drink tea, green tea, every day.

A: Lunch? Well, I don't often eat a big lunch. In the morning I make a sandwich. I really like cheese sandwiches or egg sandwiches. I sometimes eat my sandwich at my desk or I sometimes go to the park. Then I have an apple. I love apples. After lunch I drink a cup of tea. Always tea. I never drink coffee. I hate it.

C **Refer Ss to the table to tick the food they think they heard. They can discuss this in pairs. While they are doing the activity, copy or project the table onto the board. You can go through the answers, but don't confirm them as correct yet.**

EXTRA SUPPORT: TEACHER The purpose of this activity is to give exposure to the vocabulary in the listening and provide a focus for listening. Ss will not necessarily remember everything and you could let them know this is OK if they are unsure or can't recall much.

D **4.02 | Play the recording and ask Ss to check their answers. Then go through the answers as a class and write them in the table on the board.**

EXTRA SUPPORT This task is demanding because it requires Ss to listen as well as associate a (new) spoken word with an image. The table format is something that Ss should be getting used to, but it's still worthwhile spending some time looking at how we read down for the items and that each person is represented in a different column.

ANSWERS:

	Isabel	Miki	Aiden
pasta	✓		
rice		✓	
tomato	✓	✓	
sandwich			✓
cheese	✓		✓
fish	✓	✓	
chicken		✓	
apple	✓		✓
egg		✓	✓
tea		✓	✓

GRAMMAR

adverbs of frequency

4A Write: *I always drink tea.* on the board and point out that the speakers in the listening talk about how often they eat and drink things. Ask Ss to identify the word in the sentence that tells us how often (*always*) and tell Ss this is an adverb. Draw a vertical line on the board and put the percentages *0%* at the top and *100%* at the bottom. Ask Ss to place *always* (100%). Read the sentences with the class and elicit the position of the other adverbs (*usually*, at 80%, is already given). Drill them and get Ss to copy the completed line into their notebooks.

EXTRA SUPPORT: TEACHER Ss may get a bit fixated on the percentages. Explain that these are approximate! There is also a conceptual difficulty with *usually*, which expresses that a behaviour is regular (= normally) and *often* which is more truly related to frequency (= many times). At this level it should help Ss to see the adverbs in relation to others on a scale. Note that *be* with adverbs of frequency is covered at A2.

ANSWERS:
1 never **2** sometimes **3** often
4 *usually* **5** always

B The Grammar Bank on page 104 can be used in the lesson or for homework. Decide how and when the exercises will benefit your class.

GB ⏩ page 104 **GRAMMAR BANK**

This focuses on both the use and form of the present simple with adverbs of frequency. Go through the notes with Ss or let them read them alone. Check understanding where necessary, especially of the word order when using adverbs. In A1, *be* with adverbs of frequency isn't covered. This is because we want Ss to focus on the use of the present simple for routines rather than with state verbs.

1 This exercise practises the use and form of adverbs of frequency with the present simple. Use the example to check Ss understand they need to put the adverbs in brackets in the right places and remind them that they need to use *don't/doesn't* to make negatives. Ss complete the rest of the exercise alone then check in pairs. Check answers with the class. Ask individuals to read sentences aloud to the class.

ANSWERS:
2 We **usually** have breakfast at eight.
3 My parents **always** eat dinner at nine.
4 I **don't often** have an umbrella in my bag.
5 My children **never** listen to the radio.
6 I **often** choose green apples.
7 Do you **always** write in a notebook?
9 I **sometimes** look at our old family photos.
9 I **don't usually** read newspapers.
10 Do Barry and Olivia **often** speak Spanish?

2 This exercise focuses on the meaning of adverbs of frequency in context, along with the present simple. Check Ss understand that they should use the information in the table to complete the conversation. Ask Ss to complete the exercise alone, then check answers with the class. You could then put Ss in pairs to practise saying the conversation.

EXTRA SUPPORT: DYSLEXIA This exercise requires Ss to process visual information and transfer it into written form, which is a challenge for dyslexic learners who have processing difficulties. Break down the task by first asking Ss to write the adverb beside each row of the table and agreeing this with you, then asking them to insert the adverbs into the conversation. For further support you could list the adverbs on the board before they do this, for reference.

ANSWERS:
2 usually **3** never **4** often
5 sometimes **6** always **7** often
8 sometimes

EXTRA CHALLENGE Ss complete the table for themselves, then ask and answer with a partner (e.g. 'Do you eat chocolate?', 'Yes, I often eat chocolate.'). Stronger classes could write the information using the conversation for ideas.

5A Look at the example, pointing out that the subject (or subject + auxiliary verb for negatives) is immediately followed by the adverb of frequency, which is then followed by the main verb. Then ask Ss to write the remaining sentences, before putting them in pairs to compare answers. Check answers with the class and write them on the board (or invite Ss to come up and do so).

EXTRA SUPPORT It's worth reinforcing the typical *Subject + Verb + Object* (*SVO*) word order that occurs in English, particularly if working with Ss with a very different language structure. The position of the adverb after the subject (and auxiliary verb) is worth reinforcing, though, of course, it can sometimes go in different places.

EXTRA SUPPORT To support beginner literacy and dyslexic learners, provide the complete sentences with the adverb separately. Ss should indicate where the adverb goes. This reinforces the word order without requiring too much writing. Fast finishers can rewrite a few sentences in full.

ANSWERS:
2 I don't often eat at home.
3 I sometimes have vegetables for dinner.
4 I always eat steak on my birthday.
5 I usually drink tea with milk.
6 I never eat chicken.
7 I always have coffee after lunch.
8 I never eat eggs for breakfast.

B Ask Ss to tick the sentences that are true for them and change the other sentences to make them true for themselves. Write an example on the board, e.g. *I never eat fruit. I often eat cheese.* to show how they can change either the adverb or other elements. Allow time for this and move around the class and help. When they have finished, ask Ss to compare in pairs.

EXTRA CHALLENGE Some Ss may notice the prepositions in the sentences. With stronger classes, write these phrases from Ex 5A on the board: *at home, for dinner/breakfast, (tea) with milk*. Highlight the prepositions and use these to generalise and elicit more ideas (e.g. *at home/school/work*; *for breakfast/lunch/dinner*; *tea/coffee with milk/sugar*; *chicken with vegetables*). Ss create their own sentences.

EXTRA IDEA: DIGITAL Ss can record themselves saying the sentences, then listen back to check for correct pronunciation.

SPEAKING

6A Read the instruction with the class and elicit another example of a type of fruit (e.g. *bananas*). Ask Ss to complete the box with their own ideas, using the Vocabulary Bank or their device/dictionary to help them. When they have finished, elicit a few answers to the board.

B Model the activity by saying an example yourself and showing how you use and link the information in the boxes to make a sentence, e.g. 'I never eat bananas in the morning.' Point out how we say *in the morning/afternoon/evening*. Introduce the phrases *Me too.* and *Me neither.* for agreement and disagreement. Put Ss in pairs to tell each other five things, using the prompts in Ex 6A to help them. Monitor while they practise and check Ss are making correct sentences. Give feedback on any errors when they have finished.

EXTRA SUPPORT With weaker classes or classes with beginner literacy needs, Ss can usefully write their sentences before telling each other. If you complete the speaking activity and Ss have made a lot of errors, they can write a few sentences after you have given them feedback, for consolidation.

C Put Ss in new pairs to repeat the activity without looking at the prompts. Move around and see how they manage, then give feedback at the end.

7 Ss read the instruction. Remind them to make a few notes to help them talk about their lunch in the next lesson.

EXTRA: OUT OF CLASS Ss write one or two sentences about their lunch (e.g. 'This is my lunch today. I usually have a sandwich with tomato and cheese in the afternoon.') and upload the picture and text to an online forum.

WRITING

write an email to a friend

8A Look at the exercise as a class and elicit what type of text it contains (an email). Tell Ss the email is from Stacy to Jade and that they are making a plan. Ss read the questions and then the email to find the answers to questions 1 and 2. They then answer Stacy's questions for themselves in question 3. Ask Ss to compare in pairs before going through the answers as a class and eliciting some answers for question 3.

EXTRA SUPPORT With weaker or beginner literacy Ss, it's worth spending time looking at the organisation of the email. Ask Ss to say who it is from (Stacy) and to (Jade), and note how the names are positioned at the beginning and end, as well as the layout of the greeting and the sign off. Look at the content of the first paragraph (Stacy's news) and the second (Stacy's questions for Jade about her visit).

EXTRA SUPPORT: DYSLEXIA Ss with dyslexia may have difficulty processing questions and text and writing the answers. As this is a reading task, ask them simply to identify in the text where the answers to questions 1 and 2 are found. They don't need to write the answers.

ANSWERS:

1 Pete has a new job and Susie has a new apartment.
2 How are you? What do you like for breakfast? Do you eat meat and fish?
3 Students' own answers

B Refer Ss to the Writing Bank on page 89.

WB ▶▶ page 89 **WRITING BANK**

1 A Explain to Ss that here they have the email from Stacy they saw before, and also the sentences from Jade's reply (a–g), which are not in the correct order. They are going to put the sentences in order. The topics and answers should follow the order of the information and questions in Stacy's email. Ask Ss to locate the start (e), and then continue. Check the answer with the class.

EXTRA SUPPORT: TEACHER Checking the answer to this task and doing those that follow will be much easier if you supply Ss with an ordered version of Jade's email.

EXTRA SUPPORT: DYSLEXIA Putting the jumbled text in order is challenging. You could provide Ss with cut-up strips of email to physically move into order. When checking the answers, provide Ss with a complete ordered text to refer to.

ANSWER:

The correct order is e, a, g, b, f, d, c.

B Give Ss two minutes to find the answers to questions 1 and 2 in Stacy's email individually, then check in pairs. Check answers with the class.

ANSWERS:

1 cereal or toast, and coffee **2** meat, but not fish

C Ss put the topics in order alone, then check in pairs. Check the answer with the class. Elicit that they follow the same order as Stacy's email.

ANSWER:

The correct order is b, c, a.

D Do this activity together as a class and write the answers on the board. Explain that, with the exception of 'Love', the terms are informal greetings/goodbyes also used in speaking.

ANSWERS:

starting an email: Hi Jeff, Hey Paola, Hello Ed
finishing an email: See you soon, Love, Speak soon

EXTRA SUPPORT: TEACHER When you focus on the start/end of emails it may be helpful to point out that a comma traditionally comes after these sorts of openings and closings to emails and letters. Increasingly, many people do not use this punctuation in emails, but they do still start the text on a new line. It's common to close an email to a friend with *x* or *xxx*, as we see in the example, which means a kiss or kisses. Ss may like to know other suitable semi-formal closing phrases (*Kind regards, Regards, Best regards, Best wishes*).

2 Read the instruction with the class and point out that they have studied how to start and finish an email, and seen the order to include the information in. Ss should reply to Stacy's email and answer the questions for themselves. You could tell Ss that they should aim to write 50–60 words. Go round and offer help where necessary. Stronger Ss can use their own ideas, weaker ones can use the model provided and copy it more closely.

EXTRA IDEA Put Ss in pairs to swap emails and read them. You could give them a checklist to tick off, ensuring appropriate start and finish phrases are used and that the topics in Ex 1C are covered.

TO FINISH

Put Ss in pairs to discuss their favourite weekend lunch or meal to cook for friends. Move around the class and be available to help with any vocabulary they need.

4B A day in the life

GRAMMAR | present simple: regular verbs (*he*, *she*, *it*)
VOCABULARY | everyday activities (1); telling the time
PRONUNCIATION | third person *-s*

LESSON OVERVIEW

In this lesson, Ss learn vocabulary of everyday activities and ways to express the time. The context is a reading where they read a text about a YouTuber. This leads into the grammar of regular verbs in the present simple third person form. The lesson ends with a speaking activity where Ss exchange information about their routines.

Online Teaching

If you're teaching this lesson online, you might find the following tips useful:

- **Ex 2B:** Share your screen and have Ss type their answers in. Use the annotate function to highlight the sections of text where the answers are found.
- **Ex 4A:** Rather than underlining, Ss write the verbs in the chat and compare with others.
- **Ex 6A:** Ss work in groups in breakout rooms then summarise their findings by reporting back in the chat.

Additional Materials

For Teachers:
Presentation Tool Lesson 4B
Photocopiable Activities 4B
Grammar Bank 4B
Vocabulary Bank 4B

For Students:
Online Practice 4B
Workbook 4B

TO START

Write the following questions on the board: *What do you do before class? What do you do after class?* Tell the class your answers to the questions (e.g. 'Before class, I go to the gym. After class, I meet my friends for a cup of coffee.'), then put Ss in pairs or small groups to ask each other.

EXTRA SUPPORT: DYSLEXIA Dyslexic learners in particular benefit from understanding exactly what they are learning in a lesson so that they understand what they are working towards. In this and every lesson, explain clearly what the learning objectives of the lesson are near the start.

VOCABULARY

everyday activities (1)

1 A Look at the pictures (A–I) as a class, then put Ss in pairs to match the phrases in the box with the pictures. You could do *get up* – *A* as an example (and point out that *get up* is crossed out in the box as it is used in the example for Ex 1B). When Ss have finished, elicit answers and drill. With weaker classes, first introduce the phrases and then have Ss do the matching as confirmation.

ANSWERS:

A get up
B leave home
C go to work
D finish work
E get home
F have lunch
G go to bed
H make dinner
I watch TV

'start work' is not in the pictures.

B Tell Ss they should write the phrases into the sentences. They can do this alone then check in pairs. Check answers with the class.

EXTRA SUPPORT: DYSLEXIA Provide dyslexic learners with two alternatives for each gap. Remind them to cover the parts of the exercise they are not doing to reduce distraction.

ANSWERS:

2 leave home
3 go to work
4 start work
5 have lunch
6 finish work
7 get home
8 make dinner
9 watch TV
10 go to bed

C With weaker classes, read through the example. Demonstrate the continuation of the conversation in the example with a stronger student (e.g. 'I go to work at nine.', 'Me too!'). Ss change the sentences individually, then compare in pairs. If Ss don't go to work, they can substitute *school* or another regular daily activity for *work*. Tell them they should use approximate times for now, using just the hours (highlight *about 8 a.m./1 p.m.* in Ex 1B) and that they will learn more detailed ways to say the time in the Vocabulary Bank.

EXTRA IDEA: DIGITAL Ask Ss to record themselves on their devices talking about their routine. They can then listen to each other's recordings and compare.

D Refer Ss to the Vocabulary Bank on page 132.

VB page 132 **VOCABULARY BANK** telling the time

Note that the Vocabulary Bank activities are an important part of the lesson. They should only be omitted if you are confident that your Ss already know this vocabulary. If you don't use the exercises in class, it would be a good idea to set them as homework.

1 A VB 4.02 | Refer Ss to the pictures of the clocks before they listen to the times. Play the recording. Then play the recording again and ask Ss to repeat after each time.

B Look at the example conversation with the class. If necessary, drill 'What's the time in … ?', 'It's …'. (You could use the clock times A–E in Ex 1A for practice.) Put Ss in pairs to practise asking and saying the times (1–8). Monitor and step in to correct where necessary.

2 A Ask Ss to choose the correct definitions for *a.m.* and *p.m.* Check the answers. Drill *a.m.* and *p.m.*

EXTRA SUPPORT: TEACHER Ss may wonder what *a.m.* and *p.m.* mean. The expressions come from the Latin, *ante* (before) and *post* (after) *meridiem* (midday). Nobody uses these full forms! *a.m.* and *p.m.* are usually lower case and can be separated by full stops (*a.m.*) or not (*am*).

ANSWERS:
1 a.m. **2** p.m.

EXTRA IDEA For extra practice and to reinforce understanding, refer Ss to the clocks in Exs 1A and 1B and ask them to work in pairs and take turns to choose a time to add *a.m.* or *p.m.* to. Their partner then says what part of the day it is in.

B Ss work alone to write times, as in the example given.

C Demonstrate the activity by asking a stronger student and writing the time they give. Then put Ss in pairs to ask and write times, as in the example given.

D Put Ss in pairs to ask and answer. Stronger classes can write more questions to ask each other.

2 Refer Ss back to page 40 and then put them in new pairs (different to those for Ex 1C) to ask and answer. Monitor and listen for language, especially telling the time. If they have done the Vocabulary Bank activities, they should now be able to give more precise times. When they have finished, hold brief class feedback.

EXTRA IDEA: DIGITAL Ss record themselves asking and answering the questions. When they have finished, they should play back their recording and listen to their pronunciation.

READING

EXTRA SUPPORT: DYSLEXIA There is a recording of the reading text available to help dyslexic learners.

3 A Tell Ss they will see the daily routine verbs they studied in a reading text. Depending on your class, you may need to explain what a YouTuber is. You could most easily show a short clip of a currently popular YouTuber and discuss what they do (make videos about their daily life that can be humorous or are of interest). Refer Ss to the photos and ask them to discuss the questions in pairs. When they have finished, elicit their answers and write them on the board. Don't confirm if they are correct. Then ask them to read and check. Elicit the answers and see who was closest in their predictions.

ANSWERS:
1 a YouTuber **2** nineteen **3** yes

B Explain that Ss will read the text again more carefully. Refer Ss to the statements and ask them to read the text to find out if they are true or false.

EXTRA SUPPORT Remind Ss when they read to mark where they find the answers in the text. Then, when you take feedback, annotate the text so they can see it. This technique aids reading skills development and is helpful to those who perhaps did not get the answers correct first time and can look over it later.

EXTRA SUPPORT: DYSLEXIA Read the statements aloud to help Ss with dyslexia identify what information they need to find in the text. They can listen again to the recording as they read.

ANSWERS:
2 F **3** T **4** T **5** T **6** F **7** F

C Put Ss in pairs to find two things that they do the same and two that are different. (e.g. 'I have breakfast.' = different from MP). When they have finished, elicit a few answers. Ask Ss if they like MP's life.

GRAMMAR

present simple: regular verbs (*he*, *she*, *it*)

4 A Explain that you will now use the reading about MP to study some grammar. Ask Ss to identify the verbs individually, then check in pairs. If necessary, you could elicit or remind Ss that verbs are action words – the first (*gets up*) has been done as an example. Check answers with the class.

EXTRA: ALTERNATIVE IDEA This task introduces positive and negative forms at the same time. With weaker classes, you could introduce just the positive form by writing the following two sentences on the board: *I go on social media for about twenty minutes. At twelve she goes to a café.* Ask Ss to identify the verb and subject and say how they are different (first person / third person) then introduce further examples from the text. Move on to the negative form separately after this.

ANSWERS:

2 loves	**4** finishes
3 goes	**5** doesn't have

B Put Ss in pairs to complete the rules, using the examples in Ex 4A to help. Check answers with the class. With weaker classes you could do this as a class.

ANSWERS:

2 es **3** doesn't

EXTRA CHALLENGE With stronger classes, you could ask Ss to suggest other verbs ending in *-sh* (e.g. *wash*, *push*). You could extend this further by asking them to suggest verbs ending in *-ch* (e.g. *watch*, *match*), *-x* (e.g. *mix*, *tax*) or *-ss* (e.g. *dress*, *guess*), all of which also follow the *-es* rule. Note, though, that these are above A1 level.

C Ask Ss to look back at the text and find eight more examples of the third person form. (They shouldn't count *has* which also occurs.) When they have finished, elicit these and drill them before highlighting them in the text.

ANSWERS:

Any eight from: talks, checks, starts, makes, gets, does, makes, thinks, writes, listens

D The Grammar Bank on page 105 can be used in the lesson or for homework. Decide how and when the exercises will benefit your class.

page 105 **GRAMMAR BANK**

This focuses on the form and use of third person verbs in the present simple, including positive and negative forms. Go through the notes as a class, with individuals reading sections out, or ask Ss to read them alone and then check understanding, especially of the use of *doesn't* in the negative form.

EXTRA SUPPORT: TEACHER At A1 level, no verbs which end in *-x* or *-ss* (e.g. *fix*, *kiss*) are taught, and so we cannot exemplify here. A fuller range is covered in A2 level, where more verbs become available. If you feel your Ss need to use or recognise such a verb, then you could add this information.

1 Look at the example, noting that the change is to make the verb third person. Ss correct the rest of the verbs alone, then check in pairs. Check answers with the class. Point out that *has* is irregular and in *looks at*, the verb is *look*, so that is where the *-s* is added. At this point you could read the text to the class for listening practice.

EXTRA SUPPORT: DYSLEXIA Provide a vertical list of the verbs separately for Ss to put into the third person form. They can then get the context through you reading the text to the class. Alternatively, you could record the text before the class for Ss to listen on their personal devices (either with the verbs in the infinitive for them to listen before they do the exercise, or in the correct form for them to listen after they have completed the task).

ANSWERS:

2 has	**3** checks	**4** answers
5 does	**6** works	**7** makes
8 chooses	**9** watches	**10** goes
11 reads	**12** looks at	

2 Read the example with the class. Ss complete the sentences individually, then compare answers in pairs. Check answers with the class.

EXTRA SUPPORT With weaker classes or if you are short of time, you could divide the exercise among the class, giving each pair a few sentences to complete. When they have finished, read the correct sentences out for them to check before going through the answers and writing them on the board.

ANSWERS:

1 *doesn't drink*, loves
2 makes, goes
3 doesn't like, has
4 understands, doesn't speak
5 doesn't eat, reads
6 works, studies
7 doesn't know, says
8 asks, listens

GB 3 **Read the example with the class. Elicit that the mistake is with the verb form. Ss work alone to find and correct the remaining mistakes (there are seven). Let them compare in pairs, then go through the answers as a class.**

EXTRA SUPPORT: DYSLEXIA To ease the load for Ss with dyslexia, you could tell them which sentences are correct so they can focus on the error correction. They need only write the correct form of the verb for each, not the whole sentence. Remind them to cover the sentences they are not working on to reduce distraction.

ANSWERS:

2 Dr Lund doesn't ~~likes~~ **like** it.
3 Rachel ~~studys~~ **studies** in the evening.
4 correct
5 My brother ~~no hates~~ **doesn't hate** cats.
6 Ms Rodriguez ~~starts work always~~ **always starts work** at eight o'clock.
7 Sam ~~never doesn't write~~ **never writes / doesn't write** emails.
8 correct
9 Mr Hart ~~think~~ **thinks** phones are bad in class.
10 My son ~~gos~~ **goes** to bed at nine o'clock.

PRONUNCIATION

third person *-s*

5 A 4.03 | Explain that the focus is on listening and pronunciation. Play the recording. Ss should write the verbs that they hear. Pairs can compare then check as a class. Write the words on the board to ensure correct spelling.

EXTRA SUPPORT: DYSLEXIA Ss can find simultaneous listening and writing a challenge. In this case you could give Ss a vertical list of the verbs with two or three distractors mixed in and they tick the ones they hear. Give them plenty of time to read the list before the activity, or you or a partner could read the list with them first to help them identify what to listen for.

ANSWERS AND AUDIOSCRIPT:

1 makes	**2** gets up	**3** writes
4 leaves	**5** goes	**6** listens
7 finishes	**8** watches	

B 4.03 | Draw attention to the three ending sounds and drill them in isolation. Point out that Ss have seen these before in relation to plurals. Play the recording again. Ss should identify the endings of the verbs that they hear. Go through the answers and add them to the board, then play the recording again for Ss to repeat.

EXTRA SUPPORT: TEACHER The focus here on the sound is quite subtle. The aim at this level is for Ss to recognise and produce /ɪz/, with /s/ and /z/ barely differentiated. If Ss have studied Sounds and Spelling 3, they will, however, be aware of voiced and unvoiced consonants. You could show (or remind) them that /s/ follows an unvoiced consonant (e.g. *makes* /ks/; *gets*, *writes* /ts/) and /z/ follows a voiced consonant (e.g. *leaves* /vz/, *listens* /nz/). You could use the same method as there (i.e. hand on throat) to help them notice the difference.

EXTRA: ALTERNATIVE IDEA With stronger classes, you could get Ss to draw a table with three columns and put each sound at the top of a column. Before they listen, they should say the words to each other in pairs and decide what the final sound is, then write the word in its column. They then listen to the recording and tick or cross if they change their mind. Finally, go through the answers.

ANSWERS:

1 /s/ **2** /s/ **3** /s/ **4** /z/ **5** /z/ **6** /z/ **7** /ɪz/ **8** /ɪz/

C Demonstrate by looking at the verb list and eliciting the start (as in the example 'MP makes videos about her life …'). Elicit some possible sentences for the next verb, *gets up*, (e.g. 'She gets up at six …') then ask pairs to continue.

EXTRA CHALLENGE Retell a typical day for MP across the class, with individuals taking turns. This gives an opportunity to assess and drill again. Then put Ss in pairs to retell it at their own pace.

SPEAKING

6 A Tell Ss they will now talk about their routine. Refer Ss to the table and give them time to read it through. Explain that Ss need to find people who answer *yes* to the questions. Demonstrate the start of the activity with a stronger student by asking them 'Do you get up at eight?' If the student says 'no', then ask the same question to another until you hear the answer 'yes'. Only then should you write the name. Once this is clear, ask Ss to start. Monitor while they do the activity and check they are asking questions correctly. Make notes on any common errors or examples of good language use for later class feedback.

EXTRA SUPPORT Some Ss will tend to read the words from the table, but they need to use a question form starting with *Do … ?* If your class is weaker, get them to write the beginning of the questions at the side before they start this activity.

B **Once they have completed the survey and got names for all questions, put Ss in pairs to compare answers and add their own information. Look at the example and encourage stronger classes to use *and* where they are the same and *but* where they differ. When they have finished, ask a few pairs to report back to the class.**

TO FINISH

Write on the board: *What do you like about MP's day and what don't you like? Why?* Put Ss in pairs to discuss the questions. Take whole class feedback to see what Ss think about the YouTuber's lifestyle.

HOW TO ... | order in a café
VOCABULARY | café words
PRONUNCIATION | intonation in *or* phrases

LESSON OVERVIEW

In this lesson, Ss learn functional language for ordering in a café. They start with vocabulary related to café items. The context is a listening where they hear conversations about ordering such food. Ss then learn phrases for ordering in a café and focus on intonation in *or* phrases. The lesson ends with a speaking activity where Ss roleplay a conversation asking for food and drink in a café.

Online Teaching

If you're teaching this lesson online, you might find the following tips useful:

- **Ex 1A:** In the main room, cameras on, Ss ask across the class and listen to each other's answers. Then put them in breakout rooms for further practice.
- **Ex 3B:** Show the conversations on your device and share your screen. Ask Ss to annotate the correct answers, then play the recording for them to check in Ex 3C.
- **Ex 6A:** Ss could share their browsers, showing menus from local cafés to choose from.

Additional Materials

For Teachers:
Presentation Tool Lesson 4C
Photocopiable Activity 4C
Grammar Bank 4C
Vocabulary Bank 4C

For Students:
Online Practice 4C
Workbook 4C

TO START

Write the following questions on the board: *Do you have coffee/breakfast/lunch/dinner out or at home? Why?* Tell the class your answers (e.g. 'I usually have breakfast or coffee in a café, but I have dinner at home because I like dinner with my family.'), then put Ss in small groups to discuss the questions.

EXTRA SUPPORT: DYSLEXIA Dyslexic learners in particular benefit from understanding exactly what they are learning in a lesson so that they understand what they are working towards. In this and every lesson, explain clearly what the learning objectives of the lesson are near the start.

VOCABULARY

café words

1 A Look at the photo and read the questions with the class. If *coffee bar* or *coffee shop* is used more commonly than *café* in your situation, you could use this alternative form during the lesson. Ss discuss in pairs. When they have finished, ask different pairs around the class for their answers.

EXTRA IDEA If you prefer, you could first focus on pronunciation of the questions. Before they ask, Ss identify the stressed words. Check the answers as a class and drill. Then they ask each other with improved confidence.

ANSWERS:

1 Do you like the food in the photo?
2 Do you often go to cafés?
3 When do you go, in the morning or afternoon?
4 What's your favourite café?
5 What do you eat and drink there?

EXTRA IDEA: DIGITAL Ss use their devices to audio/video record themselves asking the questions in an interview vox-pop style to check their pronunciation and stress.

B Refer Ss to the words in the box and ask them to see which things they can find in the main photo, then compare answers in pairs. Check answers with the class.

ANSWERS:
cup, fork, pastry, sugar, toast

EXTRA IDEA Fast finishers can name more things in the photo, using their device or dictionary if needed.

C Refer Ss to the Vocabulary Bank on page 132.

VB page 132 **VOCABULARY BANK** café words

Note that the Vocabulary Bank activities are an important part of the lesson. They should only be omitted if you are confident that your Ss already know this vocabulary. If you don't use the exercises in class, it would be a good idea to set them as homework.

1 A Ss match the words (1–12) with the items (A–L) individually, then check in pairs. Go through the answers, drilling chorally.

ANSWERS:
1 E **2** C **3** F **4** H **5** A **6** B
7 D **8** G **9** L **10** K **11** J **12** I

B VB4.03 | Refer Ss to the photos (not the words) and ask them to listen and repeat.

C Refer Ss to the photos and give an example (e.g. 'I always have a spoon, a bowl and a cup on my table at breakfast. I have napkins, but I don't often use them. I have most of the other things at home, but I don't have any chopsticks.'). Ask them to discuss the questions in pairs. When they have finished, ask a few pairs to tell the class about their home.

EXTRA IDEA Encourage Ss to add new words as they come across them to individual pages or sections organised by topic (e.g. 'food') in their notebooks and draw or find a picture to illustrate each word.

2 A Ss match the phrases (1–8) with the pictures (A–H) individually, then check in pairs. Go through the answers, drilling the phrases.

ANSWERS:
1 C **2** F **3** E **4** B **5** G **6** A **7** D **8** H

B Put Ss in A/B pairs and ask a stronger pair to read the example. Teach and drill the phrase *Here you are.* by gesturing as you say it. Tell Student As they should order and Student Bs should point at the menu items as they 'give' them, saying *Here you are.* Move around the class and listen. Then tell them to change roles. When they have finished, give some feedback and drill problem words.

EXTRA: ALTERNATIVE IDEA If you have access to picture cards, pairs of Ss can be given a range to order from. When Student A chooses, Student B can give them the picture card as they say *Here you are.* Rotate the sets of picture cards so Ss can practise different vocabulary.

How to ...

order in a café

3 A 4.04 | Explain that Ss will now hear people ordering things from the menu in Ex 2A. Tell them they need to write the conversation number (1–3) with the food and drink (A–H). Then play the recording. Tell them the conversations can be about more than one of the pictures. Ask Ss to compare in pairs, then check answers with the class.

ANSWERS:
1 E **2** A **3** B, H

AUDIOSCRIPT 4.04

W = waiter C = customer

Conversation 1

W: Can I help you?
C: Yes. Can I have a coffee, please?
W: With milk and sugar?
C: Just milk, thank you.
W: OK, a coffee with milk. Here you go.
C: How much is that?
W: That's three pounds.
C: Thanks.

Conversation 2

C: Hi.
W: Hi.
C: Can I have a tea and a pastry, please?
W: Yes, just a moment. Here you are.
C: Thank you. Oh, can I have a fork, please?
W: It's on the table.
C: Oh yes. Thank you.
W: Anything else?
C: No, thank you. How much is that?
W: Erm, that's four pounds eighty.
C: Four pounds eighty.
W: Thank you.

Conversation 3

C: Excuse me. What's the breakfast special today?
W: The breakfast specials are here, on the menu.
C: OK … So a sandwich and a coffee is five pounds fifty?
W: Yes, a sandwich and a coffee … or a tea.
C: Great. Can I have the sandwich breakfast special, please?
W: Coffee or tea?
C: Coffee, please.
W: Coffee. Anything else?
C: Oh, can I have a mineral water, please?
W: Still or sparkling?
C: Oh, sparkling, please. How much is that?
W: Just a moment. Let me check. One sandwich breakfast special with a coffee, and a sparkling mineral water.
C: Yes.
W: That's … seven pounds fifty.

B Refer Ss to the conversations to choose the correct phrases from what they can remember from the listening. Pairs can compare answers. Don't give any answers yet.

C 4.05 | Play the recording for Ss to listen and check their answers. Check answers with the class and write them on the board. Drill key phrases.

EXTRA SUPPORT: TEACHER Ss may want to know the meaning of specific words such as 'let' in *Let me check.* or 'else' in *Anything else?* Explain that these are to be learnt as phrases and drill them that way. Seen in context, the meaning is clear.

ANSWERS:

1 Can I	**2** please	**3** you
4 How	**5** That's	**6** moment
7 are	**8** Anything	**9** thank
10 or	**11** that	**12** check

EXTRA IDEA Put Ss in pairs to roleplay the conversations, reading them and then remembering as much as they can. When they have finished, ask a few pairs to perform their roleplays to the class. After this, you may want to play the recording again for Ss to compare.

EXTRA IDEA: DIGITAL Ask Ss to record their conversations. They can then use these to compare against the original recording for homework.

4A Ask Ss to complete the table using the conversations they just heard to help them. With weaker classes, you could do this together. When they have finished, check answers with the class.

ANSWERS:

1 Can **2** or **3** please

B The Grammar Bank on page 106 can be used in the lesson or for homework. Decide how and when the exercises will benefit your class.

page 106 **GRAMMAR BANK** **GB**

This focuses on the form and use of phrases for ordering in a café. Go through the notes with the class, especially the pronunciation and use of fixed expressions such as *Here you are.*

1 This exercise focuses on the correct form of the phrases. Remind Ss how the capital letters and final punctuation can help them with word order. Ss order the phrases alone, then check in pairs. Check answers with the class and write them on the board (or invite different Ss to come up and do so).

EXTRA SUPPORT: DYSLEXIA You could make this reordering exercise more manageable for Ss with dyslexia by giving them the first and last word, or just the first word, in each case.

GB

ANSWERS:
2 How much is it?
3 It's one pound fifty.
4 Just a moment.
5 Here you go.
6 Can we have four pastries, please?
7 Let me check.
8 Here you are.

2 **This focuses on correct use of phrases for ordering in a conversation. Ss complete the conversation alone, then check in pairs. Check answers with the class.**

EXTRA SUPPORT: DYSLEXIA As gap-filling can be hard for Ss with dyslexia, remove the two extra words (*much* and *no*). You could have the remaining words on slips of paper for Ss to try in the gaps before deciding or provide them as a vertical list that Ss can move up and down the sentences to find the right words.

ANSWERS:

1 help	**2** can	**3** please
4 or	**5** else	**6** we
7 cold	**8** that	**9** a
10 That's		

3 **This exercise extends practice of phrases for ordering. Ss complete the conversations alone, using the initial letters to help, then check in pairs. Check answers with the class.**

EXTRA SUPPORT: DYSLEXIA Provide a vertical list of the words needed for Ss to fit into each of the conversations.

ANSWERS:
2 knife
3 fork
4 Just
5 mineral
6 sparkling
7 me
8 Here
9 much
10 euros (*euro* is also possible as a plural)
11 or
12 pastry

EXTRA CHALLENGE Read the conversations to the class as a dictogloss dictation. Ss listen and write, then work together to complete the conversations before listening again. This integrates intensive listening practice.

PRONUNCIATION

intonation in *or* phrases

5A **4.06 | Focus attention on where the arrow rises or falls in the questions. Ss listen and tick the intonation they hear. Check the answer with the class before asking Ss to repeat chorally.**

ANSWER:
2

EXTRA SUPPORT To encourage movement in the voice, use your hand to show how the voice goes up or down. You could also stand up and sit down or raise your eyebrows.

B **Look at the example and ask a strong pair to read it to the class, encouraging them to use the correct intonation, especially a rise–fall intonation for 'Apple or orange?'. Then put Ss in pairs to ask and answer questions in the same way. Remind them to include *or* between the two words and say the alternatives with a rise–fall intonation.**

EXTRA CHALLENGE If you have a strong class, you might offer additional pairs for them to use, e.g. *regular/decaf*, *eat-in/takeaway*, *large/small*, *white/brown* (bread), etc.

SPEAKING

6A **Put Ss in A/B pairs and refer them to the relevant pages. Remind them not to show each other their information. Give Ss time to read their information and ask you any questions they have. When they have read their role, demonstrate the activity with a stronger student, then ask them to start.**

EXTRA SUPPORT: TEACHER With activities of this type, it's worth asking a few check questions when you set the activity up so that it runs smoothly, e.g. 'Who is the customer, Student A or Student B?' (A), 'Who speaks first?' (B), 'What do they say?' (Can I help you?), 'Are you talking or writing?' (talking), etc. Get a stronger pair to demonstrate to reinforce the instruction.

EXTRA SUPPORT With weaker classes, put Ss in A/A and B/B pairs to prepare their role and practise, then re-pair them in A/B pairs for the roleplay.

B **Pause the roleplay and refer Ss to their relevant instructions. Remind weaker classes of the phrase, *Can I have a ..., please?* before the singular nouns (e.g. 'Can I have a spoon, please?'), and *some* before *sugar*, *salt* and *pepper*. Ss then continue with the roleplay.**

c **When Ss are ready, ask them to change roles and refer the new customers (Student Bs) back to page 43, and the new waiters (Student As) to page 145. Repeat the clarifying instructions as needed (see Extra Support: Teacher, above). Ss then work through the exercises again in their new roles. Move around the class and listen for errors and examples of good language to use in feedback. When they have finished, ask Ss if they liked being a waiter or a customer more.**

EXTRA: HOW TO ... Ss work in their pairs to agree on and write out a similar conversation. They then hold the conversation, trying not to look at their scripts or the prompts. They can use the menu from earlier in the lesson.

You can either extend this or increase the challenge by having Ss as customers order for more than one person, e.g. themselves and one other person. They could also ask for more things from the Vocabulary Bank.

TO FINISH

Tell the class about your favourite café, when you go there and why you like it, e.g. 'My favourite café is called Margaux. I like going there for breakfast. The coffee is very good.' Put Ss in pairs to share similar information about their favourite café and say what they like about it. Refer Ss to the Vocabulary Bank for ideas.

EXTRA IDEA: SPEAK ANYWHERE Encourage Ss to practise using the Speak Anywhere interactive roleplay.

4D BBC Documentary

Earth From Space

GRAMMAR | present simple: *yes/no* questions (*he, she, it*)
SPEAKING | ask about someone's routine
WRITING | write a quiz

LESSON OVERVIEW

In this lesson, Ss learn more about the form and use of the present simple, third person. The context is a video clip of the Earth from space. Ss learn present simple question forms and short answers and then do a speaking activity where they practise asking about someone's routine. The lesson ends with a writing activity where Ss write a quiz.

Online Teaching

If you're teaching this lesson online, you might find the following tips useful:

- **Ex 2C:** Share your screen and enable the annotation tool for Ss to complete the sentences.
- **Ex 2B:** Sometimes videos can be a little slow or jumpy when streamed in an online class environment. If you know this is an issue for you, give Ss time to watch the video on their own device before moving on.
- **Exs 4B and 4C:** Remind Ss to mute their microphones while they listen.
- **Ex 5:** Ss complete this activity in breakout rooms. Try to visit each breakout room briefly to listen in.

Additional Materials

For Teachers:
Presentation Tool Lesson 4D
Online Digital Resources
Grammar Bank 4D
Videoscript 4D: BBC Documentary

For Students:
Online Practice 4D
Workbook 4D

TO START

Show a picture of the Earth and ask Ss to identify what they can see. Teach *the Earth* and *space*. Tell Ss today's lesson is about different places on Earth.

EXTRA SUPPORT: DYSLEXIA Dyslexic learners in particular benefit from understanding exactly what they are learning in a lesson so that they understand what they are working towards. In this and every lesson, explain clearly what the learning objectives of the lesson are near the start.

EXTRA SUPPORT There are some unusual new words in the lesson that you could preteach, using pictures. These include *parakeet* and *manatee*, which could be introduced in Ex 1A, and *tower* and *firefighter*.

PREVIEW

1 A Put Ss in pairs to discuss the questions. Ss may not know animal names, so move around and help where necessary. When they have finished, briefly discuss which animals are popular with the class.

B Refer Ss to the BBC programme information. Put them in pairs to read it, then discuss and answer the questions. When they have finished, go through the answers. If Ss ask, explain that a fire lookout (or firewatcher) is a job where a person in a remote area looks for signs of the start of wildfires to inform firefighters. They usually do this from a high place, like a mountain or tower, with a good view of surrounding areas.

EXTRA SUPPORT: DYSLEXIA Read the text aloud, or have another student read it out to support dyslexic learners while they read.

ANSWERS:

1 A a village in Peru	**2** A Elvira
B Colorado, USA	B Billy Ellis
C a big city in India	C Joseph Sekar

VIEW

2 A Refer Ss to the words in the box. Use pictures to teach and check the meanings. Explain that they should connect them to each of the parts of the programme (1–3). Ask Ss to write the words beside the numbers in their notebooks. Don't go through the answers yet.

EXTRA SUPPORT Turn on the subtitles if you feel it would benefit learners.

B ▶ Ss watch the video clip and check their answers in pairs. Then check answers with the whole class.

ANSWERS:
1 breakfast, rice **2** forest, steps **3** lake, rivers

C ▶ Refer Ss to the sentences, which come from the video clip. Explain that they should complete them with the correct form of the verbs in the box. Ask Ss to work alone, then compare in pairs. Play the video clip, pausing as needed, then ask pairs to compare again before going through the answers.

EXTRA SUPPORT With weaker or less confident classes, discuss why the *-s* is added in the example (third person verb – *he*). Remind Ss that some verb endings change in the third person, for example *watch, watches* and elicit the third person form and its spelling for each of the verbs in the box, writing these on the board.

EXTRA SUPPORT: DYSLEXIA Supply Ss with a vertical list of the missing verbs in the box to hold alongside the exercise and reduce the distance between the gaps and the words. Remind Ss to mask the sentences they are not working on to focus their attention.

ANSWERS:

2 come	**3** get up	**4** watches
5 sees	**6** live	**7** says

D Put Ss in pairs to discuss. When they have finished, have a show of hands to see which story they like best.

GRAMMAR

present simple: *yes/no* questions (*he, she, it*)

3 A Ask Ss to read the three question forms alone and decide which is correct, then check in pairs. If you're short of time, you could do this exercise together as a class. Check answers with the class. Remind Ss how questions are formed for other subjects with *do*.

ANSWER:
b

EXTRA SUPPORT: TEACHER Sounds and Spelling 4 focuses on the weak and strong pronunciation of *does*.

B The Grammar Bank on page 107 can be used in the lesson or for homework. Decide how and when the exercises will benefit your class.

GB page 107 **GRAMMAR BANK**

Check understanding of the notes with the class, and especially focus on the movement of *-s* in the positive form to *does* in the question form.

1 **This exercise focuses on form. Look at the first answer, done as an example, with the class and point out the capital letter to start and the question mark to end. Then ask Ss to order the rest of the questions individually and then check in pairs. Check answers with the class and write them on the board. Remind Ss that a capital letter is required to start a question or a sentence as well as with names, nationalities, languages, etc.**

EXTRA SUPPORT: DYSLEXIA Provide dyslexic learners with the correctly formed questions, with one or two key words (e.g. *does* / main verb) gapped.

ANSWERS:

2 Does Megan like pastries?
3 Does Mrs Wood speak Italian?
4 Does Julia often write to you?
5 Does Mr Baker have any children?
6 Matt, does your phone have a good camera?
7 Liz, does your mother live with you?
8 Tessa, does the lesson start at nine?

2 **Ss match the answers with the correct questions in Ex 1 in pairs. They should ignore the gaps in the first part for the moment. Check answers with the class. Ask pairs to read out the questions and answers across the class.**

EXTRA SUPPORT: DYSLEXIA Provide dyslexic learners with the answers cut up, so they can place them beside the completed questions. (Include the line to write the short answer as they will need this for Ex 3.) Remind Ss to cover the sentences they are not working on to reduce distraction.

ANSWERS:

b 4 **c** 8 **d** 1 **e** 3 **f** 6 **g** 7 **h** 2

3 **Look at the example as a class. Point out the tick for positive and elicit the negative short answer. Add this to the board. Remind Ss they need to change the form according to the subject (given at the start of the second sentence in each answer). Ss write the short answers. Ask them to compare their answers in pairs then go through the answers as a class.**

ANSWERS:

b Yes, she does.
c No, it doesn't.
d Yes, he does.
e No, she doesn't.
f Yes, it does.
g No, she doesn't.
h Yes, she does.

EXTRA IDEA Ss practise the questions and short and extended answers in pairs, taking turns at both roles.

4 **This exercise practises form. Ss complete the questions individually, then compare in pairs. Check answers with the class.**

EXTRA SUPPORT: DYSLEXIA Provide dyslexic learners with two alternatives for each gap, one correct and one distractor.

ANSWERS:

2 Do **3** Is **4** Does **5** Do
6 Are **7** Does **8** Is

5 **This exercise builds on Ex 4. Look at the example and point out the verb change and addition of *a*. Ss write the conversations individually, then compare in pairs. Check answers with the class. Ask pairs to practise the conversations.**

EXTRA SUPPORT: DYSLEXIA Provide dyslexic learners with the completed conversations with a reduced number of gaps to complete (e.g. you could provide all of B's part of the conversations and include one gap in each of A's lines). Provide the words for the gaps in a vertical list if needed.

ANSWERS:

1 B: No, he isn't. He's a businessman.
A: Does he like his job?
B: No, he doesn't.
A: Does he work in the city?
B: Yes, he does.
A: Is he married?
B: No, he isn't.

2 A: Are your Chinese classes good?
B: Yes, they are.
A: Does your teacher speak English?
B: Yes, she does, but she never speaks English in class.
A: Is Chinese easy?
B: No, it isn't, but I love it!
A: Do you understand everything in class?
B: Yes, I do, but I don't understand films in Chinese.

SPEAKING

ask about someone's routine

4A **Ask a pair of stronger Ss to read the conversation aloud, then ask pairs to discuss who the person is, of the three seen in the video clip. Elicit the answer.**

ANSWER:
Elvira

B **4.07 | Refer Ss to page 125, where they can see a range of jobs. Ask them to listen and identify the job along with the speaker who is guessing. Play the recording again and ask Ss to compare answers. Play the recording once more if needed, then check the answer.**

ANSWER:
police officer

AUDIOSCRIPT 4.07

A: OK, ask me questions.
B: Let me see. OK, is it a man or a woman?
A: A woman. And now it's easy for you.
B: Not so easy. Does she work in a hospital?
A: No, she doesn't.
B: Does she work outdoors?
A: Yes, sometimes.
B: Does she drive in her job?
A: Yes, she does.
B: OK, she doesn't work in a hospital, so she isn't a nurse. She sometimes works outdoors and she drives in her job.
A: So, who is it?
B: Hmm. The bus driver in the photo is a man, so I think she's the police officer.
A: You're right. Now it's my turn.

C **4.07 | Refer Ss to the Key phrases and read them with the class. Check Ss understand the word *guess* (= to give your idea, e.g. 'How old is he?', 'You can guess.', 'Twenty-five? Thirty?'). Play the recording again and ask Ss to identify the Key phrases they hear. Ask Ss to compare their answers then play the recording again. Go through the answers and drill any phrases that Ss are unsure of.**

EXTRA IDEA Provide the phrases on slips of paper. Ss should select the ones they hear and move them to one side.

ANSWERS:
All the phrases are used, except: 'Does she wear special clothes in her job?' and 'You're wrong. Guess again.'

5 **Put Ss in A/B pairs. Read the instruction with the class and refer Ss to the relevant pages. Ask Ss to look at the question prompts. Point out that they need to form questions and need to ask three different questions before they can guess. Ask a stronger A/B pair to demonstrate the activity and include some of the Key phrases, then pairs do the task. Move around the class and check Ss are forming third person questions correctly. When they have finished, ask them to change roles. Stronger pairs can do more than one turn or re-pair with a new partner.**

EXTRA: ALTERNATIVE IDEA With lively classes, you could turn this into a team guessing game where each team chooses a job and another team has ten questions to guess the job. There could be a *yes/no* answer rule.

WRITING

write a quiz

6A **Explain that a *quiz* is some questions that you ask someone, often for fun, to find out how many they can answer correctly. Focus attention on the quiz, then ask Ss to read and choose answers in pairs. Give them a few minutes. Don't go through the answers yet.**

B **Ask Ss to turn to the videoscript on page 173 to check their answers. Go through the answers as a class. Ask if any pairs got them all right.**

ANSWERS:
1 b **2** b **3** c

C **Ask Ss to use the information in the videoscript to write quiz questions and multiple-choice answers about Billy and Elvira as in the example quiz in Ex 6A. They should try to write three for each person. Move around and help, making sure Ss are forming questions correctly.**

EXTRA IDEA: DIGITAL Ss could record their quiz questions to play them to another pair.

D **When they have finished, ask Ss to exchange questions with another pair who should complete their answers.**

EXTRA IDEA: DIGITAL Ask Ss to share their quizzes online, in a collaborative document or a webpage.

TO FINISH

Put Ss in new pairs to ask and answer questions about the routine of someone important in their life (e.g. a member of their family or a friend). You could start them off by eliciting and writing some questions on the board, e.g. *What time does he/she get up?*

4 REVIEW

LESSON OVERVIEW

This lesson is a review of the language – both grammar and vocabulary – presented in this unit. It also includes a link to the Sounds and Spelling section for this unit, which focuses on short vowels: /e/, /æ/, /ʌ/; and the pronunciation of *does* as /dʌz/ or /dəz/. The notes below assume that the tasks are completed in class. However, the self-study type exercises (i.e. Exs 1A, 1B, 2A, 3A, 3B, 4A and 6A) could be done out of class and then checked in the following lesson when the communicative tasks are then completed.

Online Teaching

If you're teaching this lesson online, you might find the following tips useful:

- **Ex 1A:** In feedback, share your screen and when checking answers ask Ss to annotate.
- **Ex 1B:** Ss write their sentences in the chat, so they can compare ideas in Ex 1C.

Additional Materials

For Teachers:

Sounds and Spelling 4

Unit Test in test package

TO START

Ask Ss to work in pairs and try to remember what language they studied in Unit 4 (Grammar: adverbs of frequency, present simple: regular verbs (*he, she, it*), present simple: *yes/no* questions (*he, she, it*); Vocabulary: food and drink, everyday activities, telling the time, café words; How to … order in a café). Ask them to look at the unit lesson headings to check their ideas.

GRAMMAR

1 A Ask Ss to work alone and number the adverbs, starting with *never* = 1. Check answers with the class and write them on the board in order (or invite different Ss to come up and do so).

ANSWERS:

a 6 **b** 1 **c** 2 **d** 4 **e** 3 **f** 5

EXTRA SUPPORT: TEACHER There are several stages to Exs 1B, 1C and 1D. Think about when and whether you ask Ss to write as this decision makes the activity longer/shorter. Weaker classes may want to write, but it could be overlong if you allow this at every step. Make it clear when you instruct what Ss should do so that all are working at the same pace.

B Give an example yourself (e.g. 'I sometimes go to a café for lunch.') and elicit or remind Ss that the adverb goes between the subject and the main verb, then Ss add adverbs of frequency to make true sentences about themselves. They don't need to write the sentences in full.

C Ss discuss the questions in pairs and write their partner's answers. Again they don't have to write full sentences, they could just note the adverb.

D Re-pair Ss to tell each other their partner's answers. Elicit an example to show that they need to use a third person verb here (e.g. 'Marisa never goes to a café for lunch.'). In feedback, ask them to tell the class how similar their two partners were.

2 A Demonstrate the activity by sharing some of your own answers with the class and writing the notes on the board (e.g. 3 *Maria – cheese, cola, the news*). Ask Ss to work alone and make their notes. Move around the room as you may need to help with vocabulary.

B Put Ss in pairs. Demonstrate the activity by asking questions to a stronger student. Remind weaker classes of the short answers (*Yes, he/she/it does. / No, he/she/it doesn't.*). Pairs take turns to ask and answer. When they have finished, ask a few pairs to report back briefly on what they learnt.

VOCABULARY

3 A Read the example with the class, then ask Ss to add the missing letters alone. Make sure Ss understand the missing letters are both vowels and consonants and there is one missing letter in each word. When they have finished, ask pairs to compare, then go through the answers.

EXTRA SUPPORT This activity may be challenging for Ss with beginner literacy and dyslexia as they can tend to miss small sounds in words or not see letters. You could provide two words – one spelt correctly and the other not, (e.g. *chiken, chicken*) for Ss to choose from.

ANSWERS:

2 mush**r**oom	**3** sal**t**	**4** **k**nife
5 chi**c**ken	**6** or**a**nge	**7** pep**p**er
8 fo**r**k	**9** me**a**t	**10** bre**a**d
11 sug**a**r	**12** **s**poon	

B Explain that Ss should write the words according to their own tastes and habits. There are no correct answers. Refer weaker classes to page 131 for ideas. Move around the class and help. Stronger classes may ask you for vocabulary. Ss should not share their answers yet.

EXTRA IDEA There are no correct answers here. To provide a goal, you could ask Ss to find three things in common with their partner while doing Ex 3C.

C **Read the example with the class and demonstrate the activity with a stronger student. Ss work in pairs to take turns guessing. Monitor and listen to Ss' pronunciation. When they have finished, give feedback on any words they had trouble with.**

4A **Look at the word webs as a class and show how they work by looking at the example and then eliciting the answer for 2 and writing it on the board. Ss complete the rest of the word webs individually then check in pairs. Check answers with the class.**

EXTRA SUPPORT: DYSLEXIA Word webs can be problematic for Ss with dyslexia to process. In addition, the initial letters as prompts may be confusing. Provide Ss with a version of the word webs organised so that they read in the correct order, i.e. *2 _____ home*, with the spaces for the verbs to the left and the words/ phrases they collocate with to the right. Leave out the initial letters in the places for the verbs and provide a vertical list of the complete verbs. Ss should decide which verbs go with the words. Their answers may be in a different order to the key.

ANSWERS:

2 get	**3** go	**4** start
5 finish	**6** make	**7** have

EXTRA CHALLENGE Stronger classes can add more words to each word web (e.g. stay at / go home, like/enjoy/hate work; eat/start/finish breakfast).

B **Read the example with the class, then demonstrate by saying three more phrases and asking Ss to put them in order (e.g. *have dinner, start work, get home*). Point out that answers can vary. Ask Ss to continue in pairs, taking turns. (Younger classes or Ss can substitute 'work' with 'school' if it is more relevant for them.)**

EXTRA: ALTERNATIVE IDEA Stronger classes can report back on their partner using third person verb forms. You could introduce *then* to sequence the sentence, e.g. 'Jack makes breakfast, has breakfast, then goes to work.'

5A **Ask Ss to say the words and phrases in pairs and decide on the sound. Don't expect them to be perfect at this point, it's mainly to get them thinking about and trying sounds. The answers below are for the teacher's benefit and we don't expect Ss to be able to write the phonetic symbols.**

ANSWERS:

apple /æ/ napkin /æ/ lunch /ʌ/ money /ʌ/
breakfast /e/ red /e/ Does he understand? /ə/
Yes, he does. /ʌ/

B **Refer Ss to Sounds and Spelling on page 154.**

page 154 **SOUNDS AND SPELLING**
short vowels: /e/, /æ/, /ʌ/; *does*: /dʌz/ or /dəz/?

The Sounds and Spelling section can be used to help with particular problems. You might want to select the sections or even particular sounds that are most useful for your Ss. The vocabulary used in each section comes from the current unit or previous units.

SOUNDS AND SPELLING TEACHER'S NOTES page 210

6A **Refer Ss to the text and ask them to complete the words. If you are short of time, ask half the class to do half the words each, then help each other. Put Ss in pairs to compare answers.**

EXTRA SUPPORT: DYSLEXIA Incomplete words can present a challenge for Ss with dyslexia. It might be better for Ss to be provided with two completed alternatives for each of the gaps. You could also reduce the number of gaps.

B **R4.01 | Play the recording for Ss to listen and check. Ask individuals to read sections aloud, then write the answers on the board so they can check their spelling.**

ANSWERS:

1 banana	**2** eggs	**3** fruit
4 half	**5** bowl	**6** cereal
7 sandwich	**8** pasta	**9** quarter
10 steak	**11** rice	**12** cheese
13 vegetables	**14** potato	**15** carrots
16 tomatoes		

EXTRA IDEA When you have corrected the text, Ss read it aloud to each other. Paired reading is useful practice for beginner literacy Ss as well as a confidence builder.

TO FINISH

Ask Ss to reflect on their learning in this unit. They should write an exit slip – you can give them a piece of paper for this – with one thing they learnt, one thing they want to practise more and (optional) a question. This reflective practice can be useful at the end of individual lessons as well as units.

5 action

GSE LEARNING OBJECTIVES

5A Good colleagues

- READING | Read about a good colleague: common verbs (1)
- Talk about people: object pronouns
- Pronunciation: linking with object pronouns
- Write about a good friend; use pronouns

GSE INFORMATION

VOCABULARY

10–29 Can use language related to work activities.

READING

29 Can understand basic factual statements relating to pictures or simple texts.

29 Can understand simple phrases related to familiar, everyday activities.

GRAMMAR

27 Can use personal pronouns as objects and complements.

SPEAKING

28 Can ask and answer simple questions about people they know in a limited way.

WRITING

30 Can write simple sentences about what they and other people do.

5B Yes, I can!

- LISTENING | Listen to everyday conversations: verbs of ability
- Do a quiz and talk about your abilities: *can* for ability
- Pronunciation: *can*: weak and strong forms

GSE INFORMATION

VOCABULARY

10–29 Can use language related to aptitude, ability, knowledge, and skills.

LISTENING

24 Can distinguish between 'can' and 'can't'.

29 Can understand what people say they can or can't do from simple sentences spoken slowly and clearly.

GRAMMAR

29 Can use 'can' to refer to ability in the present.

SPEAKING

27 Can express ability or lack of ability with regard to basic activities using 'can' or 'can't'.

5C Can you help me?

- HOW TO … | make requests and offers: common adjectives (2)
- Pronunciation: weak forms: *could you*

GSE INFORMATION

VOCABULARY

10–29 Can use language related to describing something's quality.

HOW TO …

29 Can follow simple, everyday transactions (e.g. shopping and eating out) if carried out slowly and clearly.

26 Can recognise words and simple phrases related to familiar topics, if spoken slowly and clearly and supported by pictures.

SPEAKING

32 Can make offers using basic fixed expressions.

27 Can accept offers using basic fixed expressions.

27 Can ask for help using basic fixed expressions.

28 Can ask people for things and give people things.

5D Birthday!

- BBC STREET INTERVIEWS | Understand street interviews about birthdays: months
- Talk about your birthday: ordinal numbers; dates
- Write about your birthday

GSE INFORMATION

PREVIEW

10–29 Can use language related to point or period of time.

VIEW

35 Can understand short, basic descriptions of familiar topics and situations, if delivered slowly and clearly.

GRAMMAR

28 Can give dates (e.g. their date of birth) using ordinal numbers in the form day-month-year or month-day-year.

SPEAKING

24 Can give dates using standard formats (day and month).

29 Can answer simple questions about habits and routines.

WRITING

28 Can write dates using both digits and words.

28 Can write simple sentences about their life and routines.

For full coverage of GSE Learning Objectives go to page 222.

BBC VLOGS

This is a short activity that can be used as an introduction to the unit topic and a warm-up to Lesson 5A. It shouldn't be exploited or taught at length, just played once or twice in class.

Put Ss in pairs to tell each other about their jobs (or family members' jobs if they are not working). Help with vocabulary as needed. When they have finished, ask a few Ss for their answers and have a brief class discussion before they watch the video. At this point you may also want to preteach *work from home*, *stay-at-home mum* and *BBC* (British Broadcasting Corporation) as these are in the video. When they are ready, play the video for Ss to answer the question. Ask a few Ss for their answer and see if others agree.

ANSWER:
Two speakers work for the BBC.

EXTRA SUPPORT: TEACHER If Ss ask about it, you can tell them that the BBC is the national broadcaster of the UK. It provides television, radio and online content and services, including entertainment, news and education.

EXTRA CHALLENGE If Ss want to watch the video again outside class, you could ask them to note how many people say they are students (three) or make a list of other jobs that they hear. You may also want to exploit the video further, focusing on individual jobs, for example by doing an ordering exercise. You would need to give the jobs, listed here (currently in order) for Ss to order as they watch: *student doctor, work in IT, teacher, news reporter, stay-at-home mum, student, teacher and student, journalist*.

NOTE The vlogs have been provided by people from around the world in response to the same question. The video content was filmed by them on their own mobile phones, so the picture quality varies considerably and in some cases is of a lower quality. However, this adds to the authenticity of the content.

The locations labelled on the vlogs show where the speaker was when they filmed the video. It does not reflect where the speaker comes from (necessarily).

As many of the speakers are non-native, the videos expose Ss to a range of different accents and varieties of English. This could be used as a way to highlight interesting or useful differences.

Additional Materials

For Teachers:

Presentation Tool Unit 5

Online Digital Resources

Videoscript Unit 5 Opener: BBC Vlogs

5A Good colleagues

GRAMMAR | object pronouns

VOCABULARY | common verbs (1)

PRONUNCIATION | linking with object pronouns

LESSON OVERVIEW

In this lesson, Ss learn some common verbs. The context is a reading where Ss read about what makes a good colleague. This then leads to a focus on object pronouns. Ss also practise the pronunciation of object pronouns when they link to verbs in a sentence. Ss then practise speaking by asking and answering about different people in their lives. The lesson ends with a writing activity where Ss write about a good friend using the pronouns and vocabulary from this lesson.

Online Teaching

If you're teaching this lesson online, you might find the following tips useful:

- **Ex 1A:** Ss write their answers to the questions in the chat for others to see before having a whole class discussion.
- **Exs 3A and 3B:** Put Ss in breakout rooms, Student As together and Student Bs together, to read and discuss, then regroup them for Exs 3C and 3D.
- **Ex 4B:** Share your screen and enable annotations so that Ss can add their answers.

Additional Materials

For Teachers:

Presentation Tool Lesson 5A

Photocopiable Activities 5A

Grammar Bank 5A

Writing Bank 5A

For Students:

Online Practice 5A

Workbook 5A

TO START

Write on the board: *family, friends, classmates* and *colleagues*. Check Ss understand the words *classmate* (someone you are in class with) and *colleague* (someone you work with). Ask Ss to discuss the question: *Who do you talk to about the following: money, problems, work, relationships?* in small groups. Give an example yourself, e.g. 'I talk to my mum about work. I don't talk to her about money.' When they have finished, discuss answers with the class to see if there are similarities.

EXTRA SUPPORT: DYSLEXIA Dyslexic learners in particular benefit from understanding exactly what they are learning in a lesson so that they understand what they are working towards. In this and every lesson, explain clearly what the learning objectives of the lesson are near the start.

VOCABULARY

common verbs (1)

1 A If you didn't check understanding of *classmate* and *colleague* in the To start activity, you should do so now. Put Ss in pairs to look at the main photo and discuss the questions. When they have finished, ask a few pairs to share their ideas.

EXTRA SUPPORT: TEACHER You could point out that a *colleague* is less formally known as a *workmate* – a similar word pattern to *classmate* – and that *mate* means friend. You can also introduce *flatmate* as a member of this group of compound nouns as it appears later in the lesson. All these words are stressed on the first syllable, as is common in two-syllable nouns.

ANSWERS:
1 at work
2 colleagues
3 Students' own answers

B Focus attention on the sentence starters and ask for ideas. Ensure Ss apply third person *-s* to the positive verb and remind them that after *doesn't* we need the infinitive, so there is no *-s*. Ask pairs to discuss and write sentence endings. When they have finished, elicit their ideas. There are no fixed answers.

EXTRA CHALLENGE With stronger classes, you could extend this activity and ask Ss to write similar sentences about a good friend / parent / teacher / language learner, etc. This is useful consolidation practice of third person present simple.

2 A Tell Ss they are going to compare their ideas about a good colleague with a short text. Refer Ss to the words in the box and explain that they must use them to complete the sentences in the list. Look at the example and remind them about third person verb formation. Ask Ss to start alone, then help each other in pairs. When they have finished, elicit answers from pairs of Ss and write them on the board.

EXTRA SUPPORT: DYSLEXIA Ss with dyslexia can struggle with moving words from one place to another, as text is already quite unstable for them visually. Make the words less physically distant by writing them in a vertical list for Ss to place alongside the text with gaps. They can move this up and down to help them make their choices.

ANSWERS:
2 helps **3** gets **4** forget
5 call **6** thanks **7** take
8 sends

EXTRA SUPPORT: TEACHER 'Get' is an extremely useful verb because of its many meanings and uses. Here, in the context of requesting and doing things for someone, it means *go + make/buy/obtain + bring back* all in one concept. The easiest way to show this is through example and mime, e.g. getting something for Ss, like a book, a pen or a cup of water.

EXTRA IDEA: DIGITAL Ss make a recording of the list. They can do this as a group, taking turns to read lines, or individually. With stronger classes, Ss could go on to create their own text about a good friend/husband/parent, etc. and record it in the same way.

B This task invites Ss to respond personally to the ideas in the list. Give Ss a few minutes to identify the ideas they think are more/less important, then discuss as a class. There are no fixed answers.

FUTURE SKILLS | Self-management 

C Read the Future Skills box with the class, then put Ss in pairs to complete the phrases, referring to the list in Ex 2A if they need to. When they have finished, elicit answers.

ANSWERS:
1 for **2** for

EXTRA IDEA: FUTURE SKILLS Stronger classes can suggest other verb + preposition combinations (e.g. *ask for, look at*, etc.). Write these on the board for Ss to add to their notebooks and generate their own examples.

D Put Ss in A/B pairs and read the instruction and example together. Ask a pair to demonstrate. Explain that Student As can look at the list but not Student Bs, then ask them to start. After a few turns, change roles.

EXTRA CHALLENGE Stronger classes or pairs could 'BEEP' prepositions in the sentences as well.

READING

EXTRA SUPPORT: DYSLEXIA There are recordings of the reading texts available to help dyslexic learners.

3A **Explain that Ss will now read about two different colleagues and decide which of the rules in Ex 2A are true for each of them. Put Ss in A/B pairs and refer them to the relevant pages. Ss read and answer the question. Don't check answers yet.**

EXTRA SUPPORT: DYSLEXIA If possible, divide the class into pairs and allocate them Student A or B roles before the class and share the relevant audio file with learners with dyslexia. As Ss work on their own in Ex 3A, they can then read and listen to the text if they prefer.

EXTRA SUPPORT With weaker classes, put Ss in A/A and B/B pairs and ask them to read the text together then discuss the answers. Each student in the pair could work on a different paragraph or they can practise paired reading, where one reads a section aloud with the other listening and tracking the text. This is particularly effective for beginner literacy learners. Ss can also complete Ex 3B together, supporting each other.

ANSWERS:

René: says 'good morning' with a smile.
listens to their colleagues.
never sends work emails at the weekend.
(Text states that René never gets coffee for people.)

Claudia: starts work at nine o'clock and leaves at five (in a 9–5 job).
helps people with their work problems.
doesn't forget important dates, for example birthdays.
doesn't call friends in work time.
never sends work emails at the weekend.
(Text states that Claudia doesn't often thank people for their help.)

B **Explain that Ss will now write questions to find out about their partner's text. Look at the example and remind Ss to use *does* + infinitive when asking in the third person. While Ss are writing, move around the class and check they are forming questions correctly. Fast finishers can write more questions. With weaker classes, four questions would be sufficient.**

C **Put Ss in A/B pairs to ask questions and find out about their partner's text (either Student A or Student B should ask all their questions before their partner asks theirs). First elicit the short answers: *Yes, he/she does., No, he/she doesn't.* and *I don't know.* and write these on the board for Ss to refer to. They don't need to write the answers.**

D **Ss should now have enough information about both René and Claudia in order to discuss the questions. When they have finished, discuss as a class and display the answers in Ex 3A, above, to confirm the similarity. They can use their ideas for Ex 2B as well, to discuss question 2.**

ANSWERS:

1 Both René and Claudia never send work emails at the weekend.

2 Students' own answers

EXTRA IDEA Pairs that finish quickly can read each other's texts. They can swap questions and ask and answer about the other person for further speaking practice.

GRAMMAR

object pronouns

4A **Explain that Ss will now use sentences from the texts in Ex 3A to study some grammar. Give them a few minutes to choose the correct alternatives, then check answers with the class.**

EXTRA: ALTERNATIVE IDEA With weaker classes, as an alternative to Exs 4A and 4B, write a simple sentence on the board and ask Ss to identify the subject and object (e.g. *Jane drinks coffee.* – subject = *Jane*, object = *coffee*). Remind Ss that English sentences typically follow this *SVO* pattern. Ask Ss to replace *Jane* and *coffee* with pronouns (Jane = *she*, coffee = *it*). With weaker classes, you could then elicit all the subject pronouns and build a list of these on the board, then introduce the object pronouns alongside (e.g. *she – her, he – him*, etc.). Leave them on the board for reference during the lesson. Ss could then do Ex 4A as practise. You can then proceed with Ex 4C and the Grammar Bank.

ANSWERS:

1 it **2** him, us **3** her **4** them

B **This exercise summarises the form of subject and object pronouns. Ss complete the table, referring to Ex 4A where necessary, then check in pairs. Check answers with the class. Drill chorally by saying the subject pronouns in random order and Ss reply with the correct object pronoun.**

ANSWERS:

subject pronouns	I	he	she	we	they
object pronouns	*me*	him	her	us	them

C **Work as a class and use the examples seen to complete the rules. Elicit the answers and write them on the board.**

ANSWERS:
1 before **2** after

D **The Grammar Bank on page 108 can be used in the lesson or for homework. Decide how and when the exercises will benefit your class.**

GB page 108 **GRAMMAR BANK**

Go through the notes with Ss or let them read them alone. Check understanding where necessary to ensure Ss are clear on the basic grammar terms introduced.

1 **This exercise focuses on recognition of gender and number for the correct use of pronouns. Point out if necessary that Ed Sheeran is a male singer and Emma Stone is an actress. Discuss the first answer provided and the fact that male pronouns are used. Ss continue alone, then check in pairs. Check answers with the class. If you have time, pairs can practise asking and answering the questions.**

EXTRA SUPPORT: DYSLEXIA Work as a class to highlight the subject in each question. You could reduce the scope of the exercise so that Ss have to choose just one answer (object pronoun) for each question. Positioning the questions and answers side-by-side in two columns will also help Ss to process the information.

ANSWERS:
2 a, g **3** d, i **4** c, h **5** e, j

2 **This exercise focuses on selecting pronouns. Look at the example with the class, and discuss why each pronoun is used, then ask Ss to rewrite the rest of the sentences. Refer Ss to the table in the notes to help them if necessary. Check answers with the class.**

EXTRA SUPPORT Weaker classes or Ss with dyslexia could just write the pronouns rather than rewrite the whole sentence, to reduce the writing load.

ANSWERS:
2 ~~Kevin and Neil~~ **They**'re brothers. I like ~~Kevin and Neil~~ **them** a lot.
3 … Are you happy with ~~your new apartment~~ **it**?
4 ~~Alice and I~~ **We**'re sisters. Ms Dexter teaches ~~Alice and me~~ **us**.
5 … Can I help ~~Nisha and Dimitry~~ **you**?
6 Do you know ~~Mr Baros~~ **him**? ~~Mr Baros~~ **He**'s from Greece.
7 ~~My mother~~ **She**'s a teacher. The students like ~~my mother~~ **her**.
8 ~~Red~~ **It**'s my favourite colour. I like ~~red~~ **it** a lot.

3 **This exercise focuses on accuracy in using pronouns. Look at the example with the class and discuss why we need *me* here (it's the object), then ask Ss to correct the rest of the mistakes. Point out that two sentences are correct. Move around and support as needed, e.g. by prompting 'Is it singular or plural?' Check answers with the class.**

EXTRA SUPPORT: DYSLEXIA Remove the two correct sentences and provide two alternatives for each of the incorrect pronouns to choose from in each case (e.g. *I like* ***him*** */* ***her*** *a lot.*). Encourage Ss to cover the sentences they are not working on to avoid distraction.

ANSWERS:
2 … She's great and I like ~~him~~ **her** a lot.
3 … I have lunch with ~~he~~ **him** every Friday.
4 We live in Madrid and my sister lives with ~~we~~ **us**.
5 correct
6 I don't drink milk because I don't like ~~them~~ **it**.
7 … I read to ~~they~~ **them** for half an hour.
8 correct
9 Who is Harry? I don't know ~~it~~ **him**.
10 We help Jennifer a lot but she never thanks ~~them~~ **us**.

4 **This exercise gives practice in the position of object pronouns. Remind Ss of the typical *SVO* word order – *subject → verb → object*. Look at the example with the class and discuss why we need *them* here (*keys* = plural), then ask Ss to insert object pronouns in the rest of the sentences where they are missing. Move around and support as needed, e.g. by discussing with Ss where the missing word should go. Ask Ss to compare in pairs then go through the answers and write them on the board.**

EXTRA SUPPORT: DYSLEXIA You could help Ss with dyslexia focus on the position of the pronouns by providing them with the correct pronoun for each sentence which they then need to position in the correct place.

ANSWERS:
2 Yes, but I don't always understand **him**.
3 I don't like **it** very much.
4 Thank **you** for your help.
5 No, she doesn't, but I speak to **her** every day.
6 For **me**? Oh, it's beautiful. Thanks!
7 Me too, she always helps **us** with our problems.
8 I love **them**. I think they're great.

EXTRA IDEA Ss work in pairs, reading the completed conversations. They should take turns at each role. If they want to, they can read the conversations in front of the class or record themselves.

PRONUNCIATION

linking with object pronouns

5 A 5.01 | Read the examples with the class and demonstrate the linking either yourself or by playing the recording. Play the recording again for Ss to listen and repeat.

EXTRA SUPPORT: TEACHER Ss should note that the linking occurs where a vowel sound meets a consonant sound. This is clearly seen in example 1: *call us*. Ss may wonder why *h* is crossed out in the examples. The sound /h/ is not a hard sound, it is considered a voiceless vowel. Between two vowels it can be voiced (e.g. *a hat*).

B 5.02 | Ss listen and write. Pause after listening so they can compare and check their spelling, then go through the answers.

EXTRA SUPPORT Provide weaker classes and/or Ss with dyslexia with the sentences. They can then listen only for the linking and mark this in, as in the examples seen in Ex 5A.

ANSWERS AND AUDIOSCRIPT:

1 We like him.
2 She helps us with our English.
3 I don't have it with me.
4 Don't call her at the weekend.

C 5.02 | Ss listen and practise saying the sentences. At this level it's probably sufficient to have Ss listen and repeat, but you may feel it useful to get Ss to mark the links themselves by drawing a line from the end of the verb to the beginning of the object pronoun, and even crossing out the *h* where it isn't pronounced.

EXTRA SUPPORT If Ss are struggling with linking, try a backchain drill. This involves repeating segments of the sentence from the end, e.g … *English.*, … *our English.*, … *with our English.* and so on, building up to Ss saying the whole sentence.

EXTRA IDEA: DIGITAL Ss use their phones to record themselves pronouncing the phrases, then listen back to check their own pronunciation. Finally, they can listen again to the recording and compare.

D Ask a stronger pair to model the first pair of matching sentences as an example, then ask Ss to take turns to match the rest of the sentences orally. Check answers with the class and write them on the board (or invite different Ss to come up and do so).

EXTRA SUPPORT: DYSLEXIA It can be a challenge for Ss with dyslexia to locate text on different parts of the page. Provide a vertical list of the responses from Ex 5B. Ask Ss to first write the correct sentences from Ex 5B beside sentences 1–4 in Ex 5D, then practise saying them. They can cover these after a first practice reading them.

ANSWERS:

2 I don't have it with me.
3 Don't call her at the weekend.
4 She helps us with our English.

EXTRA CHALLENGE With a strong class, you could extend Ex 5D as follows. First, Ss work in pairs and write four more sentences that match with the sentences in Exs 5A and 5B. Then they work with a new partner and take turns to read one of their sentences. Their partner says the sentence from Ex 5A or 5B that matches.

SPEAKING

6 A If you didn't introduce *flatmate* in conjunction with *classmate* in Ex 1A, check understanding of the term now. Look at the list of people and give an example to demonstrate the activity (e.g. 'This person cleans the bathroom.'). Point out that Ss should choose one person from the list and not go through it in order. Put Ss in pairs to choose and write a sentence starting *This person …*.

B Use your example again (e.g. 'This person cleans the bathroom.') and ask Ss to guess (e.g. 'Is it a parent?', 'Is it a flatmate?'). Put Ss in new pairs to read their sentences and guess.

EXTRA IDEA If time allows, Ss can read their sentences to several partners. If space allows, this can be done as a class mingle.

EXTRA: ALTERNATIVE IDEA You could set this activity up as a game in small groups. Put three pairs of Ss from Ex 6A together to read their sentences to the others. The pair who guesses the person first wins a point. Ss could play a number of rounds of the game with each pair choosing a different person each time (they are not allowed to repeat any of the ideas already given).

WRITING

write about a good friend; use pronouns

7 A Tell Ss they are now going to write about the qualities of a good friend. Give them a few minutes to think of someone, then refer them to the prompts and ask them to complete them with their own ideas. Move around the class, helping where needed and reminding Ss of the third person *-s* if necessary. Ss should complete the four sentences.

EXTRA CHALLENGE Stronger Ss can think of other information about a friend and write more.

B **Put Ss in pairs to tell each other.**

C **Refer Ss to the Writing Bank on page 90.**

WB ⏩ page 90 **WRITING BANK**

1 A **Explain that Ss should read the text *My friend Dwayne* and use the information to complete the sentences. Complete the first part to ensure they know what to do (*His name is Dwayne*) then Ss continue alone. Go through the answers as a class and write them on the board.**

EXTRA SUPPORT: DYSLEXIA Record the text before the class so that Ss with dyslexia can listen and read at the same time. If you don't have time to do this, you could read it aloud. Then play (or read) it again while Ss focus on the incomplete sentences. Put them in pairs to help each other and refer back to the text. Then elicit the answers and highlight where they are found in the text.

ANSWERS:

1 Dwayne, school
2 and I play football and have lunch in a restaurant
3 always gives me a big present
4 listens to me, asks questions and helps me

B **Look at the text (it is another version of the first two sentences of the text in Ex 1A) and discuss as a class what the differences are. Ask Ss which text they think is better. Hopefully they should choose the one with pronouns as it's less repetitive.**

ANSWERS:

The text uses pronouns. It doesn't repeat the name 'Dwayne' over and over again.

2 **Ask Ss to replace the words in bold (1–7) in the sentences with pronouns. They should work alone then check in pairs. Go through the answers as a class.**

EXTRA SUPPORT: DYSLEXIA Encourage Ss to cover the phrases or sentences they are not working on to reduce distraction.

EXTRA IDEA During the pair-check stage, ask Ss to take turns to read the text to each other. It will be more obvious where they have an incorrect pronoun.

ANSWERS:

2 we **3** him **4** He **5** He **6** he **7** his

3 A **Tell Ss that they will use what they have studied so far to write a description of their friend. Remind them of their completed sentences from Ex 7A. Weaker classes can rely closely on the model text about Dwayne, stronger Ss can use more of their own ideas. Ss should aim to write at least five sentences, or about 50 words. Allow time for Ss to think, and move around the class to be available to help and support. Tell them that they should write neatly as another person will read their text. When they have finished, encourage them to check their work.**

B **Ask Ss to exchange their descriptions with a partner. They should pay attention to pronouns and decide if they are used correctly. Be available to consult on this as Ss sometimes correct something that is actually fine!**

C **Put Ss in groups of three or four to share their descriptions and find similarities and differences. When they have finished, ask each group for a similarity that they found.**

EXTRA: ALTERNATIVE IDEA If your Ss need more speaking and listening practice, put them in groups and ask them to take turns to read their description to each other aloud, then afterwards ask and answer questions. When they have all read, they can discuss what the similarities are.

TO FINISH

Write on the board: *A good student* … . and *A good student doesn't* … . Put Ss in pairs to complete the two sentences and then discuss as a class. This can be a good opportunity to talk about homework, study habits and note-taking. If you are brave, you can repeat the exercise with *A good teacher* … !

5B Yes, I can!

GRAMMAR | *can* for ability
VOCABULARY | verbs of ability
PRONUNCIATION | *can*: weak and strong forms

LESSON OVERVIEW

In this lesson, Ss learn verbs to express ability. The context is a listening where they listen to people talking about what they can and can't do. This leads into the grammar, using *can* and *can't* for ability and where Ss also practise the weak and strong forms of this verb. Ss then talk about their own abilities. The lesson ends with a speaking activity where Ss complete a quiz about abilities in different areas of life.

Online Teaching

If you're teaching this lesson online, you might find the following tips useful:

- **Ex 1A:** Share your screen and enable annotations. Invite Ss to take turns writing the words in the correct place and have a whole class confirmation.
- **Ex 4A:** Remind Ss to put their microphones on mute to ensure there is no disturbance when they are listening for sounds.
- **Ex 6B:** Put pairs in breakout rooms to ask and answer. Try to visit one or two breakout rooms while you monitor and make a note to visit others next time.

Additional Materials

For Teachers:
Presentation Tool Lesson 5B
Photocopiable Activities 5B
Grammar Bank 5B
Vocabulary Bank 5B

For Students:
Online Practice 5B
Workbook 5B

TO START

Show photos or write the names of internationally well-known people with special skills that you think Ss will recognise (e.g. Usain Bolt, the Jamaican runner; Lang Lang, the Chinese pianist; Serena Williams, the American tennis player; Carlos Acosta, the Cuban dancer; etc.). Put Ss in pairs to discuss who they are, where they are from and why they are famous. This has the benefit of potentially previewing some of the vocabulary in the lesson and also the theme. Write useful vocabulary on the board. When they have finished, ask pairs to identify the people and say which one they think is the most impressive. Tell Ss that in today's lesson they will be talking about people's abilities.

EXTRA SUPPORT: DYSLEXIA Dyslexic learners in particular benefit from understanding exactly what they are learning in a lesson so that they understand what they are working towards. In this and every lesson, explain clearly what the learning objectives of the lesson are near the start.

VOCABULARY

verbs of ability

1 A Focus attention on the word webs and explain that Ss should complete them with the words in the box. Check Ss remember what *chopsticks* are. Some Ss may not know what *salsa* and *the tango* are (Latin American partner dances: salsa is attributed to several Latin American countries, including Cuba and Puerto Rico; the tango originates in Argentina). Put Ss in pairs to compare answers. Fast finishers and stronger classes could add more words. When they have finished, elicit answers from the class and write the words on the board.

EXTRA IDEA If the load isn't too much for your Ss, you could get them to add more items to each verb, either from their own ideas (if they have this level of resource) or by feeding items in (e.g. via dictation).

EXTRA SUPPORT: DYSLEXIA Dyslexic learners may find word webs visually confusing. Provide a version in which the collocations appear in reading order, with the verbs in a column on the left and the phrases on the right, e.g. *1 ______ Japanese, a map*. Write the verbs to insert in a vertical list, ideally on a piece of paper so Ss can place it near the word webs. Encourage Ss to cover the other items and focus attention on sections of the task as they complete them to avoid distraction.

ANSWERS:

2 play	**3** remember	**4** sleep
5 dance	**6** use	

EXTRA SUPPORT: TEACHER Note that the Vocabulary Bank, with an additional set of verbs, is located at the end of the Grammar section. It is there and not in this main Vocabulary section so that Ss can practise the items using the grammar right away.

B This task is a kind of memory game. Look at the example as a class and put Ss in A/B pairs. Student Bs can look at their book and say the verb; Student As cannot look at their book and they need to remember the verb and its collocations. Be on hand to adjudicate if they come up with other (correct) collocations not given in Ex 1A, e.g. *remember my friend's birthday*. After a few turns they change roles. Move around and listen. When they have finished, drill any words that caused problems.

LISTENING

2 A 5.03 | Refer Ss to the main photo and ask them to look at it while they listen to the conversations and decide which one matches it. Play the recording. Ask Ss to compare in pairs. Check the answer with the class. If they can, ask Ss to say why they chose that photo.

ANSWER:
Conversation 2

AUDIOSCRIPT 5.03

Conversation 1

A: Hi, Cindy. It's Neil …
B: Oh hi, Neil.
A: Listen, is it Andy's birthday this month?
B: Yes, it is.
A: I always forget birthdays. Can you remember the date?
B: Yes, I can. His birthday's on the twenty-second of March.
A: Great. Thank you.
B: I write down birthdays. So I remember them.
A: And how old is he?
B: Oh I can't remember. Maybe thirty-five?
A: OK, thanks.
B: That's all right.
A: Speak soon. Bye.
B: Bye.

Conversation 2

C: Look, we're nearly there!
D: Are we?
C: What's the problem? Are you OK?
D: I'm really tired. I can't sleep on buses.
C: Really? I can sleep everywhere. I can sleep on buses, in cars, in hotels …
D: Hotels! I can sleep in hotels. But not on buses.
C: Here, I have some chocolate in my bag.
D: Oh perfect! Thanks.

Conversation 3

E: Ash, can you dance salsa?
F: Yes, I can. A little. Why?
E: Look. A salsa class on Wednesday and … it's for six weeks.
F: What time does it start?
E: Er … it starts at half past seven and finishes at ten.
F: Hmm … What about you? Can you dance salsa?
E: No, I can't. But I love the music!
F: OK … let's do it!
E: Great!

B 5.03 | Tell Ss they will listen again more carefully. Go through the table with the class and establish that they need to tick or cross for the man and the woman in each conversation. Play the recording, ask Ss to compare, then play it again before checking the answers.

ANSWERS:

	he	she
remember birthdays	✗	✓
sleep on buses	✗	✓
dance salsa	✓	✗

GRAMMAR

can for ability

3 A Ss have met *can* in the listening, so tell them you're now going to use some sentences from that to focus on it. Point out that Ss will see positive, negative and question examples. Ask Ss to use the words in bold to help them complete the table with *can* and *can't*. They can do this in pairs then check as a class. With weaker classes, do it together as a class and write the answers on the board.

EXTRA SUPPORT: DYSLEXIA The missing words are either *can* or *can't*. You could provide a set of these on slips of paper for Ss to try in the gaps before deciding.

ANSWERS:

1 can **2** can't **3** Can
4 can **5** can't

B The Grammar Bank on page 109 can be used in the lesson or for homework. Decide how and when the exercises will benefit your class.

page 109 **GRAMMAR BANK** **GB**

Go through the notes with Ss or let them read them alone. Check understanding where necessary, especially of the change to word order in questions.

1 This focuses on the form and meaning of *can* and *can't*. Explain that Ss should read the conversation and fill each gap with a form of *can*. Elicit the first answer as an example, then ask Ss to complete the rest of the conversation alone, then compare in pairs. Check answers with the class and deal with any questions. If time allows, Ss can read out the conversation in pairs.

GB

ANSWERS:

1 can't **2** Can **3** can't
4 can **5** can **6** can't
7 Can **8** can **9** can't
10 can't

2 Read the example with the class and discuss why it's wrong (*can* is followed by the infinitive). Tell Ss that the mistakes can be in form, structure, word order or meaning. Ask Ss to correct the rest of the sentences alone using the Grammar Bank notes to help them, then check in pairs. Check answers with the class and refer them back to the notes if they have any questions.

EXTRA SUPPORT: DYSLEXIA Finding mistakes can be challenging. You could highlight the errors for Ss to focus on just the error correction part of the activity.

ANSWERS:

2 Hans, ~~do you can~~ **can you** sleep in the daytime? I can't!
3 I'm sorry. I ~~no can~~ **can't** remember your name.
4 Susan understands French, but she ~~doesn't can~~ **can't** speak it.
5 Mary ~~cans~~ **can** dance very well – she's good!
6 Can ~~make Isabella~~ **Isabella make** a good pizza?
7 Zhen and Mei Hui can write in English but ~~no~~ **not** very well.
8 Can Chloe ~~says~~ **say** 'hello' in Japanese?

3 Read the example with the class and point out that they should use *can* or *can't* and a verb from the box. Ask Ss to complete the rest of the sentences alone, then check in pairs. Check answers with the class and ask individuals to read whole sentences aloud, drilling as needed.

EXTRA SUPPORT: DYSLEXIA To support dyslexic learners, break down the stages. First Ss should identify which verb to use, then decide on the form of *can* needed. To further assist, provide the verbs in a vertical list that can be placed alongside the sentences to help Ss choose. Alternatively, you could provide the verb for each sentence to allow Ss to focus on the correct formation of *can/can't*.

ANSWERS:

2 can play **6** can't spell
3 Can, read **7** Can, use
4 can't help **8** can't give
5 Can, sleep

PRONUNCIATION

can: weak and strong forms

4A 5.04 | Remind Ss of the weak sound /ə/ and explain that while they have previously seen this in multi-syllable words it also occurs in one of the possible pronunciations of *can*. At this point you can either model the pronunciation of the verbs yourself or play the first part of the recording to model them (i.e. items 1–3). Ss then listen and tick the table for items 4–8, then check in pairs. Check answers with the class and write them on the board.

ANSWERS:

	can /kæn/	can /kən/	can't /kɑːnt/
1	✓		
2		✓	
3			✓
4		✓	
5			✓
6			✓
7		✓	
8	✓		

AUDIOSCRIPT 5.04

1 /kæn/
2 /kən/
3 /kɑːnt/
4 Can you make a cake?
5 No, I can't.
6 I can't read Japanese writing.
7 I can play the guitar.
8 Yes, I can.

B 5.04 | Ss listen again and repeat after the recording.

C Ask Ss to use the table in Ex 4A to complete the rule. With stronger classes they can do this in pairs before checking as a class, and with weaker classes you can do it together as a class and drill examples. You could use the sentences from Ex 3A.

EXTRA SUPPORT: TEACHER Ss may struggle to distinguish the two options for *can*, though they should have less difficulty with the longer sound in *can't*. This pronunciation is British English. Note that in US English the distinction is a bit different and the long sound in *can't* is less clear. The main thing at this stage is raising Ss' awareness of the sounds for recognition; they might not be able to produce the sounds as accurately.

ANSWERS:

positive, questions

5 A Put Ss in pairs. Drill the example question and answer and elicit a further example. To note the differences, Ss should tick or cross the verb phrases in Ex 1A.

B Put Ss in new pairs. Drill the example and elicit a further example from a stronger student, then pairs tell each other their three differences. When they have finished, ask pairs to tell the class about a difference using *but*, e.g. 'I can use chopsticks, but Mark can't.'

EXTRA SUPPORT With weaker classes or those with beginner literacy needs, ask Ss to write sentences with *but* before telling each other. Ss often capitalise linking words, so remind them that *but* does not have a capital letter as it is in the middle of a sentence. While the example has a comma before *but*, it is not strictly needed.

C Refer Ss to the Vocabulary Bank on page 133.

VB page 133 **VOCABULARY BANK** verbs of ability

Note that the Vocabulary Bank activities are an important part of the lesson. They should only be omitted if you are confident that your Ss already know this vocabulary. If you don't use the exercises in class, it would be a good idea to set them as homework.

1 A Refer Ss to the photos (A–H) and ask them to match them with the verbs. Ss should work alone, then in pairs to check their answers. Check answers with the class.

EXTRA: ALTERNATIVE IDEA If your class won't know any of the verbs, go through them as a class and teach them first, then use the matching as a check.

ANSWERS:
1 D **2** H **3** F **4** B **5** C **6** A **7** E **8** G

B **VB5.01** | Ask Ss to look at the photos and repeat the verbs as you play the recording. Further drill individually if you think Ss need it.

EXTRA IDEA Mime the verbs for Ss to call out what you are doing. Put Ss in groups to do the same.

2 A Put Ss in pairs to make one list as in the example, about both of them. They should write eight sentences starting with *I*. Move around and check they are doing the activity correctly.

B Ask Ss to exchange their list with another pair and then discuss, as in the example, which person each sentence refers to.

C Put the two pairs of Ss together. They should check their ideas, as in the example. Introduce *You're right.* and *You're wrong.* and write these on the board for Ss to refer to. When they have finished, ask Ss how many they guessed correctly.

EXTRA IDEA Ss can exchange lists with others in the class to extend the activity.

SPEAKING

6 A Tell Ss they will do a fun question activity (remind them of the word *quiz*) about abilities. Read the instruction to the class, then give an example for yourself. Write on the board: *play tennis?* ✗, and elicit that it means 'You can't play tennis.' Read the lists of abilities with the class and check understanding. Ask Ss to answer the questions for themselves.

B Explain that Ss should now ask each other. Look at the example and ask a stronger pair to demonstrate another exchange. Encourage them to extend their answers. Put Ss in pairs to ask and answer. You could put Ss in new pairs, i.e. different from the pairs that worked together in Vocabulary Bank Ex 2, to minimise any feeling of overlap. Move around the class and listen to them. At the end, give brief feedback on their language and drill pronunciation as needed.

C Refer Ss to the key and ask them to work with a partner to add up their scores then discuss the questions. Provide support with vocabulary as needed. When they have finished, have a show of hands to see which skills are stronger in the class and elicit other activities that could fit into each area.

EXTRA IDEA: DIGITAL Ss write a summary of the information that they found out from their partner, then post it online in a shared chat.

D This is a freer practice activity and a chance for Ss to share some of their other ideas from Ex 6C, question 2. Give Ss a few minutes to prepare, then put them in groups of three or four to have a conversation similar to the example. Fast finishers can talk about what they can't do as well. When they have finished, have a whole class discussion to see what interesting skills Ss have.

EXTRA SUPPORT Weaker classes will need more time to think about their abilities. Encourage them to use devices/dictionaries or to ask you to help them prepare to speak about what they can do. Move around the class and help with vocabulary. Then put them in groups to discuss.

TO FINISH

Write on the board: *What can you do in English? What can't you do?* and give an example (e.g. 'I can talk about my job and I can understand numbers 1–100.'). Ask Ss to discuss. Make a note of what Ss think they can't do to address in future lessons.

5C Can you help me?

HOW TO … | make requests and offers
VOCABULARY | common adjectives (2)
PRONUNCIATION | weak forms: *could you*

LESSON OVERVIEW

In this lesson, Ss build on their knowledge of common adjectives. They also learn functional language for making requests and offers, and practise the pronunciation of the weak form of *could you*. The context is a listening where they listen to people asking for help in different situations. The lesson ends with a speaking activity where Ss roleplay making requests and offers and responding to them in social situations.

Online Teaching

If you're teaching this lesson online, you might find the following tips useful:

- **Ex 1A:** Display the photos and sentences by sharing your screen. Ask Ss to note their answers individually, then put them in breakout rooms in pairs to discuss them.
- **Ex 1B:** Display the activity by sharing your screen and make sure the annotate feature is on. Ss can then take turns to draw lines connecting the two parts.
- **Ex 3B:** Make sure Ss have switched their microphones off. When they have listened, they write their answers in the chat or a shared document.

Additional Materials

For Teachers:
Presentation Tool Lesson 5C
Photocopiable Activity 5C
Grammar Bank 5C

For Students:
Online Practice 5C
Workbook 5C

TO START

Start the lesson by making a few requests to individual Ss and waiting for them to carry them out, e.g. 'Can you take my book, Pedro?', 'Can you open the window, John?', 'Can you pass me a pen, Mary?', etc. When Ss have done what you asked, tell them today's lesson includes practice of asking people for help and that these questions are called *requests*.

EXTRA SUPPORT: DYSLEXIA Dyslexic learners in particular benefit from understanding exactly what they are learning in a lesson so that they understand what they are working towards. In this and every lesson, explain clearly what the learning objectives of the lesson are near the start.

VOCABULARY

common adjectives (2)

1 A Check understanding of *shopping list* (= a list of things to buy that you take to the supermarket or shops). Focus attention on the photos. Ss then discuss the question and match the sentences with the photos. Check answers with the class.

ANSWERS:
1 at work, B
2 at a language school, D
3 at a supermarket, C
4 in a street, A

EXTRA IDEA If you have time, there's an opportunity for vocabulary revision: things on your desk and clothes have both been taught in previous lessons. Ask Ss to write down what they can see in the photos. Give them a time limit such as two minutes. If your class are competitive, make it a team game and give them each category in turn to see who can make the longest list.

B Read the example with the class and establish that Ss are matching a statement or question (1–8) with a response (a–h). Ask Ss to complete the exercise, then check in pairs. Encourage them to use a process of elimination and not check the meaning of individual words. Check answers with the class, with pairs of Ss reading the exchanges aloud.

EXTRA SUPPORT: DYSLEXIA Exercises like this, where Ss have to choose from options and read up and down can be challenging. You could reduce the load by reorganising the exercise so Ss match a few exchanges (e.g. four) at a time. Putting the statements/questions and responses in two columns side by side will also help them process the information.

ANSWERS:
2 c **3** a **4** b **5** e **6** d **7** h **8** f

C Read the example with the class, then put Ss in pairs to find the remaining adjectives. Remind Ss that an adjective is a describing word. When they have finished, check the answers. Write them on the board.

ANSWERS:
2 cheap **3** right **4** wrong
5 open **6** closed **7** early
8 late

D **Look at the example, ask a stronger pair to say another adjective and its opposite, then put Ss in pairs to continue in turns. They can repeat the same words more than once. Move around and listen to their pronunciation. When they have finished, drill any problem words.**

EXTRA: ALTERNATIVE IDEA For a change from closed pairwork, you could do this activity across the class as a fun way of involving Ss and building class cooperation. Student A says an adjective then names another student (B) in the room to give the opposite. Student B then gives a new adjective and calls on another student (C) for the opposite and so on. They can repeat the same words more than once.

How to …

make requests and offers

2 A **5.05 | Explain that Ss will listen to people in three of the situations in the photos discussed in Ex 1A. Play the recording. Pause after each one for Ss to discuss in pairs. Go through the answers at the end and ask what things helped them to identify the situations.**

ANSWERS:
1 C **2** B **3** D

AUDIOSCRIPT 5.05

Conversation 1

A: Hello?
B: Hi, it's me.
A: Where are you?
B: I'm in the shop.
A: So it's open. Good.
B: Yes, it's open. But I don't have the shopping list.
A: OK … Ah, it's here. What do you have?
B: I have … milk, cereal and apples. I can't remember anything else.
A: Yes, that's right, and pasta. Can you get three big steaks?
B: All right. Just a moment. Erm. They're expensive.
A: How much are they?
B: Thirty-nine euros for three. And they're small.
A: Yeah, that is expensive. OK, don't get the steaks.
B: OK, no steaks.
A: Just get the pasta. Pasta's cheap.
B: Do we have any eggs at home?
A: Oh, no we don't. Could you get some eggs? And also some tomatoes?
B: OK. Eggs, pasta and tomatoes. Is that everything?
A: Yes. Great.
B: OK. See you soon.

Conversation 2

C: I can't do this! I hate computers! Oh Susie! Could you help me?
D: Sure, what's the problem, Kayla?
C: I can't send this email. It has a video in it, and I can't send it.
D: Can I do it for you?
C: Yes, please.
D: Can I look?
C: Oh yes. Here.
D: OK. The problem is the video. It's really big. Send this link, not the video.
C: This link?
D: No, Kayla. Here, just click here and …
C: Oh, no, it's ten o'clock. I'm late. Susie, could you do it for me?
D: Yes, no problem. Give me two minutes.
C: Thank you so much!
D: No problem. Go!

Conversation 3

E: Do you have a problem, Nancy?
F: Yes, Mr Santos. I don't understand some words in this reading.
E: Can I help?
F: Yes, what does 'easy' mean?
E: Easy. Not difficult. You can do it.
F: Oh, yeah, I remember. Thank you. Can I ask another question?
E: Of course.
F: On this one, is the answer right?
E: Can I see it? Yes, the answer is right, but the spelling is wrong. It's not y-u-n-g. It's y-o-u-n-g, the opposite of old.

B **5.05 | Tell the class they're going to match the words in the list (1–6) from the recording with the adjectives in the box. Point out that there are eight words in the box, so two are not needed. When they have finished, they should compare answers, then listen again to the conversations. Check answers with the class.**

EXTRA SUPPORT: DYSLEXIA Multiple matching can be hard for Ss with dyslexia, particularly where words are not near to each other. Remove the two extra words and write the remaining adjectives in a vertical list that Ss can hold beside the options (1–6).

ANSWERS:

1 open	**2** expensive	**3** cheap
4 late	**5** right	**6** wrong

C 5.06 | Tell Ss they should use the conversations they heard in Exs 2A and 2B to help them complete the conversations. When they have finished, put them in pairs to help each other then play the recording, pausing after each segment for Ss to check or correct their answers then check in pairs. Check answers with the class.

EXTRA SUPPORT For weaker classes you could simplify this by providing the missing words to choose from, either on a handout or on the board, before Ss listen and check. Alternatively, you could reduce the number of gaps and treat it as a straightforward listening, pausing after each segment for Ss to complete the segments based on what they have just heard. You may need to repeat the recording a few times. This will be intensive listening for Ss and will take longer than normal listening tasks.

EXTRA SUPPORT: DYSLEXIA Provide dyslexic learners with a vertical list of the missing words for each conversation. Tell them to cover the other segments when they are working on one, to avoid distraction.

ANSWERS:

1 Can	**2** right	**3** you
4 OK	**5** me	**6** problem
7 much	**8** ask	**9** course

D The Grammar Bank on page 110 can be used in the lesson or for homework. Decide how and when the exercises will benefit your class.

GB page 110 **GRAMMAR BANK**

This focuses on the form and use of phrases for requesting, offering, accepting and refusing. Read the notes with the class or give them a few minutes to read alone then ask any questions they have. Point out that unlike the other use of *can* (ability) they have studied, the correct response is not a short answer, but a fixed phrase.

1 This practices the form of requests. Look at the example as a class and point out the capital letter and punctuation that will help Ss put the words in order. Ask Ss to continue alone, writing the words in order, then check in pairs. Check answers with the class. After checking answers, drill Ss in tone.

EXTRA SUPPORT Provide dyslexic and beginner literacy learners with cut up requests to put in order. You could make meaningful chunks larger than one word (e.g. *Can I | try this | jacket on?*). The completed sentences can then be copied into their notebooks.

ANSWERS:

2 Can I try this jacket on?
3 Megan, can you help me?
4 Can you thank Juan for me?
5 Could I have another fork, please?
6 Angela, can you call your sister?
7 Lorenzo, can you make lunch today?
8 Karen, can you drive us to the supermarket?
9 Could I have an espresso, please?
10 Could I leave work early tomorrow, Mrs Barton?

2 This exercise practises the form and use of requests and responses. Ss use the words in the box to complete the conversations alone and then check in pairs. Check the answers with the class, asking pairs to read each conversation aloud. If time allows, pairs can practise the conversations.

EXTRA SUPPORT: DYSLEXIA Provide the words from the box in a vertical list that Ss can place alongside the conversations. Alternatively, provide two alternatives for each gap for Ss to choose from.

ANSWERS:

2 I	**3** of	**4** you
5 could	**6** try	**7** Sure
8 get	**9** All	**10** Thanks

3 This exercise introduces practice of offers as well as requests. Ss complete the conversations with *I*, *me* and *you* alone, then check in pairs. Go through the answers with different pairs reading each conversation aloud.

EXTRA SUPPORT: DYSLEXIA You could provide two alternatives (one correct, the other not) for each gap for Ss with dyslexia. Encourage them to cover the conversations they are not working on to help them focus.

ANSWERS:

1 you, me	**2** I, you	**3** I, you
4 I, you	**5** you, me	**6** you, I
7 you, me	**8** you, I	

EXTRA IDEA Ss could work in pairs to take turns reading the requests and offers and adding their own responses.

PRONUNCIATION

weak forms: *could you*

3A 5.07 | Tell Ss you will use two requests from the conversations they heard in Ex 2A to focus on pronunciation. Model the pronunciation of *could you* (/kədjə/). Ss should listen to the recording and identify the stressed words, then check in pairs. Remind them (or elicit) that words that carry meaning (e.g. nouns, adjectives) are stressed and unstressed words include auxiliary verbs.

ANSWERS:

1 Could you get some eggs?
2 Could you help me?

B 5.08 | Explain to Ss that they will listen to some requests and they should write the words they hear. Tell them to write the words spaced out along the line, then on a second listen they can add any they missed. After they have listened a second time, put Ss in pairs to compare and decide on the stressed words. Play the recording again to check the answers as a class. Write them on the board and drill, paying attention to stress and showing this with your arm. Point out that they need to speak quite quickly to pronounce *could you* in this way.

EXTRA SUPPORT: DYSLEXIA Ss can find it a challenge to listen and write simultaneously. In this case, you could give them the requests for them just to mark the stress.

ANSWERS AND AUDIOSCRIPT:

1 Could you get me a coffee?
2 Could you say that again?
3 Could you call me in the evening?
4 Could you make breakfast?

C Put Ss in pairs to take turns to make and respond to the requests in Ex 3B. Refer them back to the Grammar Bank or remind them of the possible answers so they can decide how to respond. Move around the class and monitor how they pronounce *could you* as well as the overall accuracy. When they have finished, give some feedback and drill as needed. If a few pairs would like to, ask them to repeat requests in front of the class.

EXTRA: HOW TO … Refer Ss back to Ex 3 in the Grammar Bank practice section. Ss use one request or offer as a starting point and individually write a three-line conversation that follows. Put them in pairs to rehearse their conversations, before they take turns to perform them for the class.

SPEAKING

4A Put Ss in pairs and give them a minute or two to read the prompts and think about what questions are being asked in 1–4. Weaker classes may need time to write the questions in full. Elicit the questions and write them on the board.

EXTRA SUPPORT: DYSLEXIA Pair a dyslexic learner with a partner who can support them in forming the questions from the prompts. It will help if they cover the parts they are not working on.

ANSWERS:

1 Can I make you some/a tea?
2 Could you make me some/a coffee, please?
3 Can I make you a sandwich?
4 Could I have an egg sandwich, please?

B Ss practise saying the questions, reading from the board. Gradually rub words out and leave key prompts there to see if they can remember them.

C Ss allocate roles as Student A and Student B then roleplay the conversation in pairs. Monitor and check they are using the phrases correctly. When they have finished, ask Ss to swap roles and repeat.

5 Tell Ss they will now roleplay two more conversations. Put Ss in A/B pairs and refer them to the relevant pages.

Give Ss time to read their instructions for Situation 1 and think about how to make their requests/ offers. Remind Ss of the language in the Grammar and Vocabulary Banks to help them if they need it. When they are ready, Ss roleplay Situation 1. Student A speaks first and after they have made their requests, Student B makes their offers.

Once they have completed Situation 1, Ss read their instructions and prepare for Situation 2, with Student B speaking first this time. Monitor and notice any common errors and examples of good language use for later class feedback.

EXTRA IDEA: DIGITAL Ask Ss to record their roleplays and play them back, listening particularly for how they pronounce *could you*.

TO FINISH

Put Ss in groups to discuss what requests they usually make at home, work or school.

EXTRA IDEA: SPEAK ANYWHERE Encourage Ss to practise using the Speak Anywhere interactive roleplay.

5D BBC Street Interviews Birthday!

GRAMMAR | ordinal numbers; dates
SPEAKING | talk about your birthday
WRITING | write about your birthday

LESSON OVERVIEW

In this lesson, Ss learn ordinal numbers and dates. They also learn the vocabulary of months. The context is a video of people talking about what they do on their birthday. Ss then do a speaking activity where they tell each other about what they usually do on their birthday. The lesson ends with a writing activity where Ss write about their birthday.

Online Teaching

If you're teaching this lesson online, you might find the following tips useful:

- **Ex 1A:** Share your screen and elicit the answers to the questions. Write the date and encourage Ss to copy it down.
- **Exs 2B and 3A:** Sometimes videos can be a little slow or jumpy when streamed in an online class environment. If you know this is an issue for you, give Ss time to watch the video on their own device before moving on.
- **Ex 5A:** Ss write their birthday in the chat then work as a group to put them in order on an online whiteboard.
- **Ex 6B:** Ss write their descriptions and add them to an online noticeboard where they can read each other's and comment.

Additional Materials

For Teachers:
Presentation Tool Lesson 5D
Online Digital Resources
Grammar Bank 5D
Vocabulary Bank 5D
Videoscript 5D: BBC Street Interviews

For Students:
Online Practice 5D
Workbook 5D

TO START

Say the days of the week around the class, pointing at different Ss to say the next one. (Days of the week were covered on the Lead-in page.) Write the days on the board. Then ask Ss to discuss in pairs: *What's your favourite day? Why?* When they have finished, have a vote to see which day is the most popular. Tell Ss today's lesson is about dates.

EXTRA SUPPORT: DYSLEXIA Dyslexic learners in particular benefit from understanding exactly what they are learning in a lesson so that they understand what they are working towards. In this and every lesson, explain clearly what the learning objectives of the lesson are near the start.

PREVIEW

1 A Put Ss in pairs to discuss. When they have finished, elicit the answers to the first two questions, writing the days of the week on the board if you didn't use the To start activity. Ask Ss if they can name the month and add this, then to make a list of months if they can.

EXTRA SUPPORT With weaker classes, ignore question 3 and go straight to the Vocabulary Bank.

EXTRA IDEA With stronger classes, you can also write the full date in simple format (e.g. 2nd February 2022). If Ss have questions about this, explain that today's lesson will be helpful. It's good practice to write the date and lesson objectives at the start of each lesson, to reinforce and aid their notekeeping.

B Refer Ss to the Vocabulary Bank on page 133 to check their ideas.

page 133 **VOCABULARY BANK** months

VB

Note that the Vocabulary Bank activities are an important part of the lesson. They should only be omitted if you are confident that your Ss already know this vocabulary. If you don't use the exercises in class, it would be a good idea to set them as homework.

1 A Focus attention on the calendar and explain that the names of the months have been abbreviated on it. Then ask Ss to number the months in order. Elicit that January is numbered 1 as the first month. Ss work individually, then check in pairs. Don't check the answers yet.

B VB5.02 | Play the recording for Ss to listen and check. Then play the recording again, for Ss to listen and repeat.

ANSWERS AND AUDIOSCRIPT:

1 *January*	**2** February	**3** March
4 April	**5** May	**6** June
7 July	**8** August	**9** September
10 October	**11** November	**12** December

C Put Ss in A/B pairs and focus on the example. Ss should take turns to say a month and supply the following month. Ask a stronger pair to provide a further example, then let pairs start. Move around and listen. When they have finished, drill any months they had trouble with as necessary.

VIEW

2A Read the two questions in the BBC programme information box with the class and explain that Ss are going to watch different people answering these questions. Then put Ss in pairs to ask 'When's your birthday?' While they do this, write the names of the months in a list on the board. In feedback, write the names of the Ss beside the months on the board.

B ▶ Ss watch the first part of the video and answer the question. Refer to the board to see who has a birthday in the same months. Ss can refer to the photos at the top of the page to check the names of the speakers.

EXTRA SUPPORT Turn on the subtitles if you feel it would benefit learners.

C ▶ Refer Ss to the names from the video and the months. Explain that they should watch the first part of the video again and identify the correct birthday month for each speaker. Play the video, pausing as needed, then ask pairs to compare their answers before you go through them.

EXTRA SUPPORT Provide Ss with several small pieces of blank paper. Dyslexic learners and beginner literacy Ss can place a slip of paper over the wrong answers as they watch. This removes the need for writing so that Ss can focus completely on listening. Alternatively, they could mark the correct answers with a highlighter pen.

EXTRA IDEA The work on the ordinal numbers is the grammar focus of this lesson, so you could come back to the first part of the video later in the lesson and check the dates once Ss have studied the ordinals.

ANSWERS:

1 Ama: September
2 Ryan: May
3 Elijah: August
4 Sautebh: June
5 Anna: April
6 Kielan: November
7 William: February
8 Anna: April
9 Joe: November
10 Josh: March
11 Tom: September

3A ▶ Explain that Ss should watch the second part of the video and count how many speakers do things with friends on their birthdays. They don't need to write, they can just count on their fingers. Play the video, ask pairs to compare then check the answer.

ANSWERS:
Seven speakers do things with their friends on their birthdays.

B Refer Ss to the incomplete sentences and ask them to complete them from what they can remember. Don't check the answers yet.

EXTRA SUPPORT For weaker classes, write the missing words jumbled on the board. Ss with dyslexia may find it easier to have a vertical list of the words to place beside their book.

C ▶ Play the video again for Ss to check their answers. Elicit the answers from individuals and write them on the board. Get Ss to answer in full sentences as this will help prepare them for the speaking activities later in this lesson. Point out that we say *go for a meal* but *go to a restaurant*.

ANSWERS:
2 meal **3** restaurant **4** lunch
5 picnic **6** family

GRAMMAR

ordinal numbers; dates

4A Ask Ss to read the sentences, identify the numbers as in the example, then check in pairs. (Numbers 0–10 were covered in the Lead-in section and 11–100 in Lesson 2A.) If you're short of time, you could do this exercise together as a class. Check answers with the class. Remind Ss that we usually use *on* before dates, but we don't need *on* before *today*.

ANSWERS:
2 9 **3** 21 **4** 8 **5** 3

B The Grammar Bank on page 111 can be used in the lesson or for homework. Decide how and when the exercises will benefit your class.

GB page 111 **GRAMMAR BANK**

Check understanding of the notes with the class, especially focusing on the changes between the written and spoken format of dates and the spelling changes of irregular ordinals.

EXTRA SUPPORT: TEACHER In English, dates can be given in different ways, e.g. BrE: 14.11.2023 (day, month, year); AmE: 11.14.2023 (month, day, year); internet: 2023.11.14 (year, month, day). At this level, it may be simpler for Ss to stick to one version, e.g. *the* + ordinal number + month + year, e.g. *2nd February 2023* ('the second of February twenty twenty-three'). The pronunciation of the *-th* in ordinals and *of* is developed in Sounds and Spelling 5.

1 **Look at the first answer, done as an example, with the class and remind them of the hyphen in higher numbers. Then ask Ss to complete the rest of the dates individually, using the number in brackets, then check in pairs. Check answers with the class and write them on the board. Point out spelling changes as you do so.**

EXTRA SUPPORT: DYSLEXIA You could reduce the number of items to write for dyslexic learners. Alternatively, you could present the exercise with the numbers, enlarged if possible, at the beginning of each gap for Ss to write the ordinal next to.

ANSWERS:

2 seventh	**3** twelfth	**4** third
5 second	**6** first	**7** thirtieth
8 Fifth	**9** sixth	**10** nineteenth

2 **Ss write the next ordinal number. Check answers with the class. Ask pairs to read out the first and following number.**

EXTRA SUPPORT Provide dyslexic and beginner literacy learners with the answers in a vertical list in jumbled order, so they can copy them in the correct place.

ANSWERS:

2 sixteenth	**6** twenty-sixth
3 twentieth	**7** eighteenth
4 twenty-second	**8** tenth
5 fourteenth	

3 **Point out the two examples and make sure Ss understand that 1–6 match the first possible format in the Dates table in the notes, and that 7–12 match the second possible format. Ss write the full dates in words. Note that the final *-st, -nd, -rd* and *-th* have intentionally been left off the days in this exercise so that Ss are required to think about these themselves. Go through the answers.**

EXTRA SUPPORT: DYSLEXIA Provide dyslexic learners with the full form of the dates, with a gap for a key word missing in each one.

EXTRA IDEA: DIGITAL Ss record themselves saying the full forms. They listen back and check they have included all the required words.

ANSWERS:

2 The twenty-fourth of October nineteen eighty-three
3 The second of June twenty twelve
4 The eleventh of August two thousand and six
5 The thirty-first of January twenty twenty-seven
6 The eighth of March eighteen ninety-nine
8 November the second nineteen ninety-four
9 December the twenty-fifth twenty nineteen
10 September the fifth two thousand
11 May the twenty-third two thousand and six
12 July the fourth nineteen seventy-four

SPEAKING

talk about your birthday

5 A **Remind Ss of the question: When's your birthday? and work with them as a class as they try to put themselves in order. They don't need to include the year.**

EXTRA: ALTERNATIVE IDEA If Ss can move around the room, ask the class to move around and ask each other, with the aim of standing in a line from January to December. When they are in a line, each student says their birthday (day and month) to ensure they are in the correct order. It's nice to make a note of these so you can celebrate each birthday as it comes.

B **Refer Ss to the Key phrases and read them with the class, then give them a minute or two to read them again. Give an example yourself to show that several phrases may be used, e.g. 'I usually have a big cake and I sometimes have a party.' Ask Ss to compare what they do in pairs. They don't need to write. Move around to help with vocabulary as needed.**

C **Put Ss in groups of three or four to tell each other about their birthdays, using the Key phrases. Move around and listen. When they have finished, ask each group to tell the class one thing from their discussion, then give feedback on how well they did the activity.**

WRITING

write about your birthday

6 A Explain that Ss should read the description and identify differences to their birthday, e.g, the date is likely to be different. Give Ss a few minutes. Elicit a few answers around the class.

EXTRA SUPPORT If you have dyslexic or beginner literacy learners in your class, read the description with the class so they can listen while they read, or put them in pairs with a partner who can read it with them.

B Ask Ss to write about their birthday, using the description they read as a model. With weaker classes, you could provide a partial skeleton text for Ss to complete with their own details. Ss should aim for about 50 words. Stronger Ss can write more than this.

EXTRA IDEA Ss share their descriptions on a class noticeboard or digital noticeboard.

EXTRA IDEA: DIGITAL Ss record a short talk about their birthday, using a video platform or their phone. They share this with others who then ask follow-up questions.

TO FINISH

Put Ss in pairs to talk about other special dates in their lives (elicit examples relevant to your Ss' culture(s), e.g. wedding anniversary, religious festivals, Valentine's Day, etc.) and what they do on those occasions.

5 REVIEW

LESSON OVERVIEW

This lesson is a review of the language – both grammar and vocabulary – presented in this unit. It also includes a link to the Sounds and Spelling section for this unit, which focuses on voiced and unvoiced consonants: /f/ and /v/, /θ/ and /ð/; and silent *e*: /ɪ/ to /aɪ/. The notes below assume that the tasks are completed in class. However, the self-study type exercises (i.e. Exs 1A, 1B, 2A, 3A, 3B, 4A and 6A) could be done out of class and then checked in the following lesson when the communicative tasks are then completed.

Online Teaching

If you're teaching this lesson online, you might find the following tip useful:

- **Ex 3A:** Ask Ss to write the pairs of verbs in an online collaborative document so you can check spelling.

Additional Materials

For Teachers:

Sounds and Spelling 5

Unit Test in test package

TO START

Ask Ss to work in pairs and try to remember what language they studied in Unit 5 (Grammar: object pronouns, *can* for ability, ordinal numbers, dates; Vocabulary: common verbs, verbs of ability, common adjectives, months; How to … make requests and offers). Ask them to look at the unit lesson objectives to check their ideas.

GRAMMAR

1 A Refer Ss to the list of subject and object pronouns in the Grammar Bank on page 108 to help them if they need it. Look at the example and point out that Ss need to think about gender and singular or plural to make the correct choices. Tell them that Clara Bow was an actress. Ss match the sentences alone then check in pairs. Check answers with the class.

ANSWERS:
1 e **2** b **3** c **4** a **5** d

B Look at the example. Demonstrate the activity by saying some people and things that are true for you, e.g. 'I love it with coffee: a biscuit.' Ss work individually to write their people and things. Help them with vocabulary as needed.

C **Read the example with the class, then put Ss in A/B pairs. Ss take turns at saying who or what the person or thing is and guessing the sentence. When they have finished, ask if they had similar ideas.**

2 A **Refer Ss to the table and ask them to make a sentence about the information they can see there (e.g. 'Jenna can tell the time in English.'). Refer Ss to the gapped conversations and ask them to use the information in the table to complete them. Ss should work alone then compare in pairs. Go through the answers as a class with pairs of Ss reading the conversations. Write the answers on the board so Ss can check their spelling.**

EXTRA SUPPORT: DYSLEXIA It could be helpful to break the activity down into stages and write these on the board, i.e. *1 Identify the information in the table* (can or can't) *you need for each gap. 2 Transfer the relevant information to the sentences.* Ss might find it helpful to highlight each gap and the relevant information for it in the same colour to help them match them up.

ANSWERS:

2 I can
3 I can't
4 can't tell
5 can spell
6 can't understand
7 can say
8 can't

B **Read the example with the class and, if necessary, also demonstrate with a stronger student. If Ss choose Anna and Paulo, tell them to talk about one of them, not both. Put Ss in pairs for the activity. When they have finished, ask Ss to swap roles and repeat.**

C **Demonstrate with a stronger student by asking them a question. Then put Ss in pairs to complete the activity, taking turns to ask and answer questions about the things in the table.**

EXTRA IDEA Ask Ss to copy the table in Ex 2A into their notebooks and draw two extra columns. Stronger classes can also add two or three more rows with additional information to ask about. Then pairs ask each other and put ticks and crosses in the first new column according to their partner's answer. They then ask another classmate and complete the second new column. If possible, provide an opportunity for Ss to use both the male and female pronouns. Then Ss report to the class using *He/She can* … and *They can both* … as appropriate.

VOCABULARY

3 A **Read the example with the class, then ask Ss to complete the rest of the verbs. Point out that the missing letters are the same in each pair, but are not necessarily in the same in order in both words. Monitor and offer help where necessary. When they have finished, check answers with the class and write them, including the two verbs in the example, on the board. Draw attention to patterns in silent letters such as the silent *e* at the end of a word (e.g. *type, take*).**

EXTRA SUPPORT: DYSLEXIA The incomplete words in this exercise might challenge Ss with dyslexia. In this case, reduce the scope and provide a separate numbered list of the pairs of missing letters for them to complete the verbs. Ss should also cover the lines they are not working on to reduce distraction. If possible, pair Ss with a non-dyslexic partner to read the words out.

ANSWERS:

2 drive, dance
3 type, take
4 swim, sing
5 catch, thank
6 paint, listen
7 remember, read
8 forget, throw

B **Ss should refer to their answers in Ex 3A or to the answers on the board to choose the correct verbs. Point out that there are three or four verbs for numbers 2–4. They can work alone then compare in pairs. When they have finished, check answers with the class.**

ANSWERS:

2 play, dance, sing, listen (*read* is also possible)
3 play, type, read
4 play, catch, throw

C **Read the example with the class, then ask Ss to make sentences similar to those in Ex 3B. Put Ss in A/B pairs to take turns to say their sentences and guess.**

EXTRA SUPPORT For weaker classes and Ss who would benefit from writing practice, put Ss in pairs to write their sentences first and monitor them to ensure accuracy.

EXTRA: ALTERNATIVE IDEA This can become a team game if your class is competitive, with groups of Ss guessing another team's verbs for points.

4A **Read the instruction with the class and elicit the first answer to check understanding. Ask Ss to work alone and then in pairs to compare. Invite Ss to record words they got wrong in their notebooks and to use a *Look Say Cover Write Check* method (see page 27) for memorising spelling.**

EXTRA SUPPORT: DYSLEXIA Spelling can cause difficulty for Ss with dyslexia. In this case, provide two alternatives, one correct, for them to choose from for each item (e.g: *wrong/rong*). They should also cover the lines they are not working on to reduce distraction.

ANSWERS:

1 wrong	**2** open	**3** late
4 right	**5** early	**6** closed

B **This activity is a chance for spoken practice. Ask Ss to say the sentences in Ex 4A and then discuss if they are true for them.**

5A **Ask Ss to say the words in pairs, then identify the sounds. Say the words yourself then check answers with the class. The answers below are for the teacher's benefit. We don't expect Ss to be able to write the phonetic symbols, so simply ask them to say the words and isolate the sounds.**

ANSWERS:

phone /f/	never /v/	think /θ/
mother /ð/	bike /aɪ/	time /aɪ/

B **Refer Ss to Sounds and Spelling on page 155.**

page 155 **SOUNDS AND SPELLING**
voiced and unvoiced consonants (2): /f/ and /v/, /θ/ and /ð/; silent *e* (1): /ɪ/ to /aɪ/

The Sounds and Spelling section can be used to help with particular problems. You might want to select the sections or even particular sounds that are most useful for your Ss. The vocabulary used in each section comes from the current unit or previous units.

SOUNDS AND SPELLING TEACHER'S NOTES page 212

6A **Explain that Ss should read the text through and then choose the correct alternatives to complete it. Ask Ss to work alone then compare in pairs. Don't go through the answers yet.**

EXTRA SUPPORT: DYSLEXIA Remind Ss to cover the part of the text they are not focusing on, to reduce distraction.

B **R5.01 | Play the recording and ask Ss to check their answers. Go through the answers as a class and deal with any questions.**

ANSWERS:

1 her	**2** open	**3** first
4 second	**5** us	**6** them
7 gets	**8** an expensive	**9** can't
10 thanks		

EXTRA IDEA: DIGITAL Ss read the text aloud, taking turns to read sections. They then record themselves reading it and listen back. Finally, play the recording again for them to compare.

TO FINISH

Ask Ss to decide what skills work (reading/writing/listening/speaking) they found most interesting in Unit 5 and what they are less confident about. Give them a minute or two to look back over the unit and decide, then put them in pairs to compare. Then discuss as a class. You can use this information to inform future teaching.

6 where?

GSE LEARNING OBJECTIVES

6A Lost

- READING | Read an article about lost things: rooms and furniture
- Say where things are: prepositions of place
- Pronunciation: sentence stress

GSE INFORMATION

VOCABULARY

10–29 Can use language related to furniture and decoration.

10–29 Can use language related to rooms and parts of a building.

READING

27 Can understand simple descriptions of places.

GRAMMAR

26 Can use basic prepositions of place with nouns and noun phrases.

SPEAKING

23 Can describe the position of something in a very basic way.

6B A great place to live

- LISTENING | Listen to people talking about their neighbourhood: places in town (1)
- Talk about your perfect town: *there is, there are*
- Pronunciation: linking with *there*
- Write a post about your area; use commas

GSE INFORMATION

VOCABULARY

10–29 Can use language related to public buildings and places.

LISTENING

27 Can recognise familiar key words and phrases in short, basic descriptions (e.g. of objects, places or people), if spoken slowly and clearly.

GRAMMAR

27 Can use 'there' + 'be' to express presence/absence.

SPEAKING

26 Can describe where they live.

25 Can ask and answer simple questions in areas of immediate need or on very familiar topics.

WRITING

27 Can write simple sentences about their family and where they live.

26 Can use basic punctuation (e.g. commas, full stops, question marks).

6C Where are you?

- HOW TO … | ask where a place is: places in town (2); signs in buildings
- Pronunciation: weak forms with *to*, *of* and *the*

GSE INFORMATION

VOCABULARY

10–29 Can use language related to public buildings and places.

10–29 Can use language related to location and position.

27 Can understand short written notices, signs and instructions with visual support.

HOW TO …

28 Can answer simple questions about the location of people or things in a limited way.

29 Can ask for simple directions, referring to a map or plan.

24 Can understand basic statements about where things or people are, if spoken slowly and clearly and supported by pictures.

26 Can use basic prepositions of place with nouns and noun phrases.

SPEAKING

26 Can understand simple directions from X to Y on foot or public transport.

6D The Travel Show

- BBC PROGRAMME | Understand a show about Ade Adepitan in Rome
- Talk about six hours in a city: *the*
- Describe a city tour

GSE INFORMATION

VIEW

30 Can identify simple information in a short video, provided that the visual supports this information and the delivery is slow and clear.

27 Can understand simple descriptions of places.

GRAMMAR

32 Can use the definite article to refer to a specific person, thing, or situation.

SPEAKING

28 Can answer simple questions about the location of people or things in a limited way.

WRITING

35 Can write a simple text containing key information, given a model.

For full coverage of GSE Learning Objectives go to page 222.

BBC VLOGS

This is a short activity that can be used as an introduction to the unit topic and a warm-up to Lesson 6A. It shouldn't be exploited or taught at length, just played once or twice in class.

Refer Ss to the question in the programme information box and put Ss in pairs to discuss it. When they have finished, ask a few Ss for their answers and have a brief class discussion if they are in different places or have different answers. If they are online, the discussion might be longer and more varied. When they are ready, play the video for Ss to watch and answer the questions in part 2.

ANSWERS:

Two speakers can see trees.

Two speakers can see books.

EXTRA IDEA If Ss want to watch the video again outside class, they can note how many speakers are outside and how many are inside (three of each), as well as other vocabulary.

NOTE The vlogs have been provided by people from around the world in response to the same question. The video content was filmed by them on their own mobile phones, so the picture quality varies considerably and in some cases is of a lower quality. However, this adds to the authenticity of the content.

The locations labelled on the vlogs show where the speaker was when they filmed the video. It does not reflect where the speaker comes from (necessarily).

As many of the speakers are non-native, the videos expose Ss to a range of different accents and varieties of English. This could be used as a way to highlight interesting or useful differences.

Additional Materials

For Teachers:

Presentation Tool Unit 6

Online Digital Resources

Videoscript Unit 6 Opener: BBC Vlogs

6A Lost

GRAMMAR | prepositions of place
VOCABULARY | rooms and furniture
PRONUNCIATION | sentence stress

LESSON OVERVIEW

In this lesson, Ss learn vocabulary related to rooms and furniture and prepositions of place. The context is a reading about where to look for lost items at home. They also practise sentence stress. Ss then do a communicative activity where they ask and tell each other about lost items in pairs. The lesson ends with a speaking activity where they tell each other about their favourite room at home.

Online Teaching

If you're teaching this lesson online, you might find the following tips useful:

- **Ex 1:** Ask Ss to point at or show the different furniture in the room they are in.
- **Ex 3C:** Display the sentences and photo on your device and share your screen. Use the annotate function for Ss to take turns to match the places with the arrows in the photo.
- **Ex 7B:** Ss talk about the room they are in, in breakout rooms. If they are comfortable having cameras on, they can move around and show their furniture on their device.

Additional Materials

For Teachers:

Presentation Tool Lesson 6A

Photocopiable Activities 6A

Grammar Bank 6A

Vocabulary Bank 6A

For Students:

Online Practice 6A

Workbook 6A

TO START

When you come in the classroom, pretend that you have lost something and mime looking for it, then find it. Elicit or teach *lose* and *find*. Ask Ss if they sometimes lose things and what they do to find them. On the board, write the questions: *Do you usually lose things? What do you lose? How do you find them?* and ask pairs to discuss. Take brief feedback to see which items are usually lost. Tell Ss today's class is about losing things.

EXTRA SUPPORT: DYSLEXIA Dyslexic learners in particular benefit from understanding exactly what they are learning in a lesson so that they understand what they are working towards. In this and every lesson, explain clearly what the learning objectives of the lesson are near the start.

VOCABULARY

rooms and furniture

1 **You may want to preteach *furniture*, e.g. via the furniture in the classroom. You can show that we don't use it in the plural, i.e. it doesn't take an 's'. Refer Ss to the table and talk through how it is organised into rooms and furniture, then put them in pairs to put the words in the box in the correct column. Monitor and help with any new vocabulary. Fast finishers can extend the table. When they have finished, go through the answers and drill, marking stress on the multi-syllable words and inviting Ss to note this down.**

EXTRA SUPPORT If your Ss are real beginners, draw a sketch of a house on the board and elicit the rooms, teaching the words *upstairs*, *downstairs*, *bedroom*, *bathroom*, *living room* and *kitchen*. Ask Ss what rooms are usually upstairs (e.g. *bedrooms*) and downstairs (e.g. *kitchen*). After this, move on to Ex 1 and complete it as a class.

EXTRA SUPPORT: DYSLEXIA Give dyslexic learners the words in a vertical list or provide them on separate slips of paper that they can move around.

EXTRA SUPPORT: TEACHER Ss may have come across different vocabulary, so, if necessary, point out that we can say *living room* or *sitting room*, and *sofa* or *couch*. There are no significant differences in meaning or use. An *armchair* is similar to a *sofa*, but for one person. The stress on *television* is either *television* or *television*. Most people just say *TV*. *Shelf* has an unusual plural – *shelves* – common to a few words that end with the /f/ sound (e.g. *wife*, *knife*, *roof*, etc.).

ANSWERS:
rooms: *bathroom*, bedroom, kitchen, living room
furniture: *armchair*, bed, chair, desk, shelf, sofa, table, television

2A **Read the questions with the class, then ask Ss to discuss in pairs. Point out that they should look for the items in the table in Ex 1. When they have finished, elicit their answers and correct any mispronunciations. Be prepared to name other items Ss are interested in.**

ANSWERS:
1 a living room
2 armchair, chair, desk, shelf, sofa, table

B **In their pairs, Ss list any other words for rooms or furniture they know. Refer them to the Vocabulary Bank on page 134 to check their ideas.**

page 134 **VOCABULARY BANK** rooms and furniture

Note that the Vocabulary Bank activities are an important part of the lesson. They should only be omitted if you are confident that your Ss already know this vocabulary. If you don't use the exercises in class, it would be a good idea to set them as homework.

1A **Ss match the words (1–5) with the photos (A–E) individually, then check in pairs. When they have finished, elicit the answers.**

ANSWERS:
1 D **2** C **3** E **4** B **5** A

B **Ask Ss to identify the furniture and parts of rooms (1–18) in the photos (a–r). They should work individually then check in pairs. Go through the answers as a class.**

EXTRA SUPPORT: DYSLEXIA Encourage Ss to cover the words they are not working on each time they make a match to help them focus.

ANSWERS:

1 d	**2** r	**3** o	**4** h	**5** j	**6** l
7 k	**8** f	**9** n	**10** a	**11** g	**12** p
13 e	**14** i	**15** c	**16** q	**17** b	**18** m

C **VB6.01 | Play the recording. Ask Ss to look at the furniture and parts of rooms in the photos (a–r), listen and repeat.**

D **VB6.02 | Play the recording. Ask Ss to listen to the furniture and say the room it belongs in.**

ANSWERS:
1 living room
2 kitchen
3 bedroom
4 bathroom

AUDIOSCRIPT VB6.02

1 armchair, sofa, television
2 cooker, fridge, chair, table, shelf
3 bed, lamp, window
4 bath, shower, toilet

2 A Put Ss in A/B pairs. Ask them to cover the words in Exs 1A and 1B and to focus on the photos. Look at the example together, then ask Ss to take turns to say a colour and identify items of that colour in the photos.

EXTRA SUPPORT With weaker classes, first elicit a list of colours to the board. Refer them back to the Vocabulary Bank on page 128 if necessary. Then put Ss in pairs to complete Ex 2A.

B Keep Ss in their A/B pairs. Student As name the furniture in a room of their choice and Student Bs identify the room. Then they change.

EXTRA IDEA: DIGITAL Ss could show a picture of a room in their home or use pictures found online and work with a partner to name the room and the furniture they can see.

FUTURE SKILLS | Self-management

C Read the Future Skills box with the class. If possible, bring some sticky notes to the classroom and ask Ss to write labels for some of the furniture there. Elicit other things Ss could use sticky notes to label (e.g. items on their desk at home or work, inside their car if they have one, food in their fridge or cupboard, etc.)

READING

EXTRA SUPPORT: DYSLEXIA There is a recording of the reading text available to help dyslexic learners.

3 A Give an example yourself, e.g. 'I usually lose my keys. I look in the kitchen and the living room. I usually find them in the kitchen.' Put Ss in pairs to discuss the questions. After a few minutes take brief feedback and write the things on the board.

EXTRA SUPPORT: TEACHER As Ss haven't studied the prepositions yet, Ss' answers to questions 2 and 3 will be limited. Don't worry too much about accuracy in the feedback. The main aim here is to get Ss thinking about the topic and give them a reason for reading the article.

B Give Ss one minute to read the introduction and compare it to the items they thought of in Ex 3A, question 1. When they have finished, elicit answers and tick off the items on the board to see how many of the things in the article they mentioned. Have a brief class discussion.

C Tell Ss they'll now read the article and they should match the places named (1–8) in the article with the arrows (A–H) in the main photo. Ask them to compare in pairs then go through the answers. Use gesture and examples to further clarify the meaning of the prepositions if necessary.

ANSWERS:

1 H **2** D **3** B **4** C **5** G **6** A **7** F **8** E

D Give an example yourself, e.g. 'I never lose my car keys. I always leave them near the door. I sometimes lose my umbrella or gloves at work.' Ask Ss to discuss in pairs for a few minutes and take brief feedback on the most common places to lose things.

GRAMMAR

prepositions of place

4 A Look at the example with the class, then ask Ss to find the rest of the prepositions. Tell them to focus just on the list in the article, i.e. 1–8. Point out that there are seven more prepositions, a total of eight different ones. If necessary, elicit that a preposition of place describes where something is in relation to something else. Check answers with the class. Write them on the board.

EXTRA SUPPORT: DYSLEXIA Tell Ss to focus on the numbered items one by one and cover up the others as they read, to help them focus. Pair Ss with a partner who can read each numbered item aloud.

EXTRA SUPPORT: TEACHER If Ss ask or if you feel it is relevant here, you can point out the use of the article *the* (e.g. 'Look between the cushions on the sofa.') to talk about one thing (or set of things) that both the writer and reader know (i.e. the writer is talking about the sofa they know / are sure the reader has). This will be the grammar focus in Lesson 6D.

ANSWERS:

under, behind, in, between, on, next to, near, in front of

B The Grammar Bank on page 112 can be used in the lesson or for homework. Decide how and when the exercises will benefit your class.

GB page 112 **GRAMMAR BANK**

This focuses on the meaning and use of prepositions of place. Go through the notes with Ss or let them read them alone. Check understanding where necessary, especially of the phrases with *on* and *in*.

1 **This exercise checks Ss understand the meaning of the prepositions. Do the first one as an example with the class. Ss then continue to choose the correct alternatives alone, then check in pairs. Check answers with the class and discuss where there are any doubts.**

EXTRA SUPPORT: TEACHER Ss may confuse *near* and *next to* (numbers 4 and 8). Explain that *near* is more general, *next to* means 'by the side'. Ss may also tend to confuse *in* and *on*. Point out with examples that *in* is generally 3D ('inside') where *on* is 2D ('surface'). (Note that *opposite* is not taught until Lesson 6C.)

ANSWERS:

1 between	**2** in	**3** in front of
4 near	**7** on	**6** between
7 under	**8** next to	**9** behind
10 in		

2 **This exercise requires Ss to distinguish the prepositions in context. Ss complete the conversations alone, then check in pairs. Check answers with the class.**

EXTRA SUPPORT: DYSLEXIA Dyslexic learners can find this type of exercise, with several options to choose from, difficult. In this case, remove the extra word from each set and provide the words in a vertical list to place alongside the sentences.

ANSWERS:

2 near	**3** in	**4** on
5 next	**6** on	**7** under
8 behind	**9** on	**10** between
11 in	**12** front	

EXTRA IDEA When you have checked the answers, Ss can practise the conversations in pairs, taking turns at both roles. Stronger classes can try again without looking at their books.

PRONUNCIATION

sentence stress

5 A 6.01 | Ss listen and write the sentences. Pause the recording between each sentence so that Ss have time to write, then check in pairs. Check answers with the class.

EXTRA SUPPORT: DYSLEXIA Ss with dyslexia can find listening and writing at the same time difficult. In this case, give Ss the sentences and ask them to listen and track the text with their finger. A further challenge could be set by giving the completed sentences cut up and asking Ss to listen and put them in order.

ANSWERS:

See Ex 5B.

EXTRA IDEA You could point out the use of *the* here when there's only one of something that we both know about (e.g. *in the picture, it's on the table, next to the teacher* [there's only one of you!]). (See Extra Support: Teacher in Ex 4A.)

B 6.01 | Look at the example with the class, then ask Ss to listen and identify the stressed words in the sentences they wrote in Ex 5A. Play the recording again, then ask Ss to compare answers. When you check answers with the class, ask Ss to repeat each sentence. Play the recording again if Ss would like to hear it.

EXTRA SUPPORT: DYSLEXIA Ss with dyslexia can find underlining difficult because text is unstable visually. In this case, tell Ss to highlight in a different way, e.g. by using a coloured highlighter pen or drawing a dot on top of the stressed words.

ANSWERS AND AUDIOSCRIPT:

1 It's under the bed.	**5** Is it in your bag?
2 It's near the window.	**6** Is it between the beds?
3 It's behind the door.	**7** Is it next to the sofa?
4 Is it on the table?	**8** It's in front of you.

C Demonstrate the activity, e.g. by pointing to your phone on your desk, asking, 'Where's my phone?' and inviting answers. Put Ss in pairs to practise asking *Where's my ... ?* questions and answering, using the photo of the room and the arrows (A–H). Ask Ss to change roles after a few turns. Monitor and check Ss are stressing the questions and answers correctly, and using *the* appropriately, and when they have finished drill remedially if necessary.

EXTRA IDEA Ss revise desk objects (from Lesson 3B), and ask each other about these, (e.g. 'Where's your pen?') and give answers. To make it extra challenging, they could arrange things on their desks before they start, putting their phone under a book, etc.

SPEAKING

6 **Put Ss in A/B pairs and refer them to the relevant pages. Explain that they have the same picture, but Student A knows where some things are and Student B knows where the other things are, so they need to ask each other.**

Give Ss time to look at their picture and think about what they can see. Remind them to use *the* if there is only one of something (e.g. 'It's on the table.'). Make sure they don't show each other their pictures (they could sit face-to-face to help with this). When they are ready, ask a stronger pair to demonstrate, then they can start. Student As ask first and Student Bs answer. Then Student B asks their questions. When they have finished, they can show each other their pictures and check they have understood each other correctly.

7 A **Draw a simple line drawing of a room and furniture. It doesn't need to be real but should be very simple so that Ss know you are not expecting fantastic artwork! Tell Ss about the room and what's in it, e.g. 'This is my favourite room, it's the kitchen. It's got a table and four chairs ...'. Now ask Ss to draw their own room. Allow time for this and move around, helping with any unusual vocabulary they need.**

B **Put Ss in pairs to tell each other about the room they have drawn. When they have finished, ask which room most people chose and have a show of hands.**

EXTRA IDEA: DIGITAL Ask Ss to take a picture of a room at home and show this on their device in class. If it's not appropriate or they are not comfortable showing their home, Ss can find a picture online and talk about that instead.

TO FINISH

Write the following sentence beginnings on the board and ask Ss to look back over the lesson to complete them.

In this lesson, I like ... .
I need more practice of ... .
I have a question about ... .

Put Ss in pairs to share their ideas and then have a whole class discussion.

6B A great place to live

GRAMMAR | *there is, there are*
VOCABULARY | places in town (1)
PRONUNCIATION | linking with *there*

LESSON OVERVIEW

In this lesson, Ss learn *there is* and *there are* to describe facilities in town. They also learn vocabulary for buildings and places. The context is a listening where they hear neighbours talking about what's in the area. This leads into the grammar, where Ss also practise linking, and a speaking activity where Ss talk about their idea of a perfect town. The lesson ends with a writing activity where they describe their area.

Online Teaching

If you're teaching this lesson online, you might find the following tips useful:

- **Ex 1A:** Display the photos on your device and share your screen. Ask Ss to share their ideas in the chat, then open up to a whole class discussion.
- **Ex 5C:** Put Ss in pairs in breakout rooms. Visit each room quickly to ensure they are on track, then monitor one or two rooms more closely for language, making a note to visit different Ss next time.
- **Ex 6A:** Use a collaborative document for Ss to share their ideas in breakout rooms. They can take a screenshot of this, then come back to the main room and report back.

Additional Materials

For Teachers:

Presentation Tool Lesson 6B
Photocopiable Activities 6B
Grammar Bank 6B
Vocabulary Bank 6B
Writing Bank 6B

For Students:

Online Practice 6B
Workbook 6B

TO START

Elicit or teach *neighbours* (= the people who live in the next house/apartment). Write it on the board and tell Ss about your home and neighbours, e.g. 'I live in a house in … . I like my neighbours. They're friendly. We sometimes have coffee.' Ask Ss to talk in pairs about where they live and their neighbours. When they have finished, take brief feedback and tell Ss that in this lesson they'll be talking about where they live (i.e. their neighbourhood/area).

EXTRA SUPPORT: DYSLEXIA Dyslexic learners in particular benefit from understanding exactly what they are learning in a lesson so that they understand what they are working towards. In this and every lesson, explain clearly what the learning objectives of the lesson are near the start.

VOCABULARY

places in town (1)

1 A Refer Ss to the photos, then put them in pairs to discuss the questions. (Check understanding of *neighbours* if you didn't cover it in the To start activity.) When they have finished, ask a few Ss to share their answers with the class and have a general discussion.

POSSIBLE ANSWERS:
A on the street, neighbours
B in a garden, friends (or family)
C on a roof, friends

B Read the list with the class, checking that Ss can pronounce the words, and elicit what *other things* could be (e.g. transport links, safe area, theatre, hospital) then ask Ss to discuss in pairs. Check answers with the whole class and see if people agree.

EXTRA: ALTERNATIVE IDEA You could set up the activity slightly differently by asking Ss to make a list of features in a town, and elicit these to the board, introducing any features from Ex 1B that Ss haven't mentioned. Depending on your Ss' age and interests these could be hospital / medical centre, transport links / train station, etc. Then ask Ss to tick three that are important and cross three that are not important to them. Then start the speaking activity in Ex 1B, with pairs discussing what is important to them in the place where they live.

2 A Ss work together in pairs to identify people and places in the list in Ex 1B. As they do this, monitor for pronunciation and correct as needed. Go through the answers as a class and categorise them on the board. Drill and highlight word stress. Point out that some words are given as plural (e.g. parks) and it is a good idea to record all new vocabulary in singular form unless it is always plural.

EXTRA SUPPORT Ss sometimes have difficulty with words that are similar in their language. Point out the soft /s/ in *cinema*. Note the stress in *restaurant*: if Ss pronounce it with three syllables, it's a good idea to break this down into two syllables for them ('res' – 'tront') and practise this. A *café* is a place, not a drink.

EXTRA IDEA Stronger classes and fast finishers can add more town-related words to each category (people and places).

ANSWERS:
people: *friends*, family, neighbours
places: *supermarket*, (other) shops, parks, schools, cinema, sports centre, restaurants, cafés

B Look at the list of places on the board from Ex 2A. Elicit a further place (e.g. hospital). Ask pairs to write more places and give them a time frame of three minutes, then refer them to the Vocabulary Bank on page 135 to check their ideas.

page 135 **VOCABULARY BANK** places in town (1)

Note that the Vocabulary Bank activities are an important part of the lesson. They should only be omitted if you are confident that your Ss already know this vocabulary. If you don't use the exercises in class, it would be a good idea to set them as homework.

1 A Ss match the places (1–14) with the photos (A–N) individually, then check in pairs. Check answers with the class.

EXTRA CHALLENGE Before they do Ex 1A, ask Ss to cover the words and see how many places they can name.

EXTRA SUPPORT: DYSLEXIA Covering the words they are not currently matching with a photo will help dyslexic learners focus.

ANSWERS:
1 F **2** G **3** J **4** E **5** K **6** D **7** I
8 A **9** L **10** B **11** M **12** H **13** N **14** C

B VB6.03 | Refer Ss to the photos. Explain that they are focusing on the sound of the words rather than the spelling. Play the recording and pause for them to repeat chorally. Do further individual drills as needed.

C Check Ss recall what the circles in the patterns represent (syllables, with large circles representing the stress). Look at the examples with the class and elicit an example for patterns 3 and 4. Then ask Ss to match the words with the correct pattern. Put Ss in pairs to say the words and help each other. Don't check the answers yet.

VE

D **VB6.04 | Play the recording for Ss to listen and check. Confirm the answers as a class.**

ANSWERS:

1 *school*
2 *airport*
3 hotel
4 bus station, cinema, hospital, library, post office, sports centre, swimming pool, train station
5 museum
6 shopping centre, supermarket

2 A **Put Ss in pairs. Ask a stronger pair to demonstrate the activity. Monitor and offer help where necessary.**

B **Ss stay in their pairs and share and compare their ideas. When they have finished, ask a few pairs if they had similar answers. Remind them to use *We both …* when they talk about things that are the same.**

EXTRA SUPPORT You could write the sentence starters on the board: *I often go to … . I never go to … .* and ask weaker classes to complete the sentences, then tell each other.

LISTENING

3 A **6.02 | Explain that Ss will listen to two people talking and they need to note two places: where they are now and where they go at the end. Play the recording and ask Ss to discuss the questions in pairs. Play the recording again if Ss are unsure. Go through the answers.**

EXTRA SUPPORT: TEACHER Ss are sometimes anxious about listening and not understanding every word and this creates a further barrier to their understanding. Point out to Ss that it's not necessary or even possible to understand everything. The task is there to provide a focus for Ss to understand the key information.

ANSWERS:

They are near their homes. They go to Debbie's apartment for coffee.

AUDIOSCRIPT 6.02

S = Soraya D = Debbie

S: Excuse me.
D: Hi. Yes, can I help?
S: Yes, I'm new here.
D: New?
S: Yes, I have a new job in the area. I live in an apartment in this building.
D: Oh, so we're neighbours! I'm Debbie.
S: I'm Soraya. Nice to meet you.
D: Nice to meet you!
S: Can I ask you some questions about the area?
D: Sure.
S: Are there any shops near here?
D: Yes, there are some great shops. There's a big supermarket. There are two cafés. And a nice Italian restaurant.
S: That's good.
D: And there's a very good school. But that's not important for you.
S: No, but it's interesting. Good for a family, I mean. Erm, can I ask … Is there a swimming pool? I swim every day.
D: No, there isn't a swimming pool in the area … but there's one about three kilometres from here.
S: That's OK. And is there a park? I run at the weekends.
D: Yes, there is.
S: That's great. Well, thank you for all that.
D: No problem. Are you free now?
S: Yes.
D: Come and have a coffee. I live in apartment seventeen.
S: OK, great. Thanks.

B **6.02 | Explain that Ss will now listen again for more detail. Refer them to the list in Ex 1B and ask them to note which things are talked about. Play the recording. Ss can compare in pairs, then go through the answers as a class.**

EXTRA SUPPORT: DYSLEXIA Give Ss a vertical list of the places in Ex 1B, with each place on a new line, and they can tick or highlight the places they hear rather than writing.

ANSWERS:

shops, supermarket, cafés, restaurant, school, park

GRAMMAR

there is, there are

4 A **Explain that you will now use the listening to look at some grammar. Ask Ss to use the words in the box to complete the sentences. Check answers with the class and write them on the board. Leave the sentences on the board for later.**

EXTRA SUPPORT: DYSLEXIA Adapt the exercise to make it simpler for dyslexic learners to process. Provide two alternatives for each gap, one correct and one distractor.

EXTRA: ALTERNATIVE IDEA For classes that would benefit from extra listening practice, play Audio 6.03 to the class to check the answers. Write the sentences on the board (for use in Ex 5A).

ANSWERS:

1 Are	**2** are	**3** 's
4 isn't	**5** Is	**6** there

B The Grammar Bank on page 113 can be used in the lesson or for homework. Decide how and when the exercises will benefit your class.

GB page 113 **GRAMMAR BANK**

Go through the notes with Ss or let them read them alone. Check understanding where necessary, especially of the use of *some* and *any*.

1 **This focuses on the form and use of *there is* and *there are*. Remind Ss to use the notes to help them complete the conversations, and then check in pairs. Check answers with the class and write them on the board to check correct spelling and punctuation. If you have time, pairs can read the conversations together.**

EXTRA SUPPORT: DYSLEXIA Provide the words for each conversation separately, to reduce the amount of information Ss have to process at any one time. It would also be helpful to provide them in a vertical list rather than arranged horizontally as in the box.

ANSWERS:

1 is there	**6** is there
2 there isn't	**7** there are
3 there's	**8** is there
4 are there	**9** there's
5 there aren't	**10** is

2 **This focuses on the positive and negative forms of *there is* and *there are*. Read the example with the class. Remind Ss that we need *there's* and *there isn't* for singular and *there are* and *there aren't* for plurals. Then ask Ss to write the rest of the sentences alone, and then check in pairs. Check answers with the class and write them on the board. Ask individual Ss to read sentences aloud to practise pronunciation.**

EXTRA SUPPORT With weaker classes, you may want to go over both the singular and plural positive and negative forms (*there's a / there are some, there isn't a / there aren't any*) and write these up on the board as a support.

EXTRA SUPPORT: DYSLEXIA Reduce the amount of writing for Ss with dyslexia by providing the sentence endings so they can focus on the correct form of *there is* and *there are*, e.g ... *some cinema tickets*.

ANSWERS:

2 There's a ring.
3 There are two children in the photos.
4 There are some glasses.
5 There aren't any keys.
6 There's a music book.
7 There's an English–Spanish dictionary.
8 There isn't a phone.

PRONUNCIATION

linking with *there*

5A **6.03 | Refer Ss to the completed sentences from Ex 4A. Ss listen and draw the links between *there* or *there's* and other words in the sentences. Play the first one to demonstrate, then play the rest, pausing the recording after each one for Ss to draw the lines. When they have finished, ask Ss to compare. Then check answers and add the links to the sentences on the board from Ex 4A. Point out to Ss that linking happens in speech, when we are talking at a normal speed, between a consonant and vowel sound, or when a consonant is repeated. It is completely correct and not a sign of laziness! When speech is very slow, linking is not so likely.**

EXTRA SUPPORT: TEACHER Awareness of linking is important because even if Ss themselves speak slowly and carefully at the moment, they need to get used to hearing natural speech and aim at producing it.

ANSWERS:

2 There‿are two cafés.
3 There's‿a very good school.
4 There‿isn't a swimming pool in the area.
5 Is there‿a park?
6 Yes, there‿is.

B **6.03 | Play the recording again for Ss to listen and repeat.**

C **Read the instruction and look at the example with the class. Point out the links. Then demonstrate the activity with a stronger student. Point out that we say *Is there a ... ?* when there is likely to be just one (e.g. a library, a post office) and *Are there any ... ?* when there could be more than one (e.g. shops, cafés). Remind Ss of the two short answers (*Yes, there is/are.* and *No, there isn't/aren't.*), then put them in pairs to ask and answer. Circulate to encourage and help with linking where necessary. When they have finished, ask a few pairs to report back on what their partner told them.**

EXTRA IDEA To ensure that Ss are able to use all the vocabulary seen, you could provide a map of a local area with places marked or a list of places ticked and crossed. Ss use this information to ask and answer.

SPEAKING

6 A Read through the whole task (steps 1–4) with the class to check they understand. Before they start, tell Ss to copy the diagram into their notebooks.

1 Focus on the list of roles and check Ss understand *couple* (two people in a relationship) and *retired* (not working because you are older). Have a general discussion about what the people with different profiles need (e.g. Ss from cultures where dog owning is not usual may not realise that dogs require walking daily). Put Ss in pairs to choose the role they prefer. They don't need to select a role that is similar to their real-life profile.

EXTRA: ALTERNATIVE IDEA As an alternative to Ss deciding their roles for themselves, you could divide the different profiles among Ss, with groups working on different ones. When they have finished steps 1–4, they should present their plans to each other and explain their reasoning (as in Ex 6B). This will involve more speaking.

2 When they have decided, ask Ss to discuss and agree six places that their role is likely to need. Look at the example together and show how the negative version is formed: *I don't think … is important*. Highlight that we usually make the verb *think* negative rather than using a negative *be*, i.e. *I don't think … is …* NOT ~~*I think … isn't …*~~. Encourage them to give reasons. Move around during the discussion and prompt as needed.

3 Refer Ss to the diagram they have copied into their notebooks. They should use this for this part of the activity. Model the activity by completing a version of the diagram on the board to illustrate (e.g. *young couple with a dog – near home: park, shops, café; 3–4 kilometres from home: supermarket, sports centre, restaurants*). Leave this on the board and tell Ss to discuss in their pairs where to place the places they have chosen, bearing in mind the role they have. Draw their attention to the examples in steps 3 and 4 giving useful language for the discussion parts of the task. Show how these can be generalised for more examples by writing just the first part on the board and asking Ss for continuations: *What things can we put … ? Where can we … ? I think … . Put … .*

4 Ask Ss to decide where to add 'family' and 'friends' to the diagram. You could also add these to the model diagram you presented earlier.

B Put pairs of Ss into groups of four or six and ask them to take turns to present the perfect town for the role they chose. Listening Ss should ask questions. Refer them to the example conversation for useful language they can use and circulate as they discuss to monitor and support.

EXTRA SUPPORT Weaker classes may benefit from time to prepare what they are going to say. Pairs can make notes and practise their presentation together before giving it to others. They can also spend time writing questions.

C Ss compare their diagrams in their groups and talk about what they like about each town. In feedback, ask what is the same or similar in both/all the group's diagrams.

EXTRA IDEA If you can, put the diagrams up on the wall so that all Ss can see them. Ask Ss to move around and look at them, commenting on similarities. When they have finished, ask the class which towns they liked and why.

WRITING

write a post about your area; use commas

7 A Explain that Ss will prepare to write about their own area. Refer them to the beginning of the post and the example question. Ask them to write two questions to ask for more information about Ealing. Elicit their questions and write them on the board.

B Refer Ss to the Writing Bank on page 90.

page 90 **WRITING BANK** **WB**

1 A Tell Ss they can now see the full post. Give them two minutes to read it quickly and see if they find the answers to their questions. Take brief feedback.

EXTRA SUPPORT: DYSLEXIA For dyslexic learners, record the post before the class or read it aloud. While Ss listen, they should read silently / track the text with their finger.

B Explain that the words and phrases in the box are what the numbered paragraphs in the post talk about. They are 'topics'. Ss need to read again and choose the correct topic or description for each numbered paragraph. Two of the topics in the box are not needed. If you think it's necessary, you could read paragraph 1 with the class and then elicit the correct topic (places to buy food). Give Ss five minutes to read alone and then discuss their ideas in pairs. Go through the answers.

WB **EXTRA SUPPORT: DYSLEXIA** For Ss with dyslexia, remove the distraction of the two extra topics (cafés and schools). Write the four topics in a vertical list and encourage Ss to mask the sections of the page they are not working on to avoid distraction.

ANSWERS:
1 places to buy food **3** people
2 sport/exercise **4** transport

2 A Refer Ss to the two pairs of sentences, to read and choose the correct one in each pair. Elicit or teach the words *comma* and *list*.

ANSWERS:
1b and 2a are correct.

B Referring to the two correct sentences, ask Ss to choose the correct words to complete the rules. Go through the answers.

EXTRA SUPPORT: TEACHER You (and even some Ss) may follow the rule of the 'Oxford comma' (also known as a 'serial comma'), where a comma is placed after the penultimate item in a list (i.e. before *and* or *or*). This is used less and less these days, and we do not cover it here. It is not wrong, so if Ss use it, there's no need to correct.

ANSWERS:
1 use **2** don't use **3** don't use

3 A Refer Ss to Ex 1B and ask them to choose three topics from the box to write about. For this activity they can either write about the area where they live now or their home town.

B Refer Ss to the sentences to rewrite and complete in their notebooks to start off their own posts. They should aim for 30–50 words. Stronger Ss can be encouraged to write more. Move around and support, pointing out where a comma should or should not be used if necessary.

EXTRA IDEA After Ss write their posts, and before they share them for content, you might have pairs check each other's posts for use of commas, or you may wish to check this yourself.

C Put Ss in pairs to swap posts and then ask questions. If time allows, they can swap with more than one partner.

EXTRA IDEA: DIGITAL Create an online noticeboard where Ss can post their texts, adding photos if possible, and with the opportunity to write comments or questions on the other Ss' work.

TO FINISH

Tell Ss about a place that you know (e.g. somewhere you have been on holiday, where you were born, etc.) and why you like it or don't like it (e.g 'Liverpool is a city in the north of England. There are many different shops in the centre, a famous art gallery and lots of museums. There is also a big park near the city centre. I like it because there are a lot of things to do.'). Put Ss in groups to describe a place they know to each other. When they have finished, ask them to report back to the class.

6C Where are you?

HOW TO ... | ask where a place is
VOCABULARY | places in town (2); signs in buildings
PRONUNCIATION | weak forms with *to*, *of* and *the*

LESSON OVERVIEW

In this lesson, Ss learn more vocabulary related to places in a town. They also learn functional language for asking for and giving directions, as well as practise the weak forms of small words in directions. The context is a situation where people ask and tell each other about the location of buildings. The lesson ends with a speaking activity where Ss roleplay giving simple directions in pairs.

Online Teaching

If you're teaching this lesson online, you might find the following tips useful:

- **Ex 1A:** In the main room, share the photo of the train station on your screen and ask Ss to name the country. They can write their answers in the chat then come together as class to compare.
- **Ex 4A:** Display the sentences on your device and share your screen. Enable annotations and ask individual Ss to mark stressed words on the shared screen.
- **Ex 6A:** Ss work with their partner in breakout rooms.

Additional Materials

For Teachers:
Presentation Tool Lesson 6C
Photocopiable Activity 6C
Grammar Bank 6C
Vocabulary Bank 6C

For Students:
Online Practice 6C
Workbook 6C

TO START

Write these questions on the board: *How do you find a new place? Do you use your phone, a map or ask someone? Why?* Put Ss in small groups to discuss the questions. Tell them today they'll learn about asking for directions.

EXTRA SUPPORT: DYSLEXIA Dyslexic learners in particular benefit from understanding exactly what they are learning in a lesson so that they understand what they are working towards. In this and every lesson, explain clearly what the learning objectives of the lesson are near the start.

VOCABULARY

places in town (2)

1 A Refer Ss to the photo of the train station. Write a suggested sentence structure on the board, (e.g. *I think this is ... because ...* .). Put them in pairs to discuss the question. When they have finished, elicit their ideas and have a brief class discussion.

ANSWER:
The photo shows Bremen station in Germany.

B Focus attention on the words in the box. Ask Ss to identify these in the pictures (A–I) and point out that one word is not in the pictures. Ss can compare in pairs, then check the answers with the class. Drill pronunciation.

EXTRA SUPPORT: DYSLEXIA Encourage Ss to read the places in the box one at a time, covering over the others to help them focus. Once they have identified the thing in a picture (or not), they move on to the next word.

EXTRA SUPPORT: TEACHER It's a good idea to drill countable nouns with the article *a/an*, so *a cash machine, an exit*. Remind Ss that we use *an* before words starting with a vowel sound. Point out the silent letters: *u* in *building* and *g* in *sign*.

ANSWERS:

A car park	**B** exit	**C** cash machine
D sign	**E** building	**F** street
G bus stop	**H** entrance	**I** clock

'seat' is not in the pictures.

C Ss discuss the question in pairs. When they have finished, ask pairs what they see, eliciting answers from different Ss for them to compare. Pay attention to the pronunciation of the vocabulary in the box and drill as needed.

D Ss can draw signs they know, as they may not know what they are called. They discuss what the signs mean. When Ss have finished, refer them to the Vocabulary Bank on page 136 to check their ideas.

EXTRA: ALTERNATIVE IDEA Teach the shapes: *circle*, *triangle* and *rectangle*; and revise colours: *red*, *blue*, *yellow*, etc. Ask Ss to work in pairs, taking turns with one drawing and describing a sign (e.g. 'It's a circle, it's red with a white line.') and the other saying or guessing what it means (e.g. 'It means don't go in.').

VB page 136 **VOCABULARY BANK** signs in buildings

Note that the Vocabulary Bank activities are an important part of the lesson. They should only be omitted if you are confident that your Ss already know this vocabulary. If you don't use the exercises in class, it would be a good idea to set them as homework.

1 A Ss work in pairs to identify the signs. Don't check the answers yet.

B Ask Ss to match the words and phrases (1–10) with the signs (A–J). They should compare in pairs, then go through the answers as a class.

EXTRA SUPPORT: DYSLEXIA Encourage Ss to cover the words they are not currently working on to help reduce distraction.

ANSWERS:
1 G **2** C **3** E **4** I **5** B
6 H **7** J **8** A **9** F **10** D

C VB6.05 | Play the recording. Ask Ss to look at the signs, listen and repeat.

D Put Ss in pairs to discuss which signs in Ex 1A they can see where. Point out any signs in the room. Move around and listen. When they have finished, take brief class feedback.

ANSWERS:
1 entrance, hospital, parking area, school
2 fire exit, lift, stairs, the first floor
3 exit/way out, fire exit, information desk (sometimes), lift, stairs, the first floor
4 exit/way out, fire exit, information desk, lift, stairs, the first floor

How to ...
ask where a place is

2 A Ask Ss what kind of messages they can see (text / instant messages) and who they are from (Marta in white and Rob in blue). Then ask them to look at the messages and identify what Rob's problem is. Discuss this as a class.

ANSWER:
Rob doesn't know where the sports centre is.

B Focus attention on the map. Give Ss a few minutes to look at it in pairs, look at the places that are labelled (e.g. post office) and identify the sign for the bus stop. Then ask them to match the sentences (1–5) with the places and things on the map individually, then check in pairs. Check answers as a class.

ANSWERS:
3 bus stop **4** 8 **5** 6

C Elicit which word, or words, in the first sentence tells us the position of the cinema in relation to the supermarket (*opposite*). Tell Ss this is a preposition. Ask them to identify the prepositions in the other sentences and point out that these can be a group of words, rather than just one word. Note that *opposite*, in particular, will be new to Ss.

EXTRA SUPPORT If you feel Ss need more support with the prepositions presented here, first introduce the terms *to the left/right* and *opposite / in front of* by referring to classroom furniture and Ss. (e.g. 'The door's opposite the window. John is to the right of Gabi.' etc.). Clarify that *in front of* suggests less distance and *opposite* suggests face-to-face. You could contrast the example of people in a queue (*in front of*) with two shops on a street (*opposite*) to underline this.

ANSWERS:
1 opposite
2 to the right of
3 in front of
4 to the right of
5 to the left of

EXTRA IDEA For further practice, put Ss in pairs. Looking at the map, Ss ask each other 'Where's number 3?', 'Where's the cinema?', etc. and answer using prepositions.

3 A 6.04 | Focus attention on the map again. Explain that Rob is going to ask for directions. Ss should listen and identify the sports centre and the two bookshops (they are three of the numbers on the map). To do this, Ss will also need to refer back to the content of the messages in Ex 2A. Play the recording, then ask Ss to discuss in pairs and then go through the answers. Write them on the board. If you have an active board / projector, label them on the map.

ANSWERS:
1 place 4 **2** places 2, 7

AUDIOSCRIPT 6.04

R = Rob W = woman M = Marta

Conversation 1

R: Excuse me?
W: Yes?
R: I'm lost. Is there a sports centre near here?
W: Yes, it's next to the cinema. Can you see the cinema? Over there?
R: Oh yes. I can see it.
W: The sports centre is to the left of the cinema. It's a big building. You can't miss it.
R: Thanks a lot.
W: No problem.

Conversation 2

M: Hi Rob, where are you?
R: I'm in front of the bookshop. It's closed.
M: Yes, sorry. It closes at five.
R: Where are **you**?
M: I'm in another bookshop in the shopping centre.
R: Where's the shopping centre?
M: It's opposite the post office.
R: Oh, yes, I can see the entrance.
M: OK. Go in the main entrance and the bookshop is on the right.
R: On the right.
M: Yes, it's opposite the shoe shop.
R: OK. See you in a minute.
M: Wait. I'm on the first floor.
R: OK.
M: You can take the lift or there are some stairs.
R: OK, see you in a minute!
M: OK. See you.

B 6.05 | Focus attention on the sentences. Explain that these are extracts from the conversations just heard and that Ss should try and complete them in pairs. Move around the class and monitor. When they have finished, play the recording for Ss to listen and check individually before allowing time for them to pair check. Then go through the answers as a class.

EXTRA SUPPORT If you feel your Ss will find this too difficult, write the missing words, jumbled, on the board for them to choose from. You might decide to add this support when monitoring if they are struggling or getting a lot wrong. When checking the answers, you may need to play the recording a second time in sections.

ANSWERS:

1 there, next **2** left **3** Where, opposite
4 on **5** on, get

C The Grammar Bank on page 114 can be used in the lesson or for homework. Decide how and when the exercises will benefit your class.

page 114 **GRAMMAR BANK**

GB

This focuses on the form of phrases for asking about and saying where places are. Read the notes with the class or give them a few minutes to read alone, then ask for any questions they have.

1 **Refer Ss to the map, then ask them to choose the correct prepositions to complete the sentences alone, then check in pairs. Check answers with the class. Ask Ss to read each answer aloud so you can work on pronunciation.**

ANSWERS:

2 left **3** next to **4** opposite
5 in front of **6** near **7** opposite
8 near **9** right **10** in front of
11 near **12** left

2 **Point out the example and explain that all the examples of mistakes are grammatical (i.e. missing words, extra words, word order, incorrect words), not spelling. Ss find the rest of the mistakes alone, then check in pairs. Monitor and advise them to use the notes to help them. When they have finished, check answers with the class. If you have time, Ss can practise reading the conversations.**

EXTRA SUPPORT Spotting mistakes can be quite difficult for dyslexic and beginner literacy learners. Here, you could adapt the exercise to give the correct and a wrong alternative in each case. Ss choose which one is correct.

ANSWERS:

(Only the sentences where there is a mistake are given.)

1 A: How far is **it**?
B: It's next **to** the bank and it's opposite ~~to~~ the cinema.

2 A: … Are ~~any there~~ **there any** toilets …
B: Yes. ~~There~~ **They're** near the lift.
A: How **do** I get to the lift?
A: Where **are** the stairs?

EXTRA CHALLENGE If you think they can do it, ask Ss to change some of the places and directions when they practise the conversations in pairs.

PRONUNCIATION

weak forms with *to*, *of* and *the*

4A 6.06 | Tell Ss that they should listen and identify the stressed word or words in each sentence. Elicit the kinds of words that are usually stressed (e.g. nouns, verbs). Ask Ss to read the sentences before they listen so the task is easier. Ss listen and underline the stressed words, then check in pairs. Check answers with the whole class.

EXTRA SUPPORT: DYSLEXIA Ss with dyslexia might find listening, reading and underlining at the same time a challenge. For this activity, tell them to simply listen for the stress in the sentences to see if they can identify where it falls.

ANSWERS:

1 It's next to the cinema.
2 It's opposite the sports centre.
3 It's to the left of the supermarket.
4 It's on the right.
5 I'm in front of the bookshop.

EXTRA SUPPORT: TEACHER The focus in Ex 4A is on the stressed words rather than the weak forms so that Ss can then recognise the reason for the weak forms in Ex 4B. As well as reminding Ss that stressed words are words that carry meaning, you could also tell Ss that stressed words are spaced evenly when we speak, like a metronome. This means that the words between stressed words become squashed into the same amount of time.

B 6.06 | Remind Ss of the weak sound /ə/. Play the recording and ask Ss to notice the weak sounds.

C 6.06 | Play the recording again and pause for Ss to listen and repeat. Show the rhythm of the sentence with your hand and conduct them.

EXTRA IDEA You could use backchain drilling to practise the sentences, e.g. … *cinema.*, … *the cinema.*, … *next to the cinema.*, *It's next to the cinema.*

SPEAKING

5 Put Ss in A/B pairs and refer them to the relevant pages. Explain that they have the same map, but Student A knows where some places are and Student B knows where the other places are. They shouldn't show each other their maps but need to ask each other and write the names on their map where they have a blank space. Give them a few minutes to look at their map, then ask them to start. They take turns to ask about their places, with Student As asking first. Move around and listen, reminding them not to look at each other's maps. When they have finished, ask pairs to show each other their maps and check they have labelled them correctly.

6A Refer Ss to the flow chart. Elicit the first question, then put Ss in pairs to work out the remaining questions and answers. When they have finished, elicit the conversation by asking pairs to read across the class and build it up on the board.

EXTRA SUPPORT: DYSLEXIA It would be helpful to pair dyslexic learners with stronger Ss for this task. Dyslexic learners will also be better able to process the information if the conversation is presented as a single column of dialogue.

ANSWERS:

A: Excuse me?
B: Yes?
A: Is there a good café near here?
B: Yes, there is. There's a good Turkish café.
A: How far is it?
B: About ten minutes.
A: How do I get there?
B: Do you know the post office?
A: Yes, I do.
B: The Turkish café is opposite the post office.
A: Thank you.

EXTRA SUPPORT: TEACHER If you add the conversation to the board, it's a useful reference. However, Ss are likely to read from it in Ex 6B. If you don't want them to do so, then rub it out (possibly leaving a few key words) or use a screen to cover the words.

B Refer the pairs to the flow chart to practise the conversation using the prompts. When they have finished, they can change roles. Move around and listen to how they manage the phrases and weak forms.

7 A **Give Ss a minute or two to prepare individually. They choose two places from the list.**

B **Put Ss in pairs to take turns asking about their places and giving their directions. The listening student should draw a sketch map to show where each place they ask about is.**

C **Ask Ss to show the map they have drawn to their partner and check if it is correct.**

EXTRA: HOW TO ... Ask Ss to work in small groups and describe a room in their home, saying where the furniture is using prepositions of place. Refer them to the Vocabulary Bank for support as needed. The listening partner can ask questions and draw a plan if they enjoyed that aspect of the last activity.

TO FINISH

Write on the board:
What do you think of English pronunciation?
What is difficult for you? How can you improve?
and ask Ss to discuss. Have a general discussion.

EXTRA IDEA: SPEAK ANYWHERE Encourage Ss to practise using the Speak Anywhere interactive roleplay.

6D BBC Entertainment

The Travel Show

GRAMMAR | *the*
SPEAKING | talk about six hours in a city
WRITING | describe a city tour

LESSON OVERVIEW

In this lesson, Ss learn the form and use of the definite article *the*. The context is an extract from a BBC travel show where the presenter visits Rome for six hours. Ss also learn phrases to talk about a city tour. They then listen to somebody talk about their city and do a speaking activity where they practise talking about a city they know. The lesson ends with a writing activity where Ss describe a city tour.

Online Teaching

If you're teaching this lesson online, you might find the following tips useful:

- **Ex 1A:** Share your screen and have a whole class discussion about the photo. Ss can contribute verbally or, if a very large group, use the chat.
- **Ex 2A:** Sometimes videos can be a little slow or jumpy when streamed in an online class environment. If you know this is an issue for you, give Ss time to watch the video on their own device before moving on.
- **Ex 3A:** Display the exercise on a shared screen and enable the annotate function so that Ss can add their answers.
- **Ex 4A:** Put Ss in pairs in breakout rooms to complete this activity. Try and visit each breakout room briefly to listen in.

Additional Materials

For Teachers:
Presentation Tool Lesson 6D
Online Digital Resources
Grammar Bank 6D
Videoscript 6D: BBC Entertainment

For Students:
Online Practice 6D
Workbook 6D

TO START

Show pictures of cities including Rome and Paris, as well as other cities relevant to Ss. Ask Ss in pairs to identify the cities and say which adjective(s) suit them. Provide a list of these on the board, e.g. *romantic, fun, expensive, interesting, beautiful, lovely*). The last three adjectives appear later in the lesson, so are worth teaching at this point. When they have finished, discuss as a class. Tell Ss today's lesson is about talking about cities.

EXTRA SUPPORT: DYSLEXIA Dyslexic learners in particular benefit from understanding exactly what they are learning in a lesson so that they understand what they are working towards. In this and every lesson, explain clearly what the learning objectives of the lesson are near the start.

PREVIEW

1 A Ask Ss to identify the place in pairs and name any other tourist attractions in Rome they know. When they have finished, collect answers and write them on the board.

EXTRA SUPPORT Some classes may not have this cultural knowledge. If you think your Ss will have few ideas, you can skip this stage or provide some names of attractions for them (there is a list in the programme information).

ANSWER:
The photo shows the Colosseum.

B Refer Ss to the programme information. Check that Ss understand *tour guide* (person who leads you around tourist attractions) and *local* (from the area). Put them in pairs to read it and check the names of the attractions mentioned. When they have finished, go through the answers and tick the names of attractions they listed in Ex 1A off on the board.

EXTRA SUPPORT: DYSLEXIA Read the programme information aloud, record it before the lesson or have another student read it with a dyslexic learner to support them.

C Refer Ss to the sentences (1–4). Explain that they should read the programme information again and choose the sentence that is correct. When they have finished, ask pairs to compare then elicit the answer. Point out that the key word for sentence 4 is *local*.

ANSWER:
Sentence 4 is correct.

EXTRA IDEA Ss could correct the other three sentences according to the programme information (Ade has six hours, not seven. He goes by bus, not by car. He has five places to visit, not six.).

VIEW

2 A ▶ Ask Ss to watch the video clip and decide which tourist attraction they like best. They don't need to write. After viewing they can compare with a partner and then have a whole class show of hands to see which attraction is the most popular.

EXTRA SUPPORT Turn on the subtitles if you feel it would benefit learners.

B Ask Ss to match each sentence with an attraction from the video clip, then check their answers in pairs. Don't check answers with the whole class yet.

EXTRA SUPPORT: DYSLEXIA Provide the names of the attractions on slips of paper for Ss to place alongside the sentences and choose from.

C ▶ Play the video clip, pausing as needed, then ask pairs to compare again before going through the answers.

ANSWERS:

2 the Palatine Hill	**4** the Trevi Fountain
3 the Mouth of Truth	**5** the Colosseum

GRAMMAR

the

3 A Ask Ss to complete the sentences from the video clip with *a* or *the*, then check in pairs. If you're short of time, you could do this exercise together as a class. Check answers with the class. You could elicit Ss' ideas about why we use *the* when the answers are complete.

ANSWERS:
1 a **2** the, a **3** The **4** a, the

B The Grammar Bank on page 115 can be used in the lesson or for homework. Decide how and when the exercises will benefit your class.

⏩ page 115 **GRAMMAR BANK**

Check understanding of the notes with the class, and especially focus on the difference between *the*, where there is only one, and *a*, where we are speaking more generally, e.g. *Can I see the doctor?* (there is only one doctor) vs. *Can I see a doctor?* (there is more than one doctor, and I don't mind who I see).

1 Look at the example with the class and discuss why *the* is used (there is only one kitchen). Check that Ss remember when we use *a* and when we use *an*, then ask Ss to complete the rest of the sentences individually, then check in pairs. Check answers with the class and write them on the board. Drill phrases.

GE

ANSWERS:
2 an **3** the **4** the **5** an **6** the
7 a **8** the **9** a **10** the

2 This exercise focuses on correct usage. Ss should find three places where *a*, *an* or *the* is missing in each conversation. They can work alone, then check in pairs. Check answers with the class. Ask pairs to read out the conversations across the class. Ss could then practise the corrected conversations in pairs, taking turns at both roles.

EXTRA SUPPORT With weaker classes, first identify the places where an article is needed, then ask Ss to work in pairs and decide which one. This would also support dyslexic learners.

ANSWERS:
(Only the parts of the conversations where articles have been added are given.)

1 B: It's **an** old town in Maryland in **the** USA.
2 A: … on **the** fifth of June?
B: … at 8.00 in **the** morning … 6.00 in **the** evening.
3 A: Is there **a** bookshop near here?
B: Yes, it's to **the** left of **the** exit.
4 B: Is it in **the** kitchen?
B: Look in **the** living room.
A: … in front of **the** television.

EXTRA IDEA: DIGITAL Ss record one of the conversations in pairs. They listen back to their recording and comment on their pronunciation. If time, they can record a second conversation and upload to a sharing site.

SPEAKING

talk about six hours in a city

4A Put Ss in same nationality pairs where possible. Ask them to choose a city and make a list of attractions that could be seen in six hours.

EXTRA SUPPORT If you have a class that doesn't have much world experience, Ss can research a city that interests them online.

B 6.07 | Refer Ss to the photos of places and pronounce the names for them. Ask them to listen and identify the order that they are mentioned. They can write the letters in order in their notebooks. Play the recording, ask Ss to compare answers and play it again if needed, then check the answers.

ANSWERS:
The correct order is D, B, A, C, E.

AUDIOSCRIPT 6.07

OK, so you have six hours to see Paris. Where can you go? Well, there are a lot of beautiful places in Paris, but you can't go to all of them. Not in six hours.

First, I think it's a good idea to buy a bus ticket. There are tourist buses. They go to the important tourist attractions.

So here is my plan for Paris in six hours. Your first stop is the Eiffel Tower. The Eiffel Tower is over a hundred and thirty years old. You don't have time to climb it, but you can take some great photos.

Next you can take the bus again and go over the River Seine. The Seine is my favourite river in the world. It's really beautiful.

Next the bus goes to the Arc de Triomphe. The Arc is a very famous monument in the centre of Paris. You don't have time to stop here, but you can stop near the Tuileries Gardens. The gardens are lovely at all times of the year and you can have a coffee or lunch in a café in the park.

You can walk from the gardens to my favourite museum, the Musée d'Orsay. The Musée d'Orsay is a very famous museum. Here you can see pictures by famous artists, for example Vincent van Gogh and Claude Monet.

There are a lot of other interesting places, but you only have six hours!

C 6.07 | Refer Ss to the Key phrases and give them a minute or two to read through and ask any questions. Play the recording again and ask Ss to identify which alternatives in bold in the Key phrases they hear. Ask Ss to compare answers, then play it again. Go through the answers and drill any phrases that Ss are unsure of.

EXTRA SUPPORT: DYSLEXIA Read the Key phrases with the class to help Ss identify what they need to listen for. This would also be useful for weaker classes.

ANSWERS:
1 bus
2 first
3 climb it
4 take some great photos
5 Next
6 lovely
7 famous
8 pictures by famous artists

5A Put Ss in the same pairs as for Ex 4A. Ask them to practise talking about their tour, including the Key phrases. Move around the class and help Ss. They shouldn't write a script, just notes they can refer to.

B Put Ss with another pair, ideally one who has planned a tour of another city. Ask each pair to describe their tour, including the Key phrases, and then each pair chooses their favourite place on the tour they have heard about. They can repeat this a few times, circulating and talking to different pairs. When they have finished, ask each pair to decide which city they'd like to visit.

WRITING

describe a city tour

6 A Explain that Ss should read the tour information and identify the places that are not on Yvette's tour in Ex 4B. Give them two or three minutes, then check the answer. Ask Ss which tour they prefer and why.

EXTRA SUPPORT: DYSLEXIA You could record the tour information before the class for Ss with dyslexia to listen to on their personal devices or read it to the class. If you prerecord it, Ss can listen again for Ex 6B.

ANSWERS:
the Pont Neuf, the Louvre Museum (*a typical Paris restaurant* is also possible)

B Look at the example with the class and ask Ss to read the tour information again and find three more phrases that help order it. Go through the answers as a class.

ANSWERS:
Our second stop is Next, Finally,

C Put Ss in pairs to write their city tour. They can use the same city as before or choose a new one. They should use the text in Ex 6A as a model, aiming to write 60–80 words. They could add photos or maps.

EXTRA IDEA: DIGITAL Ss record the information about their city tour, taking the role of a tour guide. If they wish, they can share this on a video sharing platform and others can view it and comment.

D When they have finished, ask Ss to swap their tour information with other pairs and choose the one they like best.

EXTRA: ALTERNATIVE IDEA If your classroom space allows Ss to move around, number the itineraries, stick them around the room and ask Ss to move around and read them. They should note the number of the one they like best, or the top three if you have a large class. When they have finished, see which tours are the most popular.

TO FINISH

Put Ss in new pairs to discuss if they like going on guided tours when they visit another place or if they prefer to explore alone.

6 REVIEW

LESSON OVERVIEW

This lesson is a review of the language – both grammar and vocabulary – presented in this unit. It also includes a link to the Sounds and Spelling section for this unit, which focuses on voiced and unvoiced consonants: /s/ and /z/, /ʃ/ and /ʒ/; and /tʃ/ and /dʒ/. The notes below assume that the tasks are completed in class. However, the self-study type exercises (i.e. Exs 1A, 1B, 1C, 2A, 2B, 3A and 5A) could be done out of class and then checked in the following lesson when the communicative tasks are then completed.

Online Teaching

If you're teaching this lesson online, you might find the following tips useful:

- **Ex 1A:** Ask Ss to write their answers in the chat. Wait until everyone has completed every question before confirming the answers.
- **Ex 1D:** You can have Ss ask questions in the main room or in breakout rooms, pointing and referring to their surroundings.
- **Ex 5A:** Display the text on your device and share the screen. Ask individual Ss to annotate it, then play the recording before correcting on screen.

Additional Materials

For Teachers:
Sounds and Spelling 6
Unit Test in test package

TO START

Ask Ss to work in pairs and try to remember what language they studied in Unit 6 (Grammar: prepositions of place, *there is*, *there are*, *the*; Vocabulary: rooms and furniture, places in town, signs in buildings; How to … ask where a place is). Ask them to look at the unit lesson objectives to check their ideas.

GRAMMAR

1 A Ss complete the questions alone, then check in pairs. Check answers with the class and write them on the board.

ANSWERS:

1 Are there	**4** Are there
2 Is there	**5** Is there
3 Is there	**6** Are there

B **Ask Ss to match the answers (a–f) with the questions (1–6) in Ex 1A, ignoring the gaps for the moment. Do an example together to demonstrate how you want Ss to do this, getting them to write the number and letter in their notebooks (e.g. 1 d), then ask them to continue. Check the answers with the class and record them on the board.**

EXTRA SUPPORT: DYSLEXIA Provide the questions and answers in two columns, side by side, to help make the connections clearer.

ANSWERS:
1 d **2** f **3** e **4** c **5** a **6** b

C **Ss should now complete the answers in Ex 1B with a form of *there is* or *there are*. Put them in pairs to compare their answers. When they have finished, check the answers. If time allows, ask pairs to repeat the questions and answers.**

ANSWERS:

a there is	**d** there aren't
b there aren't	**e** there is, there's
c there are	**f** there isn't, there's

D **Put Ss in pairs to take turns to ask the questions in Ex 1A and to give their own answers.**

2 A **Ss complete the prepositions alone then compare in pairs. When they have finished, elicit answers and write the words on the board.**

EXTRA SUPPORT For weaker classes, you could provide the sets of missing letters, jumbled, on the board. For maximum support, provide the letters with the item number.

EXTRA SUPPORT The incomplete words will be challenging for dyslexic and beginner literacy Ss. You could provide two possible alternatives for each, for them to choose from (e.g. *1 frunt/front*). Present these in a vertical list that Ss can hold alongside the beginning of the words if possible, or if not you can write them on the board.

ANSWERS:

1 front	**2** behind	**3** opposite
4 between	**5** next to	

B **Refer Ss to the picture. Ask Ss to look at the sentences in Ex 2A and identify the different people and things being referred to. Then write the following sentences on the board to show how they can make false sentences using the sentences in Ex 2A as models, e.g. *The man is <u>behind</u> the house., The <u>car</u> is in front of the house.* Ask Ss to work alone. Monitor and discretely check their sentences.**

C **Refer Ss to the picture in Ex 2B again. Demonstrate the activity by saying a sentence and asking Ss to say 'True' or 'False', according to what they can see. Then put Ss in A/B pairs to continue, with Student As reading one of their sentences and Student Bs looking at the picture and saying if it is true or false. They then continue alternating roles until they have read all their sentences. Move around and listen to their pronunciation. Give some feedback on how they did by drilling problem words or further clarifying prepositions.**

EXTRA CHALLENGE You can extend this by getting Ss to choose another picture from the book and write more true/false sentences about that picture, and then to repeat the activity described in Ex 2C with those sentences.

VOCABULARY

3 A **Ask Ss to complete the words alone, then check in pairs. If they struggle, they can refer back to Lessons 6A–C and the Vocabulary Bank to help. Go through the answers as a class.**

EXTRA SUPPORT The incomplete words may be challenging for dyslexic and beginner literacy Ss. You could provide the complete words in a different order for each category in a vertical list for them to refer to while doing the activity. Encourage Ss to mask the parts of the exercise they are not working on to avoid distraction.

ANSWERS:
Rooms and furniture: *armchair*, lamp, shelf, shower, toilet
Places: airport, hospital, hotel, school, sports centre
Signs: entrance, lift, stairs, information desk, way out

B **Read the example with the class, then put Ss in groups of three for the activity. Ask a stronger group to demonstrate, then ask groups to continue. They should continue until they can't think of any more words in the group. The last to finish can start again with a new group. Stronger classes should be able to do the activity without looking at the lists. If you allow Ss to refer to their books to do the activity, ask them to do it again, this time with the lists covered.**

EXTRA: ALTERNATIVE IDEA Do this activity as a team game with groups taking turns to add a word to each category (they can use words that are not in Ex 3A as long as they are correct). Part of the game is remembering the words that have gone before in the correct order.

EXTRA IDEA Stronger classes can add more words to each group.

4 A Read the instruction to the class, then ask Ss to say the words in pairs. When they have finished, check answers with the class and focus on the underlined sounds.

EXTRA: ALTERNATIVE IDEA If you are short of time, write the words on the board and complete this as a whole class activity.

EXTRA SUPPORT: TEACHER The answers are here in phonetic symbols for the teacher's benefit. Ss are not expected to know the symbols, though they have met /s/ and /z/ before. You can simply get them to say the words and evaluate how well they can pronounce the sounds.

ANSWERS:

sofa /s/	museum /z/	shower /ʃ/
television /ʒ/	China /tʃ/	Japan /dʒ/

B Refer Ss to Sounds and Spelling on page 156.

page 156 **SOUNDS AND SPELLING** voiced and unvoiced consonants (3): /s/ and /z/, /ʃ/ and /ʒ/; /tʃ/ and /dʒ/

The Sounds and Spelling section can be used to help with particular problems. You might want to select the sections or even particular sounds that are most useful for your Ss. The vocabulary used in each section comes from the current unit or previous units.

SOUNDS AND SPELLING TEACHER'S NOTES page 214

5 A Refer Ss to the text and explain that it's advertising a house to rent. Ask them to work alone, read the text and choose the correct alternatives, then compare in pairs. Don't check the answers yet.

EXTRA SUPPORT: DYSLEXIA You could record the text before the class, or read it out, including the alternatives, for Ss to listen as they read. Encourage Ss to cover the sentences they are not working on to help concentrate their focus when reading and selecting the correct alternatives.

B R6.01 | Play the recording for Ss to correct their answers. Go through the answers as a class.

EXTRA: ALTERNATIVE IDEA Provide a correct version to pairs and ask one to read it to the other as they check their answers. They then swap roles.

ANSWERS:

1 There are	**5** living room
2 has	**6** behind
3 table	**7** near
4 There's	**8** supermarket

TO FINISH

Write on the board: *What do you remember most from this unit?* Ask Ss to write three specific things they remember (e.g. signs in buildings; when we use *the*). When they have finished, ask Ss to compare in pairs and look back at the unit.

7 healthy lives

GSE LEARNING OBJECTIVES

7A The little things

- LISTENING | Understand people talking about things that make them happy and healthy: everyday activities (2)
- Answer questions about everyday activities: present simple: *wh-* questions
- Pronunciation: sentence stress
- Write an online post; punctuation

GSE INFORMATION

VOCABULARY

10–29 Can use language related to everyday activities.

LISTENING

27 Can understand basic information about free-time activities.

29 Can identify objects, places or people from short spoken descriptions.

GRAMMAR

27 Can ask a range of *wh-* questions.

SPEAKING

29 Can answer simple questions about habits and routines.

WRITING

28 Can write simple sentences about someone's life and routines.

26 Can use basic punctuation (e.g. commas, full stops, question marks).

7B Heroes

- READING | Read about people's childhood heroes: common adjectives (3)
- Talk about your past: *was, were*
- Pronunciation: weak and strong forms: *was, were*

GSE INFORMATION

VOCABULARY

10–29 Can use language related to describing something's quality.

READING

25 Can understand short, simple descriptions of objects, people and animals, given visual support.

GRAMMAR

32 Can use 'was' and 'were' with a range of complement phrases.

SPEAKING

31 Can ask simple questions to find out about a subject.

33 Can make simple references to the past using 'was/were'.

7C What's wrong?

- HOW TO ... | say you're not well: parts of the body
- Pronunciation: word stress

GSE INFORMATION

VOCABULARY

10–29 Can use language related to parts of the body and mind.

HOW TO ...

10–29 Can use language related to wellness and illness.

28 Can express how they are feeling using very basic fixed expressions.

SPEAKING

28 Can use common forms of 'have got' (BrE) in the present tense.

7D Focus on fitness

- BBC STREET INTERVIEWS | Understand street interviews about keeping fit: sports and exercise
- Do a sport and exercise survey: imperatives
- Write a Top Tips post

GSE INFORMATION

VIEW

30 Can identify simple information in a short video, provided that the visual supports this information and the delivery is slow and clear.

GRAMMAR

27 Can use verbs in the imperative.

SPEAKING

34 Can ask simple questions in a face-to-face survey.

34 Can answer simple questions in a face-to-face survey.

33 Can describe skills and abilities using simple language.

34 Can exchange simple information on everyday topics, provided the other person speaks slowly and clearly and is prepared to help.

WRITING

33 Can write simple sentences about personal skills.

For full coverage of GSE Learning Objectives go to page 222.

BBC VLOGS

This is a short activity that can be used as an introduction to the unit topic and a warm-up to Lesson 7A. It shouldn't be exploited or taught at length, just played once or twice in class.

Show some pictures (or write the words) of healthy and unhealthy food, e.g. a salad, some fruit and some water on one side and a burger, a pizza and some chips on the other. Ask Ss how these foods differ and elicit/teach the words *healthy* and *unhealthy*. Put Ss in pairs to discuss the question in the programme information box. When they have finished, ask a few Ss for their answers and have a brief class discussion to find out if there is anyone particularly healthy in the class. When they are ready, play the video for Ss to watch and write how many speakers like pizza and chocolate. Check answers with the class, then have a show of hands to see how many Ss like these foods and if they think they are healthy.

ANSWERS:

Three speakers like pizza.

Two speakers like chocolate.

EXTRA CHALLENGE If Ss want to watch the video again outside class, you could ask them to note how many people mention fruit (four – three speakers say 'fruit' and one speaker says 'an apple'). You may also want to exploit the video further, e.g. by asking Ss to listen and write more foods that they recognise (foods mentioned: burgers, pizzas, fish, salad, fruit, vegetables, chocolate(s), bananas, oranges, an apple; coffee is also mentioned).

NOTE The vlogs have been provided by people from around the world in response to the same question. The video content was filmed by them on their own mobile phones, so the picture quality varies considerably and in some cases is of a lower quality. However, this adds to the authenticity of the content.

The locations labelled on the vlogs show where the speaker was when they filmed the video. It does not reflect where the speaker comes from (necessarily).

As many of the speakers are non-native, the videos expose Ss to a range of different accents and varieties of English. This could be used as a way to highlight interesting or useful differences.

Additional Materials

For Teachers:

Presentation Tool Unit 7

Online Digital Resources

Videoscript Unit 7 Opener: BBC Vlogs

7A The little things

GRAMMAR | present simple: *wh-* questions

VOCABULARY | everyday activities (2)

PRONUNCIATION | sentence stress

LESSON OVERVIEW

In this lesson, Ss learn more vocabulary for everyday activities. They also learn *wh-* questions with the present simple. The context is a listening where Ss hear about different lifestyles. They then practise pronouncing questions with the correct sentence stress. The lesson ends with Ss writing an online post, with a focus on punctuation.

Online Teaching

If you're teaching this lesson online, you might find the following tips useful:

- **Ex 1A:** Ask all Ss to type their answers in the chat box as a class rather than doing this in pairs.
- **Ex 3B:** Ask Ss to share a collaborative document to put the parts of the question in order, either in breakout rooms or as a class.
- **Ex 5C:** Put Ss in breakout rooms to discuss the questions.

Additional Materials

For Teachers:

Presentation Tool Lesson 7A

Photocopiable Activities 7A

Grammar Bank 7A

Writing Bank 7A

For Students:

Online Practice 7A

Workbook 7A

TO START

Ask Ss to work in pairs and make a list of what makes our life healthy/unhealthy apart from food. When they have finished, elicit their ideas to the board. (Possible answers: sleep, stress, exercise/sport, age, genetics, etc.). Decide as a class how important each factor is and write/number them in order of importance.

EXTRA SUPPORT: DYSLEXIA Dyslexic learners in particular benefit from understanding exactly what they are learning in a lesson so that they understand what they are working towards. In this and every lesson, explain clearly what the learning objectives of the lesson are near the start.

VOCABULARY

everyday activities (2)

1 A Focus attention on the question and three answers. Explain that Ss should identify the answer closest to their own ideas. Put Ss in pairs to discuss their answers. When they have finished, elicit Ss' ideas and take a show of hands to see which answer is the most popular.

B Ss have seen word webs before, so should be familiar with this way of organising vocabulary. Refer them to the phrases in the box and ask them to identify which verbs they go with. Monitor and help individuals as necessary.

EXTRA SUPPORT: DYSLEXIA The organisation of the word webs along with the matching exercise may create difficulties for Ss with dyslexia. They will be better able to process the information if the webs are organised in reading order, with the verbs to the left and the phrases that collocate with them to the right. Provide the missing phrases in a vertical list rather than in a box, ideally on a piece of paper that Ss can move near the gaps, or write them on the board.

EXTRA SUPPORT: TEACHER Ss may have questions about the difference between *clean* and *wash*. *Wash* usually requires water, whereas clean may not. It's also partly a question of words that usually go together (collocation). We *clean our teeth* but *wash our faces,* where in other languages people may *wash their teeth*. This sounds wrong in English. Encourage Ss to make a note of common collocations such as this, recording the whole phrase. Ss may also wonder about *feed the birds*. Refer them to photo C and explain that this is an English habit, though not necessarily good for the birds!

ANSWERS:

2 a room
3 my favourite food
4 the shopping
5 the cat
6 five minutes alone
7 some friends
8 hands

EXTRA CHALLENGE Ss should be getting used to seeing word webs by now. If they like them, show Ss how they can use them to organise other vocabulary areas, not just collocations. For example, they could organise countries (e.g. by continent: Europe, Asia, etc.), food (e.g. by type: fruit, vegetables, etc.), and so on. Point out that it's a good way to organise and revise vocabulary.

C Refer Ss to the questions and ask them to discuss them in pairs. When they have finished, ask a few pairs to feed back.

ANSWERS:

1 Photo A: have a hot drink, do nothing, spend five minutes alone

Photo B: spend an hour together, visit my grandmother

Photo C: feed the birds

2–3 Students' own answers

EXTRA IDEA If your class would benefit from extra writing practice, you could ask them to write fuller sentences about their own actions. e.g 'I never visit my grandmother, but I sometimes visit my aunt.' They can share these with a partner or with the class.

LISTENING

2 A Explain that Ss are going to listen to a podcast called *Healthy and happy*. Ask them to work in pairs, read the text about the podcast and find the question it asks. Write this on the board (*What little things do you do every day to be healthy and happy?*). Give an example yourself to show what you expect, e.g. 'I have a phone call with my grandmother.', then ask Ss to discuss in pairs. When they have finished, elicit their answers and write them on the board. There are no fixed answers, but this could help them when they listen.

EXTRA SUPPORT: DYSLEXIA Record the text about the podcast before the class, or read it aloud, and have Ss track the text as they listen.

B 7.01 | Explain that Ss will now listen to the podcast. They should identify the order of the pictures (A–C). Check the answer as a class.

ANSWER:

The correct order is B, A, C.

AUDIOSCRIPT 7.01

I = interviewer J = Jim A = Anya S = Sandra

I: Everybody is busy. Sometimes there's no time for exercise, no time to do healthy things. But it's important to be healthy and happy. In our podcast we ask three people the same question. What little things do you do every day to be healthy and happy? So Jim, you're a taxi driver, right?

J: That's right. I like my job, but I'm often very tired.

I: So, what little things do you do to … to be healthy and happy?

J: Well, in the afternoon I sometimes visit my grandmother.

I. Where does she live?

J: She lives very near me. We spend an hour together and we talk a lot.

I: What do you talk about?

J: About the family, life, everything.
I: That's great. Really nice for her.
J: And nice for me!
I: OK, and do you do anything else?
J: Well, let me think. Every week I clean a room. Just **one** room, really well. For example, I clean my kitchen. Or the bathroom.
I: Yes, I often do that. It's a good feeling. Thanks!
J: No problem.
I: Anya is a digital designer. She works in the city centre. Hi, Anya.
A: Hi.
I: What little things do you do? Little things to make you healthy and happy?
A: Well, I usually get home late. And I'm often very tired.
I: When do you get home?
A: Oh, sometimes at seven or eight.
I: So what do you do?
A: Well, I usually sit outside and do nothing for half an hour. Just relax. Or I sometimes have a long bath, a really long bath, and I wash my hair.
I: Oh, yeah … Do you do anything else?
A: I often call someone and we talk for an hour or two.
I: Who do you call?
A: Different people … my sister or a friend. That's always good.
I: I'm here with Sandra. Sandra's a mum with two children and … you work, too, is that right, Sandra?
S: Yes, I work at the library.
I: So you're very busy, but are you happy?
S: Yes, I think so.
I: And healthy?
S: Yes.
I: What do you do to be healthy and happy? What little things?
S: Well, in the morning I don't eat anything. I have a hot drink. Hot water with lemon.
I: With lemon? Why do you drink water with lemon?
S: Because it's good for you. It's very healthy.
I: OK …
S: Food is important to me. I eat a lot of fruit and vegetables. In the evening we usually cook a meal, we cook dinner together – me, my husband and the children.
I: Nice! Do you do anything else?
S: Let me think. Oh, lunchtime is really special for me. I sometimes have lunch in the park and I feed the birds.
I: How do you feel after that?
S: I feel really good. Really relaxed.

C **Ss should look back at the vocabulary in Ex 1B and identify which activities each speaker (A–C) does. Ask them to compare answers in pairs, but don't check answers as a class yet.**

D **7.01 | Play the recording again for Ss to check their answers then check the answers as a class.**

ANSWERS:
(Note that the answers are presented here in the order Ss hear them.)

Person B (Jim):	visit my grandmother, spend an hour together, clean a room, clean my kitchen
Person A (Anya):	*do nothing*, have a (long) bath, wash my hair
Person C (Sandra):	have a hot drink, cook a meal, feed the birds

GRAMMAR

present simple: *wh-* questions

3 **A** **Explain that you will now use extracts from the listening to study some grammar. Read the first conversation and elicit the question word (*Where*), then ask Ss to complete the rest of the questions with a question word, and then check in pairs. Check answers with the class.**

EXTRA SUPPORT If you think your Ss may not be sure of the question words, first check their meaning. You could write two columns on the board: the question words and what they refer to. Ss match the question words with their subject – a person, a place, a thing, a reason, etc. Pay attention to the pronunciation, especially of *who* /huː/, which has a silent *w* at the start. See Sounds and Spelling 2 for more on the pronunciation of question words.

EXTRA SUPPORT: DYSLEXIA The similar options here might be confusing for Ss with dyslexia. Give two alternatives for each gap, one correct and one distractor. Ss choose the correct question word.

ANSWERS:

1 Where	**2** What	**3** When
4 Who	**5** Why	**6** How

B **Write a question from Ex 3A on the board and analyse the form with the class. Point out that we start with the question word and see if they can name the other parts. Remind them that they have studied before that the subject goes before the verb. Ask Ss to copy this annotated sentence into their notebooks for reference.**

ANSWER:
The correct order is:
wh- question word; *do/does*; subject; infinitive.

C **The Grammar Bank on page 116 can be used in the lesson or for homework. Decide how and when the exercises will benefit your class.**

GB **page 116 GRAMMAR BANK**

This focuses on the meaning, form and use of question words. Go through the notes with Ss or let them read them alone. Check understanding where necessary, especially of the position of adverbs of frequency.

1 **Look at the example with the class. Ss write the remaining questions alone. Remind them of the word order in the reference notes or in the example sentence in their notebooks. Then check in pairs. Check answers with the class.**

EXTRA SUPPORT: DYSLEXIA Provide Ss with the parts of each question separately on pieces of paper. They can then work alone or with a partner who can help put them in the correct order. To simplify further, you could provide chunks of the correct questions together (e.g. *Where do / your parents / live?*). You could vary how the questions are chunked in different questions.

ANSWERS:

2 What does Ali do on Saturday?
3 What time does our lesson start?
4 Why does Carina feed the birds?
5 When do the children visit their grandparents?
6 Who do you play football with?
7 How do you pronounce 'international' in English?
8 What languages do you speak?
9 Where does Philippa buy her jeans?
10 How do you remember people's names?

2 **Read the example with the class and check Ss understand they should focus the question so that the answer is the word(s) in bold. Remind them that they may need to change the pronoun. Ss write the rest of the questions alone, then check in pairs. Check answers with the class. When they have finished, put Ss in pairs to practise the the questions and answers. Then ask them to swap roles and practise again.**

ANSWERS:

2 Where does your brother work?
3 What do you have for breakfast?
4 How do you spell 'building' / this word / it?
5 When do you/we finish work?
6 Who does Sofía live with?
7 Why do you always walk to work?
8 What music do you like?
9 Who do you know in class?
10 When do you usually make lunch?

PRONUNCIATION

sentence stress

4A **7.02 | Ss listen and write the sentences, then check in pairs. When you go through the answers, write them on the board to ensure Ss have them correctly. (They will also need to refer to them in Ex 4C.)**

EXTRA SUPPORT: DYSLEXIA Listening and writing whole sentences at the same time can be difficult for Ss with dyslexia. You could give Ss the sentences broken up into language chunks on separate pieces of paper (e.g. *Who / do you / call?*) and ask them to listen and put them in order. Alternatively, you could just give them the complete sentences and ask them to listen and try to identify the stress.

ANSWERS:
See Ex 4B.

B **7.02 | Ss listen again to identify the stressed words. Remind Ss again how the stress in a sentence usually falls on the words that carry the main meaning. Go through the answers. Play the recording again if necessary, and drill.**

ANSWERS AND AUDIOSCRIPT:

1 <u>Who</u> do you <u>call</u>?
2 <u>What</u> do you <u>talk</u> about?
3 <u>What</u> do you <u>drink</u>?
4 <u>Why</u> do you <u>drink</u> it?
5 <u>Where</u> do you <u>go</u>?
6 <u>When</u> do you <u>eat</u>?

EXTRA IDEA You may want to revise the use of the weak form /dəjə/, here. However, the important thing is to get the stress and rhythm right.

C **Look at the example. Remind Ss that we say *on* with days (e.g. *on Saturday*), and *in* with parts of days (e.g. *in the morning*). Point out that in their questions these days / parts of days will be stressed and drill an example. Ask a stronger pair to demonstrate with a further example, then put Ss in pairs to continue. Move around the class and listen particularly for correct word order and stress. When they have finished, give some feedback and ask a few pairs to repeat for the class.**

EXTRA CHALLENGE Stronger classes could write a few more questions and then ask a partner.

SPEAKING

5 A Look at the questions (1–8) as a class. Tell them to ignore the gaps for the moment. Identify that in most cases there are both questions and follow-up questions. They should read the questions and identify the correct answers and follow-up answers (a-h). Ask Ss to work in pairs then go through the answers as a class, using numbering (e.g. 1 h). Don't read them out or drill just yet as the questions are incomplete.

EXTRA SUPPORT: DYSLEXIA Adapt the exercise and provide Ss with the questions and corresponding answers in two sets of four for them to match. This will help reduce the amount of information they need to process at one time. The sets of questions could be in a list with the sets of answers individually cut up, so they can move them around to match.

ANSWERS:
1 h **2** a **3** d **4** b **5** c **6** e **7** g **8** f

B Explain that in 1–8 the second question is a follow-up for more detail when we say 'yes' or give an answer to the first question. The task is to write the correct question word. The answers they identified in Ex 5A will help them with this. Ask Ss to work alone then check in pairs before going through the answers as a class. Ask pairs of Ss to read the correct sets of questions and answers across the class (initial question, initial answer, follow-up question, follow-up answer). Demonstrate this with a stronger student first.

EXTRA SUPPORT With weaker classes, stage the activity as follows. Put Ss in pairs and provide them with a set of matched questions and answers. Ask them to highlight the part of the answer that identifies the missing question word (a person, place, thing, etc.). Agree these as a class, then ask pairs to insert the correct question word in each case before going through the answers as a class. If you have dyslexic learners in your class, you could stage the activity in this way with them individually.

ANSWERS:
1 What **2** Where **3** What
4 What **5** What, Where **6** Who
7 How **8** Why

C Put Ss in pairs. Explain that they should now ask and give their own answers to the questions (1–8). Remind them to use short answers and ask the follow-up question only when there is a 'yes' answer to the inital *Do you … ?* question. Move around the class and listen. When they have finished, ask a few Ss to report back on something interesting they learnt from their partner. Finally, point out any examples of good language or common errors to the class.

EXTRA IDEA: DIGITAL Ss choose some of the questions and video each other or other English-speaking people outside the class answering them. They then bring their videos to class to show others and compare answers.

WRITING

write an online post; punctuation

6 A Look at the introduction and part of an answer as a class and explain/elicit that it's part of an online discussion. Read the instruction and two questions to the class or ask a confident student to read it. Ss should answer the questions alone, then discuss in pairs. Elicit their ideas and write them on the board.

B Explain that Ss will now find out how Beni76 finishes his answer and will then write about what they do to stay happy and healthy. Refer them to the Writing Bank on page 91.

page 91 **WRITING BANK**

1 Explain that Ss should read the online post and check their ideas from Ex 6A. If you wrote them on the board, tick off those that were correct.

EXTRA SUPPORT: DYSLEXIA If possible, record the online post before the lesson so dyslexic learners can listen to it as they read. Alternatively, you can read the post with the class.

ANSWERS:
1 old things
2 He talks about listening to music from his university days, looking at old photos and watching old films.

2 A Explain that the words (1–6) are the names for the punctuation marks (a–f). Do this matching as a class if time is short or the class is weaker. There's no need to drill these words as they are mainly for recognition.

ANSWERS:
1 d **2** b **3** c **4** f **5** e **6** a

B **Ask Ss to find an example of each punctuation mark in the post. Elicit these to the board and clarify any doubts.**

ANSWERS:

1 The (or any other capital letter)
2 … a difficult question, but I … ; Well, for me, the past … ; … old photos, for example … ; … my childhood, photos of …
3 … I buy something!
4 Write and tell us about three things. (or any other full stop)
5 (and sometimes I buy something!)
6 … happy AND healthy?; What little things do I do?

EXTRA: ALTERNATIVE IDEA With strong or lively classes, an alternative task here is to have a competition to count all the examples and find out who can find the most or the correct number quickest.

ANSWERS:

capital letters: 22 (including the title, 'AND', 'Benji76' and 'I')

comma: 5

exclamation mark: 1

full stop: 8

brackets: 1 pair (or 2 individual)

question mark: 2

C **Go over the basic rules of punctuation: that we start a sentence with a capital letter and end it with a full stop, question mark or exclamation mark, and that a pause in speech is represented by a comma. Point out the inverted commas that we use to show speech. Tell Ss that the pronoun *I* is always capital, but other pronouns don't need a capital letter unless at the start of a sentence. Explain that Ss should find three cases where the letter is small but it should be a capital letter and insert the missing punctuation marks in the gaps. Ask them to work alone to correct the punctuation, then compare in pairs. Elicit the answers and show them on the board.**

EXTRA SUPPORT: DYSLEXIA Break the activity down into stages to help Ss process the information. Tell them to focus on identifying and correcting the capital letters first, then completing the punctuation. Give alternatives for each punctuation gap, one correct and one distractor, and encourage Ss to cover over the parts of the text they are not focusing on.

ANSWERS:

1 ? **2** , **3** . **4**) **5** , **6** . **7** !

Capital letters: So, Well, It's

3A **Refer Ss to the question again (*What little things do you do … ?*). Explain that Ss will now write their own answer. Give plenty of time for them to think of their ideas. Tell Ss they should aim to write 50–60 words. Move around the class and help/correct as needed.**

B **Put Ss in groups of three or four and ask them to read their posts to each other. Explain that Ss should listen to their classmates and choose one new idea they'd like to try.**

EXTRA IDEA: DIGITAL Ss share their posts on a website. They can read each other's and comment on them.

C **Ask groups to feed back to the class about the most popular or best new ideas.**

TO FINISH

Write on the board:
Why do you study English?
When and where do you speak English?
Where do you study?

Put Ss in pairs to discuss the questions. In feedback, you could open up a wider discussion on how Ss could practise outside class as it's very important for them to seek opportunities to do that.

7B Heroes

GRAMMAR | *was, were*
VOCABULARY | common adjectives (3)
PRONUNCIATION | weak and strong forms: *was, were*

LESSON OVERVIEW

In this lesson, Ss learn some adjectives to describe quality. They also learn to express the past using *was* and *were*. The context is a reading where people talk about their heroes. This leads into the grammar where they learn the past simple of the verb *be*. They also practise weak and strong forms of *was* and *were*. Finally, they do a speaking activity where they ask and tell each other about different past experiences.

Online Teaching

If you're teaching this lesson online, you might find the following tips useful:

- **Ex 4A:** Display the photos on your device and share your screen. Ask Ss to put their answers in the chat. Discuss as a class.
- **Ex 6B:** Display the sentences on your device and share your screen. When checking answers, highlight the weak forms for everyone to see.
- **Ex 9A:** Display the sentences on your device and share your screen. Ask Ss to take turns to ask a question to different people in the group. They can repeat the activity in pairs in breakout rooms for further practice.

Additional Materials

For Teachers:
Presentation Tool Lesson 7B
Photocopiable Activities 7B
Grammar Bank 7B
Vocabulary Bank 7B

For Students:
Online Practice 7B
Workbook 7B

TO START

Write the following questions on the board: *Who are your heroes? Why do you like them?* Explain that a hero is someone you like who does something very well or who does good things. You could mention superheroes, or a relevant well-known public figure, if this suits your group. They should choose someone who is living and they don't need to be famous. Give Ss a few minutes to think, then put them in small groups to discuss the questions. When they have finished, nominate a student from each group to share their ideas with the class. Explain that today's lesson is about people's heroes.

EXTRA SUPPORT: DYSLEXIA Dyslexic learners in particular benefit from understanding exactly what they are learning in a lesson so that they understand what they are working towards. In this and every lesson, explain clearly what the learning objectives of the lesson are near the start.

VOCABULARY

common adjectives (3)

1 A **Check Ss know the meaning of *famous*. You can do this by giving examples and checking, e.g. 'Is X famous?', and including questions to elicit a negative, e.g. 'Am I famous?' This can also begin the brainstorm of famous people that they do in groups. Ss should make a list in small groups. If you have a multicultural class, try to put people from different countries together, as they may have different ideas.**

B **Ss should take turns to choose someone from the list and say two sentences. The others listen and identify who the person is.**

EXTRA CHALLENGE Ss say their sentences to other groups, who cannot see their list of names. This makes it more of a guessing game and could be suited to monolingual classes who are likely to have quite similar cultural references.

2 A **Put Ss in pairs. Explain that they should match the pairs of sentences. When they have finished, elicit answers by asking pairs to read the sentences aloud. Drill words that cause problems.**

EXTRA SUPPORT: DYSLEXIA Ss with dyslexia may find the information for the matching easier to process if you present the two lists side-by-side in two columns.

ANSWERS:
1 d **2** f **3** b **4** a **5** e **6** c

B **Ss should work in pairs to think of two people for each sentence, one man and one woman. Encourage them to give some more information, as in the example. There might be fruitful discussion about who is the best football player, etc. Stronger classes can think of more names. You could have a few photos/names of internationally famous people ready to support this task (e.g. Bill Gates, Beyoncé, etc.) if Ss look to be running out of ideas.**

EXTRA SUPPORT: TEACHER You may want to think about pairings for this task, pairing Ss of similar ages and backgrounds who will have shared knowledge to achieve the task.

3 A **Ss should work in pairs to identify the adjectives in sentences 1–6 in Ex 2A. Stronger Ss will be able to add more. When they have finished, go through the answers. Remind Ss that in English adjectives don't have a plural form and go before the noun.**

ANSWERS:

1 famous	**2** best	**3** rich
4 positive	**5** fast	**6** amazing

B **Refer Ss to the Vocabulary Bank on page 136.**

VB page 136 **VOCABULARY BANK** common adjectives (3)

Note that the Vocabulary Bank activities are an important part of the lesson. They should only be omitted if you are confident that your Ss already know this vocabulary. If you don't use the exercises in class, it would be a good idea to set them as homework.

1 A **Refer Ss to the photos (A–J) and ask them to match the adjectives (1–10) with them alone, then check in pairs. Go through the answers and use the photos to further confirm meaning. Drill and elicit stress.**

EXTRA SUPPORT With weaker classes, ask Ss to first match the words they are confident about, then check in pairs. Ss could use a dictionary or a process of elimination for the remaining words.

EXTRA SUPPORT: TEACHER If Ss don't know the word *(the) best*, explain that it's the superlative of *good*, so it means very, very good. Because it's a superlative form, it needs *the* (unlike the other normal adjectives). *Amazing* also means very good.

EXTRA SUPPORT: DYSLEXIA Encourage Ss to cover the adjectives they are not currently matching to help them focus.

ANSWERS:

1 E	**2** G	**3** C	**4** A	**5** J
6 H	**7** B	**8** I	**9** F	**10** D

B **VB7.01 | Ask Ss to focus on the photos and not the words. Play the recording for them to listen and repeat.**

C **Look at the example with the class and ask Ss to identify the two other pairs of opposites. Do this as a class if time is short.**

ANSWERS:

fast – slow, poor – rich, strong – weak

2 **This is an opportunity for Ss to personalise the adjectives. Demonstrate the task by writing on the board: *A song can be …* and eliciting completions. Ss discuss the remaining items in pairs then have whole class feedback and discussion.**

EXTRA SUPPORT: TEACHER *Famous* is mostly used for people, important places, works of architecture and art. We can also say a country 'is famous for' something, e.g. 'Switzerland is famous for chocolate.'

A wifi signal can be *strong* or *weak*; we don't usually say it's *fast* or *slow*, rather that the internet or the broadband is fast or slow.

POSSIBLE ANSWERS:

a song – amazing, (the) best, famous, fast, positive, slow

a car – amazing, (the) best, fast, slow

a country – amazing, poor, rich

a wifi signal – strong, weak

an animal – amazing, fast, slow, strong, weak

coffee – amazing, (the) best, strong, weak

an actor – amazing, (the) best, famous, poor, rich

3 A **Ask Ss to work alone and write their answers for as many of the things as they can.**

B **Read the example conversation with the class. Ask a stronger pair to compare their answers in the same way, then put Ss in pairs to discuss. When they have finished, select some of the categories that you think most relevant to your Ss and have a whole class discussion.**

READING

EXTRA SUPPORT: DYSLEXIA There is a recording of the reading text available to help dyslexic learners.

4 A **Refer Ss to the photos and ask them to discuss the questions in pairs. If the people are likely to be unknown, introduce *Maybe …* . When they have finished, ask a few Ss to share their ideas with the class and write useful vocabulary on the board (e.g. *hockey*). You don't need to confirm if their answers are correct.**

POSSIBLE ANSWERS:

From the photos, Ss might guess, or they might know, that:

Carlos Acosta is famous because he was a great dancer, from Cuba.

Luciana Aymar is famous because she was a great field hockey player, from Argentina.

B **Tell Ss they will now read and check their ideas. If you didn't explain the meaning of *hero* in the To start activity, you should do so now. While they read, Ss should find out how each writer is similar to their hero (i.e. what they have in common), then check in pairs. Tell them they have two minutes for this. Check answers with the class, reminding them that they can make sentences using *both*.**

EXTRA SUPPORT: TEACHER When Ss will read a text a few times, it's a good idea to give them a time frame that lets them know *how* to read. In this case, it's not a deep focus so a short time frame should be suitable. In Ex 4C they need to read more carefully, so they need more time. If Ss have too long, they can start to notice words they don't know and become panicked.

ANSWERS:

Carlos Acosta and CarlosCuba2020 were both born in Cuba, are from big families, weren't rich but were happy, have the same name and both love dance.

Luciana Aymar and Martina2000 are both from Rosario, Argentina. Martina2000 was in the hockey team in school (but she wasn't very good).

C **Tell Ss they will now read again more carefully. Refer them to the statements. Check they understand the adjective *retired* (no longer working due to age). While they read, they should mark the statements True or False and correct the false ones. Ask Ss to read alone then compare answers. Go through the answers as a class.**

EXTRA SUPPORT Point out that the questions are in order, first about Acosta and then about Aymar, and that they are in the same order as the information is given in the text. Ss should note where they find the answers to enable them to compare and for feedback. Some Ss may notice the past verbs in the texts as they read and ask about them. Reassure them that they can answer the questions without these and that you will look at this in detail shortly.

ANSWERS:

2 T
3 F (in the UK)
4 F (a famous hockey player)
5 F (Lionel Messi is also from her city.)
6 T

EXTRA IDEA Ss should generally read silently, but texts of this length are ideal for paired reading (i.e. reading aloud to a partner) if you have time, after they have been read for comprehension. The texts are short and similar to spoken language. Paired reading can be useful for Ss with beginner literacy as they do not face the exposure of stumbling over words in the class but can be gently corrected by their partner, and vice versa.

D **Give Ss a few minutes to think first and write any key vocabulary they need. Move around and offer help as needed. Put Ss in groups of three to talk about their heroes. When they have finished, ask a few groups who they talked about.**

GRAMMAR

was, were

5 A **Explain that you will now use some sentences from the texts to study some grammar. Ask Ss to identify the verbs alone, then check in pairs. Check answers with the class and write them on the board.**

ANSWERS:

1 was **2** was **3** weren't, were
4 wasn't **5** was

B **Ss discuss the questions in pairs. Check answers with the class. With weaker classes, you could do this exercise together as a class.**

ANSWERS:

1 the past
2 add *-n't* to *was* or *were*
3 question word + *was/were* + subject

C **Complete the rules as a class and write the answers on the board for Ss to copy. You could point out that *was/were* are the past of *is/are* and questions and negatives are formed in the same way.**

ANSWERS:

1 I, he/she/it **2** you, we, they

D **The Grammar Bank on page 117 can be used in the lesson or for homework. Decide how and when the exercises will benefit your class.**

page 117 **GRAMMAR BANK**

GB

This focuses on the differences in form and use of *was* and *were*. Go through the notes with Ss or let them read them alone. Check understanding where necessary, especially of the form of short answers.

1 **Elicit the answers in the first sentence as an example, then ask Ss to choose the remaining correct alternatives alone, then check in pairs. Check answers with the class and write them on the board to ensure correct answers.**

ANSWERS:

1 isn't, was **5** are, weren't
2 wasn't, is **6** isn't, wasn't
3 I was, I'm **7** were, aren't
4 weren't, we're **8** was, is

2 **Read the example with the class and point out the use of the past tense *was*. Then ask Ss to make the rest of the questions alone, then check in pairs. Check answers as a class.**

EXTRA SUPPORT: DYSLEXIA The form of the prompts could cause some difficulty for dyslexic learners. Instead, provide the correct sentences, leaving a gap for *was* or *were* for Ss to complete. (You could also insert the ticks and crosses from Ex 3 at the end of each sentence for Ss to write the short answers when you come to do that exercise.)

ANSWERS:
2 Were your sandwiches nice?
3 Was your jacket expensive?
4 Were you at home yesterday?
5 Were your parents born in the USA?
6 Was Mrs Green at school yesterday?
7 Was your phone in the car?
8 Were the shops closed yesterday?

3 **Read the example with the class and elicit the short answer forms to the board, including the negative. Then ask Ss to write the rest of the short answers alone, then check the answers with the class.**

ANSWERS:
2 Yes, they were.
3 No, it wasn't.
4 Yes, I was / we were.
5 No, they weren't.
6 No, she wasn't.
7 Yes, it was.
8 No, they weren't.

4 **Read the example with the class, then ask Ss to write the rest of the questions alone, then check the answers with the class.**

EXTRA SUPPORT Stage the exercise for weaker classes. First, work as a class to agree and write in the question words, then ask Ss to work in pairs to write the full questions. This staging would also help to support dyslexic learners.

ANSWERS:
2 When were you born?
3 Where was your family home?
4 Who was your favourite person?
5 Why was she / your aunt your favourite person?
6 What were the names of your best friends?

EXTRA IDEA Ss work in pairs to ask the questions from Ex 4 and provide their own answers. Tell them they will need to change the subject of question 5 depending on the answer to question 4.

PRONUNCIATION

weak and strong forms: *was, were*

6 A **7.03 | Play the recording for Ss to listen and identify the stressed words. Elicit from Ss what kinds of words are stressed (words that carry meaning). Ask pairs to compare answers then check the answers with the class.**

EXTRA SUPPORT: DYSLEXIA Underlining can cause difficulty for Ss with dyslexia. In this case Ss can use a coloured highlighter to mark the words that are stressed.

ANSWERS:
1 <u>Where</u> were you <u>born</u>?
2 I was <u>born</u> in <u>England</u>.
3 Were you a <u>happy</u> <u>child</u>?
4 <u>Yes</u>, I <u>was</u>. I was <u>very</u> <u>happy</u>.
5 Were your <u>teachers</u> at school <u>good</u>?
6 <u>Yes</u>, they <u>were</u>. They were <u>amazing</u>.

B **7.03 | Read the instruction with the class and model the /wəz/ and /wə/ sounds they are listening for. Point out that Ss only need to focus on *was* and *were*. Play the first sentence and ask Ss if they can identify the weak sound. Then play the rest of the recording. Ask Ss to compare in pairs, then go through the answers.**

EXTRA SUPPORT: TEACHER Ss may struggle with the concept that a word can have different pronunciations depending on its position in the sentence. Point out that they have seen this before, with *does* and *can*. If the sound changes, it's often to the schwa /ə/ sound, which is the most common sound in English. Ss should be familiar with its use in unstressed syllables. Help them with the strong/stressed sound of *Yes, I was*. (/wɒz/) / *No, I wasn't*. (/wɒzənt/) and of the strong form of *were* (/wɜː/).

ANSWERS:
weak /wəz/ in sentences 2, 4 (second sentence)
weak /wə/ in sentences 1, 3, 5, 6 (second sentence)

C **7.03 | Play the recording again, pausing for Ss to repeat.**

7 A **Put Ss in pairs to ask and give their own answers to the questions in Ex 6A. Monitor and check Ss are using weak forms where appropriate. When they have finished, ask a few Ss to share some of their sentences with the class.**

EXTRA IDEA: DIGITAL Put Ss in pairs to interview each other and record themselves on their devices. When they have finished, they should listen back for their pronunciation of /wəz/ and /wə/, rerecord if they want to, then listen again to the recording and compare.

FUTURE SKILLS | Collaboration

B Read the Future Skills box with the class, then ask them to complete the question. Elicit the other question words and write them on the board to support the next activity.

ANSWER:

when

SPEAKING

8 Explain that Ss will now practise asking and answering about different famous people. Put Ss in A/A and B/B pairs and refer them to the relevant pages to read their instructions.

1 Give Ss a few minutes to read the information and work together to prepare their questions for the missing information using the prompts in brackets. Weaker Ss may need to write their questions, but stronger Ss can do this orally. Point out to Ss that some questions are in the past and some are in the present. Move around the class and support/correct as needed.

EXTRA SUPPORT If Ss do need to write their questions, allow this, but enourage them to do steps 2 and 3 without looking at their written questions as far as possible.

ANSWERS:

Student A questions

1 *Where was he born?*
When was he born?
2 Where were his parents from?
3 What was his father's sport?
4 Where does he play now?
5 What year was his first NBA game?
6 Why is he your hero?

Student B questions

1 *When was she born?*
Where was she born?
2 Where was her favourite place?
3 How old was she in 2005?
4 Who does she work with?
5 What is her foundation (called)? / What is the name of her foundation?
6 Why is she your hero?

2 Put Ss in A/B pairs. Give Student Bs some time to read the information they have (while they are doing this their partner can continue to prepare to ask their questions). Student As should ask and Student Bs answer. Encourage Student Bs to answer with full sentences. Make sure they don't show their information, but listen to each other. Ss may work through this activity at different speeds, so move around the class and prompt them if necessary to move on to step 3.

3 Keep Ss in their A/B pairs. Give Student As some time to read their information while Student Bs review their questions. Student Bs should ask and Student As answer. Again, encourage them to answer with full sentences and make sure they don't show their information, but listen to each other. When Ss have completed the activity, they can show each other the answers to the questions.

EXTRA SUPPORT: DYSLEXIA To help Ss focus on the information they need to answer each of their partner's questions, tell them to cover the other sentences.

EXTRA CHALLENGE If some pairs finish quickly, they can swap information and ask different questions. They don't need to write.

POSSIBLE ANSWERS:

Answers to Student A questions

1 *He was born in Greece.*
He was born in 1994.
2 They were from Nigeria.
3 His father was a football player. / His sport was football.
4 He plays in the USA in the NBA.
5 His first NBA game was in 2013.
6 He's my hero because he's strong and fast and he's amazing to watch.

Answers to Student B questions

1 *She was born in 1976.*
She was born in England.
2 Her favourite place was on a boat, with her aunt.
3 She was twenty-eight in 2005.
4 She works with young people after their time in hospital.
5 Her foundation is called the Ellen MacArthur Foundation.
6 She's my hero because she's strong and positive. She's an amazing woman.

9 A **Give Ss a few minutes to read the instructions and the sentences. Ask them to identify which ones are negative (5, 7). Point out that they are not questions and draw attention to the example question. Demonstrate the activity with a stronger student, eliciting the short answers *Yes, I was.* and *No, I wasn't.* You could also elicit the second question for weaker classes (*Were you good at sports in school?*). Remind Ss that they need to write the name of the person, not the answers, and they need a different name for each sentence if possible. Ss ask each other. Move around the class and listen, correcting as needed.**

EXTRA SUPPORT: DYSLEXIA Read through sentences 1–8 with the class before they begin the activity to help Ss with dyslexia identify what they should ask about.

EXTRA SUPPORT: TEACHER In the sentences, there are examples of *be* + adjective (e.g. *was good*) and *be* + preposition + noun (e.g. *wasn't in a shop*). Grammatically aware Ss may ask about the unusual form *was born.* You could explain that this is a kind of passive and it is always past. (Though it's true we can say *many babies are born every year,* we can't say *I am born* because this is always a single past event.)

B **Put Ss in pairs to tell each other the information they learnt about their classmates. When they have finished, ask for sentences around the class.**

EXTRA CHALLENGE Stronger Ss can write follow-up questions to ask (e.g. *What hospital were you born in? What sport were you good at? What country were you in last summer?* etc.). Then they can ask and answer the questions in Ex 9A in pairs, asking follow-up questions where they can.

TO FINISH

Write the following questions on the board: *Where were you yesterday / last week / last year?* and ask Ss to discuss.

7C What's wrong?

HOW TO ... | say you're not well
VOCABULARY | parts of the body
PRONUNCIATION | word stress

LESSON OVERVIEW

In this lesson, Ss learn vocabulary for parts of the body and how to say they are unwell, as well as how to offer simple advice. The context is a listening where they listen to people talking about being unwell. Ss then roleplay similar situations. The lesson ends with a speaking activity where Ss say what they do when they have different ailments.

Online Teaching

If you're teaching this lesson online, you might find the following tips useful:

- **Ex 2A:** Display the pictures on your device and share your screen. Ss write the words they know in the chat then come together as a class to check them.
- **Ex 4A:** When checking answers, use a collaborative document to display the four stress patterns and nominate different Ss to supply the answers by typing them in.
- **Ex 5A:** Remind Ss to mute their microphones when listening. Use the chat box for Ss to compare ideas before feedback.

Additional Materials

For Teachers:
Presentation Tool Lesson 7C
Photocopiable Activity 7C
Grammar Bank 7C
Vocabulary Bank 7C

For Students:
Online Practice 7C
Workbook 7C

TO START

Start the lesson by asking Ss how they are feeling today and invite them to ask you. Give a more extended answer than just 'I'm fine', e.g. 'I'm OK. I'm a bit tired today. I was out late last night.' Then put Ss in pairs to ask each other. When they have finished, elicit Ss' answers and have a brief class discussion. Tell Ss today's lesson is about how to say they are not well.

EXTRA SUPPORT: DYSLEXIA Dyslexic learners in particular benefit from understanding exactly what they are learning in a lesson so that they understand what they are working towards. In this and every lesson, explain clearly what the learning objectives of the lesson are near the start.

VOCABULARY

parts of the body

1 **Ask Ss to make a list of responses in pairs (they should have got some ideas from the To start activity). When they have finished, ask for their answers and write useful vocabulary on the board. If appropriate, point out the pattern of *be* + adjective and how we often soften it by including *a bit*, e.g. *I'm a bit tired.***

POSSIBLE ANSWERS:

Ss might give answers they learnt in Unit 2, e.g. 'I'm not very good/well.', 'I'm OK / not bad.', 'I'm well/ good/fine.', 'I'm very well / really good.', 'I'm great.' Also, 'I'm cold.', 'I'm tired.'

2 A **Refer Ss to the pictures and ask them to discuss in pairs. Don't let this go on too long unless the class is strong. Don't go through the answers as Ss will use the Vocabulary Bank to check.**

B **Refer Ss to the Vocabulary Bank on page 137 to check their answers.**

VB page 137 **VOCABULARY BANK** parts of the body

Note that the Vocabulary Bank activities are an important part of the lesson. They should only be omitted if you are confident that your Ss already know this vocabulary. If you don't use the exercises in class, it would be a good idea to set them as homework.

1 A **Refer Ss to the photos and ask them to identify the parts of the body (1–15). Point out the irregular plurals (*feet* and *teeth*). Ss should work alone, then check in pairs. Go through the answers as a class.**

EXTRA SUPPORT: DYSLEXIA Divide the task and provide the photos and labels separately for 1–5, 6–10 and 11–15 to help Ss focus on the answers. Remind Ss to focus on one word at a time and cover the others to help them do this.

ANSWERS:

1 C **2** B **3** N **4** H **5** A **6** I **7** J **8** E
9 L **10** O **11** D **12** K **13** M **14** G **15** F

B **VB7.02 | Ask Ss to look at the photos, not the words. Play the recording for them to repeat.**

C **Put Ss in A/B pairs. Ask them to take turns to point and identify the parts of the body.**

EXTRA CHALLENGE Play a version of the game 'Simon Says'. Put Ss in groups of four. Nominate one as leader to say, 'Please touch your … .' Their partners must touch the named part of the body. If the leader doesn't say 'please', then they must stay still. Anybody who touches is out, and the last person out becomes the next leader.

How to …

say you're not well

3 **Refer Ss to the pictures (A–H) and explain they show people that are unwell. Ss should work alone to match them with the problems (1–8), then check in pairs. Go through the answers with the class and clarify any queries. (Ss may notice *hurt* and *hurts* – this is because *hurt* is a verb and conjugates accordingly). Point out and drill the unusual pronunciation of *ache*, with its /k/ sound.**

EXTRA SUPPORT If you think your Ss might not know the problems, mime having backache. Elicit/Teach and drill: *I've got backache, toothache,* etc. through miming. Then ask Ss to look at the pictures (A–H) and match them with the words. Introducing the problems this way, before seeing the written form, is a good way to help Ss get over the mismatch of sound and spelling of *ache*.

EXTRA SUPPORT: TEACHER Ss may notice the use of the article with some ailments, but not others. Point out that we always say *a headache* and *a cold* (NOT ~~'He's got headache.'~~, ~~'She's got cold.'~~), but the other ailments don't need an article. It is, however, also possible and correct to say: 'I've got a backache / a toothache / an earache.'; and to omit the article in 'I've got stomachache.' This is also highlighted in the Grammar section.

ANSWERS:

1 F **2** E **3** B **4** D **5** A **6** H **7** C **8** G

PRONUNCIATION

word stress

4A 7.04 | Remind Ss that words with more than one syllable have a stressed syllable that is pronounced more strongly. Read the example *backache* and place the stress alternately on the first or second syllable to show that it is correctly stressed on the first. Play the recording for Ss to match the words with the patterns individually, then compare answers. Go through the answers as a class, drilling as needed.

EXTRA SUPPORT This exercise requires Ss to do several things at once: listen, read and write. For weaker classes, break it down into stages as follows:

1 Provide (or get Ss to draw) a table with four columns headed with the four possible patterns.

2 Before listening, ask pairs to work together saying the words in Ex 3 and placing them in a column.

3 Play the recording. Ss should tick if they have the word in the right column.

4 After listening, Ss can compare and move words they didn't tick, then listen again.

Finally, check the answers and write them in the table on the board. Drill down the column to help Ss hear the pattern. This staging process would also help to support learners with dyslexia in doing this activity.

ANSWERS AND AUDIOSCRIPT:

a Oo *backache*, toothache, earache
b oO a cold
c oOoo a stomachache
d oOo a headache

B Demonstrate the activity by pointing to a picture and eliciting the phrase with the correct stress. Aim for Ss to say a whole sentence, e.g. 'I've got backache.' rather than just 'backache'. Put Ss in pairs, with Student As pointing and Student Bs identifying the problem. Ask them to change roles after a few turns. When they have finished, if there have been particular problems, point at those pictures and drill again.

EXTRA: ALTERNATIVE IDEA You could ask Ss to take turns to mime a problem for their partner to say what it is, e.g. 'You've got … .' This is suitable for lively classes.

5A 7.05 | Tell Ss they are going to listen to some people talking about their problems. Ask them to look at the pictures in Ex 3, then listen and identify the problems. When they are ready, play the recording. Ask Ss to compare their answers in pairs. Check answers with the class.

ANSWERS:

Alex has got a headache and his eyes hurt.
Paola's son has got a cold.

AUDIOSCRIPT 7.05

A = Alex L = Lucy N = Nina P = Paola

Conversation 1

A: Hi, Lucy. I'm really sorry, but I can't come to the cinema tonight. I don't feel very well. Call me. Bye.

Conversation 2

L: Hello?
A: Hello, Lucy.
L: Hi, Alex. What's wrong?
A: I feel terrible. I've got a really bad headache.
L: Oh, no! Poor you.
A: I'm so sorry about the cinema.
L: No problem. I can ask Jo. You go to bed and maybe watch a film on your laptop.
A: Ooh no. My eyes hurt. I just want to sleep.
L: OK. Go to bed. Get well soon.
A: Thanks. Enjoy the film. Bye.
L: Bye.

Conversation 3

N: Hello, Central College. Can I help you?
P: Yes, this is Paola. I'm really sorry, but I can't come to work today. Can you tell Chris?
N: Hi, Paola. What's the problem?
P: My son isn't well. He's got a cold. A really bad cold and he can't go to school.
N: OK. I hope he gets well soon. Phone us this afternoon.
P: OK. Thanks, Nina. Goodbye.
N: Bye, Paola.

B 7.06 | Tell Ss they are going to hear some extracts from the conversations again. Before they listen, they should use the words in the box to complete the conversations, then compare in pairs. Play the recording for them to listen and check. Go through the answers.

EXTRA SUPPORT: DYSLEXIA Give Ss the sentences with two possible alternatives for each gap. This reduces the need for Ss to move their eyes from the word choice box to the sentences.

EXTRA SUPPORT: TEACHER Ss have recently learnt *poor* (having little or no money, the opposite of 'rich'), and here it's used with a different meaning, to express sympathy. This is the case in some other languages – the same word is used for both – so there may not be any confusion. However, if you think this might be a problem, it may be useful to highlight the difference.

ANSWERS:

1 well	**2** wrong	**3** headache
4 you	**5** eyes	**6** well
7 problem	**8** well	

C **The Grammar Bank on page 118 can be used in the lesson or for homework. Decide how and when the exercises will benefit your class.**

GB page 118 **GRAMMAR BANK**

This focuses on the form and use of phrases for saying we're not well. Read the notes with the class or give them a few minutes to read alone then ask any questions they have. Emphasise the difference between *He's cold.* and *He's got a cold.*

1 **Elicit the first answer as an example, then ask Ss to continue to choose the correct alternatives in the conversations, then check in pairs. Check answers as a class.**

ANSWERS:

1 wrong	**6** 's got
2 cold	**7** wrong
3 don't feel	**8** feet
4 poor	**9** the problem
5 Is	**10** a bad headache

2 **Look at the example with the class, then ask Ss to complete the remaining sentences using the words in the box, then check in pairs. Check answers as a class.**

EXTRA SUPPORT: DYSLEXIA Give Ss a vertical list of the words from the box that they can place alongside the sentences. This reduces the need for Ss to move their eyes from the word choice box to the sentences.

ANSWERS:

2 Get	**3** backache	**4** feel
5 earache	**6** arms	**7** tooth
8 problem	**9** wrong	**10** you

3 **Make sure Ss understand that there are six mistakes in the conversation. Ss correct the mistakes alone, then check in pairs. Check answers with the class. When they have finished, put Ss in pairs to practise the conversation, then swap roles and repeat.**

EXTRA SUPPORT: DYSLEXIA Supply the conversation with the sentences that contain the mistakes highlighted. This will help Ss to focus on the necessary parts.

ANSWERS:

(Only the sentences where there is a mistake are given.)

A: What ~~does~~ **'s/is** the problem?
B: I ~~not~~ **don't** feel well.
B: ~~I'm~~ **I've got** really bad stomachache.
A: I'm so ~~so~~ **sorry**.
A: ~~Not~~ **No** problem.
A: Get ~~good~~ **well** soon.

EXTRA CHALLENGE Ask Ss to practise the conversation again but get them to change details such as the problem and the advice.

SPEAKING

6A **Put Ss in pairs. Focus attention on the flow chart and give Ss time to think about what Students A and B can say. When they are ready, take feedback and elicit the conversation to the board. Drill expressions.**

EXTRA SUPPORT: DYSLEXIA Ensure dyslexic learners are paired with a student who can provide them with the support they need when forming the phrases and sentences from the prompts for this activity. Presenting the conversation as a single column of dialogue may also help.

ANSWERS:

A: Hi, it's (name).
B: Hi, (name). How are you?
A: I don't feel well.
B: What's wrong?
A: I've got a bad headache.
B: Poor you!
A: And my eyes hurt.
B: Oh, no.
A: I'm sorry, but I can't go to the cinema tonight.
B: I understand.
A: I'm really sorry.
B: No problem. I hope you get well soon.
A: Bye.
B: Goodbye.

B **Ss practise the conversation in pairs, taking turns as Student A and Student B. When they have finished, ask different Ss to repeat the conversation in open pairs across the class.**

EXTRA SUPPORT Depending on your class, you may want to leave the conversation on the board. Ideally, Ss should be able to have a conversation without it. One strategy is to take away a few words from the board at a time until Ss are left with just a skeleton of key word prompts in the pattern of the conversation. Weaker classes will still need to read and that is acceptable as they are still speaking English.

C **Ss change partners and create a new conversation in their pairs, taking turns as Student A and Student B. When they have finished, ask one or two pairs to perform their conversation for the class.**

EXTRA SUPPORT Give Ss time to write their conversation in pairs first, then practise and then see if they can do it without their written conversation, using just the prompts. Monitor and offer help where necessary. They could then try again without any support.

7 **A** **Ask Ss what they do when they feel unwell. Some may say they go to the hospital! Explain that we are talking about small everyday illness such as a headache. Elicit a few ideas then ask Ss to choose an illness or a part of the body to complete the first clause in the first box, then write sentences about it using the words in the other two boxes. Look at the examples provided and give an example yourself, showing how you can connect the phrases in the boxes, e.g. 'When I've got a headache, I usually stay at home.' Move around the class and be available to help.**

EXTRA SUPPORT: TEACHER Here, you might want to point out that *When you've got …* means 'When a person has got', so it is the general meaning and use of 'you' and not the person the student is talking to. There will likely be an equivalent in the Ss' own language.

B **Put Ss in pairs to tell each other what they do. It could be good to pair Ss from different backgrounds (e.g. age, gender, nationality) where possible. When they have finished, ask a few pairs if they had similar or different approaches.**

C **This activity is a bit freer, and Ss don't have preparation time. Put Ss in groups of three or four to discuss. Stress that they should not go into any serious health problems. Move around the class and listen. When they have finished, ask if groups have learnt any new ideas and go over any problem areas that you noted.**

EXTRA: HOW TO … Put Ss in pairs to write a new conversation about a health problem using phrases from the lesson. Encourage them to include suggestions and advice for how to deal with the problem. When they have finished, they should practise and some can perform for the class.

TO FINISH

Ask Ss to discuss the following questions in pairs or threes:
What was useful in today's lesson?
How can you remember it?
How can you use this language outside the class?

When they have finished, discuss the questions as a class.

EXTRA IDEA: SPEAK ANYWHERE Encourage Ss to practise using the Speak Anywhere interactive roleplay.

7D BBC Street Interviews

Focus on fitness

GRAMMAR | imperatives
SPEAKING | do a sport and exercise survey
WRITING | write a Top Tips post

LESSON OVERVIEW

In this lesson, Ss learn the names of different sports and forms of exercise and also learn to express tips with imperatives. The context is a video of interviews with people in the street talking about what exercise they do. Ss then do a speaking activity where they practise asking each other about their own attitudes to exercise. The lesson ends with a writing activity where Ss write a list of Top Tips for a topic of their choice.

Online Teaching

If you're teaching this lesson online, you might find the following tips useful:

- **Exs 2A and 3A:** Sometimes videos can be a little slow or jumpy when streamed in an online class environment. If you know this is an issue for you, give Ss time to watch the video on their own device before moving on.
- **Ex 3B:** Create a two-column task with the names and the topics in jumbled order. Share your screen and enable the annotation tool for individual Ss to match, then confirm the answers.
- **Ex 4A:** Project the exercise and share your screen. Enable the annotate function. Ask Ss to take turns to complete the sentences. Discuss as a class before confirming as correct, to involve all Ss.
- **Ex 5:** Ss write their question words in the chat and compare answers.

Additional Materials

For Teachers:
Presentation Tool Lesson 7D
Online Digital Resources
Grammar Bank 7D
Vocabulary Bank 7D
Videoscript 7D: BBC Street Interviews

For Students:
Online Practice 7D
Workbook 7D

TO START

Write these questions on the board: *Are you healthy? How do you stay healthy?* and ask pairs to discuss. You could display some photos of healthy food and people doing different activities to prompt them. When Ss have finished, ask for their feedback and include key vocabulary for the lesson such as *exercise* and *go to the gym*. Tell Ss that this is today's topic.

EXTRA SUPPORT: DYSLEXIA Dyslexic learners in particular benefit from understanding exactly what they are learning in a lesson so that they understand what they are working towards. In this and every lesson, explain clearly what the learning objectives of the lesson are near the start.

PREVIEW

1 A Refer Ss to the questions. Give an example yourself to start them off, e.g. 'I go to the gym and I play football. It's important to me and I like it.' Put Ss in pairs to ask and answer the questions. Encourage them to give extended answers where possible. When they have finished, take general feedback to see what kind of activities are popular.

B Put Ss in pairs to make a list of sports. Give a five-minute time limit. If you like, you could display some images to prompt them. Don't give answers, though, as Ss will check their ideas in the Vocabulary Bank.

EXTRA SUPPORT If your class is weaker and you think they may not know any vocabulary, you can go straight to the Vocabulary Bank.

C When they have finished, refer Ss to the Vocabulary Bank on page 138 to check their ideas.

page 138 **VOCABULARY BANK** sports and exercise

VB

Note that the Vocabulary Bank activities are an important part of the lesson. They should only be omitted if you are confident that your Ss already know this vocabulary. If you don't use the exercises in class, it would be a good idea to set them as homework.

1 A Focus attention on the photos and ask Ss to match them with the activities. Elicit the first answer as an example. Ss work individually, then check in pairs. Don't check the answers yet.

B VB7.03 | Play the recording for students to listen and check. Remind Ss that we *do* most sports and exercise, but we *play* games with a ball and we *go* to the gym, for a walk, etc. Drill the activities.

ANSWERS:
1 C **2** D **3** H **4** G **5** A **6** E **7** B **8** F

EXTRA IDEA You may also want to teach more sports that Ss do or want to know.

C **Model the conversation with a strong student and highlight the short answers. Put Ss in pairs to ask and answer. When they have finished, ask a few Ss to tell the class about their partner.**

VIEW

2A **Refer Ss to the two questions in the programme information box and explain that they will see and hear people answering them. Ask them to count how many speakers go to the gym as they watch the first part of the video. Tell Ss to count with their fingers, there's no need to write. Ss watch then check their answer in pairs. Check the answer with the whole class.**

EXTRA SUPPORT Turn on the subtitles if you feel it would benefit learners.

ANSWER:
Two speakers go to the gym.

B **Put Ss in pairs to try and remember what the speakers said. Then play the video again and ask them to identify what was said. Ask them to compare in pairs, then elicit their answers. Point out that *twice* = two times. Elicit *once* and explain that, apart from these two, we say *three times, four times,* etc. Draw attention to the pattern, *once/twice a week/month,* etc. Drill several examples.**

EXTRA SUPPORT: DYSLEXIA This type of activity can pose a challenge for Ss with dyslexia as they need to do a number of things at the same time. To simplify the process for them, provide some blank slips of paper for Ss to cover the wrong alternatives as they watch.

ANSWERS:
1 do yoga
2 football
3 run
4 walks
5 run
6 at the weekends

3A **Refer Ss to the question. Ss watch the second part of the video in which the speakers give their exercise tips, then compare in pairs. Play the video again if Ss want you to.**

ANSWER:
Five speakers talk about clothes (including shoes).

B **Refer Ss to the topics. Suggest they write these in their notebooks and write the names beside them. They can refer to the pictures at the top of the page to check people's names. Don't go through the answers yet.**

EXTRA SUPPORT: DYSLEXIA Provide Ss with a grid with the names across the top and the topics down the side. Ss tick the relevant boxes and check their answers as they watch in Ex 3C.

C **Ss watch the video to check their ideas, then compare in pairs. Play the video again if Ss want you to. Go through the answers as a class.**

ANSWERS:
1 Gaia
2 Gaia, Chris, Rachael
3 Ryan
4 Chris, Lucy, Sautebh
5 Tracey, Vincent, Rachael
6 Tracey

GRAMMAR

imperatives

4A **Tell Ss you are going to look at some tips from the video. Ask Ss to look at the sentences and identify which verbs in the box match them. If you're short of time, you could do this exercise as a class. Check answers with the class. Ask Ss what is different about these sentences (there's no subject before the verb).**

ANSWERS:
1 Drink **2** Wear **3** Be **4** eat **5** Don't

B **The Grammar Bank on page 119 can be used in the lesson or for homework. Decide how and when the exercises will benefit your class.**

page 119 **GRAMMAR BANK**

GB

Check understanding of the notes with the class and especially ensure Ss understand that imperatives can sound rude and it can therefore help to include *please* at the beginning or end, or use a request form.

1 **Look at the example with the class and point out that Ss don't need to change the form of the verbs in the box for positive answers but they do for negatives. Then ask Ss to continue individually, selecting the correct verbs, then check in pairs. Check answers with the class and write them on the board. Deal with any questions as they come up and refer Ss back to the notes as needed.**

EXTRA SUPPORT: DYSLEXIA Support dyslexic learners by giving two alternatives per gap, one correct and one distractor, for Ss to choose from. You could also reduce the number of items.

GB

ANSWERS:

2 Use	**3** Don't speak	**4** Don't swim
5 Throw	**6** don't feed	**7** Never play
8 Call	**9** come	**10** Never leave

2 **Look at the example. Point out that the mistakes could be with word order, grammar or logic. There are five mistakes in each of the three sections. Ss find the mistakes individually, then compare in pairs. Check answers with the class.**

EXTRA SUPPORT: DYSLEXIA Reduce the reading load for dyslexic learners by reducing the number of items in each section to four. Make two sentences correct and two incorrect in each section. Ss should read and tick the correct ones and cross the wrong ones. They then correct the mistakes.

ANSWERS:

Things that parents say to their children

2 ~~Don't say~~ **Say** please and thank you.
3 ~~Never don't look~~ **Never look / Don't look** at your phone at dinner time.
4 ~~Be always~~ **Always be** nice to your sister.
5 correct
6 ~~Always~~ Go to your room! Now!

On the plane

1 ~~Don't remember~~ **Don't forget / Remember** your passport.
2 correct
3 Always ~~to~~ drink a lot of water.
4 ~~Not~~ **Don't** eat a lot.
5 Change ~~you~~ your watch on the plane.
6 Never ~~running~~ **run** to the toilet.

Test instructions

1 ~~Write please~~ **Please write** your first name.
2 ~~Never read~~ **(Always) Read** the instructions.
3 Answer ~~you~~ all the questions.
4 ~~Check always~~ **Always check** your answers.
5 Don't ~~to~~ speak in the test.
6 correct

EXTRA IDEA Ss write their own list for things that parents say or instructions for a plane/bus.

SPEAKING

do a sport and exercise survey

5 **Refer Ss to questions 1–4 and explain they should complete each one with a question word. When they have finished, go through the answers as a class and drill. If you are short of time, complete the activity as a class.**

EXTRA SUPPORT Ss should be familiar with the question words and their use by now, but, if necessary, with weaker classes, first elicit the question words to the board, then review what they are used for and write these alongside (e.g. *Who* = person, *What* = thing, *When* = time, *Where* = place). Leave this on the board as a reference while Ss complete the exercise.

ANSWERS:

1 What **2** When **3** Where **4** Who

6A **Demonstrate the activity by matching the first phrase in the Key phrases box with one of the questions in Ex 5 (question 1). Ask Ss to continue. When they have finished, ask pairs to compare then go through the answers as a class.**

ANSWERS:

I really like football/basketball … 1
I don't do sport, but I exercise a lot. For example, I do yoga. 1
I don't do sport or exercise. 1
I go for a walk every day/every week/on Saturday. 2
I only have time at the weekend. 2
I walk near my apartment. 3
I run in the park. 3
I run with a friend. 4
I go to the gym alone. 4

B **Ss should rewrite the Key phrases so that they are true for them. Give an example yourself, (e.g. 'I really like tennis.'). Go round and help with vocabulary where necessary, adding any useful new words/phrases to the board.**

EXTRA SUPPORT: DYSLEXIA Provide dyslexic learners with some of the Key phrases with gaps for them to complete with their own ideas, rather than needing to rewrite whole sentences. This is also suitable for weaker classes.

C **Put Ss in pairs to ask the questions in Ex 5 and answer with the sentences they adapted from the Key phrases. Move around and listen.**

EXTRA IDEA: DIGITAL Ss video record themselves talking about their sports activities, as in the interviews at the beginning of the lesson. Encourage them to roleplay for the camera. When they have finished, Ss can play their interviews to another pair who should watch/listen and note the sports mentioned.

D **Put Ss in a different pair and ask them to report back about their previous partner. Remind them to use third person verb forms. When they have finished, ask a few groups to report back something interesting to the class.**

WRITING

write a Top Tips post

7 A **Explain that a *tip* is a good idea for doing something. Ask Ss if they have any tips for doing exercise (e.g. wear the right shoes). Read through the tips as a class. Ask Ss to identify two that are not relevant. Go through the answers.**

ANSWERS:
Bad tips: Clean your room first. Don't wash your hair.

B **Read the instruction and topics with the class. Put Ss in pairs and tell them to agree on a topic from the box, then write five or more Top Tips. They should aim to write 30–40 words. Make sure both Ss write the tips as they will need to refer to them in Ex 7C. Remind them to use the imperative verb form. Move around the class and help them with vocabulary and check spelling/grammar.**

C **Put Ss in groups, with partners from Ex 7B in different groups. Ask them to read out their tips one by one for the group to identify the topic.**

EXTRA IDEA: DIGITAL Ss write their tips on a webpage or make a simple poster for the classroom.

TO FINISH

Put Ss in small groups to discuss and make a list of their top tips for learning English (e.g. keep a vocabulary notebook, read your notes after the lesson, etc.). Ask groups to share these with the class and have a general discussion about what Ss can do to improve their skills.

7 REVIEW

LESSON OVERVIEW

This lesson is a review of the language – both grammar and vocabulary – presented in this unit. It also includes a link to the Sounds and Spelling section for this unit, which focuses on consonants: /b/, /v/, /w/, /l/ and /r/; and silent *e*: /æ/ to /eɪ/. The notes below assume that the tasks are completed in class. However, the self-study type exercises (i.e. Exs 1A, 2A, 3A, 4A, 5A and 7A) could be done out of class and then checked in the following lesson when the communicative tasks are then completed.

Online Teaching

If you're teaching this lesson online, you might find the following tips useful:

- **Exs 1A and 1B:** Ss write their questions in the chat and compare before confirming as a class. Put pairs together in groups of four to six (depending on your class size) in breakout rooms to ask each other and answer using the information in the text.
- **Exs 2A and 2B:** In the main room, Ss take turns to nominate a classmate to answer. Then put Ss in breakout rooms to ask and answer all the questions.

Additional Materials

For Teachers:

Sounds and Spelling 7

Unit Test in test package

TO START

Ask Ss to work in pairs and try to remember what language they studied in Unit 7 (Grammar: present simple: *wh-* questions, *was*, *were*, imperatives; Vocabulary: everyday activities, common adjectives, parts of the body, sports and exercise; How to … say you're not well). Ask them to look at the unit lesson objectives to check their ideas.

GRAMMAR

1 A **Read the example with the class and check Ss know that they must write questions that can be answered by the words in bold. Point out that numbers 3 and 4, and 5 and 6 all require a question each. Ss complete the questions alone, then check in pairs. Check the questions with the class and write them on the board.**

EXTRA SUPPORT With weaker classes, do this together as a class. Ss may want to put the preposition first (in 8, and possibly 7, depending on how the question is worded), but it is more usual to place it at the end. When you have finished, drill the questions.

EXTRA SUPPORT: DYSLEXIA Encourage Ss to mask the parts of the text they are not working on to help them identify and focus on the words and phrases in bold.

ANSWERS:

2 Where do you have dinner?
3 When / What time do you meet?
4 Where do you meet?
5 What do you eat?
6 Why do you eat pizza/it?
7 Where do you know him from? / How do you know him?
8 What do you talk about?
9 When / What time do you go home?

B Read the instruction with the class and put Ss in pairs to take turns to tell each other and ask questions. Ask a stronger pair to model this first, using the text and questions from Ex 1A as prompts. Point out that Student A should start and that Student B should ask all their questions before they swap roles. Monitor and check Ss are asking the questions correctly.

EXTRA: ALTERNATIVE IDEA Weaker classes can first write a short text, using the one in Ex 1A as a guide. When they have finished, they read this to their partner who then asks questions.

2 A Look at the first sentence and discuss the options. Point out that there is sometimes more than one possible answer (as Ss may still be at school [*is*] or may not [*was*]). Ss complete the questions alone, then compare their answers in pairs. Monitor and check they're using the correct verb forms. When they have finished, go through the answers with the class.

ANSWERS:

1 was	**2** Were	**3** Were
4 is	**5** Are	**6** were

If Ss are still at school, then the answers to 1, 2 and 3 will be: *is*, *Are*, *Are*

B Put Ss in pairs to ask and answer. When they have finished, ask a few pairs to say something about their partner. If (some) Ss are still at school, then remind them to adapt the verb to the present for questions 1–3.

VOCABULARY

3 A Ss complete the sentences by moving the verbs in bold to the correct sentence, then check in pairs. You could point out that all the verbs are used. Check answers with the class and write them on the board to check spelling.

EXTRA SUPPORT: DYSLEXIA Ss with dyslexia may find this activity difficult as the wrong word in the sentence is a distraction. In this case you could simply gap the sentences and provide Ss with a vertical list of the missing words to insert.

ANSWERS:

2 cook	**3** feed	**4** have	**5** spend
6 visit	**7** wash	**8** do	

B Explain that Ss should give their own answers, and that there are no correct answers. Give an example yourself to demonstrate, e.g. 'I clean my room every week.' Then put Ss in pairs to tell each other. When they have finished, ask for a few examples.

EXTRA SUPPORT Weaker classes will benefit from staging the activity. First, they tick sentences that are true for them and then change the sentences that are not. When they have finished, they tell their partner.

EXTRA CHALLENGE Ss change the sentences about themselves to a mixture of true and untrue. They say a sentence to their partner who decides if it's true or false.

EXTRA IDEA: DIGITAL Ss record themselves saying their sentences. They should listen back and try and evaluate their pronunciation, then record again.

4 A Complete the first word as an example with the class and point out that all the words in focus are adjectives and all the missing letters are vowels. Ss complete the adjectives individually, then check in pairs. Go through the answers as a class, writing them on the board so Ss can check spelling.

EXTRA SUPPORT: DYSLEXIA Ss with dyslexia may be uncertain about spelling in this exercise. In this case, provide two alternatives, one with the correct spelling and one wrong (e.g. *por/poor*), for Ss to choose from.

ANSWERS:

1 poor, rich	**3** slow, fast
2 weak, strong	**4** famous, amazing

B **Ss work in pairs to give each other examples. When they have finished, take brief feedback.**

5 A **Look at the word square with the class and point out that all the words are vertical or horizontal. Ss can circle words or otherwise highlight them. Go through the answers. You might want to write them on the board for Ss to refer to in Ex 5B.**

EXTRA SUPPORT: DYSLEXIA Ss with dyslexia may find it useful to use a mask to cover the grid as they work through it line by line systematically, first horizontally and then vertically.

ANSWERS:

A	F	A	C	E	E	Y	E	H
N	O	S	E	M	O	U	T	H
U	E	F	O	O	T	R	O	E
H	A	N	D	B	T	H	O	A
W	R	T	O	E	A	A	T	D
L	E	G	V	C	R	I	H	R
E	N	E	C	K	M	R	M	M

B **Ss work in pairs to give each other examples. When they have finished, take brief feedback.**

6 A **Put Ss in pairs to take turns to say the words and sounds. Go through the answers. Stronger classes may be able to identify silent letters. The answers below are for the teacher's benefit. We don't expect Ss to be able to write the phonetic symbols, so simply ask them to say the words and isolate the sounds.**

ANSWERS:

back /b/ | visit /v/ | when /w/
right /r/ | leave /l/ | headache /eɪk/
late /eɪt/

B **Refer Ss to Sounds and Spelling on page 157.**

page 157 **SOUNDS AND SPELLING** consonants: /b/, /v/, /w/, /l/ and /r/; silent *e* (2): /æ/ to /eɪ/

The Sounds and Spelling section can be used to help with particular problems. You might want to select the sections or even particular sounds that are most useful for your Ss. The vocabulary used in each section comes from the current unit or previous units.

SOUNDS AND SPELLING TEACHER'S NOTES page 216

7 A **Tell Ss the text is about how to be a good student. Choose the first answer together as a class, then ask Ss to continue alone. Ask them to compare in pairs but don't go through the answers yet.**

EXTRA SUPPORT: DYSLEXIA You could provide the activity divided into two sections with four gaps in each with the corresponding options presented directly below each section. In this way, the eye doesn't need to travel far between the gap and the options. Remind Ss to cover any information they are not referring to, to reduce distraction.

B **R7.01 | Play the recording for Ss to check their answers. Go through the answers as a class, discussing why each one is correct.**

ANSWERS:

1 C **2** A **3** C **4** B **5** C **6** A **7** C **8** A

C **Put Ss in pairs to discuss, then discuss as a class and elicit further ideas.**

TO FINISH

Ask Ss to work in groups of three or four to make a simple poster about learning English. They can use some of the ideas from Ex 7A as well as their own ideas. When they have finished, Ss can regroup to tell each other or you could put the posters on the classroom wall. Ss could vote on the top three ideas and copy them into their notebooks.

8 time out

GSE LEARNING OBJECTIVES

8A Weekend break

- LISTENING | Listen to someone talking about a weekend break: common verbs (2)
- Talk about past actions: past simple: regular verbs
- Pronunciation: *-ed* endings

GSE INFORMATION

VOCABULARY

10–29 Can use language related to holidays.

10–29 Can use language related to moving in a direction.

LISTENING

32 Can identify basic factual information in short, simple dialogues or narratives on familiar everyday topics, if spoken slowly and clearly.

GRAMMAR

30 Can make affirmative statements using common regular past simple forms.

29 Can use negative forms of the simple past.

SPEAKING

30 Can talk about familiar topics using a few basic words and phrases.

8B Going out, staying in

- READING | Read about people's weekends: free-time activities; time phrases
- Talk about past activities: past simple: irregular verbs
- Pronunciation: silent letters: *didn't*
- Write a group chat; linkers: *and, but, then*

GSE INFORMATION

VOCABULARY

10–29 Can use language related to hobbies and interests.

READING

27 Can understand basic phrases in short, simple texts.

GRAMMAR

30 Can make affirmative statements using common irregular past simple forms.

WRITING

28 Can write simple sentences about their life and routines.

31 Can use very basic connectors like 'and', 'but', 'so' and 'then'.

SPEAKING

25 Can indicate time by such phrases as 'next week', 'last Friday', 'in November', 'three o'clock'.

8C A ticket to ... ?

- HOW TO ... | buy a travel ticket: transport and tickets
- Pronunciation: word stress in prices

GSE INFORMATION

VOCABULARY

10–29 Can use language related to public transport.

10–29 Can use language related to trains, train travel, and stations.

HOW TO ...

27 Can understand basic information about prices, times, and dates in familiar contexts, if spoken slowly and clearly.

29 Can follow simple, everyday transactions (e.g. shopping and eating out) if carried out slowly and clearly.

SPEAKING

24 Can buy tickets on public transport using basic fixed expressions.

28 Can ask people for things and give people things.

8D Kodo drummers

- BBC PROGRAMME | Understand a show about two people trying Kodo drumming
- Talk about something you want to try: *want, would like*
- Complete a questionnaire

GSE INFORMATION

VIEW

30 Can identify simple information in a short video, provided that the visual supports this information and the delivery is slow and clear.

GRAMMAR

29 Can use 'I'd like ... / I want ...' to express wants and wishes.

31 Can use 'want to' + infinitive to express intentions.

SPEAKING

34 Can take part in a very simple conversation on a familiar topic if the other speaker repeats questions and answers as necessary and speaks slowly and clearly.

WRITING

27 Can write simple sentences about personal interests.

For full coverage of GSE Learning Objectives go to page 222.

BBC VLOGS

This is a short activity that can be used as an introduction to the unit topic and a warm-up to Lesson 8A. It shouldn't be exploited or taught at length, just played once or twice in class.

You may want to check the words related to weather mentioned in the video (i.e. *sunny*, *hot*) and elicit some other words Ss could use to describe a holiday (e.g. *fun*, *relaxing*, *cold*, etc.). Put Ss in pairs to discuss the question in the programme information box. If your Ss may not have much experience of holidays, make this a general discussion of ways that people could describe a holiday. When they have finished, ask a few Ss for their answers and take brief class feedback. When they are ready, play the video for Ss to watch and answer the question in part 2. Ask them to compare in pairs then check answers with the class.

ANSWERS:

Four speakers talk about the weather. (Two use the word *weather*; two others talk about specific types of weather.)

EXTRA IDEA If Ss want to watch the video again outside class, you could ask them to note the countries that the speakers mention (Greece, Portugal, Australia, Holland, Spain, Sweden, Mexico).

NOTE The vlogs have been provided by people from around the world in response to the same question. The video content was filmed by them on their own mobile phones, so the picture quality varies considerably and in some cases is of a lower quality. However, this adds to the authenticity of the content.

The locations labelled on the vlogs show where the speaker was when they filmed the video. It does not reflect where the speaker comes from (necessarily).

As many of the speakers are non-native, the videos expose Ss to a range of different accents and varieties of English. This could be used as a way to highlight interesting or useful differences.

Additional Materials

For Teachers:

Presentation Tool Unit 8

Online Digital Resources

Videoscript Unit 8 Opener: BBC Vlogs

8A Weekend break

GRAMMAR | past simple: regular verbs
VOCABULARY | common verbs (2)
PRONUNCIATION | *-ed* endings

LESSON OVERVIEW

In this lesson, Ss learn vocabulary related to arranging short holidays. They also learn the past simple of regular verbs. The context is a listening where the speaker describes their weekend away. This leads into the grammar, where Ss also practise the different possible pronunciations of *ed* endings: /t/, /d/ and /ɪd/. The lesson ends with a speaking activity where Ss practise telling each other about their recent activities in pairs.

Online Teaching

If you're teaching this lesson online, you might find the following tips useful:

- **Ex 1A:** Display the adverts on your device and have a whole class discussion of the questions in the main room.
- **Exs 2A and 2B:** Remind Ss to mute their microphones. Use a collaborative document containing the T/F statements for Ss to write the answers.
- **Exs 5A and 5B:** Ask Ss to write their sentences in the chat, then set up breakout rooms for them to discuss them.

Additional Materials

For Teachers:

Presentation Tool Lesson 8A

Photocopiable Activities 8A

Grammar Bank 8A

For Students:

Online Practice 8A

Workbook 8A

TO START

Ask Ss if they like to go away with friends or family and where they like to stay. Elicit/Teach places to stay: *hotel*, *(rented) house*, *with friends or family*, *(rented) apartment*, *campsite*, etc. and ask Ss which they like. Give an example yourself, e.g. 'I like staying in a rented house because I like cooking.' Then put Ss in pairs to discuss which they like and why. When they have finished, ask a few Ss to share anything interesting they found out about their partner with the class.

EXTRA SUPPORT: DYSLEXIA Dyslexic learners in particular benefit from understanding exactly what they are learning in a lesson so that they understand what they are working towards. In this and every lesson, explain clearly what the learning objectives of the lesson are near the start.

VOCABULARY

common verbs (2)

1 A Check understanding of *break* (a short holiday) and use the photos to teach other key words including *glamping* (camping in a permanent tent that is luxurious; formed from *glamorous* + *camping*). Ask Ss to read and discuss the questions in pairs. When they have finished, elicit their answers and take a show of hands to see which is the most popular weekend break advertised. Ask a few Ss to share something about where they go (and why). Ideas could include mountains or the countryside (walking), cities (sightseeing, shopping, visit friends/family), etc.

EXTRA SUPPORT: DYSLEXIA You could record the adverts before the class so that Ss can listen on their devices as they read. Alternatively, pair dyslexic learners with a partner who can read the adverts with them.

EXTRA SUPPORT: TEACHER If there are Ss who don't have the opportunity to go away, for question 2 they could talk about things they do in their local area, e.g. 'I don't (often) go away at the weekend, but I go to the park to walk/talk with friends / go to the town centre to shop.'

EXTRA CHALLENGE With stronger classes, you could ask Ss to rank the weekends away in order of preference and to say why.

B Focus attention on the words in the box and point out that these appear in the adverts, too (in bold). Ss should use the adverts to help them understand the meaning of the words and then complete the sentences. Ask Ss to work alone then compare in pairs. Check answers as a class.

EXTRA SUPPORT With weaker classes, you could read out the short texts so that Ss can follow at the same time. As you do so, draw attention to the prepositions that are dependent on the verbs and can act as clues in Ex 1B (e.g. *stay in a tent*).

ANSWERS:

2 plan, change	**3** stay	**4** want, relax
5 arrive	**6** walk	**7** try
8 travel		

C Explain that Ss should tell each other the sentences that are true for them. Give an example yourself, e.g. 'I usually book my room online. This is true for me.' Stronger classes could also change those that are not true to make them true for them.

EXTRA CHALLENGE Put Ss in A/B pairs. Student A says the verb and Student B supplies a suitable complement, e.g. *stay – in an apartment, arrive – early*, etc. After a few turns they change roles.

LISTENING

2 A 8.01 | Explain that Ss will hear someone talking about their weekend away and they should listen and decide which one it was from the adverts in Ex 1A. At the same time they should listen for the problem the person had. Play the recording, then ask Ss to compare in pairs. Play it again if they need it, then go through the answers.

ANSWERS:

Advert 3

The problem was that he went to the wrong house.

AUDIOSCRIPT 8.01

My wife and I wanted a weekend break. We work in the city and we wanted a nice weekend by the sea, with sun and good food.

We looked online. There was a place about two hours from us by car. It was perfect. It was a white beach house next to the sea. We booked the house on Thursday. An email arrived on Friday with the address and the code for the door. An easy code, 1-2-3-4.

We arrived on Friday evening. It was a beautiful place, but there was a problem. There were **two** houses at the address. Two white beach houses. House number one and house number two. I didn't remember our house number, but the code, 1-2-3-4, opened the door of house number one, so there wasn't a problem. Right?

Wrong! Maria, my wife, walked into the house. 'Oh no … ,' she said. It was really bad. There was food on the kitchen table, the floor was dirty and the *bathroom*! I tried to phone the owner, but he didn't answer. We washed some cups for a cup of tea and then we walked on the beach for an hour.

At ten o'clock I called the owner again. This time he answered the phone. He was very surprised about the problem and he said 'I'm sorry' five times. He lived about thirty minutes away. He arrived and walked … to house number two! He looked at me and asked, 'Why are you at number one? **This** is your house – house number two. 'But the code was right for this house,' I said. 'Yes, they have the same code, 1-2-3-4. And you're in the wrong house!'

B Refer Ss to the True/False statements. They should discuss what they can remember in their pairs. If they ask questions about the verb forms, tell them that they will see those later. Move around and see how they are doing. Don't check answers yet.

C 8.01 | Now play the recording again for Ss to check their ideas. Ask pairs to compare, then check answers with the class. If Ss got a lot wrong, play the recording again, pausing at times to focus attention on the answers.

ANSWERS:
1 F **2** T **3** T **4** F **5** T **6** F

D Put Ss in pairs to discuss, then take whole class feedback. You could see what the three most common problems are. If this topic is not relevant for your Ss, you can leave it out.

GRAMMAR

past simple: regular verbs

3A Look at the sentences as a class and ask Ss if they are about the present or the past (past). Then ask Ss to look at the verbs in bold and use these to help them complete the rules (a–d) in pairs. With weaker classes, you may prefer to do this as a whole class activity, highlighting spelling changes on the board. Check answers with the class and write them on the board.

ANSWERS:
a -ed **b** -d **c** -i, -ed **d** didn't

B The Grammar Bank on page 120 can be used in the lesson or for homework. Decide how and when the exercises will benefit your class.

GB page 120 **GRAMMAR BANK**

Go through the notes with Ss or let them read them alone. Check understanding where necessary, especially of the spelling rules.

1 This exercise practises the form of verbs in the past simple. Look at the example with the class and elicit the second answer in the first sentence, then ask Ss to continue alone. Check answers with the class. In feedback, ask individual Ss to read the whole sentence aloud and drill as needed.

EXTRA SUPPORT: DYSLEXIA Encourage Ss to cover the sentences they are not working on, to avoid distraction.

ANSWERS:
1 *opened*, closed
2 cleaned, cooked
3 started, finished
4 changed, didn't wash
5 liked, loved
6 studied, didn't like
7 asked, didn't answer
8 called, thanked
9 played, stopped
10 painted, didn't help

2 This exercise practises the meaning and form of past simple regular verbs. Read the example with the class. Ss complete the rest of the text, then check in pairs. Check answers with the class.

EXTRA SUPPORT: DYSLEXIA You could record the text before the class, indicating where the gaps occur, for Ss to listen as they read. You could also divide the text into two halves and provide the verbs for each half separately in a vertical list to support Ss in focusing on the form rather than the choice of verb. Ask them to write the past forms (either positive or negative) beside the verbs in the list before attempting the exercise.

ANSWERS:
2 booked **3** travelled **4** weren't
5 walked **6** looked at **7** tried
8 stayed **9** was **10** didn't want

3 This exercise practises the form of past simple regular verbs as well as the verb *be* and correct use of prepositions. Elicit the first answer then ask Ss to continue alone before checking in pairs. Go through the answers as a class, with pairs of Ss reading the conversation across the class. Write the answers on the board to ensure Ss have correct spelling.

EXTRA SUPPORT: DYSLEXIA You could adapt the conversation, leaving gaps for the correct form of the verbs only and giving the infinitive of each verb immediately after each gap.

ANSWERS:
A: How was your day?
B: It was busy. I started work at ten and I worked all day.
I finished at six o'clock and (I) cooked dinner.
I didn't stop all day!
How was your day?
A: It wasn't bad.
In the morning I checked the/my children's homework and I listened to them read.
In the afternoon we studied spelling and we walked in the park.

EXTRA IDEA Ss read the conversation in pairs. If this is easy for your group, they can repeat and change the answers to their own ideas. When you monitor, listen out for pronunciation of the past simple verb endings and drill these at the end if necessary.

PRONUNCIATION

-ed endings

4 A 8.02 | Focus attention on the three sounds /t/, /d/ and /ɪd/, then play the recording for Ss to listen and identify which sounds they hear in each verb. Ss could draw a table in their notebooks with three columns, one sound at the top of each, then listen and write the verbs in. Play the recording a second time if necessary.

EXTRA SUPPORT: DYSLEXIA Provide the verbs written on slips of paper. Ss should listen and place them in the correct category.

EXTRA: ALTERNATIVE IDEA You could get Ss to try to categorise the past forms by sound before listening to them, e.g. by putting the verbs (in the past) on the board, demonstrating the categorisation and letting Ss practise saying them in pairs to help identify the differentiation. This can help raise their sensitivity to the underlying rules without actually articulating those rules. The issue of voiced and unvoiced consonants will be familiar to any Ss who have been working with the Sounds and Spelling pages, as it is a recurring focus there (/t/ and /d/ have already been covered as single sounds).

ANSWERS:
/t/ *walked*, washed, asked, looked, finished, liked, stopped
/d/ *arrived*, changed, travelled, lived
/ɪd/ *wanted*, started, hated, texted

AUDIOSCRIPT 8.02
walked, arrived, wanted, changed, travelled, washed, asked, looked, started, finished, lived, liked, hated, stopped, texted

B 8.02 | Play the recording again for Ss to listen and repeat.

C 8.03 | Play the sentences one by one, pausing for Ss to listen and repeat.

AUDIOSCRIPT 8.03
1 This morning I washed my hair.
2 I walked to class.
3 The lesson started at nine.
4 I arrived late.
5 We asked a lot of questions.
6 The teacher answered our questions.

EXTRA IDEA You might find it useful to highlight the consonant–vowel linking that occurs after the past forms when they're followed by a word starting with a vowel, often a preposition. There are a few examples in the recording: *started at, asked a, answered our.*

D In pairs, Ss try and remember the verbs from the sentences in Ex 4C. Weaker classes can write them, stronger classes just say them. Go through the answers. You could play the recording from Ex 4C again to check.

EXTRA IDEA: DIGITAL Ask Ss to record themselves saying the sentences in Ex 4C, then listen to the recording again and compare it with their pronunciation.

SPEAKING

5 A Read the instructions as a class. Point out that Ss need to change the verb forms. Give a positive and a negative example yourself, e.g. 'Last summer, I played tennis with my friends.', 'Yesterday evening, I didn't talk to my mum.', to show how to use the prompts in the boxes. Give Ss a few minutes to think and write. Move around the class to support and check they are completing the exercise correctly.

EXTRA SUPPORT When moving around, remind Ss to write on alternate lines, giving themselves plenty of space to make changes to their writing.

EXTRA SUPPORT: TEACHER In this activity, encourage Ss to use the verbs in the prompts. They may, however, naturally want to use *went*, which is not taught until the next lesson. As with any new language, simply teach it if the need arises.

B Put Ss into pairs to tell each other their sentences.

C Ss help each other in their pairs to change two sentences. You could demonstrate this by changing the examples you gave in Ex 5A, e.g. 'Last summer, I didn't play tennis with my friends.', 'Yesterday evening, I talked to my mum.' Encourage them to change verb forms from positive to negative or vice versa. Move around the class to support and check.

D Put Ss in new groups of three or four to read out their sentences in turn, for other Ss to say if they're true or false. Move around the class to listen for how they are pronouncing and how confidently they are using the past forms. In feedback, ask Ss how many they guessed correctly and drill any pronunciation problems.

TO FINISH

Write on the board: *What did you study today? How can you use this outside the class?* Put Ss in pairs to discuss the questions.

8B Going out, staying in

GRAMMAR | past simple: irregular verbs
VOCABULARY | free-time activities; time phrases
PRONUNCIATION | silent letters: *didn't*

LESSON OVERVIEW

In this lesson, Ss learn vocabulary related to free-time activities. They also learn past simple irregular verbs. The context is a reading where people talk about how they spend their weekends. This leads into the grammar, where Ss also learn about the pronunciation of *didn't*. They then do a writing activity where they write about their weekends using linking words. The lesson ends with a speaking activity where Ss discuss past activities using time phrases.

Online Teaching

If you're teaching this lesson online, you might find the following tips useful:

- **Ex 1B:** Use a collaborative document to brainstorm ideas, using a different colour for each category.
- **Ex 1C:** Ss write their answers in the chat and comment on what others have written.
- **Ex 3A:** Make the document available for collaboration on your device and share the screen. Individual Ss add answers.

Additional Materials

For Teachers:
Presentation Tool Lesson 8B
Photocopiable Activities 8B
Grammar Bank 8B
Vocabulary Bank 8B
Writing Bank 8B

For Students:
Online Practice 8B
Workbook 8B

TO START

Go round the class naming the days of the week. Write them on the board as well as the following questions:
What's your favourite day? Why?
What do you usually do on that day?

Put Ss in small groups to discuss, then take whole class feedback to see if people have similar ideas.

EXTRA SUPPORT: DYSLEXIA Dyslexic learners in particular benefit from understanding exactly what they are learning in a lesson so that they understand what they are working towards. In this and every lesson, explain clearly what the learning objectives of the lesson are near the start.

EXTRA SUPPORT: TEACHER Depending on who and where you are teaching, the weekend may not mean Saturday and Sunday. In the Muslim world, countries such as Somalia and Yemen traditionally observe the weekend on Thursday and Friday, though in recent years there has been a change to Friday and Saturday, to facilitate business with western countries.

VOCABULARY

free-time activities

1 A Put Ss in pairs to discuss. When they have finished, take brief class feedback to see which activities are popular.

EXTRA SUPPORT If you think your Ss won't have much to say, because they lack vocabulary, go over some of the free-time activities in Ex 1B first, eliciting them using pictures. With weaker classes, you may simply want to start with Ex 1B, then move to Ex 1A as a discussion, to practise the free-time activities taught.

B Give Ss plenty of time to read through the activities, then discuss in pairs where people do them. While they are talking, monitor and observe how they pronounce the new vocabulary.

EXTRA: ALTERNATIVE IDEA If you feel your class would benefit from recording their answers, you could structure the activity as follows. Create a ticking grid with activities 1–8 written vertically and the four places heading columns at the top. Ss discuss and tick whichever columns are relevant. This will facilitate feedback and discussion and be a good way of checking understanding.

POSSIBLE ANSWERS:
outdoors: have a barbecue, play a game, meet a friend, do a sport
indoors/at home: go to a party, play a game, see a film, meet a friend, watch television
online: play a game, see a film, buy clothes
alone: see a film, buy clothes, watch television

C Explain that Ss should think of more words that go with each verb. Elicit an example with the class (e.g. *go to the shops*), then ask Ss to continue in pairs. Check answers with the class. Be careful only to accept verb/noun combinations that really go together, as a combination that may be acceptable in the Ss' own language may not be so in English.

EXTRA SUPPORT: TEACHER Both *see* and *watch* can be used with 'film'. Generally, we *see a film* at the cinema, and we *watch a film* on TV. We also use *see* to mean 'meet or visit'. We can *go to* or *have* 'a party'. When we 'go to a party', we are a guest; when we 'have a party', we are the host. You can check understanding by asking Ss which they prefer or which is easier – most people prefer to go to a party as it's easier! We speak generally about *doing sport*, but we *play* some specific sports (usually those with a ball, such as tennis or football).

POSSIBLE ANSWERS:

have: a shower, a meal, an apple
go to: a/the park, school, work, the office
play: football, tennis, a computer game, the guitar
see: a friend, my mother
meet: a person, my brother
buy: music, food, a car
watch: a film, sport, a match/game, a box-set, the children, a video, YouTube
do: yoga, nothing, exercise, the shopping, homework

READING

EXTRA SUPPORT: DYSLEXIA There is a recording of the reading text available to help dyslexic learners.

2 A Read the title with the class and point out that here *stay in* means 'stay at home'. Explain that 'go out' is the opposite, but doesn't necessarily mean you have to be outside. Then focus attention on the photos and explain that Ss should read the group chat and identify a writer for each photo, A and B. Give them two minutes for this, then ask them to check in pairs. Check answers with the class.

ANSWERS:

A Sentry607 **B** Alexa950

B Refer Ss to the questions and explain that they should read the group chat again more carefully and identify one or more writer for each question (1–3). Give them three minutes, then ask them to compare answers with a partner. Go through the answers as a class.

ANSWERS:

1 Alexa950
2 Sentry607, Alexa950
3 Heather829

EXTRA IDEA: DIGITAL Ss work in threes and record themselves reading one of the user responses. Ask them to listen back and give each other feedback, then record themselves reading a different response.

GRAMMAR

past simple: irregular verbs

3 A Ss have probably already noticed the verbs in bold in the text. Ask them why they are in bold. If they have no idea, ask them if they are about the present or the past (past). Focus attention on the infinitive column and ask Ss to identify the past forms that match, then check in pairs. Check answers with the whole class and write them on the board. Drill for pronunciation.

EXTRA SUPPORT: DYSLEXIA Encourage Ss with dyslexia to follow the texts line by line, covering the lines they are not checking, until they find a word in bold. Then they should cover everything else in the text to help them focus on the word to match it with an infinitive in the table. You could provide the infinitives as a vertical list on a separate piece of paper they can hold next to the text as additional support.

ANSWERS:

buy – *bought*
do – did
get – got
go – went
have – had
make – made
meet – met
see – saw

B Ss use the examples to complete the rule alone, then check in pairs. Check answers with the class. This exercise can be done as a class if your class is weaker or you don't have much time.

ANSWER:

didn't

C The Grammar Bank on page 121 can be used in the lesson or for homework. Decide how and when the exercises will benefit your class.

page 121 **GRAMMAR BANK**

This focuses on the past simple form and use of some common irregular verbs. Go through the notes with Ss or let them read them alone. Drill the pronunciation of the infinitive and the past forms. Point out that the spelling of the infinitive and the past is the same for the verb *read* but the pronunciation differs /riːd/ vs. /red/. Check understanding where necessary, especially of the negative form, which is formed in the same way as for regular past verbs, but is a tricky form to master.

1 **Read the example with the class, then ask Ss to complete the sentences individually, then check in pairs. Check answers with the class and write them on the board or invite different Ss to come up and do so.**

EXTRA SUPPORT: DYSLEXIA Dyslexic learners might find this type of exercise difficult. In this case, adapt the exercise: remove the two extra verbs and provide the others in a vertical list that Ss can place alongside the gapped sentences. They then need to write the past simple form in the gap.

ANSWERS:

2 gave **3** did **4** took
5 knew **6** ate

2 **Look at the example together. Remind Ss that *but* is used to contrast and has a small letter, not a capital. Ss complete the sentences alone, then check in pairs. Check answers with the class.**

EXTRA SUPPORT: DYSLEXIA To reduce the writing load, provide the completed sentences with the verbs in brackets in the infinitive with a gap for Ss to complete them in the correct tense.

ANSWERS:

2 but last week we bought our food online
3 but on Thursday morning she left home at ten
4 but yesterday I had lunch in/at a restaurant
5 but last Wednesday I met some friends in the afternoon
6 but yesterday I didn't write any emails
7 but we went to the cinema yesterday evening
8 but yesterday she went (to bed) at half past nine
9 but last Sunday I slept for ten hours
10 but yesterday he didn't do his homework

EXTRA IDEA If your class would benefit from extra writing practice, Ss write their own endings for some of the sentence beginnings (e.g. 1, 2, 4, 5, 6, 7, 9), changing the first part of the sentence a little if needed. When they have finished, put them in pairs to tell each other and respond with their own sentences.

3 **This exercise is to practise the negative form. Look at the example together. Remind Ss that the negative uses the infinitive after *didn't*. Ss write the sentences alone, then check in pairs. Check answers with the class.**

EXTRA SUPPORT: DYSLEXIA Provide the complete sentences with just the verbs gapped for Ss to complete with the negative form to reduce the writing load.

ANSWERS:

2 I didn't read a newspaper last Sunday.
3 Stefan didn't know me.
4 Wasim didn't go to work on Monday.
5 We didn't come to this city in 1998.

4 **This exercise is to practise the positive form. Look at the example together. Remind Ss that they can refer to the verb list if they need to. Ss write the sentences alone, then check in pairs. Check answers with the class.**

EXTRA SUPPORT: DYSLEXIA Provide the complete sentences with just the verbs gapped for Ss to complete.

ANSWERS:

2 Kim left university in 2004.
3 I wrote messages to all my friends.
4 I saw a good film last week.
5 I had two showers yesterday.

PRONUNCIATION

silent letters: *didn't*

4A **8.04 | Ss have seen silent letters before, so ask them if they can think of any (e.g. the final 'e' in *take*). Write *didn't* on the board and ask them which letter they think may be silent, then play the recorded sentences one by one. Ask them to listen for the final *t*, to see if they can hear it.**

ANSWER:

No, you can't hear the *t*.

B **8.04 | Play the recording again, pausing after each sentence for Ss to listen and repeat.**

C **Read the instruction to the class. Ask them what tense they will use (past simple) and refer them to the vocabulary seen in Ex 1B and the activities they came up with in Ex 1C for ideas. Move around and help/support Ss as they write. With stronger classes, feed in new vocabulary that they ask you for.**

EXTRA SUPPORT: TEACHER While the main aim is to practise the vocabulary in this lesson, it's also good to enable stronger Ss to express their real activities, as this will be more memorable for them. Encourage them to use you as a resource and also to check vocabulary with their devices or dictionaries. Stronger Ss can also write more sentences.

D **Ss work in pairs and take turns to say what their partner did, using their own list of activities from Ex 4C. Their partner says if they did each activity or not. Encourage them to use full sentences when replying with the negative forms, for practice. Monitor and check they're pronouncing the verbs correctly. When they have finished, ask a few Ss to share what they found out about their partner's weekend with the class.**

WRITING

write a group chat; linkers: *and, but, then*

5 A **Explain that Ss should read the extract and choose the correct option from the words in bold alone, then check in pairs. Elicit the answer. Point out the answer is 'go out' because it is followed by *but* which indicates a contrast with what follows ('… but first I relax at home.').**

ANSWER:
go out

B **Explain that Ss will now write about their own weekend. Refer them to the Writing Bank on page 91.**

WB page 91 **WRITING BANK**

1 A **Ss read jovi2047K's full answer and answer the question alone, then compare their ideas in pairs. Check the answer and have a brief class discussion.**

EXTRA SUPPORT: DYSLEXIA If possible, record the text before the class, indicating where the gaps occur, for Ss to listen to as they read. This could be on individual devices. They could use the recording again for Ex 1B. Alternatively, read the text with the class.

ANSWER:
played football

B **Check that Ss know or remember that *and* adds more information and *but* introduces a contrast. Ss complete the text alone, then check their answers with a partner. Check answers with the class.**

EXTRA SUPPORT With weaker classes, first review the meaning of *and* and *but* by writing the following sentences on the board:
1 *I had a coffee … I ate a cake at eleven o'clock.*
2 *I went to John's house, … he wasn't at home.*

Elicit the word that goes in each gap (1 *and*; 2 *but*) to demonstrate that *and* links two clauses to give additional information whereas *but* links two contrasting clauses. Use (+) and (-) to emphasise. Remind Ss that these linking words do not have a capital letter as they are placed in the middle of a sentence.

ANSWERS:

1 but	**2** and	**3** and
4 but	**5** and	

C **Put Ss into pairs. They should cover the text in Ex 1A and complete the sentence, then check in the text. Check answers with the class.**

ANSWER:
Then

D **Demonstrate the meaning of *then* by giving an example, e.g. 'I clean my teeth, then I wash my face.' Point out that we don't start a sentence with *and* or *but*, but we can start with *then*. Then ask Ss to complete the sentences alone. When they have finished, put Ss in pairs to compare, then go through the answers as a class.**

EXTRA SUPPORT With weaker classes, first review the meaning of *and* and *then* by writing the following sentences on the board:
1 *I had a coffee … I ate a cake at eleven o'clock.*
2 *I went to John's house, … I went to Peter's house.*

Elicit the word that goes in each gap (1 *and*; 2 *then*) to demonstrate that *and* links two clauses of simultaneous or connected actions whereas *then* links two clauses with successive actions, one after the other. So we could say, *I had a coffee, then I ate a cake* if these actions were in sequence. A fuller range of linkers is taught at A2 level.

EXTRA SUPPORT: DYSLEXIA Remind Ss to cover the sentences or parts of sentences they are not working on to reduce distraction.

ANSWERS:
1 and, Then, but
2 but, Then, and
3 but, and, Then

2 **Ask Ss to write their answers individually. Encourage them to use linked sentences and to aim to write 50–60 words. Move around the class as they work, checking their writing and offering help where necessary.**

EXTRA IDEA: DIGITAL Ss could upload their answers to a group page, if available. Alternatively, Ss can read and record their answers, then listen to each other's recordings and ask a follow-up question.

3 **Ask Ss to return to page 81 to complete the lesson.**

SPEAKING

6 A Explain that the past simple is often used with a past time phrase. Ask Ss to identify the time phrase in the first sentence. If they can do this, they can continue alone. If not, complete the exercise as a class. Go through the answers, pointing out that the time phrase usually goes at the beginning or end of a sentence, not in the middle.

ANSWERS:
On Sunday, Last Saturday, Yesterday morning, 2 months ago

B Write the four prompts on the board and elicit one idea for each, then ask Ss to work in pairs and think of more. Monitor and support as they do this. Don't check the answers yet.

C Refer Ss to the Vocabulary Bank on page 138 to check their ideas.

VB page 138 **VOCABULARY BANK** time phrases

Note that the Vocabulary Bank activities are an important part of the lesson. They should only be omitted if you are confident that your Ss already know this vocabulary. If you don't use the exercises in class, it would be a good idea to set them as homework.

1 A Look at the word webs and elicit a further example with a word or phrase from the box, then ask Ss to continue. Go through the answers as a class.

EXTRA SUPPORT: DYSLEXIA Provide the words in the box as a vertical list for Ss and encourage them to try each word in turn with the words from the time phrases in the word webs, crossing off each one as they find a match and writing it after (or before) the word given. Highlight that words going with *ago* come before it not after it.

ANSWERS:
yesterday: *afternoon*, evening, morning
last: *April*, Friday, month, night, Saturday, weekend, year
on: *Friday*, Saturday
in: *1969*, 2020 (*two years*, *a week* and *three days* are also possible but these are about the future, not the past)
two years, a week, three days **ago**

B Look at the example and ask a stronger pair to demonstrate a further example then put Ss in pairs to continue taking turns saying two time phrases and working out which comes first. Monitor and be available for questions.

7 A Look at the example and ask a stronger pair to demonstrate a further example with their own answers. Put Ss in pairs to take turns to ask and answer. Encourage them to extend their answers as in the example if possible. When they have finished, ask a few Ss to report back on something interesting their partner said.

EXTRA IDEA To encourage Ss to focus on good pronunciation, write the first question on the board and ask Ss to tell you where the main stresses are: *<u>When</u> was the <u>last</u> <u>time</u> you <u>went</u> to a <u>really</u> <u>good</u> <u>party</u>?* Drill chorally. Then put them in pairs to ask each other.

FUTURE SKILLS | Communication

B Refer Ss to the Future Skills box and read it through. Write the phrases on the board, drill them and elicit any more that Ss can suggest. Explain that Ss should try to use at least two when they talk to each other. Put Ss in small groups to take turns to ask each other different questions from Ex 7A, using the phrases from the Future Skills box when they answer. When they have finished, ask a few Ss to share some of their questions and answers with the class.

EXTRA: ALTERNATIVE IDEA Depending on your class and if space allows, you could set the discussion part of Ex 7B up as a mingling activity, where Ss move freely around the room and talk to different Ss.

EXTRA CHALLENGE Stronger classes can make changes to the questions (e.g. '… went to a really good <u>restaurant</u>?'), then ask each other.

TO FINISH

Put Ss in groups to talk about their last day trip / weekend away / birthday and the activities they did. When they have finished, ask a few to report back and see how they use the past simple.

8C A ticket to … ?

HOW TO … | buy a travel ticket
VOCABULARY | transport and tickets
PRONUNCIATION | word stress in prices

LESSON OVERVIEW

In this lesson, after first learning vocabulary related to transport, Ss learn functional language for buying a ticket on public transport, as well as practising the word stress when saying and checking prices. The context is a listening where they listen to three conversations in different transport situations. The lesson ends with a speaking activity where Ss roleplay a conversation between a customer and a staff member in which they ask for and give travel information.

Online Teaching

If you're teaching this lesson online, you might find the following tips useful:

- **Ex 1A:** Ss write their answers in the chat, then discuss and compare as a class in the main room.
- **Ex 2B:** Display the task on your device and share your screen. Make sure the annotate function is switched on. Ask individual Ss to complete the answers and confirm as a class.

Additional Materials

For Teachers:
Presentation Tool Lesson 8C
Photocopiable Activity 8C
Grammar Bank 8C
Vocabulary Bank 8C

For Students:
Online Practice 8C
Workbook 8C

TO START

Write the following questions on the board:
How do you come to class?
What time do you leave home (or work)?
What time do you arrive (here)?

Tell Ss your answers, e.g. 'I come to school by bus. I leave at eight and I arrive at nine.'). Put Ss in pairs to do the same. Take brief class feedback. Tell Ss today's lesson is about transport.

EXTRA SUPPORT: DYSLEXIA Dyslexic learners in particular benefit from understanding exactly what they are learning in a lesson so that they understand what they are working towards. In this and every lesson, explain clearly what the learning objectives of the lesson are near the start.

VOCABULARY

transport and tickets

1 A Use pictures to elicit/teach *car, bus, train* and *plane*. Ask Ss to discuss the questions in pairs. When they have finished, have a show of hands to see which form of transport is the most popular for different distances. Ask a few individual Ss to share their experiences for question 2.

EXTRA IDEA Ss complete a transport survey. As well as asking several Ss about their favourite kind of transport, they could ask: *How do you usually travel to work/class? When was the last time you took a taxi?* etc.

B Put Ss in pairs to make a list of types of transport. Give them two minutes. When they have finished, ask how many they have, then refer them to the Vocabulary Bank on page 139 to check their ideas.

page 139 **VOCABULARY BANK** transport

Note that the Vocabulary Bank activities are an important part of the lesson. They should only be omitted if you are confident that your Ss already know this vocabulary. If you don't use the exercises in class, it would be a good idea to set them as homework.

1 A Refer Ss to the photos (A–J) and ask them to match them with the types of transport (1–10). Ss should work alone, then check in pairs. Go through the answers as a class, drilling and marking stress.

EXTRA SUPPORT: DYSLEXIA Covering the words they are not currently working on will help reduce distraction for dyslexic learners.

ANSWERS:
1 C **2** G **3** A **4** F **5** B
6 J **7** H **8** D **9** I **10** E

B VB8.01 | Focus Ss on the photos and ask them to listen and repeat.

C Demonstrate the activity by pointing to a type of transport and asking Ss to identify it. Ss continue in pairs, taking turns to point. Listen for mispronunciations and drill these when they have finished.

D Put Ss in pairs to discuss the questions. Ss may need support when answering *Why? / Why not?*, in terms of some relevant vocabulary (e.g. *expensive, far, near*). When they have finished, take whole class feedback to see which forms of transport are the most and least popular.

2 A Refer Ss to the photos and the words in the box, and ask them to work in pairs to identify what they can see in the photos. Go through the answers, pointing at the photos to elicit the words. Elicit or explain the meaning of the words not shown in the photos, i.e. *monthly pass*, *return* and *single*. Make sure Ss understand *monthly* (i.e. every month) and preteach *weekly* and *daily*, which appear in Ex 2C.

EXTRA SUPPORT: DYSLEXIA Supply the words as a vertical list which is easier to read for dyslexic learners. They can then also use this in the gap-fill activity in Ex 2B.

EXTRA CHALLENGE Ask Ss to discuss what they can see in the photos without referring to the words in the box and then uncover the box to help them.

ANSWERS:
gate (B), passenger (A), platform (D), ticket machine (C), ticket office (D)

B Ask Ss to complete the sentences alone, then check in pairs. Check answers with the class.

EXTRA SUPPORT: DYSLEXIA Dyslexic learners can use the list of words they were provided with in Ex 2A to place alongside the sentences. Ask their partner from Ex 2A to read each sentence aloud to help them decide which word fits each gap.

ANSWERS:
2 platform
3 gate
4 single
5 return
6 monthly pass
7 ticket office
8 ticket machine

EXTRA IDEA Depending on where you are or your Ss are from, you may want to introduce extra relevant vocabulary such as *travelcard* (e.g. Oyster/Zip card) and *railcard* (e.g. student / older person discounted pass).

C Ss discuss the questions in pairs. They can talk about where they are now or where they are from. If you haven't covered them already, you could elicit the meaning of *weekly* and *daily*, based on Ss' awareness of *monthly* in Ex 2A. This is an opportunity to practise the new vocabulary, so move around and listen to Ss. When they have finished, ask a few pairs for their answers then give brief feedback on any problems.

How to …
buy a travel ticket

3 A 8.05 | Explain that Ss will listen to three conversations about transport situations. Refer them to the three sets of items and allow time for them to read through the sentences and alternatives. Then play the recording. Ss listen and identify the correct alternatives, then check their answers in pairs. Play the recording again if needed, pausing after each conversation. Check answers with the class.

ANSWERS:
Conversation 1
1 Airport **2** single **3** £19.60
Conversation 2
1 12.15 **2** seven
Conversation 3
1 Oxford **2** return **3** twenty-six

AUDIOSCRIPT 8.05
Conversation 1
A: Excuse me. Can you help me?
B: Yes. What's the problem?
A: I don't understand this ticket machine.
B: Where do you want to go?
A: Manchester Airport.
B: Today?
A: Yes.
B: Do you want a single or a return?
A: A single.
B: OK, first choose the station. Manchester Airport?
A: That's right.
B: OK press there. And there.
A: OK … ?
B: And choose 'today'.
A: 'Today'.
B: And then choose 'single'.
A: 'Single ticket'.
B: And pay.
A: OK, that's nineteen pounds sixty. OK. Thanks a lot.
B: No problem.

Conversation 2
A: Excuse me.
B: Yes.
A: When's the next train to Cambridge?
B: Let me check. There's one at quarter past twelve.
A: It's twelve now. Fifteen minutes, good. What platform is it?

B: Platform seven.

A: Oh, and when does it arrive in Cambridge?

B: It arrives at half past one.

A: Thanks.

Conversation 3

A: Hello. Could I have a return ticket to Oxford, please?

B: For today?

A: That's right.

B: And the return?

A: Today.

B: So that's a return ticket to Oxford, going and coming back today?

A: That's right. How much is it?

B: That's forty-two pounds fifteen.

A: Sorry? Forty-two pounds fifty?

B: No, fifteen.

A: What gate is it?

B: Oxford buses leave from gate twenty-six.

A: And when's the next bus?

B: Just a second. Ah … It leaves in five minutes.

A: Thanks!

B Put Ss in pairs to complete the conversations from what they can remember. Don't give any answers at this stage.

C 8.06 | Play the recording for Ss to check their answers. Check answers with the class.

EXTRA SUPPORT: TEACHER If Ss ask about the tense, the present simple is correctly used here for the arrival and departure information. This use of the tense is commonly referred to as 'timetable future', i.e. the events are scheduled.

ANSWERS:

1 want	**2** next	**3** There
4 arrive	**5** arrives	**6** Could
7 today	**8** from	

EXTRA IDEA Ss practise the conversations in pairs, taking turns at both roles

D The Grammar Bank on page 122 can be used in the lesson or for homework. Decide how and when the exercises will benefit your class.

GB page 122 **GRAMMAR BANK**

This section focuses on the form and use of phrases for buying a travel ticket. Read the notes with the class or give them a few minutes to read alone and then ask any questions they have.

1 Look at the example with the class, then ask Ss to continue, finding three mistakes with the phrases in each conversation, then check in pairs. Check answers as a class.

EXTRA SUPPORT: DYSLEXIA Ss with dyslexia can find this type of error correction exercise difficult. In this case, you could highlight where the problems are as a class, then ask pairs to discuss how to correct them. Alternatively, provide the conversations with the mistakes highlighted for Ss to correct. Reading the conversations aloud can also be helpful.

ANSWERS:

(Only the sentences where there is a mistake are given.)

1 A: Yes. What platform is **it**?

B: It **is** / It**'s** platform seven.

2 A: Can I buy **a** monthly pass … ?

A: Thanks. How much is **it**?

B: **It** is / **It**'s fifty euros.

3 A: What ~~gates~~ **gate** is the bus to Lima?

A: ~~Where~~ **When**'s the next bus?

A: And what time ~~arrives~~ **does it arrive** in Lima?

EXTRA IDEA Ss practise the conversations in pairs, taking turns at both roles. Stronger Ss can try again, making substitutions.

2 Ss complete the conversation alone, then check in pairs. Check answers with the class. When they have finished, put Ss in pairs to practise the conversation, then swap roles and repeat.

EXTRA SUPPORT: DYSLEXIA Dyslexic learners can find it difficult to connect the options with the gaps. In this case, provide two alternatives for each gap, one correct and one distractor.

ANSWERS:

2 tomorrow	**3** first	**4** does
5 good	**6** much	**7** platform
8 you		

3 Ss use the prompts to make a conversation alone, then check in pairs. Check answers with the class. When they have finished, put Ss in pairs to practise the conversation, then swap roles and repeat. If you think they can do it, you could also ask them to change some of the details and respond accordingly.

EXTRA SUPPORT: DYSLEXIA Exercises such as this can present a challenge for dyslexic learners. You could give them the whole conversations, but with key words from the functional phrases gapped.

ANSWERS:
B: For today?
A: Yes. How much is it/that?
B: It's two euros.
A: When's / When is the next bus?
B: There's one at half past two.
A: When does it arrive in Lisbon?
B: At quarter to four.
A: Thanks. What gate is it?

PRONUNCIATION

word stress in prices

4A 8.07 | Write a few prices on the board, e.g. *£3.50, £4.15, £6.50*. Ss say them. Refer Ss to the sentences in Ex 4A. Play the recording and ask Ss to listen and complete the prices. Check answers with the class.

EXTRA SUPPORT With weaker classes, and to support Ss with dyslexia, to avoid Ss having to write when they listen, tell them to write the numbers 15 and 50 in each gap before playing the recording for them to circle the number they hear as they listen.

ANSWERS:
fifteen fifty fifteen

B 8.07 | Ss listen and identify the stressed syllable.

ANSWERS:
fif<u>teen</u> <u>fif</u>ty

C 8.07 | Play the recording for Ss to listen and join in with. Ss in their pairs could each take a role then swap for a second play of the recording. Pause and repeat as needed.

5A Read the instruction with the class and demonstrate with a stronger student. Put Ss in pairs to take turns saying the two prices. Remind or tell Ss how to say the different currencies.

EXTRA IDEA Ss work in pairs and take turns to say one of the prices. Their partner points to the one they think was said. They then change roles. Move around and listen.

B Refer Ss to the conversation in Ex 4A. Ask them to repeat the conversation in pairs, using the different pairs of prices from Ex 5A. They should take turns with each role.

EXTRA IDEA When they have finished, ask pairs to read the conversations across the class. Stronger Ss can try this without looking at their books.

SPEAKING

6 Put Ss in A/B pairs and refer them to the relevant pages.

EXTRA SUPPORT If your Ss need more support in the roleplays, you could ask them to prepare their questions in A/A and B/B pairs. Then re-pair them in A/B pairs to conduct the two roleplays. Give feedback between the two roleplays so that Ss can improve.

1. **Give Ss plenty of time to read their role and prepare what they're going to say. Monitor and offer help where necessary. When they are ready, Ss practise their conversations. Monitor and make notes on their language use for later class feedback. When they have finished, correct any common errors and/or highlight any examples of good language use as a class.**
2. **Ss change roles. Again give them time to read and prepare for their new roles before they complete the second roleplay. Monitor and provide feedback as for Ex 6A.**

7 Ask Ss to choose a place to visit and complete their research out of class. Point out they should make notes about the information to bring to class and tell others.

TO FINISH

Ask Ss to choose the three phrases they learnt today that are most useful and that they're most likely to use in the future. Ss then compare in pairs.

EXTRA IDEA: SPEAK ANYWHERE Encourage Ss to practise using the Speak Anywhere interactive roleplay.

8D BBC Entertainment
Kodo drummers

GRAMMAR | *want, would like*
SPEAKING | talk about something you want to try
WRITING | complete a questionnaire

LESSON OVERVIEW

In this lesson, Ss learn *want* and *would like* to express wants and wishes. The context is a video clip of two TV presenters learning how to do a kind of drumming called taiko. Ss then do a speaking activity where they tell each other about a new activity they want to try. The lesson ends with a writing activity where Ss complete a questionnaire about holiday activities.

Online Teaching

If you're teaching this lesson online, you might find the following tips useful:

- **Ex 1A:** Share your screen and discuss the question as a class.
- **Ex 2A:** Sometimes videos can be a little slow or jumpy when streamed in an online class environment. If you know this is an issue for you, give Ss time to watch the video on their own device before moving on.
- **Ex 4C:** Share your screen with the questions in Ex 4A before listening. Remind Ss to mute their microphones as you play the recording.
- **Ex 6A:** Put Ss in breakout rooms to complete the questionnaire. Try and visit each room briefly to check how they are managing.

Additional Materials

For Teachers:
Presentation Tool Lesson 8D
Online Digital Resources
Grammar Bank 8D
Videoscript 8D: BBC Entertainment

For Students:
Online Practice 8D
Workbook 8D

TO START

Write the following questions on the board and ask Ss to discuss: *Do (or did) you play a musical instrument? Which one? Do (or did) you like it?* When they have finished, take feedback and teach instrument names including *drums*. Tell Ss that in this lesson they will see some people learning to play a new instrument and talk about trying new things themselves.

EXTRA SUPPORT: DYSLEXIA Dyslexic learners in particular benefit from understanding exactly what they are learning in a lesson so that they understand what they are working towards. In this and every lesson, explain clearly what the learning objectives of the lesson are near the start.

PREVIEW

1 A Put Ss in pairs to discuss. When they have finished, elicit their answers. Use the photo in the BBC programme information to present key vocabulary that will be useful later, i.e. *drum, drummer* and *drumsticks*.

B Refer Ss to the sentences and ask them to read the BBC programme information to find the answers. Give them a few minutes, then put them in pairs to discuss before going through the answers.

EXTRA SUPPORT: DYSLEXIA Read the text aloud to the class or make a recording before the class for Ss to listen to as they read.

ANSWERS:
1 BBC presenters
2 learn drumming
3 don't have

VIEW

2 A ▶ Refer Ss to the question. Play the video clip and then ask pairs to compare answers before checking the answer as a class.

EXTRA SUPPORT Turn on the subtitles if you feel it would benefit learners.

ANSWER:
Yes

B Put Ss in pairs to discuss the order the actions from the video clip (a–g) happened. Don't go through the answer yet.

EXTRA SUPPORT Provide Ss with dyslexia and beginner literacy with a set of the actions on slips of paper that they can move around and place in order. This approach would also benefit weaker classes and those who prefer kinaesthetic activities.

C ▶ **Ss watch the video clip again and check their answer. Give them time to discuss the order of the actions in their pairs, then go through the answer as a class.**

ANSWER:
The correct order is *e*, f, c, b, g, d, a.

GRAMMAR

want, would like

3 A Refer Ss to the two incomplete sentences from the video clip. Ask them to write the missing word in each, pointing out that it's the same word in both sentences, then check in pairs. If you're short of time, you could do this exercise together as a class. Check answers with the class. Point out that the *to* goes with the following verb, which is an infinitive.

ANSWERS:
1 to **2** to

B The Grammar Bank on page 123 can be used in the lesson or for homework. Decide how and when the exercises will benefit your class.

GB ▶▶ page 123 **GRAMMAR BANK**

Check understanding of the notes with the class. Focus especially on the different ways that the two verbs make questions and negative forms.

EXTRA SUPPORT: TEACHER The negative *wouldn't like* is not very common. When talking about the present in the negative, *want* is more often used/preferred, e.g. 'I don't want an ice cream, thank you, but I'd like a coffee.'

1 This exercise practises the form of *want* and *would like*. Write the first line of the conversation with the class and point out the capital letter that starts and the punctuation mark that ends each line. Then ask Ss to write the rest of the conversation in their notebooks, then check in pairs. Check answers with the class and write the conversation on the board.

EXTRA SUPPORT: DYSLEXIA Reordering words can be a challenge for dyslexic learners. Here, you could provide them with the conversation with some words gapped (preferably from the language in focus) for Ss to complete. Depending on the words gapped, their answers may vary slightly.

ANSWERS:
A: How are you?
B: I'd like a holiday.
A: Where would you like to go?
B: I'd like to go to South Africa.
A: Why do you want to go there?
B: It's very beautiful.
A: Yes, it is.
B: And I want to see the animals.
A: Go!

EXTRA IDEA When you have checked the answers, Ss practise the conversation in pairs, taking turns at both roles. Stronger classes can repeat, making their own substitutions.

2 This exercise practises the use of *want* and *would like*. Remind Ss about the difference between *like* for things that are always true and *would like* for someone's wishes. Ss choose the correct alternatives, then check in pairs. Check answers with the class. Ask individuals to read out answers and drill the class.

ANSWERS:
1 like, don't like
2 'd like
3 Would you like
4 don't want
5 Does Stefan like
6 don't want
7 to go
8 Do

3 This exercise practises the form of *want* and *would like* in context. Refer Ss to the conversations. Elicit the first answer as an example. Ss continue alone then compare answers in pairs. Go through the answers as a class.

EXTRA SUPPORT Provide dyslexic and beginner literacy learners with the words from the box in a vertical list, so they can place this alongside the conversations and copy them in the correct place.

ANSWERS:
1 would **2** like **3** want
4 help **5** 'd **6** Do

EXTRA IDEA: DIGITAL Ss record themselves saying the conversations. They listen back and check they have included all the required words.

SPEAKING

talk about something you want to try

4A Ask Ss to think about a new activity they'd like to try. You could make a list of some categories to help them (musical instrument, sport, hobby, etc.). Allow some time for individuals to reflect and help them with vocabulary and/or allow them to look up words for activities they don't know the English word for. Then ask them to make notes for their answers to questions 1–4.

EXTRA IDEA To stimulate ideas, you could display some pictures of activities that you think Ss might find interesting.

B Put Ss in pairs to ask and answer the questions in Ex 4A. When they have finished, ask a few pairs to tell the class about their partner.

C 8.08 | Tell Ss they will listen to someone talking about trying something new. Ask them to write the numbers of the questions (1–4) from Ex 4A in their notebooks, then listen and answer the questions for the person in the recording. Ask pairs to compare before going through the answers as a class.

EXTRA SUPPORT: DYSLEXIA Dyslexic learners can just listen and then discuss what they can remember with their partner.

ANSWERS:
1 dance the tango
2 because she loves music
3 at some classes near her and her husband
4 next month

AUDIOSCRIPT 8.08

I'd like to learn to dance the tango. I want to learn because I love music. I got married last year and my husband Luis is a great dancer and he loves the tango. We went to a tango party together last week. It was terrible for me because everybody danced really well, but I can't dance the tango. I'm a disaster! Well, there are some classes near us. They start next month and I'd like to go.

D 8.08 | Refer Ss to the Key phrases and give them a minute or two to read through and ask any questions. Play the recording and ask Ss to identify the phrases in bold they hear.

EXTRA SUPPORT: DYSLEXIA Read the Key phrases through with the class, to help dyslexic learners recognise what they need to listen for.

ANSWERS:
1 dance the tango
2 I love music
3 a disaster
4 near us
5 start next month

5A Put Ss in new pairs to tell each other about the activity they made notes on in Ex 4A, using the Key phrases where appropriate. Move around and listen. When Ss have finished, give feedback on how well they did the activity and drill any of the phrases they had difficulty with.

B Put Ss in different pairs. Ask them to ask and answer the questions in Ex 4A again about the activity they want to try. Encourage Ss to work without their books here. When they have finished, ask them to change to a new partner. Monitor and move Ss on to a new partner each time they finish. Stronger Ss can do more exchanges with different partners. When they have finished, ask Ss which activity they heard about was the most interesting.

EXTRA SUPPORT If you think your Ss will struggle without using their books, you could write up prompts for the questions on the board and get Ss to practise forming them:
1 activity?
2 Why / want / try it?
3 How / where / try it?
4 When / like / try it?

EXTRA: ALTERNATIVE IDEA If you have a large classroom and a lively group, you could organise the activity as follows. Put Ss in groups of 12–16, with an even number of Ss in each, then put half of the Ss in each group in an inner circle, facing out, with their partner facing them on the outside. They complete the question and answer step, then the outside Ss all move one place to their left. The inside Ss don't move. Everybody has a new partner and they repeat the activity. This activity can be very noisy but great fun for Ss to work with new people.

WRITING

complete a questionnaire

6A Tell Ss they are going to read a questionnaire about a holiday where you do different activities. Explain that Ss should read the questions and discuss their answers in pairs. Give Ss a few minutes. When they have finished, discuss what kind of extra information they should give for question 2 (e.g. 'because I'd like to be a good cook') and question 3 (e.g. age, disability, dietary needs, etc.). Make sure Ss understand what a *no-wifi zone* is (question 6).

EXTRA SUPPORT: DYSLEXIA Pair a dyslexic learner with a partner who can support them with the reading.

B **Ask Ss to write their answers to the questions. Refer them to the example, pointing out that this is an opportunity to practise the grammar of today's lesson. Ss should write sentences and aim for 60–80 words altogether.**

C **Put Ss in groups and ask them to read each other's answers to the questions. When they have finished, ask if anyone had similar ideas.**

EXTRA: ALTERNATIVE IDEA Number the Ss' answers and pin them around the room. Ask Ss to move around and make a note of the numbers that have similar ideas to their own. When they return to their seats, they can find out which people the numbers correspond to.

EXTRA IDEA: DIGITAL Ss work in pairs, record themselves asking and answering the questions, then listen back and give each other feedback before changing roles and repeating.

EXTRA IDEA Ss share their answers/texts on a class noticeboard or digital noticeboard.

TO FINISH

Put Ss in pairs to talk about the different kinds of activity holidays they'd like to or don't want to try (e.g. skiing, safari, trekking, etc.). Be prepared to help with vocabulary.

8 REVIEW

LESSON OVERVIEW

This lesson is a review of the language – both grammar and vocabulary – presented in this unit. It also includes a link to the Sounds and Spelling section for this unit, which focuses on short and long sounds: /æ/, /ɑː/, /ɒ/, /ɔː/, /ə/ and /ɜː/; and silent *e*: /ɒ/ to /əʊ/. The notes below assume that the tasks are completed in class. However, the self-study type exercises (i.e. Exs 1A, 1B, 2A, 3A, 4A and 6A) could be done out of class and then checked in the following lesson when the communicative tasks are then completed.

Online Teaching

If you're teaching this lesson online, you might find the following tips useful:

- **Ex 1A:** Ask Ss to write their answers in the chat.
- **Ex 1C:** Ss compare answers in breakout rooms, in pairs. Visit each room in turn and listen to how accurately they are using the past simple.

Additional Materials

For Teachers:

Sounds and Spelling 8

Unit Test in test package

TO START

Ask Ss to work in pairs and try to remember what language they studied in Unit 8 (Grammar: past simple: regular verbs, past simple: irregular verbs, *want*, *would like*; Vocabulary: common verbs, free-time activities, time phrases, transport and tickets; How to ... buy a travel ticket). Ask them to look at the unit lesson objectives to check their ideas.

GRAMMAR

1 A **Look at the example. Point out that sentences may be positive or negative (*not*). Ss write the sentences alone, then check in pairs. Check answers with the class and write the answers on the board.**

EXTRA SUPPORT: DYSLEXIA Provide the words in sentence form with a gap and prompt for the verbs.

ANSWERS:
2 I wrote an email.
3 I relaxed in the evening.
4 I read an English newspaper.
5 I didn't sleep well.
6 I tried a new kind of food.
7 I met a friend.
8 I didn't do the shopping.

B **Read the example with the class, then give your own example, e.g. 'Yesterday I wrote an email to a friend.' Ask Ss to work alone and change the sentences to make them true for themselves. Monitor and check Ss are forming sentences correctly.**

C **Put Ss in pairs to compare, taking turns to read out their sentences. When they have finished, call on a few pairs to tell the class something interesting they found out from their partner. Remind them of the phrase *We both …*.**

EXTRA IDEA If Ss need writing practice, ask them to write three sentences about the similarities or differences they found, using *and* or *but*.

VOCABULARY

2A **Point out the pictures and elicit the first answer as an example (*party*). Ss complete the phrases individually, then check in pairs. Check answers with the class. Drill as needed.**

EXTRA SUPPORT To help weaker Ss, provide the missing words in jumbled order in a list.

ANSWERS:

1 party	**4** clothes
2 game	**5** television/TV
3 film	**6** a sport / sports

B **This exercise enables personalised practice. Put Ss in pairs to discuss the questions. When they have finished, ask a few pairs to report back and find out what the most popular activities are.**

3A **Remind Ss how we usually use *the* and *of* in dates. They then match the time phrases with the dates individually, then check in pairs. Go through the answers as a class.**

EXTRA SUPPORT If you think Ss are unsure about time and time phrases, you could supply either the time phrases (1–6) or the dates (a–f) in chronological order to help them organise their thoughts.

ANSWERS:
1 b **2** a **3** f **4** c **5** e **6** d

B **Elicit today's date and write it on the board. Look at the example, then ask a stronger student to demonstrate the activity with you, using today's date. Put Ss in pairs to continue, taking turns as Student A or Student B.**

4A **Elicit the five vowels and write them on the board. Look at the example, point out that the vowels are missing, and elicit a second example. Ask Ss to continue alone, then compare in pairs. Go through the answers as a class, writing them on the board so Ss can check their spelling.**

EXTRA SUPPORT: DYSLEXIA Provide Ss with the five vowels and present the words with gaps showing where the missing letters are, e.g. *t r _ m, m _ t _ r b _ k _*. If possible, read the words aloud before going through the answers, or pair dyslexic learners with a partner who can read the words out as they do the activity together.

ANSWERS:

2 tram	**8** plane
3 motorbike	**9** ticket machine
4 boat	**10** monthly pass
5 train	**11** passenger
6 bicycle	**12** single
7 subway	

B **Demonstrate the activity by drawing a bicycle on the board, then mime riding a bicycle. Refer Ss to the example description. Explain that Ss can use any of the methods to describe a word from Ex 4A. Put Ss in groups of three or four to do this.**

EXTRA SUPPORT: TEACHER Some Ss don't like too many options. In such a case, choose the method for them. In terms of ease, the easiest is mime, then drawing and finally defining, so choose according to your group.

5A **Ss have probably already noticed that the same vowel can be pronounced in various ways (e.g. c<u>a</u>t, c<u>a</u>ke, c<u>ar</u>). Ask Ss to try saying the words in Ex 5A. Don't expect Ss to be perfect at this point or write the phonetic symbols as the 'full answer' comes via the Sounds and Spelling section.**

ANSWERS:

pl<u>a</u>nned /æ/	c<u>ar</u> /ɑː/	pass<u>e</u>ng<u>er</u> /ɪ/ /ə/
w<u>or</u>ked /ɜː/	g<u>o</u>t /ɒ/	w<u>al</u>ked /ɔː/

B Refer Ss to Sounds and Spelling on page 158.

page 158 **SOUNDS AND SPELLING**
short and long sounds (2): /æ/, /ɑː/, /ɒ/, /ɔː/, /ə/ and /ɜː/; silent *e* (3): /ɒ/ to /əʊ/

The Sounds and Spelling section can be used to help with particular problems. You might want to select the sections or even particular sounds that are most useful for your Ss. The vocabulary used in each section comes from the current unit or previous units.

SOUNDS AND SPELLING TEACHER'S NOTES page 219

6 A Ask Ss to work alone, read the text and complete it with the past simple of the verbs provided in brackets. When they have finished, they can compare answers in pairs. Don't check the answers yet.

EXTRA SUPPORT: DYSLEXIA You could record the text before the class for Ss to listen to (with a personal device if it's not appropriate for all Ss to listen) or read it out in class. Supply the text with two completed past verb alternatives for each gap for Ss to select from (e.g. *started* / *stayed* for gap 2). Ss should also cover the sentences or phrases they are not working on to avoid distraction.

B R8.01 | Play the recording for Ss to check their answers. Go through the answers as a class. If you have time, Ss can read the text to each other in pairs.

ANSWERS:

2 stayed **3** walked **4** changed
5 tried **6** didn't plan **7** were
8 wanted **9** slept **10** met
11 had **12** went

TO FINISH

Put Ss in groups to discuss the last time they visited somewhere, including the transport used and where they stayed if relevant. Refer them back to the vocabulary from this unit to help if necessary.

SPEAKOUT GAME

The Speakout Game has great potential for exploitation, depending on your group and how much time you would like to spend on it. There are instructions on the board and Ss are likely to be familiar with board games. Put Ss in groups. Each group will need a dice and counters. Simply playing the game will result in lots of speaking and interaction. However, you can get more out of the game in a number of ways:

- Teach the useful phrases given in **B**. Ask Ss when they would use each one. Alternatively, check understanding by asking: 'What do you say when you don't know whose turn it is?', 'What do you say when you don't understand a word?', etc.
- Check Ss understand the instructions in **B**. You can do this by asking. 'I'm on square 7 and I don't complete the task. Where do I go?', etc.
- Check Ss understand the colour 'codes', as each of the four colours suggests a different instruction. You can do this by asking 'I'm on square 9. What do I do or say?', etc. You could also demonstrate the whole first row with the class, to make sure everyone understands what to do once they're in groups.

When Ss are playing the game, you can of course monitor for language and to make sure they are on task, and it can also be useful for Ss to self-monitor / peer monitor. You may also choose to collect examples of both good use of language and errors for review afterwards. However, consider the class atmosphere, keeping in mind that this is the end of the course.

ANSWERS:

(Only the answers to the 'Put the words in the correct order' task are given. All other squares are Students' own answers.)

3 Where are you from?
6 What is in your bag?
10 How do you spell your surname?
15 Do you have American friends?
18 Do you usually eat breakfast at home?
22 Do you like fast food restaurants?
27 Can you play the piano or the guitar?
30 When is your birthday?
34 Is there a good café near here?
39 Do you live in a house or a flat?

TO FINISH

Ask Ss what the most interesting thing they heard was while they were playing the game.

pages 160–161 **REVISION GAME**

REVISION GAME

Student's Book pages 160–161

Tell Ss that they are going to play a game to revise grammar, vocabulary and How to … language from Units 1–8. Ss can either work in pairs or groups of three (playing individually), or in two or three teams of two (playing against each other). Give out counters or ask Ss to make them from pieces of paper.

Ss choose a hexagon in the left-hand column where they would like to start. The first student/team must complete the task satisfactorily before they can move their counter onto the hexagon. The other Ss decide whether it is a correct answer. Point out that most questions have many possible answers.

If an answer is correct, the student/team can place their counter on the completed hexagon. Then play moves to the next student/team. If they answer the question incorrectly, they stay where they are, and that question is no longer available to them for their next turn. (This means that Ss may have to take a less direct route to the other side of the board.) Circulate to be available for checking any answers Ss are unsure of.

Point out that only one counter is permitted on a hexagon at any one time, so Ss can try to block the other player(s) from taking the most direct routes.

For class feedback, ask Ss to share one of their best answers or ask them to pool ideas for any questions that they found difficult.

EXTRA IDEAS Fast finishers could replay the game, starting with a different hexagon.

Alternatively, pairs could work together to complete as many hexagons as possible in a given time limit, e.g. fifteen minutes. The pair who completes the most correctly wins.

The activity can also be run as a class mingle. Ss move around and pair up with different Ss. Each time they pair up, Ss nominate a question for their partner to answer.

POSSIBLE ANSWERS:

1 Can you swim? Can you speak Spanish?
2 Are you a student?
3 I sometimes visit a museum. I often cook lunch on Sundays. Every day I spend time with my friends.
4 Yes, I do. No, I don't.
5 brother, daughter, grandmother, mother, son
6 I went to the cinema. I had pizza for dinner. I saw my friends.
7 I get up at 8 a.m. and have breakfast. I go to work on the bus. I start work at 9 a.m. and I finish work at 4 p.m. After work, I go to English class. Then I go home and I cook dinner.
8 I'm really good! I'm not bad. I'm not very well.
9 What time's the next train to London? How much is a single ticket?
10 banana, egg, fish, pasta, rice
11 Can I get you a cup of tea? Can I make you a sandwich?
12 bathroom, bedroom, kitchen, living room
13 What**'s** your phone number? It's 0-3-4-7-8-1-3-2-1-9.
~~What~~ **How do** you spell your first name? It's M-I-L-A.
14 She's rich. She's strong. She's the best!
15 Excuse me, can I try this shirt on, please?
16 What's your surname? It's Abadi.
17 When do you have lunch? Why do you like this city?
18 Excuse me, how much are these jeans, please?
19 We ~~isn't~~ **aren't** late. You**'re** early!
20 When does the next bus leave?
21 I always get up late. I sometimes have breakfast at a café. I never work!
22 Can I use your pen for a minute, please?
23 My house is near a park. It's next to some other houses. There is a big tree opposite my house.
24 My sister gets up at 7 a.m. She leaves the house at 8 a.m. She goes to school. She gets home at 3 p.m. She has dinner with the family at 7 p.m. She watches TV. Then she goes to bed at 9 p.m.
25 A good colleague helps people with their work problems. A good colleague doesn't forget to say thanks.
26 There are four windows. There are two doors. There are blue walls. There's a teacher's desk. There's a computer. There are some shelves with books. There's a plant. There are students and there's a teacher!
27 Hi! Hey! Good morning!
28 Who's your friend? How do you get to class?
29 a black shirt, blue jeans, a red jacket
30 I visit ~~me~~ **my** friends. ~~They~~ **Their** house is near here.
31 do a sport, go to a party, meet a friend, play a game
32 mouse, notebook, pencil
33 Yes, it is. How are you?
34 bicycle, bus, subway, train, tram
35 Yes. Can I have a latte, please?
36 I can play the piano and I can sing, but not very well. I can't play the guitar. I can dance salsa, but I can't dance the tango! I can sleep very well at home, but I can't sleep on a bus. I can remember people's faces, but sometimes I can't remember their names.
37 Is there a supermarket near here? How far is it?
38 doctor, singer, taxi driver, teacher, waiter
39 I have a headache and my eyes hurt!

UNIT 1

Opener: BBC Vlogs

1 Hi, I'm Beatriz and I'm from Portugal.
2 Hello, my name is Mo. I come from China.
3 Hi, my name's Anna. I'm from Queensland, Australia.
4 Hi. My name's Brian. I'm from the United States.
5 My name's Kayo. I'm from Japan.
6 Hi, I'm Phil. I'm from England.
7 Hi, I'm Holly and I'm from Nottingham in England.
8 Hi. My name is Daniel. I'm from Poland.
9 Hello. My name is Sonia and I'm from Serbia.
10 My name's Lucia. I'm from Spain.

1D: BBC Street Interviews
Exs 2A and 2B

William: My name is William and it's spelt W-I-L-L-I-A-M.
Rachael: My name is Rachael. R-A-C-H-A-E-L.
Chris: My name is Chris. C-H-R-I-S.
Sharron: Sharron. And that's S-H-A, double-R, O-N.
Ian: My name's Ian. That is spelt I-A-N.
Simnit: Simnit, and it's spelt S-I-M-N-I-T.
Biba: My first name is Biba, and I spell it B-I-B-A.
Layan: So it's Layan, and it's L-A-Y-A-N.
Tom: My name is Tom. That's T-O-M.

Exs 3A and 3C

William: I have a sandwich in my bag.
Rachael: I have a bottle of water. I have my purse, my keys.
Chris: I have a laptop and a notebook.
Sharron: I have a bottle of water, a notebook and a banana.
Ian: I have a laptop and a mobile.
Simnit: I have an umbrella, my mobile phone and my purse.
Biba: In my bag I have my phone and my wallet.
Layan: So I have my wallet and some make-up.
Tom: I have my laptop and two books.

UNIT 2

Opener: BBC Vlogs

1 Hello. My name is Jorge. I'm from Colombia. Today, I am in Bogotá.
2 Hi, I'm Sherri. I'm from California. Now, I'm in New York.
3 Hi, I'm Alison. I'm from Scotland, but now I'm in Italy.
4 Hello. My name is Anastasia. I'm American and Russian. Today I'm in London.
5 Hello. My name's Iullia and I'm from Russia. I live in Italy, in Rome.
6 Hello. I'm Rory. I'm from England. I'm now in Ireland.
7 Hello. My name is Hanan Ali. I'm from Mombasa, Kenya, and I'm currently in Columbus, Ohio.
8 Hi. I'm Jennifer. I'm from Australia, but now I'm in Florence in Italy.
9 Hi. I'm Fotis. I'm from Greece. I'm now in Madrid, Spain.

2D: BBC Food
Exs 2B, 2C and 2D

N = Narrator Cl = Claudia R = Robin E = Elisabetta
Ch = Chris M = Mary A = Angela

N: Ten home cooks. Eight weeks. Twenty-four tasks. Three judges. This is *Best Home Cook*. It's Week four. The home cooks arrive.
Cl: Hi. Hello.
R: Hi, Claudia.
E: Good morning.
N: Our presenter is Claudia Winkleman.
Cl: How are we all?
All: Good, good.
N: Next, the judges arrive.
Cl: Judges!
J: Morning!
All: Morning.
N: It's time for today's task.
Cl: You have three hours to make the ultimate birthday cake. Let's go.
N: The task is a children's birthday cake. Robin is 63. He's a manager from Bristol in the UK. He has a wife and a daughter. Suzie is 36. She has two children and she's from Northern Ireland. Georgia is 24 years old and she's from London. She's a model. Oli is a manager in a restaurant. He's 34 and he's married. He and his wife have one daughter. Katie's 33. She's married and she works in a supermarket. Elisabetta is 52. She's from Italy, but now her home is in London. Sarah's 42 and has a son. They're from Manchester.
Cl: Fifteen minutes! One minute, cooks. And that's it, time's up.
N: Finally, the cakes are finished. But are they good? So, who are the three winners?
Ch: And that is… Suzie's.
M: The one that stood out for me… It was Robin's.
A: Katie, well done.
N: And now it's time to rest before next week.

UNIT 3

Opener: BBC Vlogs

1 My favourite thing is my garden. In the summer, it's beautiful.
2 My dog. His name is Jasper. He is a labradoodle.
3 My favourite thing is my bike. It's new. I love it because it's green and yellow and it's really fast.
4 My favourite thing is my teddy bear. His name is Fred.
5 My favourite thing is this painting of Venice in Italy.
6 My favourite thing is my camera. This is a Canon digital camera.
7 My favourite thing is my bicycle.
8 My new red car. It's great!

3D: BBC Street Interviews
Exs 2A and 2C

Rachael: I buy food online and I buy make-up and clothes in shops.
Elijah: I buy things for the house online.
Gloria: I buy clothes online and I buy food in shops.
Joe: Online I buy video games and in shops I buy food.
Josh: Online I buy clothes and in shops I also buy food.
Holly: I buy make-up online and I buy food in shops.
Nic: I buy cat food online. I buy clothes in shops.
Kirsty: I buy books online and I buy shoes in the shop.
Vincent: I buy trainers online.

Exs 3A and 3B

Rachael: I love clothes shops, I hate butchers and I love cafés.
Elijah: I like restaurants, I like cafés, and I like supermarkets.
Gloria: I love clothes shops, and I hate sports shops.
Joe: I like sports shops, and I dislike clothes shops.
Josh: I like food shops, because I like food, and I don't like pet shops.
Holly: I like clothes shops. I don't like bookshops.
Nic: I like food shops. I do not like clothes shops.
Kirsty: I like clothes shops and shoe shops, and I dislike computer shops.
Vincent: I like video game shops.

UNIT 4

Opener: BBC Vlogs

1 My favourite meal is lunch. I always have tuna salad.
2 My favourite meal is dinner. I love fish.
3 Breakfast is my favourite meal. I always have coffee and fruit.
4 My favourite meal is dinner. I eat a lot of pasta with cheese.
5 My favourite meal of the day is breakfast. I have an omelette with a cup of tea.
6 My favourite meal is breakfast. I have cereal with milk, and orange juice.
7 Lunch. My favourite, er, food is pasta. I love Italian food.
8 My favourite meal is breakfast. I have breakfast at my desk. I have eggs and two cups of coffee.

4D: BBC Documentary
Exs 2B and 2C

N = Narrator B = Billy E = Elvira

N: From space we can see colours and shapes … water … and land. Zoom in and we can see many different lives.
In the city of Chennai in India, thousands of parakeets eat breakfast. This is Joseph Sekar's house. He gets up at half past five every morning and makes rice for the parakeets. He puts the rice out and waits. The first parakeet comes at six o'clock in the morning. Four thousand parakeets come to his home every day. Joseph loves the parakeets. He says, 'All living things are important.'
In Colorado, in the USA, Billy Ellis gets up early.

B: I get up, have a cup of coffee and then I'm ready to go.

N: He climbs 143 steps … to his office. Forest fires are a big problem in Colorado. Billy is a fire lookout. He watches the forest for fires. It's a difficult job. Does he see many forest fires? No, not often, but when he sees a fire, it's his job to call the firefighters.
In the north of Peru, in a national park, we can see Lake El Dorado. Elvira is nine years old. She lives in a small village near Lake El Dorado. She goes to school there. Elvira loves animals. Her favourite animals … are manatees. Manatees usually live in rivers. But sometimes they need a new home. Today is a special day. Some men bring a manatee to live in the lake. Elvira sees a manatee for the first time. She's really happy. The men put the manatee into the lake. It has a new home. Elvira watches the manatee and says goodbye.

E: Chau manatee!

UNIT 5

Opener: BBC Vlogs

1 Hello. My name's Jude. I'm a student doctor. I work in a hospital in Manchester and I study at university.
2 I work in IT and I work from home.
3 I'm a teacher. I work at a school in Ankara. I work from 8 a.m. to 5 p.m. every day. I am very lucky. I have great students and I like my job.
4 My job? I'm a news reporter at BBC. Hi.
5 My job? I'm a stay-at-home mum.
6 I don't have a job. I'm a student. I'm at university in France. And the people here are really friendly. I love the food here, especially the pastries.
7 I'm a teacher and I'm also a university student.
8 My job? I work as a journalist for the BBC.

5D: BBC Street Interviews
Exs 2B and 2C

Ama: My birthday is the fifteenth of September.
Ryan: My birthday is on the sixteenth of May.
Elijah: My birthday is on the seventeenth of August.
Sautebh: My birthday is on the ninth of June.
Anna: My birthday is today, the twenty-first of April.
Kielan: My birthday is on the eighth of November.
William: My birthday is on the fourteenth of February.
Anna: My birthday is on the twenty-third of April.
Joe: My birthday is on the seventeenth of November.
Josh: And my birthday is on the nineteenth of March.
Tom: My birthday is on the third of September.

Exs 3A and 3C

Ama: I see family and eat nice food.
Ryan: I meet my friends for a meal in London.
Elijah: On my birthday, I eat cake with my friends and my family.
Sautebh: I go to a restaurant with my friends.
Anna: I try and be outside.
Kielan: I meet my friends and family for lunch, and my friends give me presents.
William: I go for dinner with friends.
Anna: On my birthday I have a picnic with my boyfriend.
Joe: I have a party with my friends.
Josh: I go out for a meal with my friends and my family.
Tom: I have a meal with my family.

UNIT 6

Opener: BBC Vlogs

1 I'm outside. I can see trees and the sky, and my house.
2 I am at my office and I can see a lot of books.
3 I'm in the garden and I can see my house, some flowers and some rabbits.
4 Now I am in my living room and I can see a bottle of water, my cat and a sofa.
5 I'm in my kitchen, at my desk, and I can see my laptop, a tablet, my car keys, scissors, two books, a pencil and a cup of tea.
6 I'm in the garden now. I can see some trees, plants and a table and chair.

6D: BBC Documentary
Exs 2A and 2C

N = Narrator

N: BBC presenter, Ade Adepitan, is at Rome Airport. But he has a problem – his plane is late. Six hours late. So, he has six hours to see Rome. Where can he go?
Ade gets the help of a local tour guide, Esther Maurini. He has big plans for his visit! Ade wants to see … the Colosseum, the Circus Maximus, the Palatine Hill, the Mouth of Truth, and the Trevi Fountain. Everything in six hours and everything by bus! It isn't easy.
His first stop is the Circus Maximus. It's an ancient sports stadium. A place for over 250,000 people to watch … chariot races. It's now a park. There aren't any chariot races today, but sometimes they have music concerts here.
Near the Circus Maximus is the Palatine Hill. Here you can see parts of ancient palaces and gardens. Some are nearly 3,000 years old, from the start of the city of Rome.
Ade's next stop is the Mouth of Truth. So what **is** the Mouth of Truth? Nobody knows. People say that the mouth eats the hand of a person that doesn't speak the truth.
Next, Ade visits the Trevi Fountain. The Trevi Fountain is many tourists' favourite place. It's very beautiful. And people throw money in the fountain … about 3,000 euros every day. That's over one million euros a year!
And finally, Ade's last stop … the Colosseum. There's just time for a photo. Then it's back to the airport.
And Ade has time to get there and catch his plane!

UNIT 7

Opener: BBC Vlogs

1 I sometimes eat healthy food, but I also love burgers and pizzas, and I drink a lot of coffee.
2 I try to eat healthy food, but I really like pizza and burgers.
3 I try to eat healthy. I eat fish and salad.
4 I try to eat healthy food – I eat lots of fruit and vegetables, but I also like chocolate.
5 I eat healthy food for breakfast, lunch and dinner.
6 I try to eat healthy food. I have a lot of fruit and vegetables, but I also like pizza.
7 Yes, I eat a lot of fruit. Bananas and oranges are my favourite.
8 I try to eat healthy food, like an apple, but I love chocolates.

7D: BBC Street Interviews
Exs 2A and 2B

Gaia: I do yoga and I go to the gym.
Chris: I play basketball.
Lucy: I play football.
Sautebh: I play football and cricket, but I also like to run.
Eleanor: I play tennis and sometimes go for a run.
Ryan: I go to the gym most days and I enjoy walks.
Tracey: I run twice a week.
Vincent: I play football at the weekends.
Rachael: I run twice a week, and I walk every day.

Exs 3A and 3C

Gaia: Drink lots of water and wear good trousers.
Chris: Practise and drink lots of water.
Lucy: Practise a lot and play with friends.

Sautebh: Do a sport that you love and practise, practise, practise.
Eleanor: Buy good clothes and don't forget the tennis balls!
Ryan: Tips for the gym – always warm up, take a friend if you can and always eat a good healthy meal afterwards.
Tracey: Good running shoes and good music.
Vincent: Wear good shoes.
Rachael: Drink lots of water, wear good shoes, wear comfortable clothing and be positive.

UNIT 8

Opener: BBC Vlogs

1 My last holiday was great. We were in Greece. The weather was very sunny.
2 My last holiday was great. We were in Portugal. It was really hot.
3 My last holiday was great. I was in Australia with my husband's family.
4 My last holiday was fantastic. I was in Amsterdam, Holland.
5 My last holiday was wonderful. I was in Greece with my family.
6 My last holiday was really good. I was in Spain with my family. The weather was great.
7 My last holiday was in Sweden. I went to Gothenburg. And the people were really friendly, the museums were really interesting, and the food was absolutely delicious.
8 My last holiday was great. I went to Mexico. It was really hot and sunny.

8D: BBC Entertainment
Exs 2A and 2C

Na = Narrator J = Joel Ni = Nish T = Teacher

Na: Sado Island, Japan. The home of the world-famous Kodo drummers.
This is the school for the Kodo drummers. BBC presenters Nish Kumar and Joel Dommett arrive at the school. They'd like to learn taiko drumming from the Kodo teachers. They watch some drummers.
J: Am I allowed to clap? Are we allowed to clap?
Na: Then they try the drums. For Nish, it's very difficult.
Ni: Woo-hoo!
Na: But they don't stop. Their teacher gives them more practice.
Training starts early. They get up at half past five in the morning. They start the day with exercise. Then they clean the floor. After that, they run 10 kilometres around the island. The drummers at the school do this every morning. Finally, they go to the workshop and make their own drumsticks.
Then, it's time for drum practice. The teacher works with Joel and Nish. They want to play the drums with all of the group, but they're not ready. They have two days to prepare.
Finally, they are ready. Their teacher gives them special clothes.
T: Hai.
J: Arigato gozaimasu.
T: Hai.
Ni: Arigato.
Na: Now it's the big day. They can finally play with the group. Seven top Kodo teachers watch.
At the end, the teachers are happy.
And it's time for Joel and Nish to say goodbye.
Ni: Thank you, guys.
J: We've got to say goodbye. Thank you so much. You're the best.
Ni: You're amazing! Thank you very much.

Introduction

THE IMPORTANCE OF SOUNDS FOR A1 STUDENTS

At A1 level, it's important for students to become aware of some basic elements of English pronunciation which will help lay a good foundation for the rest of their learning. In the main lessons, they learn about sentence stress and intonation as well as some useful patterns such as the pronunciation of the third person *-s* in the present simple and *-ed* endings in the past simple. The lessons also include an initial introduction to how to link words in connected speech. However, for many students the sounds of a new language will present a number of specific challenges and this often depends on their first language and which sounds are very different for them or do not exist in their language. A focus on sounds at this level can help learners with all four language skills:

- **Listening:** When we know about the sounds of a language, we can become better at 'bottom-up listening', that is we can build up words and phrases from hearing their sounds. Of course, at the same time we use a lot of 'top-down listening', that is guessing what is being said from context and background knowledge.
- **Speaking:** When we learn to speak a new language, we often need a good amount of practice in making sounds and words. We may have to learn to use our mouth and voice in a way that is new to us. It's very confidence-building when we can pronounce words and phrases in a way that's understood by other people.
- **Reading:** When we're reading, most of us sub-vocalise the sound of words as part of our process of understanding what we're reading. Students need to be able to recognise the typical pronunciation of certain combinations of sounds to increase their ability to read fluently.
- **Writing:** Although these days many of us have spell-checking software and often write informally in messages and on social media where accurate spelling may not be so vital, many of us want or need to learn to write accurately in another language. Therefore it's important to focus on spelling and its relationship with sounds right from the beginning of our language learning.

THE CONTENT OF THE SOUNDS AND SPELLING SECTION

In the Sounds and Spelling section students have the opportunity to learn about some key recurrent elements of English pronunciation and writing:

- syllable stress in words and the schwa /ə/ sound often used in unstressed parts of words
- voiced and unvoiced consonant sounds
- short and long vowel sounds
- typical spellings for the three elements above
- common words which have 'special' spellings
- the final silent *e* and how this affects pronunciation

USING PHONETIC* SYMBOLS

Phonetic symbols can be a very useful tool for A1 students. They are particularly helpful:

- when students want a record of how a word is pronounced (and don't have access to an online recording!)
- when the spelling and sounds of a word are different, e.g. ***wo**men* /ˈwɪmɪn/, ***lis**ten* /ˈlɪsən/
- when two or three letters are only one sound, e.g. *re**peat*** /rɪˈpiːt/, *col**our*** /ˈkʌlə/

You may feel that it's a bit too challenging at this level for your students to learn the symbols, especially if they are coping with a new alphabet. However, we suggest that you think of the phonetic alphabet as a tool kit, and introduce the individual 'tools' to your students as needed, rather than approaching the phonetic alphabet as a system that students have to learn in its entirety as soon as possible.

**phonetic* = the sounds of all languages; *phonemic* = the sounds of one language – we use phonetic in the teacher's notes because it is a more internationally recognised word.

HOW TO USE THE SOUNDS AND SPELLING SECTION

In the Student's Book, you'll find the reference to the relevant Sounds and Spelling section on the Review page for each unit. We suggest you look ahead when you are planning because you might want to include a sounds and spelling focus earlier in the unit. The Teacher's Notes accompanying each Sounds and Spelling section will usually advise you about when the different focuses might be used.

A Sounds

Each Sounds and Spelling section has two pronunciation focuses:

- **Pronunciation Focus 1** usually introduces and practises a key principle of English pronunciation. This could be unstressed syllables with /ə/ (*teach**er**, doct**or***); long and short vowel sounds, e.g. /ɪ/ and /iː/ (*s**i**x, sixt**ee**n*); voiced and unvoiced sounds, e.g. /p/ and /b/ (***p**ea, **b**ee*); or easily confused sounds, e.g. /e/ and /æ/ (*m**e**n, m**a**n*).
- **Pronunciation Focus 2** often has something particularly relevant to a lesson in the unit. Examples include: /s/, /z/ and /ɪz/ in plurals; the pronunciation of question words with /w/ and /h/; and the strong and weak pronunciation of *does*: /dʌz/ and /dəz/ in the present simple. In Units 5, 7 and 8, Pronunciation Focus 2 introduces students to the effect of a silent *e* at the end of words (*Tim, time*; *hat, hate*; *not, note*).

You may decide to include work on the two different focuses on two different occasions in your timetable. Of course, you may also want to focus mainly on sounds which are challenging for your students. So you may decide to pick and choose from the most relevant and useful parts of the Sounds and Spelling section. You could also decide to give individual students different parts of the section to study and practise independently. This may be a good solution when you're teaching a group of students who have different first languages and different needs with sounds.

We have followed an important principle in choosing the vocabulary to introduce and practise different sounds; this vocabulary always comes from the unit that the students are studying or from previous units. This is an excellent opportunity for students to revisit vocabulary and at the same time to be able to look at it in a different way. Research shows that students have a better chance of memorising and incorporating vocabulary into their mental lexicon if they approach vocabulary regularly but in different ways. In this case they will be looking at the words from the point of view of their sounds and their spelling.

We have included a variety of practice activities for the sounds. These include minimal pairs practice to help students hear the difference between two similar sounds (e.g. ***l**ight, **r**ight*; ***t**own, **d**own*) and game-like activities such as mazes and poems.

B Spelling

The focuses on spelling in the Sounds and Spelling section fall into two categories:

- **Common spellings:** Your students may speak a language where there is a consistent correspondence between the way a sound is spelt and the way it is said. English, however, is famous for its lack of sound–spelling correspondence. In order to build students' confidence at A1, the Sounds and Spelling section aims to introduce some very common regular ways to spell each sound. This will help students with their speaking, their reading and of course, their writing. As an example, the sound /f/ has three very common spellings: ***f**irst, o**ff**ice* and ***ph**one*.
- **'Special' spellings:** We also offer students focused help with very common words which have unusual spellings. Examples of this are: ***peo**ple, an**sw**er* and *ma**ch**ine*.

We've written the Sounds and Spelling section with the intention of providing a solid foundation that will equip students to proceed through the levels with a firm handle on this aspect of the English language. We also hope that you and your students will feel motivated to explore English pronunciation further.

SOUNDS AND SPELLING

PRONUNCIATION FOCUS 1
syllables, stress and /ə/
PRONUNCIATION FOCUS 2
/s/, /z/, /ɪz/ in plurals

The Sounds and Spelling in this unit focuses on the most common unstressed sound in English, the schwa /ə/ sound, useful for all Ss of English. There is a second focus on the plural sounds, /s/, /z/ and /ɪz/, which consolidates the grammar from Lesson 1D, which included plurals.

You would probably be best to cover the schwa /ə/ sound earlier in the unit and plural /s/, /z/ and /ɪz/ in or after Lesson 1D. Afterwards, you can highlight these in any lesson to reinforce them as they appear in new words. All the vocabulary used is from Unit 1 or the Lead-in and this can provide an extra opportunity for recycling and practice.

PRONUNCIATION FOCUS 1

syllables, stress and /ə/

1 A Write the word *pronunciation* on the board and say it slowly and clearly to show how the word divides into five syllables: *pro-nun-ci-a-tion*. Point out that each syllable has a vowel sound and that usually the syllable begins with a consonant, e.g. *doc-tor*, not ~~*doct-or*~~. Ask Ss how many syllables are in their names or surnames. Read the Pronunciation tip and ask Ss to work in pairs to write the words in the correct column in the table. Don't go through the answers yet.

EXTRA SUPPORT: DYSLEXIA Provide the words as a vertical list for Ss with dyslexia as they will find this easier to read and process.

B S1.01 | Play the recording for Ss to check their answers. Play it again for Ss to listen and repeat. Use your hand to help show where the syllables are.

ANSWERS:
one syllable (bus): four, night, Spain
two syllables (doctor): number, pizza, sandwich, singer
three syllables (computer): *afternoon*, digital, internet

EXTRA IDEA You could extend this activity by looking at other words Ss have learnt and asking them to identify the number of syllables in them.

2 S1.02 | Read the Pronunciation tip as a class and tell them that they are going to hear the words from Ex 1A with two and three syllables. Then play the recording for Ss to underline the stress. Ask them to check their answers in pairs before going through them as a class. In longer words, Ss might think there are two stresses, but tell them to listen for just the main stress in this activity.

ANSWERS AND AUDIOSCRIPT:

1 doctor	**2** number	**3** pizza
4 singer	**5** computer	**6** afternoon
7 digital	**8** internet	

3 S1.03 | Read the Pronunciation tip as a class, then play the recording for Ss to listen and repeat. Pairs can repeat these again for further practice. Point out that the schwa /ə/ sound is very common in English, when a word or phrase is spoken at natural speed, and is used for many unstressed syllables.

EXTRA SUPPORT: TEACHER To make the schwa /ə/ sound, get Ss to relax the mouth, the jaw and the tongue completely. You can also demonstrate by miming gently punching your stomach and saying the sound you'd make.

4 A Ask Ss to look at the words in Ex 3 and work in pairs to complete the Spelling tip. Go through the answers as a class. More able Ss may be able to give further examples of words in each group 1–4.

ANSWERS:
2 or **3** a **4** e

B Ask pairs of Ss to complete the words. Point out that each line could be a word or part of a word, one letter or more. Each missing item has a schwa in it, which is the focus of the exercise. Allow plenty of time. Then write the answers on the board so Ss can check the spelling.

EXTRA SUPPORT: DYSLEXIA Divide the list into four sets of three items and provide the letters to complete the spelling as a separate vertical list for each section. Complete one set together as a class, as an example of what's required.

C S1.04 | Play the recording for Ss to listen and repeat. Pairs can repeat these again for further practice. Show/Tell Ss that /ə/ is pronounced the same in all the words; the spelling doesn't change the pronunciation of the sound.

EXTRA SUPPORT: TEACHER Because we pronounce many unstressed parts of words and sentences as /ə/ there are many possible spellings, but *er*, *or*, *a* and *e* are very common and are a helpful starting point for A1 Ss.

ANSWERS:

2 sev**e**n	**8** sing**er**
3 Pol**a**nd	**9** probl**e**m
4 aft**er**noon	**10** **a**n act**or**
5 Answ**er**	**11** Chin**a**
6 **a** mom**e**nt	**12** und**er**stand
7 Br**a**zil	

PRONUNCIATION FOCUS 2

/s/, /z/, /ɪz/ in plurals

5 A Ask or remind Ss how we form plurals (by adding *-s* or *-es*). Point out or remind them that the *-es* plural spelling follows certain letters (*-ch*, *-s*, *-ss*, *-sh*, *-x*) and is pronounced /ɪz/. Put Ss in pairs to write the plurals. Ignore the phonetic slashes for the moment.

EXTRA CHALLENGE With stronger classes, you could begin to raise Ss' awareness that it is the sound before the *-s* plural which affects the pronunciation of that *-s*, but you don't need to get more technical at this point unless you choose to.

ANSWERS:

A	**B**	**C**
names	books	boxes
emails	passports	buses
keys	shops	sandwiches

B S1.05 | Say the sounds /s/, /z/ and /ɪz/, then play the recording for Ss to listen and match a sound with each group A–C. Go through the answers. Show them how the sound is written between the slashes. Ss can write the symbols in their notebooks.

EXTRA SUPPORT: TEACHER To make the sounds /s/ and /z/, get Ss to place the tip of the tongue lightly against the ridge at the back of the lower teeth. Then push air through between the tongue and the top teeth, with the edge of the tongue slightly touching the roof of the mouth at the sides. It's useful to get Ss to place their hands on their throat to feel the difference between the voiced /z/ sound and the unvoiced /s/, which is only made by air and doesn't involve the vocal cords. You can exaggerate the difference for Ss to hear and begin to feel for themselves.

The voiced/unvoiced distinction, which is very important for consonants in English, is covered in various Sounds and Spelling sections (and Unit 6, Focus 1, specifically for /s/ and /z/), but here the focus is only on plurals. The main problems Ss have are not voicing the /z/ enough or having difficulty pronouncing the *-es* spelling fully as /ɪz/.

EXTRA SUPPORT You could show pictures of some bees and of a snake as prompts for the individual sounds to help Ss visualise the difference with 'bu**zz**ing bee**s**' and a 'hi**ss**ing **s**nake'. You could also use the pictures as a correction technique by holding up the relevant one where necessary.

ANSWERS:

A /z/ **B** /s/ **C** /ɪz/

C S1.05 | Play the recording again and pause for Ss to repeat. Pairs can repeat these again for further practice.

2

PRONUNCIATION FOCUS 1
short and long sounds (1): /ɪ/, /iː/, /ʊ/, /uː/

PRONUNCIATION FOCUS 2
/w/ and /h/ in question words

SPELLING
special spellings /ɪ/, /iː/, /ʊ/ and /uː/

The key principle of short and long vowel sounds, useful for all Ss of English, is the first focus here. There is a second focus on the /w/ and /h/ sounds in question words, which you might choose to use if your Ss find this area challenging.

You would probably be best to cover the two focuses in separate lessons, or even over various lessons. Once you have covered short and long sounds, you can highlight these in any lesson, asking Ss to identify where a vowel sound is short or long in new words to reinforce. All the vocabulary used is from Unit 2 or earlier units and this can provide an extra opportunity for recycling and practice.

PRONUNCIATION FOCUS 1

short and long sounds (1): /ɪ/, /iː/, /ʊ/ and /uː/

1 A S2.01 | Write the phonetic symbols on the board and say each one clearly to show how the vowel sounds can be short or long. Point out and exaggerate the shape of the mouth as you make the sounds or draw a picture of a mouth on the board. Read the Pronunciation tip as a class and draw attention to the words they are going to hear. Play the recording for Ss to listen and repeat chorally.

EXTRA SUPPORT: TEACHER A number of English vowel sounds come in pairs: a short and long version which are made in a similar way. This is an important recurring pattern in English pronunciation. A phonetic symbol with **:** at the end means the sound is long.

The pairs of sounds can be shown physically. Put your hands facing each other close together for the short sound and extend your hands wide for the long sound. In some languages, there's only one sound where English has the short and long distinction.

To make the sounds /iː/ and /ɪ/, the lips are wide for /iː/, but a little narrower and more relaxed for /ɪ/. The tongue goes back a little when we make /ɪ/.

To make /uː/, the lips are rounded (as if you are going to whistle) and the tongue is pulled back. /ʊ/ has a very similar lip shape, though slightly more relaxed, and the tongue is forward a little and more relaxed.

Showing the mouth shape helps Ss actually see the distinction, even if they can't really hear it.

B Refer Ss to the groups of words in Ex 1A. Ask them to use these examples to complete the Spelling tip. Point out that these are tendencies rather than rules. Ask Ss to compare in pairs, then go through the answers as a class.

EXTRA SUPPORT: TEACHER We pronounce *UK* and *university* with /juː/ at the start. Ss will be familiar with this from the alphabet pronunciation of *u* and *w*. There are many common words which contain this pronunciation, e.g. *men**u***, ***www***, ***U**SA*, *m**u**sic*.

EXTRA SUPPORT: DYSLEXIA Encourage dyslexic learners to cover the sounds and words they are not focusing on to reduce distraction while they transfer the information to the Spelling tip.

ANSWERS:

/ɪ/	**1** *i*	**2** e	
/iː/	**1** ee	**2** ea	**3** e
//	**1** oo	**2** u	
/uː/	**1** oo	**2** u	**3** ue

EXTRA IDEA You could extend this activity by looking at other words Ss have learnt and asking them to identify if the vowel sound is short or long, e.g. *book* (short), *meat* (long).

C **S2.02 | Look at the photos as a class, say each word clearly, then play the recording, pausing for Ss to identify which word they hear each time. They can point to the correct picture. Ask them to check their answers in pairs before confirming as a class. You may want to repeat the recording when you do this, pausing after each word to elicit the answer.**

EXTRA: ALTERNATIVE IDEA Instead of Ss pointing to the correct picture when they hear the word, you could hand out cards with copies of the pictures for them to hold up, or they could draw rough pictures themselves. Another idea might be for them to write the word or the sound on a piece of paper to hold up.

ANSWERS AND AUDIOSCRIPT:

1 *bin (a)*	**2** bean (b)	**3** bin (a)
4 bin (a)	**5** bean (b)	**6** bean (b)
7 bean (b)	**8** bin (a)	**9** bin (a)
10 bean (b)	**11** foot (c)	**12** food (d)
13 food (d)	**14** foot (c)	**15** foot (c)
16 foot (c)	**17** food (d)	**18** food (d)
19 foot (c)	**20** food (d)	

D **Put Ss in pairs and ask them to take turns to say a word for their partner to point to the photo. Move around the class and listen to how well they are producing the sounds.**

EXTRA SUPPORT If you feel your Ss may struggle to reproduce or recognise the distinction, lead this activity yourself. Say one of the words and ask Ss to raise their left hand for the short sound and their right hand for the long sound. This can be a useful and fun way to assess their perception of the sounds.

SPECIAL SPELLINGS

2 A **Look at the example as a class and discuss what is special about the spelling (the sound and letters are very different). Ask pairs to complete the words. Go through the answers and write them on the board.**

EXTRA SUPPORT If you think your class will struggle with the spelling, you could write the missing letters jumbled on the board for them to refer to if they get stuck.

EXTRA SUPPORT: DYSLEXIA Pair Ss with a partner who can help them identify and complete the words.

EXTRA SUPPORT: TEACHER Ss may be puzzled at the lack of sound–spelling correspondence. This is the first of a recurring feature looking at less usual spellings in common words and should help Ss with their pronunciation/reading as well as their writing.

There are a few rules or tendencies, but it is something Ss will need to get used to as they progress in their learning. You could suggest Ss keep a vocabulary notebook and regularly use the *Look Say Cover Write Check* system to help them memorise unusual spellings. As a reminder, Ss should look at the word, say it aloud, then cover it and write it again alongside, finally they look again and check their spelling is correct. They then repeat this process at spaced intervals. It's very important that the word is written correctly in the first instance!

ANSWERS:

2 p**eo**ple	**3** min**u**te	**4** y**ou**
5 pol**i**ce	**6** t**wo**	**7** w**o**man
8 w**o**m**e**n	**9** n**ew**	**10** b**eau**tiful

B **Ask Ss to work in pairs to look at and say the words, identifying which of the four sounds seen so far they contain. Move around the class and listen. Don't correct answers yet.**

EXTRA SUPPORT For weaker classes and Ss with dyslexia who may find processing the information in this activity challenging, provide the words with their spellings completed. Give Ss a table with the four sounds at the top (or draw a table on the board for them to copy into their notebooks). Ask Ss to work together, saying each word in turn and putting them in the correct column according to the sound.

C **S2.03 | Ask Ss to look at the words in Ex 2A and check the sounds they hear. Go through the answers as a class. Point out the pronunciation difference between the singular *woman* /ˈwʊmən/ and the irregular plural *women* /ˈwɪmɪn/. Play the recording again for Ss to listen and repeat.**

ANSWERS:

2 peo**p**le /iː/
3 min**u**te /ɪ/
4 **you** /uː/
5 pol**i**ce /iː/
6 t**wo** /uː/
7 w**o**man /ʊ/
8 w**o**m**e**n /ɪ/, /ɪ/
9 n**ew** /uː/
10 b**eau**tiful /uː/

3 Read the Pronunciation tip with the class. Point out that the sound could be one letter or more than one. Tell Ss to choose five words from Ex 2A to record in their notebooks, identifying the sound as in the example and then writing it under the difficult spelling. Allow plenty of time. Don't go through the answers as a class, but move around and check Ss are doing it correctly.

EXTRA IDEA: DIGITAL Where Ss need to refer to phonetic symbols, encourage them to use an online dictionary to access the symbols on their device.

4 **S2.04 |** **Play the recording for Ss to identify the sounds. Point out that there are two of each. After playing the recording once, ask Ss to compare in pairs then play it again. Go through the answers.**

EXTRA SUPPORT: DYSLEXIA To avoid needing to write as they listen, Ss could use a different colour to highlight each sound, highlighting the word they hear with the correct colour.

ANSWERS:

1 /ɪ/ *Kim*, offi**c**er
/iː/ thr**ee**, pol**i**ce
2 /ʊ/ diffic**u**lt, g**oo**d
/uː/ t**wo**, **U**K

EXTRA IDEA: DIGITAL Ss practise saying the two sentences. They record themselves and then listen to each other and give feedback on the pronunciation of the sounds in focus.

EXTRA IDEA It may be useful to go through some of the words on this page and remind Ss of the stress (underlined) and the places where there is a schwa (in italics): <u>chil</u>dren, e<u>le</u>ven, <u>tea</u>ch*er*, after<u>noon</u>, <u>bus</u>inessm*a*n, <u>peo</u>p*l*e, po<u>lice</u>, <u>wo</u>m*a*n. Ss may ask why *pl* in *people* is a schwa. Explain that here there is a vowel sound, even though there isn't a written vowel and that the final *e* is silent.

PRONUNCIATION FOCUS 2

/w/ and /h/ in question words

5 A **Ask Ss to complete the question words, then check in pairs. With weaker classes, complete this as a class. Write the answers on the board.**

ANSWERS:

1 **Wh**at's
2 **Wh**ere
3 **Wh**en
4 **Wh**o's
5 **H**ow

B **Say the sounds /w/ and /h/ and get Ss to repeat. Explain that the question words in Ex 5A each start with one of these sounds. Remind Ss that the spelling may not help. Ask Ss to copy the table into their notebooks, then say each question word and place it in the correct column according to the initial sound. Don't go through the answers yet.**

EXTRA SUPPORT: TEACHER Speakers of some languages have difficulties with /w/. To make the sound, ask (or show) Ss to form their lips as if they are going to whistle and then pull their lips back. This encourages the sound /uː/ followed by the next sounds, especially the vowel, e.g. /uːeə/ for *where*, and /uːɒt/ for *what*. After exaggerating this, they can put the sounds together faster and faster to get to a /w/ sound. Their teeth should never touch the lips as this would make a /v/ sound.

/h/ is similar to a vowel because there is no interruption to the air flow (similar sounds in other languages usually have some kind of interruption). You could get Ss to make this sound with their hand on their chest or stomach, and push the air out hard like a strong breath.

EXTRA SUPPORT: DYSLEXIA Provide Ss with a vertical list of the completed question words to refer to.

C **S2.05 |** **Play the recording for Ss to confirm their answers. Play and pause the recording again for Ss to repeat. (The question words are said twice before the relevant sentence to provide Ss with the opportunity to identify and practise saying them.) Drill the words to reinforce further. Ss can repeat the words again in their pairs for further practice.**

ANSWERS:

/w/ *What*, Where, When
/h/ Who, How

AUDIOSCRIPT S2.05

/w/

What, What

What's your name?

Where, Where

Where are you from?

When, When

When is your English class?

/h/

Who, Who

Who's your teacher?

How, How

How do you spell your name?

D **Keep Ss in their pairs. They should ask the questions and give their own answers. Move around the class and listen. When they have finished, ask a few Ss to ask and answer around the class and give feedback on their pronunciation.**

3

PRONUNCIATION FOCUS 1
voiced and unvoiced consonants (1): /p/ and /b/, /k/ and /g/, /t/ and /d/

PRONUNCIATION FOCUS 2
sounds at the end of words

The focus here is on the key principle of voiced and unvoiced consonants, useful for all Ss of English. You may find that some pairs of sounds are more difficult for your Ss than the others, so you could spend the time on those and leave out any pairs that do not present problems. There is a second focus on sounds at the end of words as some Ss do not pronounce these in their own language. All Ss will need to pronounce them in order to help with linking.

You would probably be best to cover the two focuses in separate lessons, or even over various lessons. Once you have covered these voiced and unvoiced consonants, you can highlight them in any lesson, asking Ss to identify where a sound is voiced or unvoiced in new words to reinforce the point. The vocabulary used is from Unit 3 or earlier units and this can provide an extra opportunity for recycling and practice.

PRONUNCIATION FOCUS 1

voiced and unvoiced consonants (1): /p/ and /b/, /k/ and /g/, /t/ and /d/

1 A **S3.01 | Read the Pronunciation tip as a class. Point out that we are talking about sounds, not letters of the alphabet, so it's /p/ and not /piː/. Play the recording for Ss to listen and repeat chorally.**

EXTRA SUPPORT: TEACHER The voiced/unvoiced distinction is very important for consonants in English. Ss have already met this distinction with /s/ and /z/. Sometimes English uses two sounds (e.g, /p/ or /b/) where in Ss' own language there may only be one.

The six sounds covered in this section are made in the same way. They are all plosives: they are made by building up air and releasing it suddenly in a (very) small 'explosion'. Each pair of sounds is made in the same place. To make /p/ and /b/, put the lips together first before releasing the air. To make /k/ and /g/, tighten the back of the throat (the glottis) first; to make /t/ and /d/, put the tip of the tongue on the ridge behind the teeth first.

It's useful to get Ss to place their hands on their throat to feel the difference between the voiced /b/, /g/ and /d/ sounds, where the vocal cords vibrate, and the unvoiced /p/, /k/ and /t/ sounds, where there is just a flow of air. The unvoiced sounds use more air, so you can ask Ss to hold up a piece of paper in front of their mouths when they make the /p/, /k/ and /t/ sounds and make it move. Ss can also do this with their hands and feel the air. You can contrast the effect with the equivalent voiced sounds: /b/, /g/ and /d/. For these voiced sounds the paper won't move and/or Ss won't be able to feel so much air on their hands.

B **Refer Ss to the groups of words in Ex 1A. Ask them to use these examples to complete the Spelling tip. Point out that these are tendencies rather than rules. Ask Ss to compare in pairs, then go through the answers as a class.**

EXTRA SUPPORT: DYSLEXIA Remind Ss to mask the parts of the activity they're not working on and the corresponding word groups in Ex 1A to reduce distraction.

ANSWERS:

/p/	**1** *p*	**2** pp	
/b/	**1** b		
/k/	**1** c	**2** ck	**3** k
/g/	**1** g	**2** gu	
/t/	**1** t	**2** tt	
/d/	**1** d	**2** dd	

EXTRA SUPPORT: TEACHER With consonants, it's important for Ss to hear and practise them in different positions in words: the beginning, middle and end. The words in this section are organised so that Exs 2A and 2B give practice of them at the beginning of words and Pronunciation Focus 2 gives practice of them at the end of words, while also extending this to other words/sounds recently studied in Lesson 3D (*think, love, like*).

2 A **S3.02 | Look at the photos as a class, say each phrase clearly, then play the recording for Ss to identify which word or phrase they hear each time. They write the number as in the examples. Ask them to check their answers in pairs before confirming as a class.**

EXTRA SUPPORT: TEACHER The only difference between each pair is whether a consonant is voiced or unvoiced. You might decide to concentrate on the pair of sounds which your Ss are having most problems with. You could give some examples yourself for Ss to distinguish between.

ANSWERS:

a *1*, 4, 6
b *2*, *3*, 5
c 7, 9, 10
d 8, 11, 12
e 13, 15, 18
f 14, 16, 17

B **Put Ss in pairs and ask them to take turns to say a phrase for their partner to point and identify the photo. Move around the class and listen to how they are reproducing the sounds. When they have finished, drill any phrase you feel needs more attention.**

EXTRA SUPPORT If Ss are struggling to reproduce the voiced/unvoiced distinction, try repeating the same sound lots of times. Then switch to its voiced/unvoiced partner and do the same. Reassure Ss that often the distinction will be made clear through context so they shouldn't worry too much about it.

PRONUNCIATION FOCUS 2

sounds at the end of words

3 A **S3.03 | Ask Ss how many letters there are in the alphabet. Elicit the five vowels (*a*, *e*, *i*, *o*, *u*) and ask Ss what the other letters are called (consonants). Read the Pronunciation tip as a class and refer them to the phrases and sentences that follow. Play the recording, pausing for Ss to repeat chorally.**

EXTRA SUPPORT: TEACHER Ss may be uncomfortable with running words together or perceive it as somehow sloppy. Reassure them that this feature of spoken language is absolutely normal and that being aware of this will aid them in listening as well as speaking.

B **Ask Ss to work in pairs and say the phrases and sentences to each other, focusing on the linking. Note that the linking happens between the sounds and not the spelling. So, in 'I love it.', the final sound is /v/ although the final spelling is *e*. Move around the class and listen. When they have finished, ask a few confident Ss to say each sentence.**

EXTRA IDEA Ss could practise further with *love*, *like*, *hate*. You (or their partner) can show a number of pictures, e.g. of activities, sports and singular things, and Ss say 'I love it.', 'I don't like it.', I hate it.', etc., concentrating on pronouncing the final consonant sound and linking this to the next vowel sound.

PRONUNCIATION FOCUS 1
short vowels: /e/, /æ/, /ʌ/

PRONUNCIATION FOCUS 2
does: /dʌz/ or /dəz/?

SPELLING
special spellings /ʌ/ and /e/

The first focus here is on three common short vowels which are often confused. You may find that one pair of sounds is more difficult for your Ss than the others, so you could spend the time on those. The second focus is on the strong and weak forms of *does*. This is a very important area for all Ss. It supplements Lesson 4D and could be covered after that lesson.

You would probably be best to cover the two focuses in separate lessons, or even over various lessons. Once you have covered these sounds you can highlight them in new words and phrases in any lesson, to reinforce the point. The pronunciation of *does* can be practised every time Ss are using the present simple. The vocabulary used is from Unit 4 or earlier units and this can provide an extra opportunity for recycling and practice.

PRONUNCIATION FOCUS 1

short vowels /e/, /æ/, /ʌ/

1 A S4.01 | Write the phonetic symbols on the board and say each one clearly to show how each sound differs. Point out how the shape of your mouth changes as you make the sounds. Play the recording for Ss to listen and repeat chorally.

EXTRA SUPPORT: TEACHER This distinction might challenge Ss, depending on your Ss' first language. Show the mouth and jaw shape, with the lips and jaw much wider for /æ/ and the jaw really dropping down for /ʌ/: this helps Ss better see the distinction even if they can't really hear it. They could try saying each sound in turn and running them together, to note the changes.

To make the sounds:

/e/ – the jaw is neutral/relaxed. The lips are relaxed, but spread more than for the schwa.

/æ/ – the jaw is dropped; the mouth is wider open. The lips are not as wide as with /e/.

/ʌ/ – the jaw is dropped down a lot. The lips are not as wide as with /æ/.

B Refer Ss to the groups of words in Ex 1A. They use these examples to complete the Spelling tip. Ask Ss to complete this in pairs, then go through the answers as a class.

EXTRA SUPPORT: DYSLEXIA Encourage Ss to cover the words and groups they are not working with to help them focus.

ANSWERS:

/e/	**1** *e*	
/æ/	**1** a	
/ʌ/	**1** u	**2** o

2 A S4.02 | Look at the photos as a class and clarify as needed, as the vocabulary may be new for Ss. Say each word clearly, then play the recording for Ss to listen, then play it again for Ss to repeat chorally.

B S4.03 | Refer Ss to the chart and explain that the first two words they will hear are given as an example. They should listen and continue the pathway. Tell Ss that the pathway may use the same word more than once. Go through the answers as a class and play the recording again if needed.

ANSWERS AND AUDIOSCRIPT:
(START) *cap, cup,* hat, cap, cup, men, man, cap, men, hat, man, men, hat, hut, hut, hat (FINISH)

C Put Ss in pairs. Explain that Student A should say a word from Ex 2A and that Student B should point to the correct photo. After a few words, they swap roles. Move around the class and listen. When they have finished, have a recap and drill of sounds you felt were causing difficulty.

EXTRA IDEA Ss work in their pairs to repeat Ex 2B with their own pathway of words from Start to Finish in the chart. Student A says words to make a pathway and Student B follows it. Model this yourself first. Ss take turns to say and to follow.

SPECIAL SPELLINGS

3 A This is the second Special spellings section Ss have seen. Elicit what is special about the spelling in these exercises (the sound and letters are very different). Ask pairs to complete the words. Go through the answers as a class.

EXTRA SUPPORT You could provide the missing sets of letters on the board, jumbled, for Ss to place in the gaps.

EXTRA SUPPORT: DYSLEXIA Dyslexic learners might find the incomplete words difficult to process. You could give them two alternative spellings for each word – one correct and one incorrect – for them to choose from.

ANSWERS:

1 br**ea**kfast	**2** y**ou**ng	**3** h**ea**dphones
4 fr**ie**nd	**5** **o**ne	**6** **a**ny
7 ag**ai**n	**8** c**ou**ntry	

B **S4.04 | Ask Ss to listen to the words and sentences in Ex 3A, then listen again and repeat chorally.**

C Ss should work in pairs and say the words with the difficult spelling in Ex 3A, identifying which of the three sounds seen so far they contain. Write the sounds on the board. Ss should write the words and the sound in their notebooks, as in the example. Move around the class and listen. When they have finished, go through the answers as a class.

EXTRA SUPPORT For weaker classes and for Ss with dyslexia who may find processing the information in this activity a challenge, you could provide the completed words from Ex 3A. Give Ss a table with the three sounds at the top (or draw a table on the board for them to copy into their notebooks). Ask Ss to work together, saying each word in turn and putting them in the correct column according to the sound.

ANSWERS:

2 y**ou**ng
/ʌ/
3 h**ea**dphones
/e/
4 fr**ie**nd
/e/
5 **o**ne
/ʌ/
6 **a**ny
/e/
7 ag**ai**n
/e/
8 c**ou**ntry
/ʌ/

EXTRA IDEA: DIGITAL Ss practise saying the sentences. Then they record themselves and listen to each other, and give feedback on the pronunciation of the sounds in focus.

PRONUNCIATION FOCUS 2

does: /dʌz/ or /dəz/?

4A Remind Ss that a feature of English pronunciation is that a sentence has some words that are stressed (i.e. said longer, louder and higher than the other words in the sentence). Elicit the kinds of words that tend to be stressed (content words – nouns and verbs). Ask Ss to identify the stressed words in the conversation in pairs. With weaker classes, complete this as a class. Write the answers on the board.

ANSWERS:

A: *Does your <u>classroom</u> have a <u>computer</u>?*
B: Yes, it <u>does</u>.
A: Does it <u>have</u> a <u>blackboard</u>?
B: No, it <u>doesn't</u>. It has a <u>whiteboard</u>.

B **S4.05 | Say the two options /dʌz/ and /dəz/ and get Ss to repeat. Ask them to look at the examples of *does* in the conversation in Ex 4A and decide in which of these two ways each one is pronounced. Ask Ss to copy the conversation into their notebooks, then say each *does* and place the sound below it, depending on how they think it's pronounced. (Tell them just to focus on the 'does' part of *doesn't* for this exercise.) Don't go through the answers yet. Play the recording, twice if necessary, then go through the answers.**

EXTRA SUPPORT: TEACHER One word having two different pronunciation options is likely to be new for many Ss. Point out that they don't need to worry too much about producing the two options, but that recognition will help them when listening to natural English as it is spoken.

ANSWERS:

A: Does your classroom have a computer?
/dəz/
B: Yes, it does.
/dʌz/
A: Does it have a blackboard?
/dəz/
B: No, it doesn't. It has a whiteboard.
/dʌz/

C Put Ss in pairs and ask them to use the conversation to complete the Pronunciation tip. Check the meaning of *always* (every time). Go through the answers and drill as needed to reinforce.

ANSWERS:

don't stress
stress

5A Ss should work alone and write two colours, two types of clothes and two types of food or drink. Move around the class, helping and making sure that they are completing the activity correctly.

B Model the activity yourself by telling Ss to use the questions to ask you about a colour that you have chosen. Ss should work in pairs, not showing their words to their partner. The purpose of this activity is to practise pronouncing *does* correctly, so when they have finished, give feedback on this.

PRONUNCIATION FOCUS 1
voiced and unvoiced consonants (2):
/f/ and /v/, /θ/ and /ð/
PRONUNCIATION FOCUS 2
silent *e* (1): /ɪ/ to /aɪ/

This develops the attention to voiced and unvoiced consonants which was started in Unit 3. Many Ss have problems with /θ/ and /ð/ and some teachers and researchers feel that the sounds may disappear altogether in English as an International Language. However, many Ss still wish to develop their ability to understand and produce these very common English sounds. There is a second focus on a typical effect of adding an *e* to the end of a word.

You would probably be best to cover the two focuses in separate lessons, or even over various lessons. Once you have covered these sounds you can highlight them in new words in any lesson, to reinforce the point. The vocabulary used is from Unit 5 or earlier units and this can provide an extra opportunity for recycling and practice.

PRONUNCIATION FOCUS 1

voiced and unvoiced consonants (2): /f/ and /v/, /θ/ and /ð/

1 A S5.01 | Read the Pronunciation tip as a class. Ask Ss if they can remember any of the pairs of voiced and unvoiced consonants studied in Unit 3 and what the difference was (vibration of the vocal cords for the voiced sounds). Remind them that we are talking about sounds, not letters of the alphabet, and that a phonetic symbol such as /θ/ and /ð/ can represent two letters (e.g. *th*). Read the tip and say the sounds. Play the recording for Ss to listen and repeat chorally.

EXTRA SUPPORT: TEACHER These four sounds are made in a similar way. They are fricatives. This means we release the air slowly through some sort of restriction of the mouth and tongue and continue the sound for a long time. Ss already know two other fricatives: /s/ and /z/.

Speakers of some languages have problems with one or two of these four sounds, so you could identify which, if any, of the four are causing problems and give more detail and practice on how to make them. To make unvoiced /f/ and voiced /v/: the upper teeth touch the lower lip. To make unvoiced /θ/ and voiced /ð/: the tip of the tongue lightly touches against the top front teeth so that the air is just able to flow between the tongue and teeth.

B Refer Ss to the groups of words in Ex 1A. Ask them to use these examples to complete the Spelling tip. Ask Ss to compare in pairs, then go through the answers as a class.

EXTRA SUPPORT: DYSLEXIA Remind Ss to cover the sounds and words they are not working on to help them focus.

ANSWERS:

/f/	**1** *f*	**2** ff	**3** ph
/v/	**1** v		
/θ/	**1** th		
/ð/	**1** th		

2 Ask Ss what the date is and write it on the board. Remind them how in British English we say *the* and *of* when saying the date. Read the Pronunciation tip and ask Ss to say the dates chorally, then in pairs.

EXTRA SUPPORT: TEACHER These sounds are very useful for dates (taught in Lesson 5D), particularly ordinal numbers (*seventh*, *eighth*, etc.) and *of*. While this is the case for British English, in American English, 'June first' would be more usual, rather than 'the first of June'. Depending on the context that your Ss are learning in, this may be worth pointing out.

3 A Put Ss in pairs and ask them to read the conversation and identify four examples of each of the four sounds in focus. (Two examples have been done for them.) Move around the class and listen to how they are reproducing the sounds. When they have finished, ask them to compare with other pairs, but don't check the answers yet.

EXTRA SUPPORT: TEACHER You need to decide how important the sounds /θ/ and /ð/ are for your Ss and whether they might need some help in trying to make them. The sounds are often confused with sounds such as /f/, /z/ or /d/ so you will know the best way to contrast the sound, according to any problems your Ss have.

B S5.02 | Play the recording. Ask Ss to look at their answers and change them if needed. Play it again and go through the answers. Then play the recording one more time and pause for Ss to repeat after each line.

ANSWERS:
/f/ *Fiona*, fourth, photo, phone
/v/ *of*, November, have, very
/θ/ the, the, mother's, This
/ð/ Thursday, fourth, Thanks, birthday

EXTRA IDEA: DIGITAL Ask Ss to practise the conversation in pairs then record themselves. They should listen back to their recording with another pair and feed back on the sounds in focus, recording again with a new partner if they want to.

PRONUNCIATION FOCUS 2

silent *e* (1): /ɪ/ to /aɪ/

4A Read the Pronunciation tip as a class. Ask Ss what happens in this case when you add the *e* (the sound changes). Look at the words (1–4) as a class and ask Ss to say and spell them. Go through the answers, writing the words on the board and pointing out the silent *e* in each one.

EXTRA SUPPORT: TEACHER Silent *e* can be a problem for spelling as many Ss omit it. Sometimes it makes no difference to the pronunciation (e.g. *have*, *leave*) but after an *i* + consonant (*like*, *rice*, *bike*) the normal pronunciation is /aɪ/. Note that the verbs *live* and *give* do not follow this rule and neither does the suffix *-ive* (e.g. *expensive*, *active*), which is pronounced /ɪv/.

ANSWERS:
1 bike **2** nice **3** size **4** price

EXTRA IDEA You could point out that *nice* is spelt with a *c* though the sound is /s/ and remind Ss that they can usefully write a phonetic symbol in their vocabulary notebooks above or below a sound, to help them remember how to pronounce it.

B Ask Ss to work in pairs and complete the words, using the Pronunciation tip to help them. Point out that one line represents one letter. Move around the class and listen. Don't give the answers yet.

EXTRA SUPPORT The lines for the missing letters may be a distraction for dyslexic and beginner literacy learners. In this case, provide the completed words without these lines. You could provide the left-hand column as a vertical list, with the completed words jumbled in another vertical list on the right. Ss place the words in the correct category. Alternatively, you could substitute the lines with boxes big enough for Ss to write comfortably in.

C S5.03 | Play the recording for Ss to check their answers. Go through the answers as a class, writing them on the board. Play the recording again for Ss to repeat chorally.

ANSWERS:
verbs: *l*ike, dr**ive**, wr**ite**
numbers: f**ive**, n**ine**
a colour: wh**ite**
a type of food: r**ice**
a person in a family: w**ife**
an adjective: f**ine**

5A S5.04 | Explain that Ss will hear six questions. They should allow one line for each question in their notebooks and prepare by writing the numbers 1–6 at the start of each line. Play the recording for Ss to write, then check their answers with a partner before you play it again. Go through the answers as a class, writing them on the board. Play the recording again for Ss to repeat.

EXTRA SUPPORT Listening and writing at the same time is a challenge for beginner literacy and dyslexic learners. In this case, provide the completed questions with one gap for Ss to complete as they listen.

ANSWERS AND AUDIOSCRIPT:
1 Do you like rice?
2 Can you drive a bus?
3 Do you have any white T-shirts?
4 Do you have a bike?
5 What's the time?
6 What's ninety-five plus five?

B Explain that Ss should ask and answer the questions. Move around the class and listen. When they have finished, ask a few pairs to repeat the questions and their answers for the class.

PRONUNCIATION FOCUS 1
voiced and unvoiced consonants (3):
/s/ and /z/, /ʃ/ and /ʒ/
PRONUNCIATION FOCUS 2
/tʃ/ and /dʒ/
SPELLING
special spellings /s/, /z/ and /ʃ/

Here, the work on voiced and unvoiced consonants from Units 3 and 5 is further developed as the first focus. The second focus is on two consonants /tʃ/ and /dʒ/ which are each made up of two sounds.

You would probably be best to cover the two focuses in separate lessons, or even over various lessons. Once you have covered these sounds you can highlight them in new words in any lesson, to reinforce the point. The vocabulary used is from Unit 6 or earlier units and this can provide an extra opportunity for recycling and practice.

PRONUNCIATION FOCUS 1

voiced and unvoiced consonants (3): /s/ and /z/, /ʃ/ and /ʒ/

1 A S6.01 | Read the Pronunciation tip as a class. Ask Ss if they can remember any of the pairs of voiced and unvoiced consonants studied in Units 3 and 5 and what the difference was (vibration of the vocal cords for the voiced sounds). Remind them that we are talking about sounds, not letters of the alphabet and that a phonetic symbol can represent two letters (e.g. /ʃ/ often represents *sh*). Then play the recording for Ss to listen and repeat chorally.

EXTRA SUPPORT: TEACHER These four sounds are also fricatives, like the sounds in Unit 5; the sound can be sustained/continued for a long time.

To make unvoiced /s/, touch the tongue lightly to the ridge behind the teeth and let air flow through. Add the voice for /z/. Remind Ss of the 'hi**ss**ing **s**nake' and the 'bu**zz**ing bee**s**' to highlight the difference. To make unvoiced /ʃ/, bring the tongue back a little from the ridge. It is the sound used to quieten people ('Shhh!'). Add the voice for /ʒ/.

B Refer Ss to the groups of words in Ex 1A. Ask them to use these examples to complete the Spelling tip. Ask Ss to compare in pairs, then go through the answers as a class.

EXTRA SUPPORT: TEACHER Remember when modelling all unvoiced sounds not to include any voice! It should be like a whisper. Ss should be familiar with /s/ and /z/ by now, so the focus is on the two new sounds and how they differ from the other two. The sound /ʒ/ is really only used in two words at A1 level but needs to be covered in order to make the sound /dʒ/. At higher levels, it is used in many words ending *-sion*.

EXTRA SUPPORT: DYSLEXIA Covering the words and sound groups they are not working on can help reduce distraction for dyslexic learners.

ANSWERS:

/s/	**1** s	**2** c	**3** ss
/z/	**1** z	**2** s	
/ʃ/	**1** sh	**2** ti	
/ʒ/	**1** s	**2** si	

2 A S6.02 | Ask Ss to listen and write the four questions that they hear. Play the recording once, ask Ss to compare in pairs and help each other, and then play it again. Check answers with the class and write the questions on the board.

EXTRA SUPPORT Listening and writing at the same time can be a challenge for beginner literacy and dyslexic learners. In this case, you could provide the completed questions cut up into two or three 'chunks', depending on the length of the question, and ask Ss to put them in order as they listen.

ANSWERS AND AUDIOSCRIPT:
1 What's your address?
2 Who lives opposite you?
3 How do I find information about international phone numbers?
4 Where do you usually watch television?

B Put Ss in pairs and ask them to read the questions and identify two examples of each of the four sounds in focus in Ex 1A. There are two examples of the same sound in each question. Ask them to draw a table with a sound at the top of each column and write the words in. Move around the class and listen to how they are reproducing the sounds. When they have finished, ask them to compare with other pairs then check the answers as a class.

ANSWERS:
1 /s/ *What'***s**, addre**ss**
2 /z/ live**s**, oppo**s**ite
3 /ʃ/ informa**ti**on, interna**ti**onal
4 /ʒ/ u**s**ually, televi**si**on

C Put Ss in pairs to ask the questions in Ex 2B and give their own answers. Move around and listen to how Ss are pronouncing the sounds. When they have finished, give some feedback and drill any troublesome words or phrases.

SP

SPECIAL SPELLINGS

3 A Ask Ss to complete the words. When they have finished, ask them to compare in pairs and then go through the answers, writing them on the board and drilling. Point out the silent letters in *answer* (*w*) and *listen* (*t*).

ANSWERS:

1 size	**2** **s**ugar	**3** an**sw**er
4 ma**ch**ine	**5** lis**t**en	

B Ask Ss to identify the sounds in the words they completed in Ex 3A. They should write the words in their notebooks with the sound(s) under them as in the example. Go through the answers.

ANSWERS:

2 **s**ugar /ʃ/	**4** ma**ch**ine /ʃ/
3 an**sw**er /s/	**5** lis**t**en /s/

EXTRA IDEA: DIGITAL Ask Ss to choose one of the sentences (1–5) and write a three-line conversation around it. The original sentence can come at any point. They should then record themselves saying the conversation with a partner, listen back to their recording with another pair and feed back on the sounds in focus, recording again with a new partner if they want to.

PRONUNCIATION FOCUS 2

/tʃ/ and /dʒ/

4 A Say /t/ and /ʃ/ separately and slowly, pretending that you are 'holding' one sound (/t/) in your right hand and the other (/ʃ/) in your left. Ss repeat. Say the sounds more and more quickly, with Ss repeating, moving your hands closer together until the sounds finally merge when your hands touch. Repeat this procedure with /d/ and /ʒ/. Read the Pronunciation tip as a class.

EXTRA SUPPORT If your Ss have problems with a particular pair of sounds, e.g. the difference between /s/ and /ʃ/, you could do a minimal pairs activity, contrasting the sounds (e.g. *Sue – shoe, seat – sheet, sore – shore*).

B S6.03 | Refer Ss to the lists of words. Play the recording and ask them to listen and repeat.

C Ask Ss to work in pairs and complete the Spelling tip, using the examples in Ex 4B to help them. Go through the answers.

EXTRA SUPPORT: DYSLEXIA Remind Ss to cover the parts of Exs 4B and 4C they are not referring to as they find and copy the information.

ANSWERS:

/tʃ/	**1** ch	**2** tch
/dʒ/	**1** j	**2** g

5 A Look at the lists as a class. Point out the sounds in bold in each list. Explain that Ss should add the words to the correct row of the table, according to the sound in the name. Look at the examples, then complete a few more words as a class before asking Ss to continue in pairs. Move around the class and listen. Don't correct yet.

EXTRA SUPPORT With beginner literacy and dyslexic learners, it's worth going over the way that we read a table across and down. Suggest that Ss use a ruler or mask to focus their attention on one row at a time to reduce distraction. You could also fill in more of the cells to make this task more supported.

B S6.04 | Play the recording for Ss to check their answers. Go through the answers as a class, writing them on the board. Play the recording again for Ss to repeat chorally.

ANSWERS:

Sam /s/: Swiss, police officer, *suits*
Zena /z/: Vietnamese, businesswoman, trousers
Shaun /ʃ/: *Turkish*, shop assistant, shirts
Jenny /dʒ/: German, digital designer, jackets
Charlie /tʃ/: Chinese, *teacher*, French clothes

AUDIOSCRIPT S6.04

Sam is Swiss. He's a police officer. He likes suits.

Zena is Vietnamese. She's a businesswoman. She loves trousers.

Shaun is Turkish. He's a shop assistant. He likes shirts.

Jenny is German. She's a digital designer. She loves jackets.

Charlie is Chinese. He's a teacher. He likes French clothes.

EXTRA IDEA You might want to point out that *likes* and *loves* are both used to talk about people's favourite clothes, e.g. *Sam likes suits.*; *Zena loves trousers*. These can also help with pronunciation because /laɪks/ ends with two unvoiced sounds and can be contrasted with /lʌvz/ which ends with two voiced sounds.

You can encourage Ss to alternate use of these two verbs in Ex 5C, i.e. 'Sam likes … ', 'Zena loves … ', 'Shaun likes … ', 'Jenny loves … ', 'Charlie likes … ', to practise production of voiced and unvoiced sounds. You could write the verbs *likes* and *loves* on the board to prompt Ss to use them.

C **Explain that Ss should think of two things for each person in Ex 5A, according to the sound in their name. They should use the categories in the box as in the example (you might want to elicit that *supermarket* is a place and *sofa* is furniture). Tell them they should not repeat the clothes that have already appeared in Ex 5A. Remind Ss that they need to use plurals after *like* and *love* (apart from months and words which don't have a plural, e.g. fish).**

Ss should work in pairs and write sentences, as in the example. Both Ss need to write or note down their ideas as they will separate for the next stage. Move around and support/check, especially that they are using plural forms and uncountable nouns correctly.

EXTRA SUPPORT: TEACHER As /z/ is most usually found in English in plurals and in third person present simple verbs, if you decide to do another example with the class, you might choose to do 'Zena' because there are few words Ss will be able to think of (e.g. 'Zena loves cheese and Brazil.'). /s/ will be the easiest.

EXTRA SUPPORT Dyslexic and beginner literacy learners should note the words but don't need to write sentences. You could also reduce the scope of the task to just three people.

POSSIBLE ANSWERS:
Sam: *supermarkets*, *sofas*, pencils
Zena: scissors, museums, Brazil
Shaun: shoes, sugar, shopping centres
Jenny: fruit juice, fridges, January
Charlie: armchairs, kitchens, China

D **Read the example as a class and give another example yourself. Point out that you don't say the name, because your partner must guess it based on the sounds used. Put Ss in new pairs, move around and listen and support as needed.**

PRONUNCIATION FOCUS 1
consonants: /b/, /v/, /w/, /l/ and /r/
PRONUNCIATION FOCUS 2
silent *e* (2): /æ/ to /eɪ/

The first focus here is on particular consonant sounds which cause problems for speakers of some languages. You can choose the sounds which are relevant to your group. The second focus, a typical effect of adding an *e* to the end of a word, extends an area of pronunciation first focused on in Unit 5.

You would probably be best to cover the two focuses in separate lessons, or even over various lessons. Once you have covered these sounds you can highlight them in new words in any lesson, to reinforce the point. The vocabulary used is from Unit 7 or earlier units and this can provide an extra opportunity for recycling and practice.

PRONUNCIATION FOCUS 1

consonants: /b/, /v/, /w/, /l/ and /r/

1 A **S7.01 | Write the phonetic symbols on the board and say each one clearly to show how the sounds are formed. Point out and exaggerate the shape of your mouth as you make the sounds. Then play the recording for Ss to listen and repeat chorally.**

EXTRA SUPPORT: TEACHER To make /b/, put your lips together and build up air behind them. Open your lips to release the air quickly. Put your hand on your throat and feel the vibration. Hold a piece of paper in front of your mouth. It will not move. To make /v/, put your top teeth on your bottom lip. Push air through the teeth continuously. Put your hand on your throat. There is a vibration because it is a voiced sound. You can continue this sound for a long time, whereas /b/ is a short plosive sound.

To make /w/, make your lips round as if you're going to kiss or whistle, then relax the lips. Another option is to make the sound /uː/ and then the sound /ə/ quickly, one after the other and this will give /w/. It is voiced.

To make /l/, the tongue touches the ridge behind the top teeth (the same place as for /t/, /d/, /s/ and /z/); leave it there.

To make /r/, the tongue is a little further back (a little behind the place for /ʃ/ and /ʒ/) and the tip does not touch anything. The air goes along the centre of the tongue.

B Refer Ss to the groups of words in Ex 1A. Ask them to use these examples to complete the Spelling tip. Point out that these are tendencies rather than rules. Ask Ss to compare in pairs, then go through the answers as a class.

EXTRA SUPPORT: DYSLEXIA When transferring the information from Ex 1A, remind Ss to cover the parts they are not currently working on to reduce distraction.

ANSWERS:

/b/	**1** *b*		
/v/	**1** v		
/w/	**1** w	**2** wh	
/l/	**1** l	**2** ll	
/r/	**1** r	**2** wr	**3** rr

EXTRA IDEA We can also spell /b/ with *bb*, but there are no A1 words to exemplify. However, you might choose to show this to Ss, e.g. *rabbit, hobby, rubber.*

2A Ask Ss to work in pairs and discuss the different sounds. They should say the examples in blue and then think about the difference. Ss won't have the words to explain the differences, but the point here is for them to think about the differences even if they can't express these fully. When they have finished, ask a few pairs to demonstrate or explain the differences. See Extra Support: Teacher in Ex 1A for ideas.

B This is an opportunity for Ss to consider their first language in relation to English. With a monolingual class, you can discuss as a group, with a multilingual class it will be interesting for Ss to hear about others' languages. There are no fixed answers.

EXTRA SUPPORT: TEACHER Depending on Ss' answers and your knowledge of the Ss' first language(s), in the following discrimination exercises you may decide to focus only on those sounds that are problematic for your learners.

3A **S7.02 |** Play the recording. Ss should identify the word they hear each time.

EXTRA: ALTERNATIVE IDEA Rather than marking the correct word each time, Ss could point to the correct picture, or, alternatively, they could create a card with the word or sound written on it to hold up. You could even allocate the right and left arm each to a word and they raise this when they hear it.

ANSWERS:

1 berry	**4** berry
2 very	**5** very
3 very	**6** berry

B **S7.03 |** Play the recording. Ss should identify the word they hear each time.

ANSWERS:

1 vest	**4** vest
2 west	**5** west
3 vest	**6** west

C **S7.04 |** Play the recording. Ss should identify the word they hear each time.

ANSWERS:

1 light	**4** light
2 right	**5** right
3 light	**6** right

D Put Ss in pairs. Student A says a word; Student B should identify the word they hear. Then they change roles. Move around and listen to observe which sounds are causing more difficulty.

EXTRA IDEA Write the words in large print on A4 cards and place them in different parts of the room. Say one of the words in focus. Ss should move to that place. Say the word again, and allow Ss to move if they want to. Then reveal who is in the right place and say a new word.

4A Look at the sentences as a class and point out that each focuses on a different sound issue (e.g. 1 focuses on /b/ and /v/). Ask pairs to choose a sentence to practise. Go round and listen to them. Fast finishers can say more than one sentence.

EXTRA IDEA: DIGITAL Ss record themselves saying one or more of the sentences, then compare with the recording.

B **S7.05 |** Play the recording for Ss to check, then play each sentence again for them to repeat chorally.

C Ask Ss to write their sentences in pairs. They can either use all five sounds, or – if you think this may be too much of a challenge – focus on just one of the pairs (i.e. /b/ and /v/, /v/ and /w/ or /l/ and /r/) as in the sentences in Ex 4A. Move around and help them as needed.

EXTRA: ALTERNATIVE IDEA If short of time or with weaker classes, you could dictate a sentence from the examples below. Ss then practise saying it.

/b/ /v/ *Everybody wants an umbrella and a wallet.*

/v/ /w/ *When do we visit Vicky? On Wednesdays every week.*

/l/ /r/ *Be careful, there's a glass in the grass.*

D Ask Ss to exchange sentences with another pair. Move around and listen. When they have finished, give feedback.

PRONUNCIATION FOCUS 2

silent *e* (2): /æ/ to /eɪ/

5A Ask Ss if they remember the silent *e* (from Sounds and Spelling Unit 5) and what impact it had on pronunciation (it changed the sound of the vowel). Ss read the Pronunciation tip and answer the question. With weaker classes, complete this as a class.

EXTRA SUPPORT: TEACHER To make the diphthong sound /eɪ/, get Ss to say the sound /e/ and then the sound /ɪ/ and gradually say them faster and faster together: /e/ + /ɪ/ = /eɪ/. You could make your right hand represent /e/ and your left hand /ɪ/ and gradually bring them together.

B Focus attention on the text (a doctor's form). Explain that the words with missing letters all contain the sound /eɪ/. Remind them that the sound may not help with the spelling. Ask Ss to work in pairs to complete the words.

EXTRA SUPPORT: DYSLEXIA Dyslexic learners may find it difficult to work with the lines for each letter. You could provide a copy of the text with boxes large enough to write the letters in as an alternative to the individual lines. Provide the full words in a vertical list for Ss to refer to for the spelling. Alternatively, you could simply leave gaps for the whole words and Ss choose from the list of words to complete the text.

ANSWERS:

1 Name	**2** Date	**3** Age
4 headache	**5** stomachache	**6** backache

6A S7.06 | Tell Ss they will hear six questions. Ask them to write the numbers 1–6 at the start of six lines in their notebooks. Play the recording for Ss to write the questions, pausing the recording to allow time to write. Ask Ss to compare in pairs, then play the recording again before going through the answers.

EXTRA SUPPORT For beginner literacy and dyslexic learners, provide the questions with one word gapped for Ss to complete. This could also help weaker classes.

ANSWERS:
See Ex 6B.

B Ss should identify the /eɪ/ sounds. To do this, it will help if they read the questions aloud. When they have finished, go through the answers and drill as needed.

ANSWERS AND AUDIOSCRIPT:

1 Can you make a cake?
2 Do you like grapes?
3 Do you take sugar in your coffee?
4 Are you often late?
5 Do you know anyone with the same birthday as you?
6 Do you often change your passwords?

C Ss should work with a partner to ask the questions and give their own answers. Move around the class and listen. When they have finished, ask a few Ss to ask and answer around the class and give feedback on their pronunciation.

8

PRONUNCIATION FOCUS 1
short and long sounds (2):
/æ/, /ɑː/, /ɒ/, /ɔː/, /ə/ and /ɜː/

PRONUNCIATION FOCUS 2
silent *e* (3): /ɒ/ to /əʊ/

SPELLING
special spellings /ə/, /ɜː/ and /ɔː/

Here, the key principle of short and long vowel sounds, first focused on in Unit 2, is developed. The second focus is on a typical effect of adding an *e* to the end of a word, also focused on in Units 5 and 7.

You would probably be best to cover the two focuses in separate lessons, or even over various lessons. Once you have covered these sounds you can highlight them in new words in any lesson, to reinforce the point. The vocabulary used is from Unit 8 or earlier units and this can provide an extra opportunity for recycling and practice.

PRONUNCIATION FOCUS 1

short and long sounds (2): /æ/, /ɑː/, /ɒ/, /ɔː/, /ə/ and /ɜː/

1 A S8.01 | Write the phonetic symbols on the board and say each one clearly to show how the vowel sounds are short or long. Point out and exaggerate the shape of your mouth as you make the sounds. Remind Ss that two dots mean a sound is long. Allow time for Ss to read through the sounds and words in Ex 1A, then play the recording for Ss to listen and repeat chorally.

EXTRA SUPPORT: TEACHER Ease Ss into this final Sounds and Spelling section gently by reminding them of the schwa from Unit 1 and /æ/ from Unit 4. While /æ/ and /ɑː/, and /ɒ/ and /ɔː/ are short and long versions of similar sounds, only /ə/ and /ɜː/ are produced in exactly the same way. It is worth remembering that, for communication, consonants are far more important than vowels, although the schwa is particularly important because it relates to stress in words and sentences, which is key for comprehension.

You can show and explain how the sounds are produced physically. To make short /æ/, drop the jaw; the tongue is central in the mouth; the mouth and the lips are spread wide. To make long /ɑː/, drop the jaw; the tongue is a little further back than in /æ/; the lips are more relaxed and not spread so wide.

To make short /ɒ/, round the lips a little; the front of the tongue is low and towards the back of the mouth; the jaw is dropped. To make long /ɔː/, round the lips more than for /ɒ/; the front of the tongue is in the same place as /ɒ/; the jaw is dropped.

To make /ə/, remind Ss that it is made with a very relaxed jaw and tongue, and that it is always unstressed. You could start by asking Ss where the stress is in the examples. /ɜː/ is /ə/ lengthened and the *r* in its spelling is not pronounced. To make short /ə/, relax the mouth, jaw and tongue. To make long /ɜː/ simply lengthen the /ə/.

EXTRA SUPPORT: TEACHER The pronunciation of the letter *a* in many common words can be either /æ/ or /ɑː/ depending on which part of the UK you come from, e.g. in *pass, last, afternoon, ask, answer,* etc. Both are correct. In other non-UK varieties of English, /æ/ is more common.

B Refer Ss to the groups of words in Ex 1A. Ask them to use these examples to complete the Spelling tip. Point out that these are tendencies rather than rules. Ask Ss to compare in pairs, then go through the answers as a class.

ANSWERS:

/æ/	**1** *a*			
/ɑː/	**1** ar	**2** a		
/ɒ/	**1** o	**2** a		
/ɔː/	**1** or	**2** oor	**3** our	**4** au
/ə/	**1** a	**2** e	**3** er	**4** or
/ɜː/	**1** ur	**2** er	**3** ir	**4** ear

C S8.02 | Ask Ss to write the numbers 1–6 at the start of six lines in their notebooks. Play the recording for Ss to listen and write the sentences. Ask them to compare in pairs before playing it again and confirming as a class.

EXTRA SUPPORT: DYSLEXIA As Ss with dyslexia can find it a challenge to simultaneously listen and write, you could simplify the activity by providing them with the sentences with just one or two gapped words to complete.

ANSWERS AND AUDIOSCRIPT:

1 I often travel by tram.
2 I love parties and barbecues.
3 I want to watch a film tonight.
4 We have four airports in my country.
5 I like machines. I love motorbikes.
6 I get up early, at six thirty.

D Put Ss in pairs and ask them to change the sentences in Ex 1C so that they are true for them. Give an example yourself, e.g, 'I never travel by tram. I usually travel by bus.' Move around the class and help as needed.

EXTRA SUPPORT You could focus on any two sounds that Ss have problems with and do different activities before continuing, e.g. you could say the pairs of words below as Ss listen and raise their right hand for one of the two sounds and their left hand for the other, then they can do the same in pairs.

/æ/ /ɑː/ cat – cart, match – March, am – arm, pack – park, hat – heart

/ɜː/ /ɑː/ first – fast, purse – pass

/ɜː/ /ɔː/ work – walk, bird – bored, shirt – short

SP

SPECIAL SPELLINGS

2 A Look at the example as a class and discuss what is special about the spelling (the sound and letters are very different). Put Ss in pairs and ask them to complete the words. Go through the answers and write them on the board.

EXTRA SUPPORT For weaker classes, you could provide the missing sets of letters jumbled on the board for them to place in the correct words.

EXTRA SUPPORT: DYSLEXIA Dyslexic learners may find both dealing with incomplete words and writing on the individual letter lines tricky. For them, you could provide boxes large enough for them to write the missing letters in and supply the complete words in a vertical list for them to refer to when writing the missing letters. Alternatively, you could provide the words in a vertical list, with two alternatives for their spellings, one correct and one distractor.

EXTRA SUPPORT: TEACHER Words ending with *-re* and *-le* in British English are pronounced with a schwa. In US English, the spelling is often *-er* (*center, meter*). *-gh* is often silent in pronunciation and is often followed by *t* – common words are: *bought, daughter, light, night, right, flight* and *height*.

ANSWERS:
2 bou**gh**t **3** wa**l**k, ta**l**k **4** sing**le**
5 cent**re** **6** s**aw**

B Ask Ss to work in pairs, and look and say the words with the difficult spellings, identifying which of the sounds in the focus each contains. Then they should write each word with the sound under the letters it belongs with. Move around the class and listen. Don't correct answers yet.

EXTRA SUPPORT With weaker classes, give Ss a table with the three sounds needed in this exercise, /ə/, /ɜː/ and /ɔː/, at the top (or draw a table on the board for them to copy into their notebooks). Ask Ss to work together, saying each word in turn and putting them in the correct column according to the sound.

C S8.03 | Ask Ss to look at the words in Ex 2A as they listen and check the sounds they hear. Go through the answers as a class. Play the recording again for Ss to listen and repeat.

ANSWERS:
2 bou**gh**t
/ɔː/
3 wa**l**k, ta**l**k
/ɔː/ /ɔː/
4 sing**le**
/ə/
5 cent**re**
/ə/
6 s**aw**
/ɔː/

D Give an example yourself, e.g. 'I work best alone.', then ask Ss to make sentences that are true for them. Point out that they can repeat the same unchanged sentences if they are true for them. Stronger classes should be able to do this verbally in pairs; weaker classes may need to write first. When they have finished, ask a few individuals to tell the class.

3 A Read the instruction with the class. Point out that the final sound is the same in pairs of sentences as these are poems, so they rhyme. Allow plenty of time. Don't go through the answers as a class but move around and check Ss are doing the exercise correctly. Don't check answers yet.

EXTRA IDEA: DIGITAL Encourage Ss to use an online dictionary to listen to the words and access phonetic symbols on their device and copy from there.

B S8.04 | Play the recording for Ss to listen and check and identify the sounds in focus. After playing it once, ask Ss to compare in pairs, saying the words and checking the symbols, then play the recording again. Go through the answers. Ss should then say the poems with the recording.

ANSWERS:

In April I plan.	/æ/
In May I'm in Japan!	/æ/
In June I'm a writer.	/ə/
In July, a firefighter.	/ə/
In August I'm hot.	/ɒ/
In December I'm not.	/ɒ/
On Monday I walk	/ɔː/
On Tuesday I talk.	/ɔː/
On Wednesday I'm fast.	/ɑː/
On Thursday I'm last.	/ɑː/
On Friday it's skirts.	/ɜː/
On Saturday, old shirts.	/ɜː/

EXTRA IDEA: DIGITAL Ss practise saying one of the two poems, perhaps adding actions or visuals. They video record themselves and then watch each other and give feedback on the pronunciation of the sounds in focus.

PRONUNCIATION FOCUS 2

silent *e* (3): /ɒ/ to /əʊ/

4A Ask Ss to read the Pronunciation tip and answer the question. Ask them to say the words to illustrate the change. With weaker classes, complete this as a class.

EXTRA SUPPORT: TEACHER To make the diphthong sound /əʊ/, get Ss to say the sound /ə/ and then the sound /ʊ/ and gradually say them faster and faster together: /ə/ + /ʊ/ = /əʊ/. You could make your right hand represent /ə/ and your left hand /ʊ/ and gradually bring them together.

ANSWER:
When an *e* is added, the short sound /ɒ/ changes to the longer diphthong sound /əʊ/.

B Explain that the incomplete words in Ex 4B all contain a silent *e*. Remind Ss that it may not be the last letter. Ask Ss to complete the words, then compare in pairs. Go through the answers and drill the questions.

EXTRA SUPPORT To support dyslexic learners who may find this challenging, and weaker classes in general, provide Ss with a vertical list of the completed words that they can place alongside the exercise to help them fill the gaps. Remind them they should also look at the context as some words have the same first letters!

ANSWERS:
2 cl**osed** **3** cl**othes** **4** ph**one**
5 al**one**

C Ss work in pairs to ask the questions in Ex 4B and give their own answers. *Clothes* is a difficult word to pronounce due to the consonant cluster /ðz/ at the end, most Ss will say /kləʊz/ but they don't need to worry too much as the main focus here is the sound of the vowel. When they have finished, ask a few Ss to ask and answer around the class and give feedback on their pronunciation.

GSE LEARNING OBJECTIVES

UNIT	READING	LISTENING	SPEAKING
1 welcome!			
Lesson A		22 Can understand the main information when people introduce themselves (e.g. name, age, where they are from). 23 Can extract the names of people or places from short, simple dialogues, if delivered slowly and clearly.	13 Can ask someone what their nationality is. 10–29 Can use language related to nation, nationality and language.
Lesson B	28 Can extract personal details in a limited way. 25 Can understand short, simple descriptions of objects, people and animals, given visual support. 27 Can understand basic phrases in short, simple texts.		27 Can say what someone's job is, using familiar common job names. 25 Can ask and answer simple questions in areas of immediate need or on very familiar topics.
Lesson C		22 Can understand the main information when people introduce themselves (e.g. name, age, where they are from). 23 Can extract the names of people or places from short, simple dialogues, if delivered slowly and clearly. 23 Can understand questions addressed carefully and slowly.	25 Can ask and answer simple questions in areas of immediate need or on very familiar topics. 12 Can use a few basic words and phrases to show politeness (e.g. 'please', 'thank you'). 22 Can ask for the spelling of a word, or for a word to be written down. 28 Can exchange personal details (e.g. where they live, things they have). 24 Can ask basic questions using 'What's your … ?' 24 Can make simple statements with 'it's/ it is'.
Lesson D		30 Can identify simple information in a short video, provided that the visual supports this information and the delivery is slow and clear. 22 Can understand the main information when people introduce themselves (e.g. name, age, where they are from). 23 Can extract the names of people or places from short, simple dialogues, if delivered slowly and clearly. 26 Can recognise words and simple phrases related to familiar topics, if spoken slowly and clearly and supported by pictures.	28 Can exchange personal details (e.g. where they live, things they have). 25 Can ask and answer simple questions in areas of immediate need or on very familiar topics.

WRITING	GRAMMAR	VOCABULARY
24 Can write a few basic sentences introducing themselves (e.g. name, age, where they are from), given prompts or a model. 24 Can use capital letters appropriately. 26 Can use basic punctuation (e.g. commas, full stops, question marks).	24 Can use subject pronouns with the correct form of the verb 'be' in the simple present. 24 Can use subject personal pronouns. 25 Can use the verb 'be' in the simple present with adjectives.	10–29 Can use language related to greeting and saying hello. 10–29 Can use language related to introductions. 10–29 Can use language related to point or period of time. 10–29 Can use language related to leave-taking and saying goodbye. 10–29 Can use language related to addressing someone.
	24 Can use subject personal pronouns. 24 Can use subject pronouns with the correct form of the verb 'be' in the simple present. 24 Can make simple statements with 'it's/ it is'.	10–29 Can use language related to jobs. 25 Can use 'a/an' with the names of jobs. 26 Can use 'a/an' with jobs to talk about work and professions.
		11 Can say the letters of the alphabet. 10 Can write the letters of the alphabet in upper and lower case.
25 Can write simple sentences about things that they and other people have. 28 Can write short, simple notes, emails and postings to friends.	25 Can use common forms of 'have' in the present tense. 24 Can use regular nouns in the plural form. 26 Can use 'a/an' with single countable nouns.	10–29 Can use language related to household objects and possessions.

UNIT	READING	LISTENING	SPEAKING
2 people			
Lesson A	27 Can understand simple descriptions of places.		22 Can say where they and other people are in a limited way. 22 Can ask and answer basic questions about family and friends in a limited way.
Lesson B		23 Can extract the names of people or places from short, simple dialogues, if delivered slowly and clearly.	22 Can ask and answer basic questions about family and friends in a limited way. 28 Can ask and answer simple questions about people they know in a limited way. 29 Can talk about the family in a basic way, given prompts.
Lesson C		23 Can understand questions addressed carefully and slowly. 26 Can recognise words and simple phrases related to familiar topics, if spoken slowly and clearly and supported by pictures.	24 Can greet people, ask how they are and react to news. 28 Can express how they are feeling using very basic fixed expressions.
Lesson D	27 Can understand basic phrases in short, simple texts.	30 Can identify simple information in a short video, provided that the visual supports this information and the delivery is slow and clear.	27 Can ask simple questions about other people (e.g. their name, age, where they live, things they have).
3 things			
Lesson A	29 Can understand basic factual statements relating to pictures or simple texts. 27 Can understand basic phrases in short, simple texts.		18 Can use a few simple words to describe objects (e.g. colour, number), if supported by pictures. 22 Can answer simple questions about objects (e.g. colour, size). 29 Can say who something belongs to. 10–29 Can use language related to differences and similarities.
Lesson B		29 Can identify objects, places or people from short spoken descriptions. 24 Can understand basic questions about objects in pictures or in their immediate surroundings.	26 Can ask basic questions about objects (e.g. colour, size). 24 Can describe objects in a basic way (e.g. colour, size). 30 Can ask for repetition and clarification when they don't understand, using basic fixed expressions.
Lesson C		26 Can identify how much something costs in short, simple dialogues about the price, if delivered slowly and clearly. 29 Can follow simple, everyday transactions (e.g. shopping and eating out) if carried out slowly and clearly.	23 Can give basic information about the price of something. 28 Can ask people for things and give people things. 26 Can say how much something costs using basic language. 29 Can ask for attention. 27 Can ask about the price of something using 'How much is/are … ?' 24 Can make simple statements with 'it's/it is'.

WRITING	GRAMMAR	VOCABULARY
	24 Can use the correct form of 'be' with singular and plural nouns. 24 Can use subject pronouns with the correct form of the verb 'be' in the simple present. 25 Can ask where other people are using 'Where is/are …?'	10–29 Can use language related to numbers. 22 Can recognise cardinal numbers from 11–100.
27 Can write simple sentences about their family and where they live. 25 Can use 'and' to link nouns and noun phrases.	25 Can use possessive adjectives such as 'my', 'your', etc.	10–29 Can use language related to family members and relationships. 10–29 Can use language related to have or not have. 25 Can use common irregular nouns in the plural form. 10–29 Can use language related to friends and friendships.
		10–29 Can use language related to asking about feelings. 25 Can use the verb 'be' in the simple present with adjectives.
27 Can write simple sentences about their family and where they live. 25 Can use 'and' to link nouns and noun phrases.	25 Can form questions with 'what' and 'who' and answer them. 25 Can ask where other people are using 'Where is/are … ?' 25 Can ask someone's age using 'How old … ?' 24 Can ask basic questions using 'What's your … ?'	
26 Can write basic sentences describing everyday objects (e.g. colour, size), given a model. 28 Can use 'but' to link clauses and sentences. 25 Can write simple sentences about things that they and other people have.	28 Can use 's' to express possession with singular nouns.	10–29 Can use language related to household objects and possessions. 10–29 Can use language related to describing something's quality. 10–29 Can use language related to colour.
	26 Can ask *yes/no* questions using the present simple. 28 Can construct short answers to questions in the present simple using the verb 'do'. 25 Can use common forms of 'have' in the present tense.	10–29 Can use language related to home office and stationery. 10–29 Can use language related to household objects and possessions.
		10–29 Can use language related to shops and buying clothes. 10–29 Can use language related to describing clothes. 10–29 Can use language related to shops and shopping experience.

UNIT	READING	LISTENING	SPEAKING
3 things (continued)			
Lesson D		25 Can understand basic information about someone's likes and dislikes. 24 Can understand basic questions about people's likes and dislikes.	28 Can describe a person's likes and dislikes using simple language. 10–29 Can use language related to shops and shopping experience.
4 every day			
Lesson A		26 Can recognise words and simple phrases related to familiar topics, if spoken slowly and clearly and supported by pictures. 25 Can understand basic information about someone's likes and dislikes. 24 Can understand basic questions about people's likes and dislikes.	28 Can express preferences about food and drink using basic fixed expressions. 28 Can describe a person's likes and dislikes using simple language.
Lesson B	25 Can understand short, simple descriptions of objects, people and animals, given visual support. 27 Can understand basic phrases in short, simple texts. 28 Can understand a few simple phrases related to familiar, everyday activities. 29 Can understand basic factual statements relating to pictures or simple texts.		28 Can answer simple questions about their daily activities or routines, given a model. 29 Can answer simple questions about habits and routines.
Lesson C	29 Can understand simple phrases related to familiar, everyday activities.	29 Can follow simple, everyday transactions (e.g. shopping and eating out) if carried out slowly and clearly. 27 Can understand basic information about prices, times, and dates in familiar contexts, if spoken slowly and clearly.	24 Can ask for a drink or food in a limited way. 28 Can express preferences about food and drink using basic fixed expressions. 24 Can agree to simple requests using a few basic fixed expressions.
Lesson D	29 Can understand basic factual statements relating to pictures or simple texts.	30 Can identify simple information in a short video, provided that the visual supports this information and the delivery is slow and clear.	27 Can ask simple questions about other people (e.g. their name, age, where they live, things they have). 29 Can answer simple questions about habits and routines. 25 Can ask and answer simple questions in areas of immediate need or on very familiar topics. 24 Can tell the time of day to the quarter hour. 28 Can ask and answer simple questions about people they know in a limited way.

WRITING	GRAMMAR	VOCABULARY
30 Can write a few simple sentences to introduce themselves and provide basic personal information, given prompts or a model. *27 Can write simple sentences about personal interests.*	27 Can use the present simple to refer to likes, dislikes and opinions. 26 Can make affirmative statements using the present simple without time reference. 26 Can make negative statements using the present simple.	
28 Can write short, simple notes, emails and postings to friends.	33 Can use a range of common adverbs of frequency. 26 Can use the present simple to refer to daily routines.	10–29 Can use language related to food and drink.
	26 Can use the present simple to refer to daily routines. 26 Can make affirmative statements using the present simple without time reference. 26 Can make negative statements using the present simple.	10–29 Can use language related to everyday activities. 10–29 Can use language related to frequency or repetition. 10–29 Can use language related to point or period of time. 24 Can tell the time of day to the quarter hour. 29 Can write times using both digits and words.
		10–29 Can use language related to food and drink. 10–29 Can use language related to utensils, appliances and tableware. 10–29 Can use language related to restaurant experience. 31 Can find specific, predictable information in everyday materials (e.g. menus, timetables).
34 Can write short descriptive texts (4–6 sentences) on familiar personal topics (e.g. family, possessions), given a model.	26 Can ask *yes/no* questions using the present simple. 26 Can use the present simple to refer to daily routines. 28 Can construct short answers to questions in the present simple using the verb 'do'.	

UNIT	READING	LISTENING	SPEAKING
5 action			
Lesson A	29 Can understand basic factual statements relating to pictures or simple texts. 29 Can understand simple phrases related to familiar, everyday activities.		28 Can ask and answer simple questions about people they know in a limited way.
Lesson B		24 Can distinguish between 'can' and 'can't'. 29 Can understand what people say they can or can't do from simple sentences spoken slowly and clearly.	27 Can express ability or lack of ability with regard to basic activities using 'can' or 'can't'.
Lesson C		29 Can follow simple, everyday transactions (e.g. shopping and eating out) if carried out slowly and clearly. 26 Can recognise words and simple phrases related to familiar topics, if spoken slowly and clearly and supported by pictures.	32 Can make offers using basic fixed expressions. 27 Can accept offers using basic fixed expressions. 27 Can ask for help using basic fixed expressions. 28 Can ask people for things and give people things.
Lesson D		35 Can understand short, basic descriptions of familiar topics and situations, if delivered slowly and clearly.	24 Can give dates using standard formats (day and month). 29 Can answer simple questions about habits and routines.
6 where?			
Lesson A	27 Can understand simple descriptions of places.		23 Can describe the position of something in a very basic way. 28 Can answer simple questions about the location of people or things in a limited way. 25 Can ask for and give very basic information about the home.
Lesson B		27 Can recognise familiar key words and phrases in short, basic descriptions (e.g. of objects, places or people), if spoken slowly and clearly. 26 Can understand basic factual statements.	26 Can describe where they live. 25 Can ask and answer simple questions in areas of immediate need or on very familiar topics.
Lesson C		24 Can understand basic statements about where things or people are, if spoken slowly and clearly and supported by pictures.	26 Can understand simple directions from X to Y on foot or public transport. 25 Can accurately repeat clearly spoken words, phrases, and short sentences. 28 Can answer simple questions about the location of people or things in a limited way. 29 Can ask for simple directions, referring to a map or plan. 26 Can use basic prepositions of place with nouns and noun phrases.
Lesson D		30 Can identify simple information in a short video, provided that the visual supports this information and the delivery is slow and clear. 27 Can understand simple descriptions of places. 29 Can understand basic factual statements relating to pictures or simple texts.	28 Can answer simple questions about the location of people or things in a limited way.

WRITING	GRAMMAR	VOCABULARY
30 Can write simple sentences about what they and other people do.	27 Can use personal pronouns as objects and complements.	10–29 Can use language related to work activities.
	29 Can use 'can' to refer to ability in the present.	10–29 Can use language related to aptitude, ability, knowledge, and skills.
		10–29 Can use language related to describing something's quality.
28 Can write dates using both digits and words. 28 Can write simple sentences about their life and routines.	28 Can give dates (e.g. their date of birth) using ordinal numbers in the form day-month-year or month-day-year.	10–29 Can use language related to point or period of time.
	26 Can use basic prepositions of place with nouns and noun phrases.	10–29 Can use language related to furniture and decoration. 10–29 Can use language related to rooms and parts of a building.
27 Can write simple sentences about their family and where they live. 26 Can use basic punctuation (e.g. commas, full stops, question marks). 28 Can write short, simple notes, emails and postings to friends.	27 Can use 'there' + 'be' to express presence/absence.	10–29 Can use language related to public buildings and places. 10–29 Can use language related to areas, districts and neighbourhoods.
		10–29 Can use language related to public buildings and places. 10–29 Can use language related to location and position. 27 Can understand short written notices, signs and instructions with visual support. 10–29 Can use language related to parts of a building. 10–29 Can use language related to direction.
35 Can write a simple text containing key information, given a model. 28 Can write short, simple notes, emails and postings to friends.	32 Can use the definite article to refer to a specific person, thing, or situation.	

UNIT	READING	LISTENING	SPEAKING
7 healthy lives			
Lesson A		27 Can understand basic information about free-time activities. 29 Can identify objects, places or people from short spoken descriptions.	29 Can answer simple questions about habits and routines.
Lesson B	25 Can understand short, simple descriptions of objects, people and animals, given visual support. 29 Can understand basic factual statements relating to pictures or simple texts.		31 Can ask simple questions to find out about a subject. 33 Can make simple references to the past using 'was/were'.
Lesson C		30 Can understand excuses if expressed in simple language.	28 Can use common forms of 'have got' (BrE) in the present tense. 26 Can recognise words and simple phrases related to familiar topics, if spoken slowly and clearly and supported by pictures. 28 Can express how they are feeling using very basic fixed expressions. 10–29 Can use language related to wellness and illness.
Lesson D		30 Can identify simple information in a short video, provided that the visual supports this information and the delivery is slow and clear. 35 Can understand short, basic descriptions of familiar topics and situations, if delivered slowly and clearly.	34 Can ask simple questions in a face-to-face survey. 34 Can answer simple questions in a face-to-face survey. 33 Can describe skills and abilities using simple language. 34 Can exchange simple information on everyday topics, provided the other person speaks slowly and clearly and is prepared to help.
8 time out			
Lesson A	27 Can understand basic phrases in short, simple texts. 27 Can understand simple descriptions of places. 29 Can understand familiar phrases in a simple text.	32 Can identify basic factual information in short, simple dialogues or narratives on familiar everyday topics, if spoken slowly and clearly. 29 Can identify objects, places or people from short spoken descriptions.	30 Can talk about familiar topics using a few basic words and phrases. 31 Can talk about everyday things (e.g. people, places, job, study) in a basic way.
Lesson B	27 Can understand basic phrases in short, simple texts.		25 Can indicate time by such phrases as 'next week', 'last Friday', 'in November', 'three o'clock'. 29 Can answer simple questions about habits and routines.
Lesson C		27 Can understand basic information about prices, times, and dates in familiar contexts, if spoken slowly and clearly. 29 Can follow simple, everyday transactions (e.g. shopping and eating out) if carried out slowly and clearly.	24 Can buy tickets on public transport using basic fixed expressions. 28 Can ask people for things and give people things. 10–29 Can use language related to when something happens. 10–29 Can use language related to point or period of time.

WRITING	GRAMMAR	VOCABULARY
28 Can write simple sentences about someone's life and routines. 26 Can use basic punctuation (e.g. commas, full stops, question marks).	27 Can ask a range of *wh-* questions. 26 Can ask *wh-* questions using the present simple. 26 Can ask *yes/no* questions using the present simple.	10–29 Can use language related to everyday activities.
	32 Can use 'was' and 'were' with a range of complement phrases.	10–29 Can use language related to describing something's quality.
		10–29 Can use language related to parts of the body and mind.
33 Can write simple sentences about personal skills.	27 Can use verbs in the imperative.	
	30 Can make affirmative statements using common regular past simple forms. 29 Can use negative forms of the simple past.	10–29 Can use language related to holidays. 10–29 Can use language related to moving in a direction.
28 Can write simple sentences about their life and routines. 31 Can use very basic connectors like 'and', 'but', 'so' and 'then'. 28 Can write short, simple notes, emails and postings to friends. 29 Can write times using both digits and words.	30 Can make affirmative statements using common irregular past simple forms.	10–29 Can use language related to hobbies and interests. 10–29 Can use language related to everyday activities.
		10–29 Can use language related to public transport. 10–29 Can use language related to trains, train travel, and stations. 10–29 Can use language related to when something happens. 10–29 Can use language related to point or period of time.

UNIT	READING	LISTENING	SPEAKING
8 time out (continued)			
Lesson D	29 Can understand basic factual statements relating to pictures or simple texts.	30 Can identify simple information in a short video, provided that the visual supports this information and the delivery is slow and clear.	34 Can take part in a very simple conversation on a familiar topic if the other speaker repeats questions and answers as necessary and speaks slowly and clearly. 34 Can exchange simple information on everyday topics, provided the other person speaks slowly and clearly and is prepared to help.

WRITING	GRAMMAR	VOCABULARY
27 Can write simple sentences about personal interests. 34 Can write short texts about their likes and dislikes using basic fixed expressions.	29 Can use 'I'd like … / I want …' to express wants and wishes. 31 Can use 'want to' + infinitive to express intentions.